Cartographic Cinema

Cartographic Cinema

Tom Conley

University of Minnesota Press
Minneapolis • London

Sections of chapter 5 were originally published in *"Les Mistons" and Undercurrents of French New Wave Cinema,* The Norman and Jane Geske Lecture Series 8 (Lincoln, Neb.: Hixson-Lied College of Fine and Performing Arts, 2003); reprinted with permission from Hixson-Lied College of Fine and Performing Arts at the University of Nebraska–Lincoln. Material in chapter 9 was originally published in "A Web of Hate," *South Central Review* 17, no. 3 (Fall 2000): 88–103; reprinted with permission.

Published by the University of Minnesota Press
111 Third Avenue South, Suite 290
Minneapolis, MN 55401-2520
http://www.upress.umn.edu

Library of Congress Cataloging-in-Publication Data

Conley, Tom.
    Cartographic cinema / Tom Conley.
        p. cm.
    Includes bibliographical references and index.
    ISBN-13: 978-0-8166-4356-1 (hc : alk. paper)
    ISBN-10: 0-8166-4356-3 (hc : alk. paper)
    ISBN-13: 978-0-8166-4357-8 (pb : alk. paper)
    ISBN-10: 0-8166-4357-1 (pb : alk. paper)
    1. Maps in motion pictures. I. Title.
    PN1995.9.M28C66 2006
    791.43′62—dc22
                                                2006032950

Printed in the United States of America on acid-free paper

The University of Minnesota is an equal-opportunity educator and employer.

12 11 10 09 08 07   10 9 8 7 6 5 4 3 2 1

Contents

Acknowledgments

For this project much is owed to many. In 1992 James Akerman, who was then organizing panels for the biennial meeting of the International Association for the History of Cartography, invited me to submit a proposal on cartography and cinema. His inspiration and encouragement, along with that of many historians and theorists of cartography, have helped to guide this work from that inception. Special thanks go to David Buisseret for his long-standing support, and to the scholars who organized and spoke at the Virginia Garrett Lectures in October 2000 on the theme "Cartography and Popular Culture," notably Richard Francaviglia, Arthur and Jan Holzheimer, and Dennis Reinhardt. In that same year some of these concepts were presented in the frame of the Germaine Brée Memorial Lecture at the Institute for Research in the Humanities at the University of Wisconsin–Madison through the kind invitation of Paul Boyer, Ullrich Langer, and Lorctta Frciling. Also in 2000 thcsc ideas found an extraordinarily helpful reception in the cadre of a seminar led by Marie-Claire Ropars-Wuilleumier at the École Normale Supérieure and the University of Paris–VIII; to her and her team, which included Dominique Château, Claude Mouchard, Jean-Michel Rey, and Pierre Sorlin, my gratitude is infinite. Raymond Gay-Crosier and Maureen Turim provided a lovely forum for this topic at the University of Florida, as did Peggy McCracken and George Hoffmann at the University of Michigan, where Richard Abel offered keen counsel. Scott Durham and Timothy Murray did the same during a seminar at Northwestern University.

Much of the research for this book developed through a core course taught at Harvard University, "Cinéma et civilisation française." The students and teaching fellows who sustained my work include Nick Nesbitt, Andrea Flores, Elisabeth Hodges, Maggie Flinn, Natasha Lee, Mahalia Gayle, Alexis Sornin, and Ludovic Cortade. Among the hundreds of wondrous students I think immediately of Melissa Lee, Jenny Lefcourt, Katherine Stirling, Raja Haddad, John Hulsey, Ally Field, and Rachel Zerner. Giuliana Bruno, Bruce Jenkins, Bob Gardner, Ross McElwee, Rob Moss, and Rick Rentschler have been exceptionally supportive colleagues. Kriss Ravetto and Mario Biagioli commented on the material, as have students and tutors at the Kirkland House at Harvard University (Reid Caroline, Tim Hardt, Sharonna Pearl, Andy Rice, John Walsh). Thanks go to Deidra Perley and Steffan Pierce for their help in scanning many of the images that accompany the text.

I thank Richard Morrison and Douglas Armato of the University of Minnesota Press, who invited me to engage the project, and to the two aquiline and overgenerous readers, T. Jefferson Kline and David Rodowick, who helped to shape the material into its current form. Thanks go to Annette Michaelson for listening to matter destined for the introduction; to Daniela Boccassini and Carlo Testa, whose good words inflected chapter 3; to Bertrand Tavernier, whose observations informed research in chapter 5; to Rosemarie Scullion and Van Kelly, for reading an early version of chapter 9; to Therese Boyd, who copyedited the work so keenly that all errors are mine alone. To this project I allotted some of the time granted by a Guggenheim Award to conduct research on topography, and I am immensely grateful to this extraordinary foundation.

Revisions were being completed in August 2004 when the devastating news of the untimely death of David Woodward arrived. A selfless sponsor of the project, a model of generosity, and the first and finest historian of cartography of his time, David encouraged my writing at every stage of this book's development. Behind his shadow stands that of Walter Conley, my father, who made my childhood an endless encounter of cinema. To Verena Conley, whose passion for the pleasures of life and film is dauntless, this book is dedicated.

Introduction

Maps appear in most of the movies we see. Even if a film does not display a map as such, by nature it bears an implicit relation with cartography. A map we see in a film may concern locale, if the film is a documentary, or, if it tells a story, an itinerary. It may belong to the places in which a viewer experiences a film. Like an intertitle or a sign that tells us where the film is taking place, what it is doing, or where its characters are going, a map in a movie provides information; it whets the imagination. It propels narrative but also, dividing our attention, prompts reverie and causes our eyes to look both inward, at our own geographies, and outward, to rove about the frame and to engage, however we wish, the space of the film.

The cinematic image possesses, like a map, a "language" of its own that does not pertain to the linguist's field of study.[1] Like the idiolect of the geographer and cartographer, the cinematic idiom, multifaceted, is composed of signs that do not transcribe speech. Riddled with speech and writing, the cinematic image, like a map, can be deciphered in a variety of ways. Maps and films might be said to be strangely coextensive. Of vastly different historical formation, cinema and cartography draw on many of the same resources and virtues of the languages that inform their creation. A film can be understood in a broad sense to be a "map" that plots and colonizes the imagination of the public it is said to "invent" and, as a result, to seek to control. A film, like a topographic projection, can be understood as an image that locates and patterns the imagination of its spectators. When it takes hold, a film encourages its public to think of the world in concert with its own articulation of space. The same could be said for the fascination that maps have elicited for their readers since the advent of print-culture or even long before. Both maps and films are powerful ideological tools that work in consort with each other. It behooves the viewer of films to see how maps are deployed in them, and with what effects and consequences.

How to discern and make use of cartography as a way of viewing cinema will be the concern of the chapters that follow. One guiding hypothesis is that a map in a film is an element at once foreign to the film but also, paradoxically, of the same essence as film. A map underlines what a film is and what it does, but it also opens a rift or brings into view a site where a critical and productively interpretive relation with the film can begin. A corollary is that films *are* maps insofar as each medium can be defined as a form of what cartographers call "locational imaging."[2] As the person who gazes upon a map works through a welter of impressions about the geographical information it puts forward—along with his or her own fantasies and pieces of past or anticipated memory in dialogue with the names, places, and forms on the map—so also do spectators of a film who see moving pictures on a screen mix and sift through souvenirs and images of other films and personal memories.

It can be said that in its first shots a film establishes a geography with which every spectator is asked to contend. It may be in the logo, preceding the credits, that is often manufactured from cartographic elements (the globe in Universal Studios, the mountain of Paramount), or it may begin from an intertitle in the field of the image indicating the time and place of the story that will follow. When a geography is given a sense of identification ("the Paris I see in *Les 400 coups* is the city I was raised in"), of difference ("I lived there, but how much it has changed"), doubt ("what the film shows is *not* the Paris I know"), a discerning gaze ("the cars on the street don't belong to the place portrayed"), or a critical reverie ("the boy in the film cannot see how he is being mapped, even determined, by his environs"). We often wait to reach the end-credits to see where films were made and how certain places are made to become the simulacra of others.

The mode of reading proposed in this monograph is as simple as the grounding premise. It begins from what we gather when we discern a map in the field of a moving image. A welter of issues comes forward, including perspective, visual style, narrative economy, scale, cinema and history, the stakes of mimesis, and reception. Involved, too, are the vital components of projection and ideology, understood here in the classical sense as the imaginary relation that we hold with real modes of production. "The map is not the territory," note many readers of Borges's celebrated—and minuscule—story about the demise of nation and its cartographers in *Dreamtigers,* but it cannot quite be said that "the map is not the film."[3] The one that is *in* the other forever betrays its differences with respect to its surrounding milieu in the field of the frame. A map is not a movie, but the former gives cause and good reason for the cinematic effects of the latter.

A map becomes the fictional territory of a film, but its alterity in the field of the image establishes a point where an effective critical relation can be inaugurated. That same relation is especially productive when the map evinces both a history and a set of formal problems of its own making, outside of the control of the film, that simultaneously summon those of the film itself.

A map that is seen in a movie bears productive analogy with cartography at the time of its emergence in early modern print-culture. Like woodcut or copper-plate illustrations illustrating printed texts, maps were tipped into books to call attention to the aspect and format of a medium for which seeing and reading were of a same character. They drew attention to the printed letter—whether majuscule or minuscule, Italic or Roman, historiated or illuminated—in their functions as both lexical and spatial markers. The latter caused the lines, contours, shadings of relief, dots, marks, and toponyms to be read as would alphabetic matter. A formal principle in the history of the printed atlas states that it breaks new ground when the space allotted to cartographic images wins over what is provided for printed words.[4] Which is not to say by way of analogy that cinema and cartography were rivals as had been, at an earlier moment in the history of print-culture, words and maps or pictures, but, rather, that when many of the historical latencies of a map are discovered in a film, myriad tensions—many not under the control of the rhetoric of the film—can lead us toward productive, critical, and even creative speculation. Elements formerly invisible become visible, and vice-versa.[5]

Included in the field of reflection, foremost, is debate about ontology and history, about being and its vicissitudes: a map in a movie begs and baits us to ponder the fact that *who we are* or whomever we believe ourselves to be depends, whether or not our locus is fixed or moving, on often unconscious perceptions about *where* we come from and may be going. To be able to say who one is depends on believing in the illusion that consciousness is in accord with where it is felt in respect at once to itself and to its milieus. Maps in films often enhance that effect when they beguile us into believing that we are naturally in the world and are adequate in respect to the moving images we are processing. When we position ourselves in relation to the effects of plotting in cinema we quickly discern that ontology is a function of geography.[6] Figures in a topographic field are as they are because geography is destiny, or else inversely (in the case, say, of the nomadic protagonist of *The Searchers* who makes it clear that humans rarely belong in the places they inhabit), their destiny, even if atopical, is limited to the cartography of the film.

A map in a film prompts every spectator to consider *bilocation,* which may indeed be cause for the resurgence of debates in which film is treated in terms of issues concerning identity. Identity can be defined in a narrow sense as the consciousness of belonging (or longing to belong) to a place and of being at a distance from it. When a map in a film locates the geography of its narrative, it also tells us that we are not where it says it is taking place. The story that is said to be there is nowhere. The map plays a role at once as a guarantee (the film is said to be "taking place" in the area seen before our eyes, "on location," in a place we might wish to be) and a sign of prevarication (a map is inserted both to establish a fallacious authenticity of a place and to invent new or other spaces). In the ensuing perplexity we often inquire of our own geographies: what brought us to the theater or to commit ourselves to watching in its dark space, or to a room equipped with a television set, or to a computer screen, and why? Does the representation of the film impel us to see ourselves wishing to let cinema lead us, as the poet Baudelaire wrote, "anywhere out of this world"?

In its most effective instants a film causes us to perceive how our belief in the truth of being where we are, as adequate agents of what we do, can be questioned. We find ourselves immediately undone by the weightless fact that we have no reason to be where we are. The giddy and unsettling effects of watching and studying cinema may indeed have to do with the way the medium brings forward and summons issues of mental geography. It would not be wrong to say that the bilocational effect that maps exert on films prompts us, in either conscious or unconscious ways, to ask if we indeed have any relation whatsoever with being.[7] The question raised by cartography in cinema attests to the psychoanalytic dictum, shared by Jacques Lacan and many others, that subjectivity is characterized by an oscillation between a narcissistic, "jubilatory" celebration of our presence in the world and a "paranoid realization" that we are here for nothing, and no doubt, too, in our own personal and professional spheres, that most of the films we study and cherish belong to a fragile construct of mental geography. Both the awesome and wondrous power and attraction of cinema and the spaces we create through it owe to our capacity to inspire in ourselves this very gamut of unsettling sensations and reflections.

At the same time a map in a film posits a commanding paradox that lies at the basis of ideology. Most narrative films tend toward a rhetoric of invisibility. They camouflage the ways they are made; their modes of production are most often seen, if at all, only indirectly in the field of the image. Some films make their process visible in the palpable difference between the technical aspects of the film—and its shooting style, its editing, its consciousness of the virtues of its apparatus—the more seductive effects of its plot, its psychology, or philosophies with which it may be affiliated. Others, self-conscious in style, mask the same relation by demonstrating allusively that they are conscious of ideology, but all the while they reproduce it simultaneously in a mosaic of fragments and self-reflective gestures. A map in a film often situates and intensifies, even glaringly, the masked relation belonging to both narrative and self-reflective cinema. Maps in films often bring to the image a history that is *not* cinematic; they are written in codes and signs that are not those of film; yet they are of a spatial scale not unlike that in which they are portrayed. And they can never be assimilated entirely into the visual narrative or other modes of rhetoric of the films in which they are deployed. They are *in* the films in which they are seen, but they are of *other* qualities.

More broadly, if account is taken of the fact that the history of cartography is marked by the appropriation, control, and administration of power (as David Buisseret [1992], Michel Foucault [1975 and 1994 (1967)], J. Brian Harley [1988 and 2001], Denis Wood [1992], and others have shown), the interpretive stakes can be raised to a degree where it can be asserted that in sum a film *is* a map, and that its symbolic and political effectiveness is a function of its identity as a cartographic diagram. Here is where work in film theory can be yoked to some of the magnificent studies emerging from overlapping areas of the history of cartography, visual studies, and literary theory. From 1970 until about 1990 film studies witnessed, first, an explosion of theory. Since then there has tended to be a retraction in favor of extensive work on canons, genres, reception, and origins. A corollary aim for the cartographer of cinema is not to let theory go unattended, to be recanted, or left in the wings of a virtual theater of interpretation. This study seeks to make film history bear upon the art of viewing and, indeed, of living, not just with film, but also with space itself, with the attendant labor of speculating over what it means to be located and discerned in the world. The beauty of cinema, no matter what its reception may be, whether or not it is received with two thumbs up or two thumbs down, or if it is consigned to canisters in an air-conditioned vault, owes in a large degree to its power to make us ponder these questions. The force and beauty of cinema are enhanced when we think of it in light of cartography.

A second grounding hypothesis, rivaling with the proposition that rare are the films that fail to contain maps, is that the occurrence of a map in a film is unique to its own context. Some general patterns can be observed, but in general it might be said: *to each film its map*. To each its own "points de capiton," or points of stress that plot its relations with space, history, and being. For this reason cinematic cartography requires close reading, not only of images of maps as they appear in the moving image, but also of the principles of montage that inform them and that make each film the webbing that contains issues of broader scope. Classical Westerns and war films tend to celebrate the logistical virtues of mapping. Topographical charts on the walls of briefing rooms or cavalry outposts signal that western science and military hardware will defeat local knowledge, or perhaps vice-versa, when natives burn wagon trains and massacre foreign settlers. The frequent projections of South Asia on the walls of travel agencies and medium-size globes on the desks behind which their agents scribble notes attest to a new international cinema, at least in films of Wong Kar Wai's signature (especially in *In the Mood for Love* [2000]) where "globalization" of the medium is underscored when the director draws on traditions established in Hollywood and the French New Wave. A "regional" picture of delicate psychology, Eric

Rohmer's *Conte d'automne* (1998) exploits viticultural cartography of the Rhône River valley to enhance the aroma and bouquet of mature human attractions. In the narrative space, rigorously plotted about Montélimar and its environs, the characters who smell each other's flesh are compared to a *vin de garde,* a mature mix of syrah, cinsault, and grenache grapes taken from the local hillsides.[8]

As a rule the films will be taken up at the points where maps are inscribed in them. The purpose is to tackle contextual issues made clear when maps visibly are "not the territory" of the movies in which they are found. Surely some films use maps to convey their genre and their style through a seamless relation of narrative space to the film (such is the case in most films seen in megaplexes and malls), while others, *in flagrante delicto* of prevailing mimetic codes, make maps resemble Lautrémont's image of "an umbrella and a sewing machine on an operating table" of their own surrealistic creations. Others are so heteroclite in form that they lead the viewer "all over the map," everywhere and nowhere, thus directing attention toward different plottings in the interstices of sounds and images. The films will be chosen to show how varied, variegated, and mottled the cinematic cartographies can be.

Theory and Cartography

An important strain of French film theory is implicitly built on cartographic principles of cinema. André Bazin, a founder of postwar film theory in France and a father of New Wave cinema, suggests that part of the ontology of film is built upon geographical and geological foundations. The title of his book of essays is telling. *What Is Cinema? (Qu'est-ce que le cinéma?).* To ask *what* it is may be equivalent to wondering *where* it is. In his appeal to a concept of the evolution of cinema Bazin sketches a historical stratigraphy, a geological map that inheres at once in his notion of the fortunes of film language and film genres and in his predilection for deep-focus photography. His metaphors are taken from a tradition of geography that reaches back to the pedagogy of maps and mapping in French schools and the tradition of Paul Vidal de la Blache.[9] A cursory reading of Bazin's writings uncovers the signature of a Christian existentialist and casual philosopher, to be sure, but also of a heightened awareness of the way that cineastes portray—and in portraying, situating, and locating—humans and animals in their ambient world.

In the preface to the four slim tomes of *What Is Cinema?* Bazin noted, "These books will not . . . claim to offer an exhaustive geography and geology of cinema, but merely to draw the reader into a succession of soundings, explorations, and overviews practiced when films are put forward for the critic's daily reflection." He proposes fieldwork, survey, and the drawing of incomplete maps in the place of a finished work or cinematic atlas. In "Cinematographic Realism and the Italian School of the Liberation" (an article first appearing in *Esprit,* January 1948) the words that "situate" cinemas of the postwar directors are couched in the same terms. "After having attempted to demarcate the geography of this cinema, so penetrating in social description, so meticulous and so perspicacious in the choice of true and significant detail, there remains the task of understanding its aesthetic geology" (1999 [1975], 7, 273).

At the center of "The Evolution of Film Language," the most telling essay in his *oeuvre* in which he builds a typology and film based on the overlapping regimes of silent and sound traditions that exploit the long take and deep-focus photography, Bazin argues that directors who had been trained in filmmaking prior to the advent of sound made use of its spatial virtues (the absence of voice and hence a manifest hieroglyphic language or a pictogrammar in the field of view in a shot) in the era that would seem to have consigned them to obsolescence. He asserts,

In 1939 the talkie had reached what geographers call the profile of equilibrium of a river. In other words, this ideal mathematical curve that results from sufficient erosion: having reached its profile of equilibrium, the river flows effortlessly from its source to its mouth and now no longer hollows out its basin. But if there intervenes some geological movement that raises the peneplain, modifying the altitude of the source: the water continues to exert force, penetrating the subjacent terrain, sinking into it, hollowing and rounding it out. Sometimes, if there are layers of limestone, a new relief is suddenly drawn on the plateau in almost invisible concavities, but it is complex and tortuous for as far and as long as we follow the path of the water. (1999 [1975], 71)

The reader wonders if cinema is drawn into an extended geographical conceit. Sound film, argues Bazin, was at such a profile, but with the work of deep-focus directors in the line of William Wyler, Fritz Lang, Orson Welles, and Jean Renoir (indeed a director who films rivers and the *chemin de l'eau* of the water that Bazin describes) a geological "event" takes place. The style of these directors refuses to shatter the filmic event into a mosaic of montage. Bazin's celebrated hypotheses about a rupture or revolution—rather than an evolution—in the language of cinema exploit the lexicon of geography to mark "a vast geological displacement of the foundation of cinema" (76).

The critic does not write of geography and geology in a solely decorative sense. The clear refusal to compare his writings to that of a surveyor attests to its geographical "peneplain." The recurrence of the figure betrays a sensibility that ties the perception (and even what Gilles Deleuze, a close reader of Bazin, calls the *prehension*) of cinematic space to the order of a philosophical *event*.[10] Bazin's penchant for deep focus and the long take are allied with that sensibility. Time and again he ties the event to the ways that the long shot in deep focus transforms the film into a dynamic field of tensions that moves from side to side and forward and backward throughout the visual field. When used artfully, as he says of the works of Orson Welles and William Wyler, deep-focus photography conveys a cinematic event by bearing on the "intellectual relations of the spectator with the image" (75). The event of *Citizen Kane* is that of its insertion into a total movement, "a vast geological displacement of the ground of cinema" (76). For Bazin the world itself becomes part and parcel of the cinematic event that in itself is defined by its "spatial unity" (59). The latter finds ultimate expression in the Western, a genre inseparable "from its geographic frame," especially in the work of Budd Boetticher, the director who knows well "how to make prodigious use of the landscape, of the varied matter of the earth, of grainy textures and the form of rocks" (218, 246).

It is the regime of the "image-fact" (*image-fait*) where Bazin makes clear his implicit cartography. Redefining the "shot" [*plan*] in Rossellini's *Paisan*—a substantive he puts between inverted commas as if to call attention to its meaning as "map"—he notes that its received meaning as "an abstract point of view on reality that is analyzed" is transformed into a "fragment of brute reality, in itself multiple and equivocal, whose meaning is disengaged only *a posteriori*, by virtue of other 'facts' among which the mind establishes relations" (281). For Bazin the fact can be understood as a landscape comprising a paradoxically lacunary totality of elements, such as the marshes near the mouth of the River Po where, in the last sequence, German soldiers murder a group of Italian partisans. Each "image-fact" stands in a paratactic relation with others, as might the fragments of a topography. Bazin is close in spirit to the first sentence of Ptolemy's *Geography* in which cosmography is likened to the construction of a world map in the way a painter executes the portrait of the sitter, while topography is seen as a local view (of a city) in the way that the same painter depicts an isolated or detached piece, such as an eye or an ear.[11] In this way, by accumulation and not by logical concatenation, an array of image-facts produces on the surface of the frame "an equal concrete density" (282), in other words, a loose or even unbound network of tensions of the same charge that are distributed *all over* the image-field. No one place or site has privilege over another.

The image-fact requires the shot to be read as might a map or, if a map or an image of smaller proportion is held within the field of view, as a detail, a detail read not as a privileged zone but as a locus of organic force equal to everything else in the frame. At the outset of *Cinema 2: The Time-Image* (*Cinéma 2: L'Image-temps*), the second panel of a diptych presenting a taxonomy of film, Gilles Deleuze invokes Bazin's concept to inaugurate a moment and style that introduce a "new, apparently dispersive, elliptical, errant, or dancing form of reality, operating by blocks, with deliberately weak linkages or floating events" (1985a, 7). A reader informed by the history of cartography immediately discerns a shift in emphasis from topography, whose partial view is autonomous and whose pieces cohere, to a greater degree of isolation where stress is placed on "événements *flottants*," or floating events. Events become singularities or, it can be inferred, unlinked "islands" of an archipelago without beginning or end. The image-fact exists because of its "isolation" in respect to others of the same kind, to shapes and situations whose tradition of spatial arrangement reaches back to images of the world seen as an open whole of islands or aggregates punctuated by "dead time and empty spaces" (15).[12] The geographic and cartographic under-pinning of Bazin's writing is invoked at a turning point in his taxonomic history of film cinema. It emerges as a foundation for Deleuze's more extensive spatial and cartographic theory of cinema.

Cinematic Taxonomy and Cartography

With the concept of the image-fact and its implicit geography of singularity, still following Bazin, Deleuze draws a line of demarcation between an "old" world of classical cinema and its "newer" counterpart.[13] Cinema of the years prior to the Second World War, in whose immediate aftermath Bazin wrote most of the essays of *What Is Cinema?*, was marked by an aesthetics of action and move-ment. With the advent of montage it realized its own potentiality and became the complete and total—the seventh—art of its name. After the war a cinema of time, argues Deleuze, tends to replace that of movement. Films that had riveted spectators to their seats give way to features encouraging reflection on the rela-tion of the medium to what it cannot represent. A regnum of duration intercedes and supplants that of action. The impact of the war, which indeed was the context in which the image-fact was conceived by way of Bazin's study of Rossellini, is strongly felt in Deleuze's schematic treatment of film. The weakening of the "movement-image" in favor of the "time-image" is marked by the fact that film could "no longer transcribe completed events but had to attain events in the process of their creation," in other words, become consonant with the "event as it was happening." The new cinema brought forward the site of what he calls an "open totality" (Deleuze 1983, 277–78). Space enters the field of view, isolating certain events in certain areas of the frame and allowing others to take place, simultaneously, in others.

Six symptoms come forward. Deleuze speculates that as an implicit result of world history the cinematic image can no longer refer to a "globalizing or syn-thetic situation"—as a *mappamundi* would offer an enclosed view of earthly space—but to scenes of dispersion or disruption. They have no apparent cause and are in no way "unanimistic" as they had been in the past with public cinema in the style of King Vidor or Renoir in *Le Crime de Monsieur Lange*.[14] The "line or fiber of the universe" that tied events together gets frayed, and as a result events become indifferent to themselves. Instead of captivating the spectator's gaze, the camera begins to travel on its own, autonomously, without respect to the point of view of the stories of the lives of the characters it recounts. It wanders and walks through the "rundown fabric of the city, in opposition to action that took place most often in the delimited space-times of the former realism" (280). Clichés overtake plotlines and the exploration of both space and psychology.[15] Finally, cinema no longer sustains "an organization that would refer to a distinct milieu, as in the *film noir* of American realism, to attributable actions by which criminals would make themselves known. . . . No longer is there a magic center from which hypnotic actions could be broadcast as they had in the first two 'Mabuse' films by Fritz Lang" (282–83). In a realm where good and evil are mixed, the spatial and visual opposition of law and order against crime no longer holds sway. An era of suspicion, one in which conspiracy is felt and denounced, takes over.

Thus begins the regime of the time-image that generally pertains to postwar cinema for the reason that, with the filming of the concentration camps, it became evident that any filmic image was in deficit in respect to what it was showing. The time-image would be that of a moment when, "nonetheless," despite the death of the former power of images, despite their frailty and facticity, images are resurrected and redeployed.[16] The "image-fact" that had embodied the contradiction of being a totality and a fragment stands at the fulcrum of the balance. A close reading of *Cinema 2: The Time-Image* reveals that the movement-image inheres indeed in the time-image, and vice-versa, and that inasmuch as the author disclaims history—"[t]his study is not a history of cinema," he asserts in the first sentence of the first volume (1983, 7)—history sustains what he calls a taxonomic project. Without working through the contradictions or elucidating the finer points of Deleuze's classifications, a reader quickly observes that they are based on "locational" or spatial logic, if not indeed on a typology that reaches back to the hemispheres of "old" and "new" worlds as they had been depicted in atlases.[17] One of the virtues of the taxonomy is analytical. Insofar as time-images and movement-images seem to belong to two different regimes, they are nonetheless inseparable. The distinction, however, helps to show how perception, action, and affect are expressed by and evinced in cinema in different ways at different moments. It engages interpretation based on a dialectics that lacks a synthetic term. At stake is a mode of "mapping" film by way of plot points of time and movement in space.[18]

Archive and Diagram

Deleuze's work as a philosopher and critical writer resembles that of a cinematic *auteur*. It needs to be read in its totality; from the linkages and ruptures of its details and from its isolated fragments productive itineraries and connections can be made.[19] In two chapters of *Foucault* (one titled "Un nouveau cartographe [A New Cartographer]") the author of *Cinéma 1* and *Cinéma 2* makes distinctions, on the one hand, between "discursive" and "visible" formations" and, on the other, between archival maps and diagrams. For Foucault a discursive forma-tion meant the array of modes of speaking and communicating in which a human subject is born and that determine much of what he or she can say. The subject tends more to be spoken by prevailing modes of discourse than to speak them in his or her own name. The same holds for visible formations. Many inherited and often inert images circulate in the midst of a public to determine how it will ascertain and collect, and even see the shapes and contours of the world at large.

At given moments visibility changes, and so do ways of speaking. From over-lapping "manners of speaking and ways of seeing" a map a sense of modern his-tory can be conceived. Strata and layers of space and time are shown through examination of pertinent differences (Deleuze 1985b, 56). Knowledge, which Foucault equates with power, becomes a practical implementation, a "mecha-nism" or a "machine," as it were, of utterances and visibilities. The creative indi-vidual is he or she who can "break open words, sentences or propositions in order to extract their statements" (59) and who can shatter "things" in the same way. The task of the archeologist, he says, is to "*crack open* words, sentences and propositions, to *crack open* qualities, things, and objects. When what is seen and what is spoken are shown not to be of the same order an archeology is engaged." Deleuze notes that "Foucault is singularly close to contemporary cin-ema" (72), no doubt for the reason that the differences of the soundtrack and the image-track can be read and plotted along both diverging and criss-crossing lines. It is in the regime of these differences where the real "map," the strategic operation of the cinema as well as its invention or its unconscious is most likely to be discovered.[20] Real artists happen to be those who turn discursive forms in the direction of visibility and, conversely, invest visible shapes and the tactil-ity of things into language. They are, like Foucault's Raymond Roussel, those who can speak and make objects visible in the same movement and gesture. They could also be filmmakers of the order of auteurs, the artists whom Deleuze admires, "great *auteurs* of cinema . . . who can be compared not only to painters, architects, musicians, but also to thinkers. *Auteurs* think with movement-images and time-images instead of concepts" (1983, 7–8).

Those who study cinema account for the rifts and overlappings of things seen and things said. In these areas a general cartography of film becomes manifest, especially where maps, themselves intermediate objects that combine visible and discursive formations on the same surface, bring forward the gaps and con-tradictions of the "tracks" of film. In *Foucault* Deleuze's remarks fall under his rubric of "Topology: 'Thinking Otherwise.'" As if in a lap-dissolve, they blend with some crucial reflections that end the section of the book, titled "From the Archive to the Diagram," which is capped by "A New Cartographer," the name given to a close reading of *Surveiller et punir* (Discipline and punish) (1975). He argues that the author draws and then superimposes multifarious maps in order to explain the rifts and shifts of power that take place in the passage from a monarchic order in France prior to 1789 to the onset of its industrial revolution. He plots the fate of law, taken not to be a set of sacrosanct rules, but a management of "illegalisms," of illegal practices that are required to be sustained in the management of law. Law "is no more a state of peace than the result of war that is won: it is war itself, and the strategy of this war in action, just as power is not a property acquired by the dominant class, but an on-going exercise of its strategy" (Deleuze 1985b, 37, 38).

Into this configuration Deleuze plugs the latent cinematic concept of discursive and visible formations. The discursive embodiment of the law would be found in the former, in codes and in juridical practice while the latter, the prison, would be its visible counterpart of a shape and form that are not necessarily congruent with the statutes that would determine it. The commentator inserts the concepts of "form of content" and "form of expression" to show that a difference is at stake between "the form of the visible" and the "form of the utterable" (1985b, 40). When the two are juxtaposed there results a "diagram," what Deleuze glosses as

> no longer the auditive or visual archive, but the map, the cartography co-extensive with the entire social field. It is an abstract machine. Defined by functions and unshaped matter, it makes no formal distinction between a content and an expression, between a discursive formation and a non-discursive formation. It is an almost mute and blind machine even though it is what makes seeing and speaking possible. (1985b, 42)

Here the diagram could qualify as a film. A film sets forward the stakes and laws of its form and proceeds to work with and against them. It overtly proposes certain modes of conduct in some areas and others in different strata, covertly, through its own illegalisms. It obeys the laws that censors apply but simultaneously perverts them, by quoting and bending them to make new and different shapes.[21] Certain laws that would be made clear on the image-track are foiled or "cracked open" by the flagrant contradictions of utterances in and out of frame on the soundtrack. As a diagram, too, given its "spatio-temporal multiplicity" (Deleuze 1985b, 42), a film would be an exposition of relations of force, not just in what is seen on screen but also in the greater space of its projection or emission. The diagram is especially cinematographic in the way that on a collective scale it can plot behavior or even, it can be argued, perception:

> [T]he diagram is profoundly unstable and in flux, endlessly mixing material and functions so as to constitute mutations. Finally, every diagram is intersocial and in a condition of becoming. It never functions in order to represent a pre-existing world, it produces a new type of reality, a new model of truth. It is not a subject of history, nor what overlooks history. It makes history in undoing preceding realities

and meanings, constituting as many points of emergence or of creativity, of unexpected conjunctions, of improbable continuums. It doubles history with a becoming. (1985b, 43)

The beauty of the cinematic diagram resides in the way its own causes at once stand coextensive with and even "program" the reality that would be a sum of its effects. What Deleuze describes through the action of doubling can be taken at once as mirroring and, as might accelerate a car on a highway, an action of passing or moving ahead.

The diagram goes beyond "history" because it is designed to make history happen, that is, to cause its events to be enveloped in its own past or archive. What "will have happened" will have happened by virtue of a programmatic mechanism.[22] At the end of the chapter the reader returns to the issue of doubling. "The history of forms, an archive, is doubled by a becoming of forces, a diagram" (1985b, 51). In the place of the subject there could be placed "the history of cinema" in such a way that the predicate—*doubler* in French—inflects the substantive to mean that cinema has already plotted its own history or has produced the visible and discursive formations that characterize the manuals, chronicles, introductions, and encyclopedias through which we are given to know how film has "become what it is." In view of this model the historian of cinema would be the exegete or archivist who ventriloquizes the forms and norms of an inherited cinematic diagram.

But the same historian can work in the context of what Deleuze calls a cartography of becoming: "A diagram is a map, or rather [a set of] maps superimposed upon one another. And, from one diagram to the other, new maps are drawn [*tirées*]. Thus no diagram fails to bear, next to the points it connects, other points, relatively free or unbound, points of creativity, of mutation, of resistance; and we move from them in order to comprehend the totality" (1985b, 51). With archival material the historian can fashion other and new—creative, mutating, resisting—shapes of interpretation. If the lexicon of Michel de Certeau were plotted over these words, the new shapes would be the result of a cartographic tactics—a diagram—that operates in the midst of strategic designs. In this rich and dense passage of *Foucault* the reader witnesses an interrogation of inherited mappings and a politics advocating new and different uses of them. Such are the stakes of the study of maps, insofar as they can be taken as diagrams, within films, that in themselves are also diagrams with multifarious objectives.

Deleuze ends his reading by quoting an interview that Foucault had led in 1975 in which he called himself a cartographer for the reason that he felt his political commitments made themselves clear as a mode of practical and tactical writing. He called it a writing equivalent to a mapping. "To write is to struggle, in other words, to resist; to write is to become; to write is to make maps [*écrire, c'est cartographier*]. 'I'm a cartographer'" (1985b, 51).[23] In the triple definition of writing that Deleuze extracts from Foucault, what goes in the name of the archive becomes a tactics because it resists any or all complacency that inheres in pregiven truth. In terms of a cinematic diagram it can be observed that where a map is seen in a film, or where a map shows how a film becomes a map, cartography can make visible the history of the strategies informing what a film is projecting.[24] Quite often maps in films are archival diagrams that tell of the history and strategy of the surrounding film. In *Saskatchewan* (1954), a feature that André Bazin praised for its fidelity to the classical order of the Western,[25] director Raoul Walsh tells the story of a quixotic member of the Canadian Mounties (Alan Ladd) and his Sancho-like companion (Leo Carillo) who are obliged to cross the Canadian Rockies to deliver a truant woman (Shelley Winters) to authorities in Montana. The two cronies, one in his fire-engine-red uniform of the Royal Canadian Mounted Police and the other wearing animal skins, report to a British captain who is clearly out of place in the barracks of a makeshift fort at a limitrophe region of the Canadian wilderness. Trained to go by the book of classical military conduct, the captain indicates to the two men how they must cross the border. The film cuts to a close-up of a map of the Saskatchewan territory. With the tip of a pencil a hand indicates an itinerary that will go from "here" (in Saskatchewan, a site given in the credits of the film and doubled in the map seen in the close-up) to "there" on the other side of an artificial line of division, to a site that he calls "Fort Walsh." *Fort . . . da:* the itinerary is effectively that of many films for which Raoul Walsh was known. On the map is drawn the trajectory of an auteur, of a director (*Saskatchewan* figured then as the 109th film in his career as a director) who mythifies himself and the "form of the content" of his oeuvre in the map-sequence in the film.[26]

The episode pertains to the narrative and the itinerary of a director. So also does the map that appears in Ridley Scott's *Gladiator* (2000). We see it after Maximus (Russell Crowe) has won the day in bloody combat against the Goths at the upper reaches of the Roman Empire. Marcus Aurelius (Richard Harris) has brought the captain into his tent in order to bestow upon him the leadership of the kingdom. He asks his centurion to "look at this map." What we see for an instant is a projection of Italy and the northern provinces, the peninsula itself as it had been known in manuscript and printed editions of Ptolemy in the fifteenth and sixteenth centuries. The flagrant disrespect for authenticity reveals a history of greater facture: the viewer immediately recalls that in Anthony Mann's *The Fall of the Roman Empire* (1964) a similar sequence portrayed Marcus Aurelius (Alec Guinness) leading Maximus (Christopher Plummer) by an easel to look at one of its sheet maps on display. The cutway shot of Ptolemy's *Italia* in Scott's epic makes clear the facticity of the map and the liberties taken with historical reconstruction, on the one hand, while it also indicates, like a footnote,[27] not only one of the principal sources of the film's conception but also a dialogue between two different directorial stakes and styles, that of Scott in 2002 and Anthony

Mann in the heyday of the Cold War in 1963. Both instances indicate that the sight of a map in a film often makes visible the history of the form producing the film, in other words, the archive held within and generating the tactics of the diagram.

Dislocation, Distance, Discretion

At the crossroads of theory and cinema in the work of Deleuze and Foucault, it is often difficult to see if and where a spectator may be. Is the diagram on or off the horizon of the viewer? If cinema is a machine or a map of forces of its construction the spectator may be, as Walter Benjamin noted about the study of the fine arts, an element unworthy of consideration.[28] Even more than Benjamin might have believed, the film can show the viewer that, perhaps with the exception of the projectionist, he or she is outside of its operation. The effect that Benjamin (and elsewhere Foucault) locates as a regime "outside" of a field of meaning bears on the effect of exclusion that maps often convey to their readers. The effect of reading on a map under a plexiglas panel, "You are here," a statement printed adjacent to an arrow on a map of a quarter near the entrance or exit of any of the major subway stations in cities around the world, bears witness to the same sense of exclusion. We are no more on the map than we may be in the space indicated by its geographic signs. Viewers of maps who seek to arrive at a destination often discover that, once their states of agitation and expectation are accounted for, they are in different places at once. Memories and fears of being lost—often associated with thoughts of being scattered in different places— interfere with cognition required to read the chart and to arrive at a destination.

In "The Uncanny," in a memorable cartography of anxiety, Freud recounts an event in which he discovered how it felt to be lost.

As I was walking, one hot summer afternoon, through the deserted streets of a provincial town in Italy which was unknown to me, I found myself in a quarter of whose character I could not long remain in doubt. Nothing but painted women were to be seen at the windows of the small houses, and I hastened to leave the narrow street at the next turning. But after having wandered about for a time without enquiring my way, I suddenly found myself back at the same street, where my presence was now beginning to excite attention. I hurried away once more, only to arrive by another *détour* at the same place yet a third time. Now, however, a feeling overcame me which I can only describe as uncanny, and I was glad enough to find myself back at the piazza I had left a short while before, without any further voyages of discovery. (1955, 17:237)

A promenade turns into a nightmare. The author is ambulating in a town whose name and place are unknown to him. He gets lost, happens upon a sight that frightens him, he recoils, sets off again, and finds himself in the same unsettling place. By way of automatic pilot (without asking an Italian pedestrian about how to get to the unnamed site from where he had begun his voyage) he regains his bearings. He settles as soon as he marshals the concept of the uncanny to explain the fear evinced at the sight of the "painted women," the women in the window or figures who could be vamps on a screen who would stand forward (*pro-situated*) and cause him to turn away and take the same detour twice, a zig-zagged itinerary, to and from a site that in the very text is foreign to the original place: the *piazza*. The point of departure and return is not a *Platz* as it would be in the familiar German idiom. It is a piazza, the site where the "uncanny" is found, where one language resides in another, and where an effect of doubling is inscribed in the twice-marked letter, the "*z-z*," that traces the author's venture ahead, his retreat, and his return.

If Freud's account can be read in the manner of a spatial story or even a film, the autobiographical narrative that leads him to and from the painted women would be the movie and the piazza the map within it.[29] The word not only traces the line of his itinerary; it also doubles it as it stands at the origin and end of the narration. As the author had said about his own physical relation with the concept, the word *translates itself* into a spatial and graphic sign of the Uncanny.[30] He marks the very topic of the essay, the sense of being without location, in the doubly inflected site. Freud further emphasizes the point by recalling how much the uncanny is reminiscent in a comic way of the "wild exaggeration" in Mark Twain, another map-like name that in the textual carpet that stands at once as an anthroponym and a toponym of doubling. The pseudonym is of two words, the Christian name an act or fact of inscription, the surname containing a letter, a *w*, a double *u*, that is an inversion of the incipient *m* of the forename, the former distinguished from the latter by the difference between upper and lower case.

Freud's narrative of a brief and frightening experience of *Wanderlust* tells much about cartographic exclusion and doubling in the realm of cinema. Freud is obliged to imagine himself in a place where he had felt himself—had he ever been there in the first place—twice displaced. In order to feel the uncanny, he had to transport or translate himself from one site to another.[31] His miniature essay in self-mapping describes some of the cartographic effects that we often feel when we are in movie theaters. We "translate" ourselves into the imagination of another time and space. We suspend disbelief only insofar as our disbelief is threatened by our suspicion that identification with the film is based on *not being there*. We gather that the film begins to work on the ways that the very crux of our being and subjectivity are tested through spatial displacement.

The anxiety of displacement experienced in a movie theater is felt to the quick in Roland Barthes's description of the sensations he experiences (in the third person) when he exits. Barthes's spectator passes by the front doors in the evening and, as might a somnambulist, walks limp, in silence, in the direction of a café, "somewhat numb, feeling cramped, sensitive to the cold, in a word, asleep: *he's drowsy,* that's what he thinks; his body has become something sopitive, soft, serene: limp as a dormant cat, he feels something inarticulate, or even (since, for the ends of a moral organization repose is required): irresponsibility. In short, it's clear, he is leaving a kind of hypnosis" (1975, 104). Barthes's spectator wants to leave an amorphous and floating state as he is searching both for an exit (in a psychoanalytical register) and a cure. Barthes's account of the spectator's entry into the movie theater makes the connections of a geography of displacement to hypnosis even clearer. The spectator who would not be on a cultural quest

> goes to the movie theater on basis of an idleness, of free time, of vacancy. Everything happens as if, even before going inside the theater, all the classical symptoms of hypnosis were manifest: emptiness, unconstrained time, there being nothing better to do: it is not in front of the film and through the film that we dream: we dream, unbeknownst to ourselves, before we become the spectator. There exists a "situation of cinema," and this situation is pre-hypnotic. Following a true metonymy, the darkness of the room is prefigured by the "crepuscular reverie" (a precondition to hypnosis in the words of Breuer-Freud) that precedes this darkness and conduces the subject, from street to street, from poster to poster, finally to get lost in an obscure, anonymous, indifferent cube in which takes place this festival of affects called a film. (104)

Barthes's spectator depicted here is idle, aimless, seeking to find something where he will lose all bearings. A *flâneur* of celluloid, he finds passing geographical markers in streets (possibly their names) and posters (that may be those of films). He is in a privileged affective zone because he is conscious of not being where he is. His affect is charged because the space of the movie theater invites a greater erotic availability, a sort of post-Gidean *disponibilité,* than the act of cruising, which for the cruiser would imply the presence of prey to be stalked in the street. But in the cinema, "in this urban darkness" is where "the freedom of the body is laboring; this invisible labor of virtual affectivity results from what is a veritable cinematic cocoon" (105).

The erotic state of being that makes viewing possible becomes a function of the spectator's displacement into an unmoored, self-detached position with respect to the geography in which he or she is situated. For this reason Barthes underscores that as a viewer he must "also be *elsewhere*" (106). If the film itself is a lure (indeed a fiction of locational imaging), it is shown in order to capture and captivate us into misrecognizing who and where we are. He suggests that the experience of displacement owes to a visual and even retinal "detachment" in which the spectator indulges in and breaks away from a fascination with filmed images. Thus the spectator can watch the film twice in the same blow: first through the image that gets attached to the narcissistic body and then through the perverse body that fetishizes not the image but that which exceeds it. It could be the granular texture of voice on the soundtrack, the space of the movie theater, the darkness, "the obscure mass of other bodies, the shafts of light, the entry, the exit" (106).

Barthes notes that in the two viewings affected by way of detachment an initial "relation" gets complicated when it becomes a "situation," that is, a sense of site that plots the space and time of a relation. Implied here is the intervention of cartography, of the mapping of the spatial traits of the experience of subjectivity. They take place within and at the margins of the movie theater. The critic's ideal spectator is he (for Barthes the shifter tends to be masculine) who is fascinated by his own awareness of displacement. The spectator is hypnotized by the distance he takes in respect to the image or the film within the frame of its captive power. Barthes calls it an amorous and not an intellectual distance, a blissful distance of *discretion* insofar as discretion is understood, he implies, in its etymological sense as *separation*. For the purpose of the arguments in these pages it should be added that, within the movie theater and within the film the spectator is watching, the map becomes the agent of the discretion and erotic distancing at the crux of visual pleasure.

Mental Mapping and Mobile Topography

The spectator who takes cognizance of being unmoored in the theater becomes conscious of at least two geographies. The one, affective, that Barthes describes with meticulous precision, is mobile. It appears to the spectator in the liminal areas of applied distraction, of free attention, of erotic reverie, of being errant but available to fix upon and discern different mental and physical sites. These sites are where an affective situation develops from a relation that the inner folds and musings of the self hold with the spaces seen on the screen in a public theater. The other, no less mobile, is cued through a mental geography the viewer or subject constructs with positions taken in respect to those being mapped and plotted in the cinema.

This geography might be related to what has been called cognitive and mental mapping. For Christian Jacob mental mapping is constituted through the spatial representation we make in our minds of the acts and actions taken in our everyday lives. In our imagination we plot our activities with reference to "a mental projection and even to a mental world map," a psychic surface that "[i]n a complex way . . . mixes the individual and intimate traits with all forms of knowledge and with images that circulate in a given society and culture" (1992, 453–54; 2006, 359–60). The mental map belongs to the individual and cannot be translated into general terms even though its substance is made from a mixture of personal and collective impressions. It might be formed by the experience of certain films at given times, and it might also be a set of variants selected, consciously and unconsciously, from masses of images with which we construct the geographical illusions that are vital to our lives.[32]

Mental mapping resembles cognitive mapping insofar as the latter describes how individuals negotiate their lives in the places in which they move. It is a practice based on spatial choices, on going here or there in one way or mode of conveyance or another, and of tying one's actions in a particular place to the idea that they might, in the best of all utopian scenarios, bear on the world at large. For Fredric Jameson the spectator is he or she, when listening to the fantasies that a film elicits, who seeks to find at deeper levels the gnawing and unsettling thoughts about the workings of political machineries determining the act of viewing. In the context of film the cognitive map accounts both for what cinema represents and in its modes of production and global circulation. Cognitive mapping of movies entails seeing how interpretation on a local scale might tap into a praxis or a politics. For Jameson the individual viewer would be a "topographer" who tries to link the contradictions found in a particular place—a sequence in a film, or the decision to study a film that belongs to a time and space entirely foreign to the context in which it is chosen to be seen—to a greater "geography" or a world map, in which an assessment of the cartography of the overall (and generally sorry) condition of our planet is tendered.[33]

The tenor of these concepts is resonant in critical work on cinema that builds on speech-acts, subject-positions, and enunciation. The spectator of a film frequently wonders—especially when speech is heard voice-off—who is speaking and from where. Unlike living dialogue, voice in cinema cannot be plotted according to the places held by speakers and listeners or utterers and their utterances. Synchrony of sound and image remains an illusion. Quite often films, like those of Robert Bresson, make clear that illusion by showing how enunciation belongs to their own "inner geography," a spatial construction that a map in a movie tends to crystallize.[34] The map seen in the film attests to what Christian Metz calls a "mobile topography," in his other words, "the changing geography" underscored when speech or gesture are discerned in the context of camera angles, intertitles, voice-in and voice-off, film-in-the-film, and other techniques that underscore how much "filmic enunciation is impersonal, textual, meta-discursive," and how much it "inflects or reflects its own statement" (1991b, 210). The late theorist offers the metaphor of a cinematic topography in terms of "folds" and "creasings" that bear witness to the very form of film. Such is, too, what a map, when seen in a film, often makes clear.

A Map in a Movie

In the parabola of film theory drawn above, which turns from André Bazin to Gilles Deleuze and from Roland Barthes to Christian Metz, variations on a mapping impulse are clear. For the author of *What Is Cinema?* an ontology of the photographic and cinematic image brings forward a relation of surface to spatiality. The long shot, the *plan-séquence* (or long take) and deep-focus photography make the very existence of the world an event of perception. For Bazin the cinematic image is endowed with simultaneously visible, tactile, and material qualities. It is in dialogue with the players and objects that move within it, and for that reason an image—at least an image worthy of its name—is not a representation but the world itself. It is a map to the degree it is at once a geography, a totality, and a form liable to contain topographies or places in the image that can be called localities with specific characters and historical traits. His descriptions often show that cinema and mapping converge in decisive areas or moments on which he bestows the names of *facts* and *events*. They produce space through the action of perception, especially perception that both perceives and perceives its ways of perceiving. The event has a haptic quality felt when the eyes scan and move about the image as they might the surface of a relief map, where they seem to touch and to travel up and down and about the lands and waters being shown. As a general rule the haptic quality of the event bears much in common with the way that maps offer themselves to the spectator: they can be seen from any angle and studied without a prescribed track as might a printed sentence or a narrative that calls attention to its peripatetic thread. When seen in a movie a map often brings forward these elements of the image in which it is found.

Bazin's coinage of the image-fact draws attention to the paratactic aspect of elements seen in an image or a sequence of a film. Whatever linkages a spectator makes are those inspired by geographies generally determined by webbings of iconic signs in the field of view and the artifice of editing. The image-fact informs Metz's idea of a "mobile geography" of cinema because it tears asunder all illusion of a necessary cause that might make what is perceived in one area of the image or heard on the soundtrack a result of an intrinsic coherence of things. When a map appears in a movie it often turns an otherwise coded and controlled image into a lacunary or isolated "fact." Now and again (as it will be seen in Renoir's cinema) the sight of the map triggers a heightened sense of perception and thus becomes a site where the event of the film itself takes place.

If these typologies and taxonomies are kept in mind, the perception of a map both in and as the film begs consideration of the rapport of the image to movement and to time. The film moves insofar as the map offers a spatial picture of a shape and duration other than those of the image in which it is found. Quite often the map locates the history of the film within itself. It has affinities with a *mise-en-abyme,* but while it may duplicate or mirror the surrounding film, the map can reveal why and how it is made and how its ideology is operating. As an "archive," a film sums up a history of its production through contextual citation.

As a "diagram" or a model that maps perception and comportment through the image-field, the map is in flux where it shows how the archival aspect of the film might also be its diagram. The fluid and shifting spaces of the film and its cognition become *terrae incognitae* that the viewer explores in different directions and from various angles.

At the outset of his work on cinema Gilles Deleuze asserted that the "great authors" of cinema could be compared to painters, architects, and philosophers. Often destroyed, silenced, or left to decay, their lives and creations bear witness to the force and fragility that mark the great works of art and thought in general. Notwithstanding the global production and circulation of cinematic rubbish, these authors have invented "irreplaceable autonomous forms" (1983, 7–8) that, we can add, mark the lives of all of us who live with them. The concept of the *auteur* is broadened to mean that the films of certain directors invent new and other types of time and space. What is made of their work, like poetry, cannot be controlled as might a planet under the aegis of global positioning systems and satellite surveillance. The auteur in this broad sense can also be understood to be a cartographer.

The plan of the chapters that follow is guided by the idea that the great auteurs make maps of their movies. They plot and chart their films in unforeseen and often unconscious ways; they also engage, singly and collectively, extensive dialogue with cartography and its history. If these filmmakers conceive and execute their films as mapped forms, it stands to reason that their works require close and detailed analysis. "Le bon Dieu est dans le detail [The grace of God is in the detail]," Gustave Flaubert reputedly said of the art of reading and writing. The proverb has never been lost upon the cartographer and, it is hoped, the student of cinema. Some of the descriptions of sequences in which maps may appear fastidious: where detail is keynote, it appears that the detail of overly close reading is preferable to the incontinence of thematic and narrative summary.

The work will build from René Clair, a cineast whose first film, *Paris qui dort* (1924) appears to be a theory of cinema, assumed to be a strategic control of perception, tied to mapping. The study will move contrastively to Jean Renoir, whose cartographic sense of the medium in the years 1932–39 is varied and sustained. A chapter on Roberto Rossellini's *Roma, città aperta* (1945), a film that tends to resist analysis, will be treated through the presence of the *theatrum mundi* in its narrative space. Attention will turn to concurrent cinemas of "desperate journeys," films in which evasion and escape provide a ground for mapping. In these pages the model of the classical director—Clair, Renoir, Rossellini—of the earlier chapters will be tested against those who figure—Michael Curtiz, Raoul Walsh, Steven Spielberg—in the domain of industrial cinema. Attention will then turn to the juvenile geographies of auteur cinema in the postwar years, specifically in François Truffaut's first two films, *Les Mistons* (1957) and *Les 400 coups* (1959). Between the one and the other, for reason of chronology and comparison, a study of affective geography will be taken up in a reading of Louis Malle's *Les Amants* (1958). The last section of the study will be given to three films, Matthieu Kassovitz's *La Haine* (1995), a feature of post–New Wave vintage, and two others, both aimed to reach an international public, Ridley Scott's *Thelma and Louise* (1992) and *Gladiator* (2000). Different films and directors could have been chosen. Fate and design have led to work on these features that serve as models for other studies.

1
Icarian Cinema:
Paris qui dort

Michel-Etienne Turgot's great map of Paris, details of which often decorate the walls of hotels and travel agencies, was completed in 1739. Composed of a key map and followed by nineteen folios on which are printed as many detailed views, the sum is an overview of an unreal city. The viewer of this first modern city-view would be looking at agglomerations of buildings and streets around the Île-de-la-Cité and the right and left banks from an altitude of not much more than a kilometer, roughly that of a hot-air balloon or else a perch near the top of the Eiffel Tower. The Tower is what is most obviously missing from the great projection. Turgot's map presents a strange adventure for its reader. The city is bathed in light that reaches into vacant and wide streets crosshatching forests of settlements of no more than five stories. Seen from a bird's eye, Paris seems to be an architect's dream. Horse-drawn vehicles are absent from the streets, and so too are pedestrians who would crowd along the sidewalks or take refuge from the rain under any of its many arcades. The city is motionless. It invites the eye move all about and over its detailed depictions of various quarters and their houses. We delight in the fantasy of wandering about spaces where nothing would interfere with the pleasure of letting the eye walk aimlessly in the streets or rove about nooks and alleys incised in the copperplate images. When its sheets are arranged on a wall, a utopian city that could be of timeless duration is given to an unimpeded gaze.

The map will serve as one of two epigraphs for a reading of René Clair's first feature, *Paris qui dort* (1923) (The Crazy Ray), a film that begins with what would seem to be a view of the contemporary city in the style of Turgot. The other is Louis-Sébastien Mercier's *L'An 2440 : Rêve s'il en fut jamais* (The year 2440 : A fanciful dream), a utopian fiction of 1770 in which a man wakes from a sleep of 700 years to discover how his city has changed and become at once familiar and strange.[1] The novel begins with a dialogue between the narrator and an Englishman, visiting Paris, who compares the city to a *monstre difforme* (a deformed monster), a "receptacle of extreme opulence and excessive misery" (1999, 29). Disgusted by the decadent state of both Paris and London, he follows Rousseau's steps in wishing to find a village where, "in pure air and with tranquil pleasure I might deplore the fate of the sad inhabitants of these lavish prisons that go by the name of cities" (31). The Englishman leaves at midnight. The narrator gets drowsy. "As soon as sleep extended itself over my eyelids, I dreamed that I had been dozing for centuries, and that I was awakening" (35). He looks about and wonders where he is:

> Tout était changé. Tous ces quartiers qui m'étaient si connus, se présentaient à moi sous une forme différente et récemment embellie. Je me perdais dans de grandes et belles rues proprement alignées. J'entrais dans des carrefours spacieux où regnait un si bon ordre que je n'y apercevais plus le plus léger embarras. Je n'entendais aucun de ces cris confusément bizarres qui déchiraient jadis mon oreille. Je ne rencontrais point de voitures prêtes à m'écraser. Un goutteux aurait pu se promener commodément. La ville avait un air animé, mais sans trouble et sans confusion. (36)

Figure 1. Michel-Etienne Turgot, map of Paris (detail: sheet 15), 1734–39. Courtesy Spenser Library, University of Kansas.

Everything had changed. All these areas that I had known so well were offered to me in a different and newly embellished form. I lost myself in the handsome and spacious streets where there reigned such a marvelous order that I couldn't glimpse the slightest obstacle. I heard none of these confusingly strange cries that used to ring in my ears. I no longer bumped into vehicles speeding to crush me. A man afflicted with gout would have been able to walk about with ease. The city had an animated air but lacked disquiet and confusion.

In awakening the narrator might have found himself staring at Turgot's seemingly utopian map.

He too might have been the protagonist of *Paris qui dort,* René Clair's first film, a short feature (about 60 minutes) that includes in its frame equally utopian and dystopian views of the City of Light. A night watchman who guards the Eiffel Tower awakens one morning, looks down from his quarters at the top of the edifice, and discovers that life has stopped; so too has his watch, whose needles are arrested at 3:25 a.m. He descends and walks through an unreal and empty city in which humans and machines have been stopped. He encounters five people who have flown from Marseille to Paris. The aviator has brought a mundane and beautiful woman of the world, a thief handcuffed to a guard, and a cagey businessman seeking to meet his mistress. They all band together, take pleasure in the freedom of the city, but soon rival each other for the attention of the young woman. As chaos begins to reign they hear a plaintive message on the wireless from the niece and assistant of a mad doctor who has devised a ray that freezes all life in the world. The group descends to meet her. They learn of the range and effects of the ray before, together, they collectively force the doctor to bring life back to the city. They accomplish their mission. The hero realizes that he needs money and that to make ends meet he must pilfer cash from people under the spell of the ray. He and the niece to whom he is attracted return to the laboratory where a battle over the machine precipitates accelerated movement and stoppage of the life and rhythms of the city. Once the hero and the niece repair to the top of the Tower where they exchange vows with a ring, they discern evidence attesting to the fact that what had taken place was indeed not a dream.

A Site of Immaculate Origin

In a powerful study that sees in *Paris qui dort* the seeds of revolutionary cinema Annette Michaelson remarks that the analytic propensities of the medium, taken up in Epstein, Eisenstein, and Léger, "find their most concentrated and elaborate expression in the work of René Clair and Dziga Vertov" (1979, 41). The two cineastes brought forward an educational program of cinema responding to Walter Benjamin, Elie Faure, and Albert Einstein, three visionaries who desired to have film serve the ends of classroom teaching and to revitalize pedagogy of traditional disciplines. They wanted, perhaps, to bring cinema into classrooms decorated with instructive wall maps. Einstein, she adds, felt that cinema would be a boon to geography.

> By means of the school film, supplemented by a simple apparatus for projection, it would be possible firstly to infuse certain subjects, *such as geography,* which is at present wound off organ-like in the form of dead descriptions, with the pulsating life of a metropolis. And the lines on a map will gain an entirely new complexion in the eyes of the pupil, if he learns, as if during a voyage, what they actually include, and what is to be read between them.[2]

In its "cascade of subtle gags" Clair's film becomes a "topography of a great city" in which scale and pace are a function of temporality grasped as "movement in space" (Michaelson 1979, 35).

A casual reading shows that the film maps out a history of modernity born in the invention of cinema. Louis Lumière had made a tracking shot from the Tower, and so also did James White. These memories seem present in Clair's feature. If, as Georges Sadoul has noted, the Eiffel Tower was the true "star" of *Paris qui dort* (1968 [1949], 196–97), its presence as character (or even prosopopoeia) of modernity is due to the invocation of recent memory of early cinema and the aftereffects of the Exposition. As of 1889 the Tower quickly became a ground zero of French history: in its design as a dazzling and overwhelming metallic erection it occluded the political presence of the French Revolution felt in the shockwaves in Paris at regular intervals in the nineteenth century (1830, 1848, 1871). Its ironwork obelisk was to commemorate a new and immaculate beginning (Ferguson 1995). An economic revolution and a utopian space were to be born at the site of the Tower. And with the Tower came the opening the Metro and the advent of new maps of the city and monuments laced with lines indicating subways completed and under construction.[3] The early films showed that the Tower could provide "not merely a general, panoramic view of the landscape but, in a manner grasped and fully exploited by Clair, a machine for the generation of infinite compositional variations" (Michaelson 1979, 57). The environs of the Tower, seen in tracking shots through a maze of girders resembling a lacework of rhumb lines, or in takes of characters sauntering through constructions of girders, became a city-view in movement and atmospheric flux.

The film has a particular affinity for cartography in its attraction not only to the tradition of Feuillade and French cinema of the First World War but also, no less remotely, to the beginnings of the medium. The historicity of *Paris qui dort*—the degree to which it makes clear its own relation to the development of the medium—shares much with a pertinent trait of the atlas in general. Most atlases preface their maps with images or textual information about creation.

They arch back to the beginnings of life ("as we know it") and the subsequent natural and human histories of the world giving rise to its cartography.[4] *Paris qui dort* does just that in an atlas-effect felt in its jumps and gaps in time that affirm its allegiance with the beginnings of the medium. Clair admitted that he had wanted to exploit cinematic effects of movement to an absurd degree. The camera would paralyze urban space and its play of stasis and movement. It would offer "a truly fresh vision of an *other,* marvelous world" (Abel 1984, 380). The other world had been one familiar not only to Edison and Lumière but also to Jean Durand in his Onésime series, shot at the Gaumont Studio, notably *Onésime l'horloger* (1912), a film that uses time-machines to accelerate the duration of the life of its protagonist.[5] Clair recalls Durand's film but, beyond its trick effects, the memory is filtered through the realistic takes and tracking shots recalling Lumière and a narrative that would be associated with the oneiric tales of Méliès.[6] The effects of the latter are made through the style of the former. No concession is given to special effects: the fantasy is engineered in daylight, in the streets of Paris, "at the intersection of two supposedly antagonistic traditions that all of a sudden happen to be complementary" (Billard 1998, 80). If Clair's recollections about the origin of the idea of the film are trustworthy, he was wishing to study how power could be afforded to those owning an icarian point of view on the world.

A Film in Flux

Paris qui dort has appeared in at least two versions. One is a thirty-five-minute "digest," accompanied by piano music on a soundtrack, which Clair made in 1971 from material he recovered from earlier work that is now appended to the Criterion Collection edition of *Sous les toits de Paris.* Another, closer in form to an original feature of over an hour's length, is composed of 1,480 meters of film and presumably is the matter of most sixteen-millimeter prints and videocassettes.[7] In 1929 a sound version, conceived to be a partial talkie, was planned but never completed (Billard 1998, 80, 84). The restored copy in the Criterion Collection tends to be a summary or even an interpretation of the longer version. More sparing in its use of intertitles, its effects are less textured and choppy. The newly digitized version invites the spectator to follow the narrative at the expense of engaging its detail.

Both the print from the Museum of Modern Art and the video copy carry copious subtitles in English that attest to the appeal made to a public outside of France. The floral design in the borders of the subtitle bear on its cartographic latency. At a lower corner in the title is a globe, perhaps a memory of the sphere adjacent to the Eiffel Tower at the time of the Universal Exposition, replete with the lines of the tropics, colures, and meridians. Its face wears an expression fitting the content of the printed remark in the field above. Now the world smiles, then it is perplexed, saddened, or aggrieved, and yet again glows with joy. Every time the intertitle recurs, the homuncular globe reflects on the state of the world at large. Although the setting in the film itself is limited to Paris, the intertitle "globalizes" its action, thus bringing forward, albeit unconsciously, Ptolemy's grounding distinction between cosmography and topography.

> Geography is a representation in picture of the whole known world together with the phenomena which are contained therein. It differs from Chorography [or topography], selecting certain places from the whole, treats more fully the particulars of each by themselves—even dealing with the smallest conceivable localities, such as harbors, farms, villages, river courses, and such like. . . . The task of Geography is to survey the whole in its just proportions, as one would the entire head. For as in an entire painting we must first put in the larger features, and afterward those detailed features which portraits and pictures may require, giving them proportion in relation to one another so that their correct measure apart can be seen by examining them, to note whether they form the whole or part of the picture. Accordingly therefore it is not unworthy of Chorography, or out of its province, to describe the smallest details of places, while Geography deals only with regions and their general features.[8]

The distinction is present in the way the world, seen in the title cards, relates to the city. It bears on the economy of the film insofar as the distinction rehearses the local-and-global operation that Meliès and Lumière had conceived in order to assure a worldwide distribution of their commodities. The subtitles are especially effective in their suggestion—averred later in the film—that what is happening in Paris could also extend to the world at large. Between the intertitles and the portrayal of Paris is contained a theory of power that ties cinema and cartography to articulations of local and global control.

For this reason the longer version of the film, despite its fuzziness and unfinished look, merits comparison with the revised counterpart. At the outset of the longer version an establishing shot fades in from the black background of the title card. It is taken of the Allée des Cygnes, an island of the Seine, from what would seem to be the mezzanine of the Eiffel Tower. Light scintillates while two barges chug upstream. Cutting across the middle of the frame is the Passy Bridge. A subway rolls on its upper trestle from left to right. A classic view, the shot resembles a postcard that eternizes the edge of the city. In the synoptic version that Clair edited in the 1950s, the first shot is taken from the top of the Eiffel Tower. The camera is tilted downward to display the Seine as it stretches westward toward the Pont Mirabeau and Pont Garigliano in the distance. The Allée des Cygnes cuts a thin line through the middle of the river and is crossed at the lower edge of the frame by the barely visible line of the Pont de Passy. In both versions the crossing of the end of the Allée and Pont de Grenelle has at its crest a tiny but visible Statue of Liberty that welcomes boats sailing toward the middle of the metropolis.

In both versions, too, the film itself awakens into duration, into an unchanging time of day of the kind felt on Turgot's map or Mercier's Paris of 2440. Title-credits on a black background give way to a city in sunshine. Movement in the shots is minimal. The boats barely make headway while the surrounding city remains immobile. The earlier version frames the beginning between two intertitles that exploit the English rendering of "Paris qui dort" as "The Crazy Ray." The first—"The sable Goddess, from her ebony throne, In rayless majesty, stretched forth Her leaden scepter"—equates darkness with "raylessness," an absence of light before the second title card intervenes (after the establishing shot) to explain the quaintness of its figure of speech: "In other words, Paris was asleep." In the re-edited copy the first intertitle follows the establishing shot. "Un soir, Paris s'endormit [One evening, Paris went to sleep]." There follows a single shot of the city that extends from the Tower to the Arc de Triomphe and beyond. Except for the sight of a car, barely visible, driving across the vacant space of the Place Trocadéro, the scene is immobile. The shot fades into black, and then an intertitle, "et, le matin suivant" (and, the following morning) fades to a medium shot of a man asleep in a modest bed.

Figure 2. *Paris qui dort* (1924): View of the Allée des Cygnes from the top of the Eiffel Tower. The Statue of Liberty is visible at the tip of the island.

The earlier version offers a telling variant. The Paris that sleeps is seen in a dissolve from a long shot, taken from the mezzanine of the Eiffel Tower, of the Seine and the Arc de Triomphe amidst a mass of buildings. An extreme long shot displays the Seine identified by the Pont-Neuf to the far right that cuts across the middle of the frame. The shot dissolves into another bird's-eye view of the city, looking directly east, that extends from the site of the Tower to the cupola of the Invalides at the Place Vauban. Three shots display a city virtually dreamt in the passage of lap-dissolves. Each view is illuminated in the daylight whose source originates from the other side of the Tower. Hence the shots were taken at different times of the day; the overall effect is crucial to the illusion of endless duration that the film imposes. They are matched by another dissolve that moves from a close-up in a sparse interior of a man sleeping in a bed to a medium shot of the same interior. It is difficult to tell whether the dissolves present the background to the narrative or if they are the dream of a city "asleep" that is being lived by the man shown.

In both copies the metallic beams and rivets on the wall convey the effect of a prison cell. A shaft of light traverses the floor. The man rises from the bed, stands in the light, stretches his arms, and walks toward the window at its source. A straight cut leads to his exit from a door and entry into daylight. After an intertitle indicating that he is the night watchman of the Eiffel Tower, the camera pans right as he lights a cigarette, walks by two telescopes poised at the edge of a gridded barrier. He flicks the match over the barrier. In the early version of the film a vertiginous countertilt shows the streets below as if they were a part of an ichnographic perspective on the Champ de Mars. An immobile view is given of a parceled space into which the match falls and disappears. Above the two legs of the tower is an avenue in white that traverses the squares of the garden plot extending from the Champ de Mars.[9]

Herein an initial and crucial paradox: in the narrative the watchman is supposed to be seeing Paris immobilized in daylight, by what will later be shown to be the effects of a "crazy ray." Yet in the distance movement is discerned, signaling that the film cannot entirely freeze the movement of the city in the view seen from the top of the Tower. In the early version the downward tilt is matched by a sudden cut to an upward pan to the top of the Tower in order, ostensibly, to mark the icarian site from which the geography of the preceding shot was taken. The camera reverses into the upward countertilt, and then to the previous ichnographic plan, before it cuts back to the watchman running along the deck to see what is happening. A still view of the Invalides (where the viewer imagines dying soldiers immobilized in their beds) and its environs confirms that nothing stirs in the city below.[10]

The dialectic of immobility and movement is engaged through the resemblance of the views of the city from the Tower to a city-view in the tradition of Turgot. The narrative will show that the "control" of the city has much to do with what might be called a cinematic and cartographic management.[11] Paris is plotted and held in the grip of a mapped image. Time is both regained and called in question in the dazzling tracking shot that follows the watchman, in search of answers to his perception that the world has stopped, who descends (in imitation of Marcel Duchamp's "Nu descendant un escalier") the spiral staircase of the Tower. Light cuts through an ironwork maze where the man enters, begins his descent, and disappears. A long downward track follows him making three full turns in his corkscrew path that descends around a central column in front of crisscrossed girders in front of the city in the haze of the background. In departing from his site of panoptic command he turns about and around the city. His point of view is of a continuous panorama and an unbroken "take" on the world around him. He turns, but the Tower does not, and yet the effect is dizzying.[12] He disappears into Piranesian network and then, in the same shot, suddenly appears on a metallic terrace in the foreground. The watchman, whom we discover is named Albert, has just traveled through a maze and a map of an unreal territory.

Figure 3. *Paris qui dort:* Albert, in a maze, descending the spiral staircase of the Eiffel Tower.

Two Spatial Stories

The narrative begins when the protagonist reaches the ground. The watchman becomes a pedestrian in search of lost time. The sequence that follows seems to be a cavalcade of images of sites and monuments evacuated of people, but that here and there are replaced by statues. Albert crosses the Pont Alexandre III and then effortlessly—without any interference of traffic—reaches the sculpted caryatids next to the arcs of running water of the fountain adjacent to the obelisk of the Place de la Concorde. The perspective from the Louvre to the Champs Elysées is empty; so also is that from the Concorde to the Madeleine. What would be a claustrophobic space at rush hour in 1923 turns into an agoraphobic "daymare." Now and again a trace of life, like residue from a dream, is visible: fresh horse manure is visible on the clean cobblestones of a street or a jet of water spurts from a hose, off-screen, aimed at the greenery of a garden. The details do not quite shatter the illusion of immobility. Reporting that Albert is thinking of what the city ought to look like, an intertitle gives way to a flashback of six shots, four of which track movement from a vehicle that rolls down the Champs Elysées and toward the Concorde (two others are of horses trotting along an avenue and a *bateau-mouche* chugging upstream toward the Île-de-la-Cité).

The hero encounters seven frozen figures: a hack sleeping at the wheel of his taxi; a man seated on a bench by a sidewalk, whom he touches, and who breathes; a janitor arrested in moving a garbage can from a doorway to the street; a driver of a car stopped in its tracks on the slope of a street. He then meets a man poised at the edge of the Seine who appears on the verge of drowning himself. The protagonist picks up a suicide note that has fallen from the hand of the statuesque figure. In the early version the film cuts to an intertitle that reproduces the text of the note. "It's the terrible pace of modern life that has driven me to this. I cannot stand the rush and roar of this city—," before the film fades out and in from black (as it does with each of the scenes) to Albert's discovery of a policeman, arrested while running around the corner of a street, about to apprehend a man who has stolen a timepiece that hangs from his left hand.

Isolated in a medium shot, the hero sits down on the curb of the sidewalk and begins to reflect. By contrast, the later version cuts directly to the episode at the airport of Paris in which a plane lands, its pilots and passengers descend, where discovery is made of personnel on the ground frozen in their tracks. The montage of the early version does not cut to the airport. (It leaves the hero sitting on the sidewalk before he runs to the taxi and puts himself at the wheel.) When he is squatting on the curb, the line of divide between the street and the walkway makes clear the spatial demarcations that were visible in each of the seven preceding encounters, especially that of the man at the edge of the river, in which a diagonal line distinguishes the hard surface of the pavement from the ripples and reflections of the water.[13]

Two spaces are made manifest. One, of everyday life, is that of the street where people would ambulate and go about their daily business; in the other, in the passages where vehicles are driven or the river flows, motion prevails. Here the film establishes other tensions as well. Death is contemplated at the edge of the water in such a way that, as Gilles Deleuze might put it, the "molar" compression of one milieu is countered by the eerie emptiness or "molecular" dispersion of the other. The editing of this version of *Paris qui dort* emphasizes how the edges of sidewalks, bulkheads, and river barriers become critical zones in a field of muted social conflict. In the later version a flashback or alternate episode of the arrival of the plane from Marseilles enhances the uncanny effect because it cannot be tied to the thoughts the hero entertains while he countenances the unreal city before his eyes. As Albert sits (in medium close-up) a passing car prompts him to run to the cab, to catch the specter he has just seen pass in front of him. He stops the car, meets the five occupants, and leads them to inspect the zombie-like cabbie in the vehicle he had just pilfered to catch up with the others. The group runs back to the taxi parked behind them. A close-up pictures one of the men putting his ear to the shoulder of the inert driver slumped in his seat next to the meter box. From the back a gentleman wearing a monocle and a handlebar mustache (a virtual stand-in for the spectator) looks on. What are they wishing to hear and see? Would it be the heartbeat of the deadened driver?

Figure 4. *Paris qui dort:* Bliss in the grid of the tower.

Or possibly the tick of the meter? In either instance the gesture makes clear that *they listen to silence.*

The intertitle in the early version suggests that they are examining the power of control that silent cinema might exert upon the imagination. "He's alive all right, but he's unconscious." The words could be those of the third voice of the medium that indirectly states how it is shaping the unconscious of the spectator at the same time, in its most diurnal aspect, it moves the narrative ahead. In its "nocturnal" aspect the intertitle brings forward the strategic virtues of the film.[14] Except for the passengers in the plane and the night watchman, everyone is under a "spell" that can only be attributed to the film in which they are the principal players.[15] In both copies the film cuts to life at the top of the Tower. The early version has the young woman, the object of everyone's lust, sitting at the edge of a girder, attended by Albert, elegantly dressed in white pants and a white shirt, who admires a leg she coyly extends outward and over the background of the city below. From her ankle dangles a string of pearls that had been removed from one of the women in the restaurant. A medium close-up shows her fawning in front of a mirror she holds against the vast view of the city below. The effect of counterpoint is enhanced where the toe of her shoe seems to touch the buildings below. The string of pearls hanging from her ankle melds into the lines of streets in the distance. Both copies are cross-cut by reference to a jealous suitor seated amidst the girders above, who looks down upon the couple. Both, too, betray the paradox of immobility and movement where a bus and a car cross a boulevard below (clearly visible in the upper right-hand corner of the screen). In the sequence depicting the suitors in pursuit of the woman near the top of the Tower (the sublime moment when one of the men who jumped from the edge climbs back up the girder against the city below), a moving car is faintly visible in the distance.[16]

A message about where the voice originates is heard; the group descends the Tower (four by elevator, one by the spiral staircase) to find the woman who spoke into the wireless. The sound cues seen in the Tower are taken up again when the group discovers the speaker. They find a pair of shutters to which a handkerchief is attached, bang on them, and then jimmy them open. At the threshold appears a young woman who puts the index finger of her left hand to her mouth to tell them to be silent, but also, in a different register, her gesture could be telling the viewers that the film itself is silent, and that its sound can only be seen in a visual language that belongs to the medium itself.[17] The *volets* or shutters that are pried open to gain access to sound are met with an affirmative gesture that reinforces the operative codes of the film. In both copies the woman exits. Everyone steps furtively to a corner where they hear what we read on the title cards, first a speech denoting the woman's explanation of the origins of the *rayon lourd* (a heavy ray), and then of a schematic picture of two arcs emanating from a house and passing below the top of the Eiffel Tower to the left and, to the right, an airplane suspended in midair. The image becomes a representation of the turning globe about which the ray is shot westward as it rotates at the top of its horizon from France toward the Americas. The woman states that the ray has *endormi le monde* (put the world to sleep). The moving picture of the globe reiterates the point. In the early version the explanation is elided in a flashback that reproduces the story of the young woman who was witness to her father's machinations. The film fades to an abstract décor where the father, dressed in an ample bathrobe of a cloth with a zigzag pattern, explained to her—with the same drawing of the Tower and the plane—how his powerful invention worked. The flashback lasts up to the point where she makes a desperate call from a telephone (she is seen in medium close-up speaking into the receiver) before walking to the window as if to hear people tampering with it (she stands before the shutters seen from the opposite side where the men had just seconds ago forced them open). In the English intertitle she explains that the mad doctor felt that with the ray he could control the world, which the schema of the rotating globe now serves to explain.

The edited copy hastens to the encounter with the mad scientist. The group compels him, at gunpoint, to reawaken the world. He scribbles a mass of equations on blackboard set to the right of the telephone on the wall. Once the surface is filled with images, numbers, square roots, and figures of a tower and circles, he pulls a lever that precipitates a montage that brings motion to all of the frozen vignettes, seen earlier, of everyday life in Paris. During his work at the blackboard everyone in the room falls asleep. Both versions coincide in the episodes depicting the group's return to the travails of everyday life, especially where they meet and depart from the Pont d'Iéna. The couple ascends in an elevator (shots of the Seine through the girders and light that projects amidst the iron beams return the narrative to cinematic fantasy) and finds the spot where courtship had first taken place. An extreme close-up of a ring left in a cranny is evidence that what happened, as the intertitle states, "was not a dream." Albert slips the ring onto her finger. Seen from behind as they face the sunlight, the couple kisses as the outline of their bodies dissolves into that of the Trocadéro Palace in a bird's-eye view from the top of the Tower. The structure and its environs city become clear before the film cuts to a black screen on which is printed "*Fin.*"

The ending of the longer copy is of a different texture. The couple walks together behind the gridded configuration of iron beams and studs that had been the foreground to a chase and fistfight earlier in the film. They reach the spot that had been an earlier site of love, discover the ring, and exchange vows before the end-title caps the film. The cutting and editing insist on a mystical voyage taken both by the five visitors from Marseilles and the couple who have discovered their love. In its classical formula a traveler goes to a space "anywhere out of this world" and returns to tell interlocutors or readers a narrative—evinced by physical traces on the body or in things in the mystic's hands—of encounters with forces beyond the reach of any form of representation.[18] In its history the mystical tale attests to the validity of subjectivity and even of the anonymous individual—the person without qualities, the nameless practitioner of everyday life—of the modern era.[19] In the early version of the film the mystical tale is enveloped in incredible or patently crazy effects of accelerated motion and stoppage that mesh love with a promise of bliss. In Clair's revised cut the mystical effect is given where the silhouette of the two bodies of the lovers, drawn against bright light, blend into the shape of architecture below the Tower and on the other side of the Seine. It attenuates the unsettling and uncanny return to the gridlocked spaces in which people had earlier been incarcerated. The revised ending mottles the fixing effects of mapped forms and the agency of control that the film has theorized. It offers slight promise of synthesis where the narrative, in reaching an ending, occludes the identity of the film itself as a "crazy ray." The mystic fable of the earlier version, in which the space-*in* of the film becomes the space-off of its memory in the apparent reflections of the two lovers and the spectators who leave the projection room, is all but missing in the later revision.

Points of Comparison

At the risk of seeming fastidious, comparison of the two versions of the film shows that where the editing in the shorter (later) copy yields convincing narrative effects, the theoretical—and both spatial and cartographic—import of the feature gets blurred. Some shots in the one are absent in the other, and vice-versa. In both the story begins and leads to the same outcome. Along the way some pertinent differences emerge: in the early version greater emphasis is placed on gags or tricks made from still photography or freeze-frames in the midst of the moving picture; high-speed takes are added of space crashing toward the vehicles that seem to drive recklessly along busy avenues and boulevards; the Eiffel Tower bears greater presence as a character and a spatial coordinate; copious insertion of English intertitles supplements a loose and often hazy narrative progression.

The implications, too, of the cues to sound and silence seem clearer in the early version. The mad rush on the part of the watchman and the travelers from Marseille to find the origin of the voice they hear resonating from a megaphone in the Eiffel Tower rehearses the imminent advent of sound cinema and coordination of spoken words and moving images. The characters look for a synchrony of speech and motion, but along the way they discover the degree of power that film is shown to exert on the masses liable to fall under its spell. Here the cartographic dimension of the film coincides with its self-reflexivity. On the one hand, the discovery of the ray is made in the words they hear in the voice of the mad doctor's niece who describes the "map" of the world as it turns under the sway of the crazy ray. On the other, the viewer's discovery is made in the expression on the face of the homuncular globe on the title cards that reacts with disquiet to what is said and shown about the range and force of the reifying ray.

The cartoon-like images in the sequence recall schemas of radio waves, from the T.S.F. (*télégraphe sans fils,* or "wireless") to radiotelegraphic broadcasts that had been mobilized from the Eiffel Tower at the outset of the First World War. They are also anticipations of the emblems that studios would deploy to convince viewers of the power of their technology. The figure of the ray emanating from a house in Paris is of the same substance as the light that radiates from the beacon in the raised arm of the statuesque persona of Columbia Studios, a variant on nineteenth-century allegorical figures in the style of "Nation" and, surely, of the "Liberty" who is said to welcome immigrants and newcomers to the United States en route to the waiting rooms of Ellis Island. The radiation from an elevated point of origin anticipates the emblem RKO Studios would invent to figure lightning bolts pulsing from the spire of an Eiffel Tower. The figure of the ray that moves over the world extending from Europe to the Americas resembles, too, the logo of Universal Studios that displays the turning globe, on whose ecliptic band, like the rings of Saturn, is spelled the name of the studio. Each an emblem of destiny itself, the devices are all part of cartographic paraphernalia—personages in cartouches, terrestrial and celestial globes, utopian city-views—marshaled to display, albeit in the sugar-coating of vanguard and modernist cinema, the virtual power of the medium at the threshold of recording sound.[20]

Liberty: A Vanishing Point

Both versions of the film began with a map-like shot of the Allée des Cygnes below and beyond the Eiffel Tower. If, as Baudelaire had shown in "Le Cygne"—the initial poem in the section of *Les Fleurs du Mal* (1857; Baudelaire 1976) titled "Tableaux de Paris," in which a swan (a *cygne*), deprived a pond on which it could glide, is a sign (*signe*) of the unhealthy times in which it lives—the name of the island can be read in the allegorical light of poetry devoted to the monuments of Paris.[21] Where a literal take of the *Allée* would include swans paddling effortlessly by its shores, in their place the viewer sees the sluggish motion of barges and river traffic inching upstream and down. And so, too, the Pont Mirabeau farther in the distance gives the lie to what the film is showing. "*Vienne la nuit sonne l'heure/les jours s'en vont je demeure* [Come the night sound the hour/The days flow away I remain]": the site is where Clair's model poet, Guillaume Apollinaire, in his celebrated poem of *Alcools* (1913) named after the bridge, had staged the hauntingly recurrent thoughts of suicide that a person entertains while he or she stands over the waters of the Seine (1965, 45). In *Paris qui dort* the voice of the suffering soul in "Le Pont Mirabeau" has as an analogue the figure of the man, frozen in his steps, who clasps a death note prior to jumping into the Seine.

The toponyms encrusted in the inaugural shot have allegorical force that resonates through the film that follows. Pertinent is the motion of the boats and the arrow-like direction that the Seine takes in arching upward and toward the left corner of the frame. At the end of the Allée des Cygnes stands a point that might qualify as a perspectival object in the cartography of the film.[22] It is, as shown above, the miniature version of the Statue of Liberty, an object whose form and meaning, like the very medium of cinema at its origins, were said to have been shared by France and America. It offers in minuscule what the Tower would be in majuscule. Two cultures and two traditions are found in a distant coordinate that stands between a long and narrow island and the waters that bifurcate at the prow where the statue stands erect. In the greater view of the city the Statue of Liberty is a sign that stands for everything *but* liberty. In the context of the control that the film establishes liberty—indeed, motion and spatial displacement—might be what the medium of cinema, felt in the fears wrought by the fantasy of the crazy ray, will obliterate.

Within a decade of the completion of *Paris qui dort* Clair completed *A nous la liberté* (1931), a feature that impugns the inherited and shopworn meanings of "freedom" through a caustic treatment of the effects of Taylorism on French factory-workers who fabricate record players. These are the machines, if not the "spiritual automata" like the film itself and early sound cinema in general, that simulate live music and living voice.[23] The mute presence of the title of the later film in the initial shot underscores how much cinematic mapping of subjects accompanies broader reflections on cinema and its control of the mental and physical lives of those who live under its effects.

Turgot's map of Paris appears to antedate these effects, and so also do Mercier's reflections in his *L'An 2440*. Both documents, like Clair's film, are bathed in an eternal light of day. In *Paris qui dort* night is limited to the black background of the intertitles. Slumber befalls the characters at any time, in the morning or daylit hours, either on the top of the Tower or in the laboratory of the mad Doctor Crase (or, as his niece names him in the later version, Dr. "lxe," the agglutination of "luce," "luxe," and "lex"). The nocturnal realm of the film belongs to the unconscious that an intertitle in the first version attributes to the effects of the crazy ray. The city in the film is made to sleep or to vegetate in their unconscious, in a domain where light cannot penetrate and purify the bodies of every inhabitant of Paris. The modernity of the film would be associated with the enlightening effects of its science, but at the same time its necessarily archaic or atavistic underside would belong to the sleep that it can represent only in the form of a dream or a mystic fable.

The cartography of *Paris qui dort* becomes a relation of motion to mapped views of the city. The background is less immobile than what the narration suggests. Life teems around the edges. The film at once prolongs and calls into question the "enlightenment" Paris had been said to bring to the world through the inventions of modernity. Historians have shown that the wish for the birth of an eternal day that had been felt in the months following the Revolution of 1789 has always carried an underside of night, obscurity, and things forever unknown.[24] Utopia of the new age depends on the dream of an eternal day in which reason cannot be shaken by fantasies spawned in tremors of sleep. It appears that the characters in the film do not know what to do in the light in which they are bathed. If they dream, their reveries are blinded by the blank aspect of a city immobilized, reified, and idealized as might a map of the kind that Turgot had drawn to enlighten citizens of the abstract beauty of the City of Light. The utopian project has its dystopian underside, and modernity, like the revolution, carries the nightmare of a world where dream, alienation, and the presence of things unknown would be absent. Part of the dystopia, too, is the projection of power and control that the medium, like the cartography that underpins the film, is shown able to exercise over the inhabitants not only of Paris but also of the world at large. An alternative cinematic cartography, one that impugns universal projects of enlightenment, progress, and science, runs through the cinema of Jean Renoir. It is time to turn to his cinema of the 1930s.

2

Jean Renoir:
Cartographies in Deep Focus

The viewer of *Paris qui dort* quickly discerns how the film uses mapping to develop its play on time, motion, and stasis. The film reflects on agencies of control where cinema and cartography are in concert. Viewers of Jean Renoir's cinema know that the director shares similar views about the power of the medium. His films become venues for extensive study of cartography, space, and subjectivity. Maps appear in them at crucial junctures, often in ways where their presence in one feature calls attention to different and sometimes inverse expression in others. It can be said that with maps the alleged master of deep-focus photography flattens the depth of the image in order to make the eye wander over its surface, now to read legible matter in the moving picture, and then to visualize what we hear in spaces in and off screen. In his films the viewer's attention moves errantly, from place to place, in the landscape of the shot. His films beg viewers to see them as human topographies in which characters are graphic elements of the spaces in which they move. Renoir's field of view often seems projected, plotted, and even striated, his establishing or long shots betraying the motivations of a camera producing cartographic effects. Sometimes the films call into question the authority that maps have obtained when, under the banner of progress, they are taken to be scientific objects. At other times archaic maps figure in latent allegories that exert critical pressure on the narrative material.

Four very different manifestations of maps in his cinema offer as many elements for a cartography of cinema. In this chapter four specific cartographic moments will be taken up. One, in *Boudu sauvé des eaux* (1932), brings forward the paradox of a flat depth of field in deep focus. From the beginning of the film folio maps beg the question about how the film can be seen and read. The same paradox ramifies into social and political areas in *Le Crime de Monsieur Lange* (1935), a feature that would otherwise seem to be a study of unanism in deep focus. In this film a map becomes the threshold of a utopia—a cartographic theme reaching back to Thomas More—that becomes a fictive revolution: a social revolution plotted by a map that cues a decisive cinematic revolution of greater ambition. A map is the site on which political contradictions are decisively focused in *La Grande Illusion* (1937), a film that swings on the creaking hinges of the Popular Front as it turns in anticipation of war. Its lines and vectors imply that a space of illusion, vital for human action, seems to be the *terrae incognitae* of times past. Scale changes radically in *La Règle du jeu* (1939), in which two stone globes make clear the coextension of the film and the arena of European wars past and present. They acquire pervasive force in the shots taken on location and remain signs of explosively charged (and indeed affective) spaces in the greater film.

Boudu cartographe

Much of the narrative of *Boudu sauvé des eaux* (1932) takes place in a bookstore adjacent to the Pont des Arts that stretches across the Seine from the Left Bank to the Louvre on the other side. The first two shots establishing the reality of the film in the here-and-now are taken on location in Paris along the Quai Conti. We see the façade of a bookstore located not far from the Institut de France, possibly where the Editions Champion, a bookstore mostly devoted to early modern French literature, once resided in view of the Pont des Arts. The first shot (the ninth in the film) follows a prologue in which two of the later leads, Lestingois (Charles Granval) and Anne-Marie Chloë (Séverine Lerczinska) play the roles, respectively, of a satyr pursuing a nymph on a modest stage behind which hangs a curtain on which is painted a perspectival view of a classical garden. Contrasting the stage and its décor of fake depth is the first shot of the bookstore, "V. Lemasle, Autographes," that specializes in "authentic" works and, as the name indicates, in manuscripts in the hand of their authors. The second shot of the store, that immediately follows (shot 9), re-establishes the same view from the other side of the Quai where vehicles cross back and forth across the frame.[1]

All of a sudden eight baroque maps come into view, all extracted from folio atlases, identifiably in the tradition of Gerard Mercator, Jodocus Hondius, Nicolas Sanson, and Guillaume and Johannes Blaeu. The face of the building appears to be a collage or even a serial display of signs and maps that resemble photograms in the dark space of the windows in the background. On either side of the doorway are four printed folio-maps with elegant cartouches. The map on the upper-left corner is a view of Africa from Johannes Blaeu's *Atlas major* of 1662 (Goss 1990, 40–41). Below it is a topographic map, possibly of Holland, and to the right, both above and below, two others of the same kind. A Mercator map of

North and South America is farther to the right and below it a map from any of a number of hand-colored folios in the *Grand Atlas*.

The spectator is asked both to read and not to read the image in the way one reads a map. The projections shown in the window are views of greater spaces in smaller confines. They are miniature worlds that invoke in the contained milieu a presence of other spaces. Yet they are of a paradoxically *flat depth,* and their immobility is set in play with the traffic that crosses the frame. Inviting the eye to wander over the lands and waters they depict, the maps are a foil to the deep-focus photography that Renoir exploits in the confines of the Lestingois household.[2] In itself a map room or a *Wunderkammer* containing books, copperplate engravings, city-views, and cartographic images, the apartment is a crowded world of framed forms. The maps prompt a spatial reading of the milieu. Everything in the field of the image is of equal valence in respect to everything else. Even if something in the depth of field or in the foreground does not seem to have the immediate value that a centered object is shown to possess, it is nonetheless plotted in an "equipollent" fashion in which all forms seem to bear equal significance and thus turn the shot into a system of loosely affiliated signs.[3] It bears

Figure 5. *Boudu sauvé des eaux* (1932): Boudu struts in front of the Lestingois Bookstore, whose windows display ten classical maps by Blaeu and others.

much in common with André Bazin's readings of Renoir and Rossellini insofar as "the entire surface of the screen has to offer an equal concrete density" (1999 [1975], 282). The cartographic impulse informs what Gilles Deleuze calls the tactility and legibility of Renoir's modes of framing, especially insofar as it is based on baroque painting, the very style that informs the maps seen in *Boudu:*

> [I]n Renoir or Welles the sum of movements is distributed in depth so as to establish linkages, actions and reactions, that are never developed the one beside the other on the same plane [*sur un même plan*], but are staggered at different distances and from one plane to another [*d'un plan à l'autre*]. The unity of the shot [*plan*] is made here from the direct linkage among elements taken in the multiplicity of superimposed planes [*plans*] that cannot be isolated from one another: such is the relation of parts seen near and far that produce the whole. The same evolution appears in the history of painting from the sixteenth to the seventeenth centuries. (1983, 42)[4]

These maps are legible. They may inspire fantasy of the faraway spaces and worlds of times past, but as decorated surfaces they do not lead to points elsewhere or beyond themselves. They can be likened to opaque windows of the monadic world the autograph merchant and his family are inhabiting.

The maps invite the viewer to plot the movement of characters on different planes of different scales. The maps become patently visible in a sequence that follows Boudu's seduction of Emma and Lestingois' subsequent award of being "decorated" with a medal (and a cuckold's horns). Boudu Michel Simon struts indolently about the façade of the bookstore. He ambulates in front of the maps, first to the right while the camera follows him and laterally reframes the scene, and then to the left—a car passes in front of the image flattened by the lens of a long focal length—before the silhouette of a man in the street enters the frame, occludes Boudu, and then crosses and exits the frame to the right. Having just walked in front of the maps, the man now approaches Boudu, displays his bowler hat and cane, peers inside, and discreetly asks, "Monsieur, je vous demande pardon, mais où pourrais-je voir Monsieur Lestingois, est-ce qu'il est là par hasard? [Excuse me, sir, but where might I find Monsieur Lestingois? Would he happen to be in?]." He continues, now putting his body in the box-like space of the adjoining window of the doorway, asserting that Lestingois had been going to procure for him an original and first edition of Baudelaire's *Les Fleurs du Mal*. As he inquires, cars continue to pass; a couple behind a parked vehicle look at the scene being shot; two pedestrians crisscross the median space of the street; a convertible filled with curious passengers stops in front of the store for a second to gaze upon what is happening. Boudu ripostes that a bookstore is not a flower shop, a *magasin de fleurs*. To which, leaving the frame, the man replies, "Je reviendrai [I'll be back]." In view of the maps the joke is not merely a quid pro quo in which things literal are exchanged for things figural. It extends to Baudelaire's own geographical world that reaches beyond the borders of France.[5]

The maps in the field of the adjacent image invite reflection on spatial expansion. Marked here is the appeal to the allegorical voyages that had perhaps caused baroque cartography to anticipate cinematography.[6] Space at once dilates and shrinks, not only in the shot-and-countershot that begins with the close-ups of the baroque projections, but also in the shots that follow. The upshot is that the contradiction of an "open" space outdoors, called into question by the mapped images of "closed" spaces from the world at large in the windows, is matched by the "closed" area indoors, in which cartographic forms invite reflection on "open" areas in times and places remote from where they are seen. The maps inspire questions concerning where the personages are and how the viewer relates to their own perception of their place in space.

Figure 6. *Boudu sauvé des eaux:* Boudu between the name of his benefactor and two maps from Blaeu's *Atlas royal* (1650).

Boudu ends with an extraordinary countertilt that catches a parade of bums crossing the frame in the foreground while in the distance, toward the clouds of the sky above, points the spire of Notre-Dame. The bums hail the "blue waters and the blue firmament" where, as the subtitles of the vocals make clear, "the violins sow their haunting strains and the love vows of the sender ever sweeter and more tender hold you in love's embrace again." Surely an ironic commentary on the film, the words have everything and nothing to do with the radical position of the shot, which is an icarian view of the sky taken from the ground. The shot registers a parade of many Boudus, bums of a collective autograph, marking a collective of classless souls who are not quite of the aesthetic order that Lestingois had found in the bum he had saved. A mixed political design is folded into the way the shot is taken and the way that it pertains to seeing the world.[7] In a strong sense it corresponds to the establishing shot of *Boudu* in which a long take of the bookstore and its maps becomes the cinematic frontispiece, façade, the "autographe" and the "orthographe" to the rest of the film.[8]

Tracking a Revolution

A cartographic presence is confirmed and more broadly invested in two crucial cartographic sequences in *Le Crime de Monsieur Lange* (1935). A map appears in the first shot of a long flashback (comprising most of the film) that represents the words of Valentine (Florelle), who has just escaped Paris and found temporary refuge in a tavern at the border of France and Belgium. Prior to the flashback the credits dissolve in and out over a background of a photograph of the cobblestones of what might be a street or a courtyard. The credits fade into an exterior shot of a closed door on whose transom a sign reads "Café-Hôtel de la Frontière." A dissolve gives way to a close-up of a bar on which are amassed two bottles, some cups, and an array of shot glasses. At the center is a half-filled liter of "genièvre pur [pure gin]," indicating that the border might be along the northwestern reaches of France.[9] The camera pulls back to record the bartender pouring a shot for an old client after a policeman had just read a description of Lange (René Lefèvre), a criminal wanted for murder. The policeman exits while the camera holds on the bar and the client's judgment about the quality of the gin.

A regional locale is displaced when Valentine tells her story, which began in Paris and has led the couple to the border. In close-up Valentine describes how Lange used to stay up at night to write "impossible stories . . . with an old-fountain pen [*avec un vieux stylo*]." The film dissolves into its long flashback. Valentine, facing the viewer, gives way to Lange, seen in profile at his desk, speaking (voice-off) the text that he seems to be conceiving: "Smiling, the nigger-killer pushed the poor black off the branch. . . . Everyone exploded in laughter. But a shot rang out; the rope split. The nigger was saved. Hands up!" The camera begins a slow upward pan to the left to a wall papered with a checkerboard floral pattern. On the wall a picture, reflecting light, is hanging and supporting a hat. It is above a pitcher and its saucer on a bureau, and to the right on the wall above are pinned a cowboy's belts and holsters. In the same shot the camera pans right, keeping in view (in soft focus) Lange's head that looks down as he is engrossed in his writing. The shot passes by a window looking onto what would be a court-yard where other windows on the back side are visible.

"Arizona Jim . . . ," he mutters, as the camera loses sight of him and of the window while continuing its panoramic to the right where the wall is now seen decorated with a gaudy pair of chaps to the left and a wall map, circa 1925, of North America. The state of Arizona is in bold outline, seen in the ellipse between the first mention of the name of Lange's hero and the second when, voice-off, he continues, "Arizona Jim kills one or two of them . . . and takes off." The camera continues its pan right until it reaches the wall on the other side of the garret. "Hell-bent for leather," utters the voice, as the camera pans left, back along the same trajectory, now showing the map in its entirety. "Carrying the nigger off . . . in a cloud of dust," he utters off, before the camera returns to find him madly waving his arms in euphoria over the image he has just created. He stops when a church bell is heard ringing off, in unison with an alarm clock that he stops just as the *plan-séquence* cuts to an extreme long shot of a church at the end of a street on the slope of a working quarter in the eighteenth *arrondissement* of Paris. The map marks the line of divide between the rampant imagination of the writer that inspires the unlikely story and the reality of the time and space in which the personage is living. It designates faraway spaces, off, that are in strong contrast to the windows, *in,* on the other side of the courtyard. On one level the map is a projection of the writer's imagination in a closed space, while on another it refers to the fortunes of cinema, especially to the American West-ern. The camera draws attention to its movement when it passes over and across the map from west and east and back again from east to west.

The map acquires a mobility and presence that rival with those of the charac-ters and their cinematic heritage. It returns, near the end of the film, with the liv-ing specter of the evil Batala (Jules Berry). The antagonist, dressed in a priest's frock and sporting a wide-brimmed hat, resembles a clerical cowboy. Reported by a radio newscaster (voice-off) to have perished in a train wreck, the corrupt director of the publishing firm returns to the place where he had caused irrepara-ble harm. He has ferreted his way into the offices of the firm that expelled him and that now celebrates, in part thanks to his demise, its new and unforeseen success as a collective enterprise. The members of the printing firm, celebrating their success, are tippling at a Christmas party. They meet in a room on the ground floor of one of the buildings facing the courtyard. In search of quiet and calm where they can share each other's affections, Valentine and Lange take leave of the revelers.

The shot (of 54 seconds) bears all the marks of the spatial play that had been the signature of *Boudu*. The flat field of the door behind the lovers at first tends to hold them in separate frames. The backlit scene has a slightly *noir*-like aspect that underscores Valentine's silver and silky hair and white blouse against Lange's dark suit. Shadows of the mullions of another door (from which they just entered from the right) are cast upon them. The plan-séquence contains the contradictions of the greater story: Lange wants to do a film but must exit before he forgets, but he momentarily forgets (or realizes the idea of his scenario) to grace his love with a kiss. When Lange reaches the stairwell he puts his left hand on the newel as if to tell the spectator that he is touching what we are seeing. The world, a newel-globe, is in his hands. Tipsy, Lange climbs the stairs to where he can put his ideas to paper.[10] He sets his palm on the newel in the last instant in the sequence. A globe, a totality in miniature, the promise of a world to come, is placed at the vanishing point in the shot.

The gesture is repeated when, in the very long take (of 65 seconds) that follows Valentine's closing of the door, Lange (in a medium close-up) approaches the double doorway of the office. He puts his hands to the two knobs on either side of the vertical line of the juncture of the door and thrusts their panels open. The space of the office appears, and all of a sudden the doors open onto the map of the United States and Arizona. Displaced from where it had been in his garret, the map now stands over the desk as if it were an emblem of the new enterprise. The back of Lange's head is framed within the map, keylit in the same way as the newel in the previous shot. The camera trucks in to follow Lange in his entry, pans by the map, and reaches a point close to the back of the hero's head and shoulders in soft focus. The unlikely hero discovers and gazes upon Batala rummaging about a large wardrobe.[11]

The map cues the displacement and success that Lange has witnessed as writer and sponsor of the new enterprise. It also anticipates a dazzling movement of the camera that will achieve in its own terms what in the midst of their utopian ambitions the members of the collective cannot envision. Camera and map become coequal. The projection stands in the room as an icon of fictive spaces off, the site of American Westerns and of extraordinarily deep space unknown to the inhabitants of a place riddled by depression and corruption. The projection then becomes the point of departure for the revolutionary career of the camera. The lens leaves the map and holds on Batala, on whom Lange gazes interminably, wondering if the man he sees is really not dead. The camera pans and travels with him when he takes a pose by the right side of the map while Lange stands at the left edge, near the outline of the Arizona territory. Batala says that he has "always felt himself at home here [chez moi ici]," home implying any number of spaces, including the office, the United States and the western territories, or the world at large. "Why I am here at home, and I want everything, the world, everything!"

Soon Batala leaves the office and, in his exit, runs into Valentine not far from where the camera had left her. Astonished by the living ghost, she is aghast at what she sees. The camera then follows the line from her eye and a strut slanting upward; it pans up to the right, by a piece of corrugated roofing, to a closed but illuminated window on the second floor where Lange's shadow comes forward as if to hear Batala's voice-off, in response to her question asking him what he is doing: "I'm on a pilgrimage."

The words apply to the journey of the camera toward the map that suddenly reappears in the image. The camera tracks and pans left to a second, open window that displays the map of America and Arizona on the wall in the background. The map that had been in Lange's (or formerly Batala's) office is now tacked on the wall of the print shop. The map has changed rooms. Has it been displaced to emphasize the haptic quality of the camera movement? Is it there to put in counterpoint to the depth of field of the window the flat but expansive space of the map on the wall? To provide ironic innuendo in which the non-place of the United States in the studio is matched by the utopian dream of it hanging in every room in the cooperative? No matter what the answer may be, the map has ambulated miraculously from Lange's garret to the director's office and now from the director's office to the wall of the printing studio.

The shot continues its career, passing by four windows and then fixing on a spiral staircase at the opposite end of the courtyard from the smaller one from where Batala exited, now panning down, as Lange quickly descends, reaches the floor, and exits right in the direction of Valentine and Batala. A cut to a close-up of Lange seeing his target (off-screen to the right) precedes a sudden and dramatic panoramic of 290 degrees, complementing the panoramic track of the same career of the windows on the second floor. Instead of following Lange as he moves to the right, the camera now sweeps left and moves quickly, all around the courtyard. Astonished, they watch Lange approach. Lange assails Batala, grabs him by the sides, and shoots him in the belly. Batala exclaims, "Quoi, tu es sonné, mon petit vieux? [What, my little friend, are you out of your head?]." Just after the gunshot, in the midst of the revelry, the cry (off) of a baby resounds. Batala falls out of frame as the couple, now reunited again, stands in disbelief over what has happened.

Thus begins their exit from the courtyard and their trip to the border of France and the café-hotel where Valentine finishes telling the story seen in flashback. The panoramic that went in the opposite direction of the action, that lost grounding in the sweep of its movement, and that recaptured the stupefied gaze of Batala and Valentine remains one of the signature moments both in *Le Crime de Monsieur Lange* and in Renoir's cinema. The shot is one in which, for an instant, all visual bearings are upset and all sense of cardinal direction is abandoned. Bazin notes that the movement is contrary to all logic and even conveys a dizzying *vertigo:*

This astonishing camera movement, apparently contrary to all logic, may perhaps have secondary dramatic or psychological justification (its impression is one of vertigo, of madness, it creates a suspense), but its *raison d'être* is more essential; it is the spatial expression of the entire staging of the film. . . . It is true that this panoramic shot that cannot be immediately justified might appear arbitrary or smack of rhetoric. Thus Renoir prepared us to admit it unconsciously with the scene of the drunken concierge dragging the garbage cans *all around the courtyard*. The circular movement is thus inscribed in our eye, and its mental persistence is probably what causes us to admit the abstraction of the panoramic that will follow.[12]

Bazin's reading of the shot is accompanied by a map. To emphasize the nature of its revolution he makes a diagram of the courtyard that includes its concentric pavement, the two spiral staircases, the four windows on the second floor, the laundry room, the concierge's quarters, the three trashcans, the entry onto the street, and the fountain below Batala's office. It does not account for the fact that the sequence began when Lange opens the double doors and discovers Batala standing below the map. Nor does it account for the chiaroscuro that results from the alternating images of illuminated rooms or windows and dark surfaces of walls and louvred shutters. On an unconscious level it might be said that Bazin's spatial reading of the courtyard plotting of the sequence is projectively identified with the displacement of the map from the garret to the central office. His chart makes the space cohere where in fact it is being bent and twisted.[13]

Bazin's map is prefaced by statements that testify to the problematic relation of local action to total or global ends or, in the terms of existential cartography, of action on a topographic scale that would enable local change to reach a global or geographic plane. Bazin recalls that in its initial form *Lange* bore the title *Sur la cour* (Over the Courtyard).

> The general idea of the film is to group a certain number of characters and activities around the inner courtyard, in short, to depict somewhat unanimistically one of these tiny Parisian communities born spontaneously of urban topography. There are those who live and work "over the courtyard": the janitors, the laundry woman, Lange and those who solely go there to work there: the typographers, Valentine's women helpers, etc. But the whole of this little world is known to us (with the exception of a few "exteriors") only through its constant or occasional relations with the *courtyard* and the activities for which it is the center. (40)

Bazin intimates that typographers generate topographies, and that within its circular frame a happy world sees the day. The way that Lange's map moves in the film leads to different conclusions. A projection and a transitional object in the monadic frame of Lange's garret, it remains a utopian representation of places, as they had been seen in the allusions to Baudelaire in *Boudu,* "anywhere out of this world." The map betrays the utopian project, it calls it into question, and it becomes a critical object that forces counter readings—both of the panoramic that leads to Batala's murder and the final shots on the beach at the border of Belgium. Enclosing circles had been everywhere in the film, not just in the camera movement but also in the strange ring of smoke that entered the frame from right to left when Valentine, seated at the table of the borderline café, began her story that would soon be told through a flashback of almost seventy-five minutes.

The end of the film responds to these enclosing forms. Batala, dying, dissolves to a shot of the moving road ahead of the car that Meunier drives across the countryside to the border. The film returns to the tavern where Valentine finishes her story and awaits judgment. In a swift transition the inside of the tavern (made large by the door that Lange opens while Valentine stands up) dissolves to a close-up of the sands of a beach and a line of footprints. The camera tilts up to show that they are tracks left by Valentine and Lange. Their backs to the camera in a long take, they walk toward what would be a vanishing point on the horizon where the beach and the sky meet in the distance. Their bodies are mirrored by their reflections on the film of water covering the beach at low tide. In the gusting wind they turn around and wave goodbye, first to the spectator, then to two of the men who had been in the tavern: after Lange and Valentine bid adieu the shot cuts 180 degrees to catch the pair who wave back. They stand by the skeleton of a boat or a circle of wooden struts arranged around a pole on which is nailed to what seems to be a sign indicating a passage to the left. A hole is drilled through it.

In the parting shot it is impossible not to visualize an allegory of circles, cartographic spots or dots, of occluded vanishing points, and of problematic sites of egress "anywhere out of this world." The final shots become the visual counterpart to the territory of "Arizona" first seen on the map of North America. The film indicates that neither the map nor the film is a real territory on which a revolution—at least of the kind that the camera itself has performed—can take place. The map figures in a tradition of utopian projections while its movement indicates that a revolution is taking place only along the cartographic edge of the frame.[14] In Renoir's world of neo-Baudelairean "correspondances" that Bazin so admired, the close-up of the beach at the beginning of the penultimate shot is a utopian place par excellence, an indistinct border between air and land or "molar" and "molecular" states of being.[15] The beach and wind (a wind of possible change) blowing against the couple belong to an atmospheric condition of things in strong contrast to the hard and enduring aspect of the cobblestones in the earlier sequences.

"Au dessous des pavés, la plage [Below the cobblestones the beach]": the famous slogan that captured the essence of May 1968 in France finds uncanny anticipations at the beginning and ending of *Lange*. After having driven Lange and Valentine to the café at the border, standing on one side of the hood, Meunier quips to Lange and Valentine on the other side, near the camera, "Là bas vous avez les dunes, et derrière les dunes il y a la frontière, et la frontière passée, la liberté, comme on dit [The dunes are over there, and just beyond the dunes there's the border, and beyond the border, there's freedom, so they say]." The beach seems to hold the promise of the erasure of the line of divide between two nations and the sky and the land below. It promises utopia "so they say." The same site of impossible bliss was discovered in the ground of sand just below the cobblestones that the protesters extracted from the streets and threw at the police in the revolution of 1968. The movement, fomented by the perception that national policies were out of synch in a world riddled by intolerable social contradictions, was known to be impossible (Lyotard 1991, 47–48). The beach below the stones, the ground for a projection of utopia, had as its inverse in *Lange* the map tacked on the walls of three different places.

La Grande Illusion: Terrae incognitae

The beginning and ending of *La Grande Illusion* (1937) are not dissimilar to *Le Crime de Monsieur Lange.* André Bazin noted that the feature belonged, like *Lange,* to the spirit of the Popular Front, and that its narrative includes the sacrifice of a French nobleman (Boëldieu, played by Pierre Fresnay) for the cause of the collective project of an escape from the prison of a remote fortress in Germany (1989, 60). He observed, too, that the film is striated with unassailable borderlines and frontiers of nation, space, attitude, language, and class. An itinerary of evasion, like that of *Lange,* takes shape in the maps seen in both the image field and in the narrative. Renoir's provisional treatment of the film contains what François Truffaut calls its essential pieces: the prisoners' efforts at escape, the taking and surrender of Douaumont, solitary confinement, the high fortress, Boëldieu's death, "the Swiss border and especially the idea that our interests in life are more important than nationalities and that humans, as Renoir was often to declare, 'divide horizontally more than vertically.'"[16] The text mentions a map that comes to the mind of Maréchal (Jean Gabin) after he "purges the pain" of sixty days of solitary confinement and returns to his comrades with the will to escape.

> The idea is forever haunting Maréchal. . . . But how? The most useful instrument would be a map of Germany, and little by little he procures one, in tiny pieces, each the size of a postage stamp, that are delivered to him in the wrappings of chocolate bars. He glues them together. But many of the bars were lost along the way and as a result there are holes in the map. (Bazin 1989, 177)

The first sequence of the film, celebrated for the gentle flow of the camera in a military canteen, establishes a geography correlative to a map. Viewers recall how the first shot fades in from black. A tilt-down in close-up of a record spinning at 78 rpm shows a Victrola, resting on a table covered with a checkerboard cloth, set at a three-quarter angle with respect to the frame. Two hands hold the machine that sings the song in female falsetto, "Frou-frou, Frou-frou, le patron est . . . [Frou-frou, the boss is . . .]" that Maréchal, the first player to be seen, repeats, humming, "Frou-frou, Frou-frou, da da da da da-dee." The camera tilts up. Dressed in a uniform and wearing a *képi*, he watches the turning record, now invisible and out of frame below. The round top of the képi, a cruciform interlaced on its top marking four cardinal directions inside of its circle, reproduces the sight of the four bars of light reflecting from the center to the periphery of the spinning record. In soft focus, in the background to the right of Maréchal, stands a table and a chair. The camera pulls up farther. The Victrola now appears to be another of Renoir's "desiring machines" (like the organ grinder in *Boudu* or the calliope in *La Règle du jeu*) that baits whoever is captive to its melodies.

The shot holds as three men, sitting down to drink, fill the space in the background. A man walks from left to right in the middle ground. Maréchal suddenly turns right and pulls back slightly (the soft focus revealing a window in the background, two tables, the three men seated below a couple of pictures behind them), barking, "Hey there, canteen-guy [*popotier*], are you going to Epernay?" The camera pans right, bringing into sharper focus the men at the table (now at the left) and a bar attended by a server who wears a soldier's cap. Because the song is emitted in the same direction as the captain's words, a mobile geography of voice and music ensues. The shot now implies that Maréchal's voice could be a recording of the same kind as "Frou . . . frou." The song is emitted in the same direction as the captain's words. Halphen, the popotier, comes into view on the right in such a way that it is unclear whether Maréchal, the music, or the camera is interpellating him.

The space of the canteen begins to dilate. Halphen responds, yes, he will be going to Epernay. A man entering from a backlit doorway emphasizes a change in venue. At the lower right-hand corner of the frame a hand brings forward a bottle of white wine that it displays to the camera and puts on the table while one of the two seated soldiers in the foreground cuts into a loaf of bread. The man who enters, dressed in a black sweater, sporting a mustache and wearing a kepi, is Captain Ringis. He walks left, ostensibly causing the camera to reverse the course of its panoramic and bring it back to Maréchal by the Victrola. The plan-séquence turns into a three-quarter two-shot that displays the crisp lines of Ringis's face as he addresses Maréchal: "Dis donc, Maréchal . . ., il y a là un type de l'Etat-Major. . . . Il faut que tu l'emmènes [Hey, Maréchal, there's a guy from headquarters over there . . . you've got to bring him along]." To which he answers, "Un gars de l'Etat-Major? . . . Hé bé! Dis donc . . ., y tombe mal! [An Etat-Major guy? Oh damn! Hurry up! What a drag!]." Ringis's look changes from irony to disbelief at the mention of Joséphine. "Allez, vite, viens

[Now, come on, let's go]," he says, as if to cue yet another—now a third—pan of the camera (in the space of almost two minutes) to the right and toward the bar and doorway.

The megaphone is held in view, paradoxically as if it were *recording* the ambient speech of the three men at the table. The two on the left are visible, the third to the right, off frame, having just displayed the bottle of wine, now utters, "Eh passe-moi donc le camembert [Come on, hand me some of that camembert]." The Victrola that had stopped (as if to allow the words about the *état-major* to resonate and the conversation to fill the frame) now starts up again.

Two shots later, while the recorded voice, off, of the woman singing "Frou-frou" continues, she intones a verse, "Que m'en direz-vous? [What would you say about this?]." Implied is that we know not what to say about the situation that unfolds before our eyes.

Before he can respond, the film suddenly cuts to a medium close-up of the "type de l'état-major," the character in medium close-up who will soon be known as Boëldieu. Elegantly dressed in an officer's uniform, wearing a woolen overcoat

Figure 7. *La Grande Illusion* (1937): Standing in front of two military maps, Boëldieu scrutinizes (and casts aspersions on) an aerial photograph whose outline is reflected on his monocle.

and a képi, he stares down at a sheet of paper. Behind him is a cadastral map of a region with towns and roads visible despite the soft focus. Over its lower edge is tacked another map whose border frames the edge of Boëldieu's right shoulder. As he scrutinizes the sheet of paper the song on the Victrola is still heard ("moi, je dis de son Frou-frou . . . [about his Frou-frou I say . . .]"), implying that the officer's space is adjacent to the tavern or that, in the mobile geography of the film, he is as much straining to see the image *over* the words of the song as we are to look at the portrait of the état-major defined by the map behind him. Wearing a dark glove, he raises a monocle to his right eye to scrutinize the sheet of paper.

We are prone to look at the map exactly as he studies the sheet. The map doubles the paper such that what he cannot quite see is exactly what we fail to discern on the map behind him. Just as the megaphone had both emitted and received speech in the previous shot, the état-major looks toward a map that has its counterpart at his backside. The film cuts to a two-shot in medium depth that re-establishes the commander in three-quarter view in front of the map on the wall behind his little desk. Ringis, after some footsteps have announced his arrival, is in view to the left, standing in front of a smaller topographic map on the wall behind him. He occupies the center, turns left, and introduces Maréchal, entering from the right, heralding, "Capitaine de Boëldieu, état-major de division." Maréchal salutes informally and utters his name (the song is still playing in the background) before Boëldieu hands the sheet to the captain, asking him if he is familiar "with this photo."

All three men focus their eyes upon it. Maréchal affirms, yes, he knows of the picture because a certain "Ricord" took it. Boëldieu asks of the whereabouts of "Ricord" and learns that he is on leave. The état-major takes a baton and points its tip at a spot on the picture that he calls "cette petite tâche grise qui m'inquiète . . . là, en dessous de la route [this little grey spot that bothers me, just below the road]." The spectator discovers that indeed two or three similar spots are also below as many roads on the map *behind* Boëldieu. Whatever it is, the spot is cause for consternation. Ringis says that "it's not a road, it's a canal," while Maréchal esteems that it is "a railroad bed." To which, in ironic rejoinder, Boëldieu notes, "a touching unanimity! This detail gives a rich idea of the perfection of our photographic equipment." Maréchal hems and haws, "Yeah, there was fog on that morning," before Boëldieu (always in front of the map) adds, "Indeed, yes, I'd like to resolve this little enigma." Ringis interprets this as an order to call for a plane as if he were ordering a taxi: he turns to ring up a dispatcher while Maréchal departs to the left, Boëldieu still standing in front of the map on the wall and holding the photograph in his left hand, scrutinizing it through the monocle held between his nose and right eyebrow. Ringis asks him if he would prefer a flying suit or a fur jacket. Still looking at the picture, Boëldieu responds in ironic quid pro quo, "No preference at all. Flying suits stink, and fur jackets lose their hair."

Ringis connects with the fighter headquarters as the shot dissolves to what will be identified as the German officer's canteen, the counterpart to the space described in the first four minutes (and as many shots) of the film. In the intermediate area of the dissolve in which cohabit the two zones—indeed the decisive area toward which the narrative will beckon, between or in the midst of the geographic and national borders—the map behind Boëldieu is placed behind a poster whose verbal shards identify the canteen (we read "der Kriegszeitung . . . Verlagers"). Three panels of surface emerge. On the left is a panel of wall behind Ringis. In the center is an open doorway that displays a great square of greyish white sky or abstraction over another rectangle of landscape bisected by the joining edge of the two walls of the French officer's quarters which reaches down to the telephone box in the lower center. On the right is the third panel where the map and poster are over each other and where the picture Boëldieu studies is cut by the doorway emerging into view. In the foreground to the right emerges the wide end of a megaphone that we discern to be the exact double of the one seen in the canteen in first shot of the film. As the shot dissolves a bald German flyer (Erich von Stroheim), dressed in a flyer's suit, his lips clasping a cigarette, enters into the space. The Rhenish landscape in the background becomes clear.

Thus end the first five shots covering two minutes and nine seconds of the film. The topographic map shown so prominently behind Boëldieu plays an ironic role in the military history informing the film. By 1916 aerial photography replaced triangulated (or "cadastral") maps dating to the seventeenth and eighteenth centuries. Their avatars were the topographic maps first drawn by *ingénieurs du roi,* kings' engineers or royal cartographers in the age of Henry IV in the final years of the Wars of Religion. Employed to redesign the fortifications along the borders of the nation, especially in northeastern France, the topographic maps served the ends of national defense. Their work marked a turning point in military affairs for reason of their innovation in the design of fortresses and lines of defense.[17]

The "little grey spot" that Boëldieu remarks on the photograph could be a decisively "petite illusion" within the frame of "la grande illusion." The captain's snide commentary on the so-called progress—that most important product— wrought by new photographic imagery replacing the cartographic fruits of the École des Ponts et Chaussées in the pre-Revolutionary Enlightenment crystallizes debate over old and new worlds taking place elsewhere in the film. Boëldieu and Rauffenstein belong to a generation of cartographers, to a world of maps in the tradition of the ingénieurs and four generations of the Cassini family who worked under the tutelage of the nobility. Maréchal and his cohorts are those who listen to popular songs recorded on discs and rely on the picture that someone named "Ricord" had taken with a camera in fog and morning mist. Boëldieu and Rauffenstein each wear monocles; thus they see the world through two perspectives. One, monocular, is "flat" and would be depthless, according equal visual value to any point in the field of view. The other, binocular, would be in depth, with attention paid to layered areas that the eyes traverse to gain a sense of three-dimensionality and of spatial illusion. In their plotting, the first shots of the film sum up and anticipate the story lines of the hermetic divisions between nations, classes, and gender. They offer, too, the effects of a thumbnail history of locational imaging in which a line of divide separates an older and seemingly aristocratic practice of warfare to a collective, murderous, and democratic counterpart of the First World War.

The men prepare their escape from the high castle of Wintersborn. One of the officers, the professor Demolder (Silvain Itkine, who played the role of Batala's cousin in *Lange*), has little desire to leave the dungeon of pleasure where he is translating Pindar. He tells the men that the poet "is what is most important in the world . . . more than the war, more than my own life." Far more idle in his trivial pursuits, Boëldieu has been playing with a deck of cards.[18] He pushes aside a couple of dictionaries to make room enough for his game of solitaire. He distributes his cards on a surface littered with a box of tea, a pot, and a couple of jars of marmalade. The irony is multiple: the état-major who will sacrifice

Figure 8. *La Grande Illusion:* Rosenthal tells Maréchal that his map, a key to their escape, is almost complete. Behind him are the prints composing a museum without walls, and a Senegalese soldier sketching an allegorical drawing.

himself to insure the success of Maréchal's and Rosenthal's escape is at once alone and entirely given to a collective project where the professor is not. Draped over his shoulders, an ample checkered dishtowel covers part of his uniform. An accoutrement of a proletarian café, the towel makes visible a multitude of little squares, *cartes,* that match the oblique view of the playing cards on the table. The professor to the left can only *read* the material in front of his eyes, while Boëldieu, center-right, and haloed by his three comrades behind him, his monocle evident, can both read and *see* greater patterns of things as they are placed on the table. He is a cartographer. He teaches the men behind him how to discern objects and issues in space.

The next shot becomes a lesson in point. Boëldieu has just put a card on the table. The film cuts to a medium close-up of Rosenthal, in a slight tilt downward, putting topographic squares on a type of canvas backcloth used for military field maps.[19] Rosenthal attends to getting the mosaic of pieces into their proper places. His hands touch the creases of the map extended over his lap and adjacent to the draping folds of a checkered cloth covering a table to his right. Behind him, along the contours of a hanging cloth, three squares of another "map" are visible: a print of a cubist work of lines and blocks to Rosenthal's right; behind his head, that of a Caravaggesque ephebe; and in back of his left shoulder, the face of Botticelli's Venus from the painting in the Uffizi Gallery depicting the birth of the Goddess on a cockleshell floating in the ocean waters. Rosenthal pulls back to look at his work: "Voilà! Ma carte est constituée ou presque! [There! My map is almost done]."[20] As the camera reframes the scene the image of another ephebe, seen obliquely, comes into view behind and to the left of the Botticelli print. Maréchal enters right, and the camera shows a portrait of a coiffed woman in the style of Rubens. As Rosenthal brings his map forward (we see its lines obliquely) an early Christian or medieval portrait of the face of the Madonna, in the mode of the mosaics in the two churches of Sant' Apollinare of Ravenna, is on the left, behind the prisoner's head. A Japanese mask adorns the cloth, and to its left is a guitar waiting for a painter to do its still-life. Directly behind him is a print in the northern style (from Roger van der Weyden) of a woman wearing a white veil over her head. Above it is a print of a baroque scene (possibly El Greco or Tintoretto). Behind the men there are visible some pots on the wall to the right over and behind a Senegalese solider who is drawing a picture.

The map in Rosenthal's hands (and, now, in Maréchal's too) foregrounds a *musée imaginaire,* a premonition of André Malraux's genial "museum without walls." The playing cards in the former shot, that surely cannot be seen without the presence of Cézanne's "Card Players," are now turned into a staging of the details taken from the art treasures of the western world. When Rosenthal affirms and indicates, his finger pointing at a spot near the left edge of the map, "You see, we're here, just above this curve, twenty-five kilometers from the River Main," the deictic *nous sommes ici* tells us that both they and we are *not here.* They are in a mosaic assemblage of works of art that constitute a map no less vital or imaginary than what they have pieced together from cartographic fragments. Rosenthal draws his itinerary across the map with his index finger ("in order to reach Switzerland above Lake Constanz, the only way to avoid crossing the Rhine, we'll have to walk 300 kilometers. . . . We'll need fifteen nights to walk the distance on six lumps of sugar and two biscuits per day") just as the Senegalese soldier draws a line on the picture he is sketching on the top of an inverted wooden crate. The artist walks over to place his picture—that he names "Justice Pursuing Crime"—next to the map, implying by spatial juxtaposition that allegory and cartography might be worthy of comparison.[21] The allegory is confirmed when Maréchal utters, after taking a detached view of the picture and returning to the map, "Non, mais, dis donc, pour aller à ton Constance [No, I mean, say, to get to your Constance]." Here, as in much of this film, and like *Lange* and *La Règle du jeu,* Maréchal makes clear the folly of people who seek a lake or a city of "constancy" in a world where relations—seen in this very shot—are mobile, in flux, and anything but constant. The itinerary actively drawn across the map bespeaks any promise of geographic or visual stability.

The end of the film responds to the sequences in which maps had figured earlier. Prior to the last shot, a variant of the beach seen at the end of *Lange,* a panoramic of a landscape of mountains in snow cuts into medium close-up of Maréchal and Rosenthal consulting the map before they make their break for the Swiss border.[22] The latter tells Maréchal that lines separating nations are one of man's artificial creations. Dismantling an allegory of space and nation, he constructs another about the smooth and undifferentiated spaces of a world where only ecological demarcations would hold.[23] Maréchal hopes for an end of "cette putain de guerre, en espérant que c'est la dernière [this goddamned war, in hoping it's the last]," parroting the usual slogans about the "war to end all wars" at a moment when the film, along with *La Bête humaine* (1938) and *La Règle du jeu* (1939), indicates that nothing could be further from the truth. Responding that he is deluding himself (*tu te fais des illusions*) while echoing the title of the film, Rosenthal asks that they return to reality with a plan in the event they encounter a German patrol. A final panoramic leads to a snowscape where a railroad cuts a slightly diagonal path across the frame below two squat buildings with Germanic roofs. Two specks or smudges in the snow are perceptible. The shot actualizes what Ringis, Boëldieu, and Maréchal had scrutinized on the photo below the map in the officer's room: a pair of grey spots (*tâches grises*) adjacent to a railroad (*une voie ferrée*). The relation of the photo to the map at the beginning of the film finds a visual correlative in the two "smudges" that bother the spectator as much as they had bothered Boëldieu. The maps thus buckle the film and, like the map of America in *Le Crime de Monsieur Lange,* indicate both the utopian and real registers of the couple's unlikely escape from the visual and historical frame in which they trudge.

Globes In and Out of Perspective

Renoir had often spoken of some of his films being "rehearsals" for others. Parts of *Lange* rehearse spatial articulations in *La Grande Illusion,* and some lines of *La Grande Illusion* plot crucial elements of *La Règle du jeu.* In the masterpiece of 1939 equally decisive maps are found. They build on what Renoir set forward in films reaching back to *Boudu.* They figure in a style that expands on the cartographical qualities of cinema made clear in front of the bookstore by the Seine, on the beach at the border of Belgium, and in the snow at the threshold of Constance. Critics have rightly noted that *Lange* especially shows how *La Règle du jeu* turns off-screen space into theatrical space. The courtyard in the earlier feature shares the same virtues as the inside of the chateau in the film of 1939, both films offering "a play of artifice whereby reality is not falsified but theatricalised without losing its realism," realism gaining presence "in the openness of the theatrical" (Rohdie 2001, 121). Theater within film, or a comic illusion in the style of Pierre Corneille's *Illusion comique,* also draws on the spatial play of the theater-in-the-theater that had marked the middle sequences of *La Grande Illusion.*[24]

Similar articulations stage the cinematic cartography of *La Règle du jeu.* After lengthy preparations and deliberations concerning the guests he has invited to spend a vacation with him in early spring at his château in the Solognes, the Marquis de la Chesnaye (Marcel Dalio), having driven through torrential rains, arrives at his estate. Things have to get settled and put in their proper place. The following day he makes his first promenade and inspection of the territory around his château. A long shot begins with the sight of the Marquis (whose given name is Robert) seated, speaking with the keeper Schumacher (Gaston Modot), about the proliferation and damage done by rabbits. He gets up, is followed by Schumacher, and stops in the middle of a path, bordered by trees on both sides, that leads to a vanishing point in the distance. The plan-séquence develops from a dissolve of the outer stairway of the château.[25]

Beginning from a dissolve displaying a row of balusters the shot (of almost 42 seconds) portrays the Marquis on his *bâton de chaise,* a cane fitted with a folding seat, on which he turns before getting up and walking toward a road that, with the converging parallel lines of its tree-lined borders, leads to a vanishing point in the distance. Rabbits are ravaging the property. Schumacher mentions local place-names. He suggests that fences need to be erected to keep rabbits from damaging the property. As soon as he mentions the need to plant a barrier the camera encloses the space within its purview by establishing the enclosing effects of a perspectival view. The shot is literally fenced at the point where Robert retorts to Schumacher that he wants no fences, but that he doesn't want any rabbits either. When he utters his contradictory order to Schumacher, "Take care of it, my friend [Arrangez-vous, mon ami]," the camera follows suit by asking the viewer to look at the shot in view of an artificial perspective that would contain and control the spatial representation where the lateral reframing and tracking movement of the camera gave an impression of a cinematic eye ambling over the space as might the owner during a walk on his property.[26] The shot implies that it must be viewed and seen no less doubly bound than the paradoxical order given to Schumacher. An impossible situation is plotted to be seen once as a flat surface and as a landscape in great depth of field, as a delineated and center-enhancing composition rife with lines distinguishing layers of relief, and as a surface over which the eye moves about in order to *read* words and things in and on what it sees. The shot requires study at once from binocular and monocular points of view.[27]

Such is one of the rules of the game that the film imposes upon its viewer. It brings forward the fabulous cartography belonging to one of the most important perspectival objects of the entire film, a pair of stone globes that decorate the two ends of the balustrade at the threshold of the perron of the left wing of the château. Almost all of the principal entries and exits to and from the inner space pass by the doorway, the steps, and the pair of globes. The latter are seen for the first time in the plan-séquence (shot 71 above) that precedes the Marquis's discussion with Schumacher about how to reach a final solution to the rabbit problem. Two panoramic shots (68 and 69) have just followed two elegant cars driving across the landscape and toward the château (itself a classified monument that enthusiasts of baroque architecture recognize as La Ferté Saint-Aubin in the Loiret). A straight cut to a medium-long shot of the cars arriving, their tires crunching the gravel path in broad daylight, includes an older guardian in the foreground next to Schumacher. Their backs face the viewer. They behold the first car that arrives from the left. The camera is aimed at the left wing of the château. Bells ring to welcome the coming. Schumacher advances and bends over to open the door of the car. He salutes the Marquis who is seated inside with Christine, his wife, who says hello; he then leans toward the inside in saluting Christine. La Chesnaye emerges from the driver's side and utters a curt "bonjour" to Schumacher before the camera tracks right to follow, in front of the first car, the Marquis who "turns about, embracing the landscape with a look of satisfaction" (Curchod 1998, 83). As he turns, a second, lightly colored car arrives, bringing into view a pair of large headlamps set on its wide front fenders. Corneille (Eddy Debray) exits from the right and then disappears behind La Chesnaye.

Schumacher, in his dark velvet guardian's uniform, takes the occasion to beg a moment of his master's time as they move upward and into profile. "M'sieur l'marquis will excuse me for speaking to him about this while at work, but it's only . . . because of my wife." He complains that he leads the life of a widower while Lisette (Paulette Dubost), his spouse who serves Christine (Nora Grégor), spends all of her time in the company of the Marquis's spouse. The remaining players arrive and greet one another. With a thick Burgundian accent the old guard tells Corneille that he has lit the stove and furnished the fireplaces, to which the majordomo responds, "Très bien, mon ami." Lisette comes forward on the steps from behind Corneille. Schumacher salutes her and walks up the steps with her as the camera pans with them in a slight countertilt. She hastens to enter the château when there comes into view, as the couple moves right and past the balustrade, "[d]ecorating the extremity of each of these posts, *two imposing globes of stone*" (Curchod 1998, 85, emphasis added). Schumacher, veiled by the balustrade in front of the width of the field of view, sighs with relief that, finally, his wife has arrived: "Ah, enfin, te voilà!" The tracking shot ends with the globes and building dissolving away as Lisette enters the château and Robert appears (shot 71) seated on his walking stick. The globes enter into view before the slightly countertilted camera displays Schumacher following his wife through a row of six balusters below and to the right of the nearer globe.[28]

Time and again the film returns to the sight and scene of the globes. As they become increasingly present—in broad daylight here and later in chiaroscuro, now obliquely, later frontally, and then obliquely again—the globes acquire explosive iconic force. They seem to be embodiments of two terrestrial and celestial spheres, of the style of classical globes that Vincenzo Coronelli and his avatars

Figure 9. *La Règle du jeu* (1939): Schumacher and Lisette enter the château in Solognes, passing by one of two decorative globes at the end of the balustrade.

manufactured for the French nobility from the 1660s all the way up to 1789.[29] They also belong to a baroque vocabulary of power by which, as commonly seen in manuals of military architecture, they were associated with the attributes of Mars and Bellona, the god and goddess of war chosen to decorate frontispieces and allegorical pictures. They are both "globes" and cannonballs that figure in festoons and sways amassing the paraphernalia of artillery and warfare.[30] They belong to a triumphal order of panache, power, and empire that belonged to the pre-Revolutionary order. The globes refer immediately to an idea of the nobility as it could be imagined in an era stretching form the age of Henry IV up to Louis XVI.

Yet they seem to be globes without the outlines of continents, oceans, and islands or those of constellations and galaxies in the heavens. The granular surface of the stone that the camera caresses in its panoramic is one of a world map without borderlines or edges, a world in which contradiction and difference are impalpable. In the historical moment of the production of the film, Neville Chamberlain's policy of appeasement and "peace in our time" with Nazi Germany had been established in Munich, and the *Sitzkrieg* itself was a term that went along with the grand illusion that the Maginot line would protect France from the German enemy (Tifft 1992). In the ambience of fear and uncertainty the globes seem to be cannonballs on the verge of bursting. In a broad sense they are icons eliciting a gamut of impressions that run from fear to uneasy anticipation. Reminders of heroic maps of times past and harbingers of future destruction, they simultaneously invite and resist typological or figural interpretation.

The spheres are inflected differently at the very end of the film. After La Chesnaye learns that Schumacher shot André Jurieu (Roland Toutain) by the greenhouse adjacent to the château a throng of guests assembles around the steps and perron where the two globes were first seen (shot 334). The camera is at a level above six onlookers who seem to be standing in the loge below a stage on which the Marquis faces the audience, viewers and participants alike, at the center. Midway on the steps, his left foot on one step below the one on which his slightly bent right leg is placed, Schumacher looks on the scene maladroitly, bending over, good subaltern that he is, as he had when opening the door of the car and greeting La Chesnaye upon his arrival at the château. In a keen treatment of the shot Stanley Cavell notes Schumacher's awkward pose and his isolation that is halfway up the stairs, between La Chesnaye and the audience below. He notes, too, that the double-barreled shotgun slung over Schumacher's shoulder "happens to be pointing exactly at the Marquis's head" (1979, 221).[31]

The sightline that runs from the two barrels of the shotgun to La Chesnaye's head can be glimpsed only if the viewer sees the staging from simultaneously monocular and binocular perspectives. From the point of view of the latter, the gun draws a line that goes from the foreground to the background (as had the trees on the right border of the path in shot 71) just as, from below and to the left,

Saint-Aubain's and the Old General's lines of sight lead in a complementary way from the left up to the Marquis's head. In this way La Chesnaye would be at the vanishing point of a scene whose interest goes into the depth of field from all sides of the frame. From the point of view of the former, Schumacher's shotgun does not really happen to be literally aimed at the Marquis but only suggestively, only when the eye can connect the gun to the standing figure along a sightline made possible when the shot is seen in its flat aspect, *before* Schumacher moves up a couple of steps, turns about, and joins his master. From this vantage point every form in the shot would be of equal valence—the four pilaster strips on the wall, the bricks and quoins that give the wall the characteristic look of the Henry IV style, the illuminated balusters—and would be grasped without attention to depth of field. In that way the two illuminated globes that for a moment mark the separation of the Marquis from his public could be fancied as two slugs from the double-barreled shotgun, indeed reminders of the projectiles that struck and felled the aviator with such murderous force that he, in Marceau's (Julien Carette's) soppy words, "a boulé comme une bête quand on est à la chasse [rolled over like an animal shot when you're hunting]" (shot 238, Curchod 1998, 264).

Figure 10. *La Règle du jeu:* Chesnaye is about to deliver a eulogy after the shooting of Jurieu. The two globes on the terrace stand in analogy with the double-barreled shotgun, slung on Schumacher's back, that is aimed at Chesnaye.

Suspended, the globes are also, in Renoir's world of optical *correspondances,* two suspended shells that are the complement to the two globes—a double hemisphere in miniature—seen at the end of the barrels of the gun Schumacher had aimed in the direction of the greenhouse (in shot 321), just after the camera moved in a half-perpendicular panoramic from the background of the target to the hunter and his accomplice looking, stalking, and waiting for the arrival of their prey. In this shot, in which care is taken to put the end of the barrels at the center of the frame before Schumacher lowers the shotgun and lets the moonlight gleam on its metal, the end of the twin pipes becomes a miniature complement to the globes. A terrifying cartography emerges from the relation of the men with the gun to the architectural décor. It has to do with the projection of the characters' fears and desires, to be sure, but also with the complicities of the camera, in its own labors, when it accounts for their projections and the pleasure we take in identifying with their murderously confused motives in a moment of extraordinary historical fragility.

Everywhere, but here especially, Renoir is a cartographer of cinema. His films are folded into and through the maps he portrays. It is a well-known fact that his cinema is a model, like a *patron* in a geographer's studio, for generations of cineasts who study his films.

3
Maps and Theaters of Torture:
Roma, città aperta

The evidence accumulated in the preceding chapter reconfirms a point obvious to adepts of auteur theory. In one way or another director are auteurs by virtue of cartography found both within each of their films and that runs across many others of their signature. Cartography is not equated with an author's "vision of the world" or of an oeuvre whose sum would be greater than any or all of its constituent topographies. The auteur merits the name because of a cartographic consciousness seen in maps shown or in shots and montage taken to be deciphered as maps. Such was the effect of the overlay of four moments in Renoir's films of the 1930s. Such, too, is the character of Roberto Rossellini's cinema in general. The salient traits of the two directors owe much to maps that embody the multifarious and often-conflicting forces that inspire their cinemas. It would seem that, at the end of the Second World War, as an Italian director dedicated to the cause of Italian film, Rossellini wanted to project to the world at large a shattered and shattering historical geography of Italy. His cinematic project was one of reconstructing the nation and infusing an Italian style into his films. Certainly *Paisan, Germany, Year Zero, Stromboli, Viva l'Italia!*, and other features attest to these ends. But what of *Roma, città aperta*, the classic that launched Rossellini as an auteur? Surely in this film a mapping impulse is clear, but so also are the contradictions that figure in the quest for power that seems to be a defining quality of the modern map, a quality that René Clair, as we saw in chapter 1, associated with cinema. *Roma, città aperta*, in which the loathsome sight of torture is excruciating, can be understood cartographically, as a staging of the yoking of locational imaging to terror.

A guiding hypothesis of this chapter is that in the film Rossellini taps into the tradition of the *theatrum mundi*, a world-theater conceived as an atlas of maps with which its owners can assuage their broadest desires for travel and displacement. The same theater is tied to one of cruelty, to a theater of torture, a subsidiary of the theatrum mundi. From 1570 and well into the seventeenth century Abraham Ortelius invented, published, and circulated the first modern atlas, the *Orbis theatrum terrarum*, which would be translated into many languages and published in epitome and grand format. Its publication was synchronous with many theaters associated with art and architectural design. The metaphor of the "theater" quickly dominated European print-culture in the sixteenth and early seventeenth centuries. It drew on the medieval notion of the world in the shape of a circular disk (*orbis terrae*) but was applied to the "sense of a scene where action takes place" and to a "setting of human life."[1] The atlas became an object that Ortelius claimed would allow the reading spectator to travel all about the world without leaving the room in which the book was placed. The theater was contained in the action of studying the maps and turning the folio pages on which they were printed and painted. Theaters and "world-stages" became the thresholds of books of anatomy, agriculture, logistics and, no less, the practice of torture.[2]

A reading of Rossellini's early masterpiece will be engaged through this tradition. Jacques Rancière (2001), for one, has suggested that in features beginning from *Roma, città aperta* cinematic compositions are as much mapped as they are staged. The films of the neorealist period draw the staging of tragedy into their texture and thus, in their doubling and duplicities, yield images of intractable violence. Heeding Rossellini's dictum to the effect that he organizes each of his films around a sequence, a single and simple shot, or sometimes even a gesture within a shot, Rancière argues that emblematic proof is found in the death of Pina (Anna Magnani), a turning point in the feature.

The apartment building in which she and her fiancé had found brief solace together has just been ransacked by a phalanx of armed soldiers sent by the Gestapo. The fiancé is captured, thrown in the back of a pickup truck, and driven away. All of a sudden, in this "highly improbable sequence," Pina breaks through a line of soldiers (bustling and fighting her way, she comically thrusts askew the helmet on the head of one of the SS soldiers), tears herself free from the crowd, and runs after the truck that speeds away. From its point of view the camera, using the flattening effect of a telephoto lens, shows her going forward without advancing. She sprints into the open, is isolated in

the middle of the roadway, a black silhouette on a great white page, tendered toward us, toward the camera, toward the guns, almost comically with her exaggerated gesticulation as if she were hailing a taxi driver who has left without waiting for his passenger. And we think too of these brides and grooms in comedies, late for their marriages, who rush to church half-dressed. And, in fact, it is the altar where the same morning she was going to rejoin Francesco. (2001, 167)[3]

The sequence, he notes, is one of a "suspension of the image of meaning" that has to fall to earth.

> For both the camera and the bullets time has come to be done with the suspense. Pina, gunned down, alights on the white asphalt like a great bird on which, like two other birds cut away by the hand of a painter, that drop down and land about her far from the presence of the militia: the crying child arches over her and the priest tries to tear the boy away from his pain. Never has there been so unified the weight of the bodies that fall with the absolute suspension of grace in this very slight parabola by which, beforehand, are abolished all pain and all disorder. (167)

A feeling of Pauline grace never intercedes to clean or to redeem either the characters or the uncanny staging of the murder. The sequence is "the exact concordance of the meeting of what or whoever was not being sought," Rossellini intending, without artistic frills, to underscore "the exact concordance of an ethical surge and an aesthetic drawing" (167). A trajectory, a path, or a line—*une courbe*—of descent is drawn in the articulation both of the shot and of other meetings and cadences. Just when Don Pietro (Aldo Rossi) holds Manfredi's head in his arms after his body has fallen from the chair of torture, doing what the torturers failed to do, his thumb sealing the victim's eyelids, he looks upward, not in just in search of the voice or light of God but in ire and anger. Aesthetics of grace are broken when he unleashes his wrath.

Rancière infers that Rossellini's sequences are vectored by movements of bodily action and of attractions that run up and down and across the field of the image. Any of Rossellini's films

> is a surface of inscription that refuses to accept the slightest trace of dissimulation; nothing is present that would need to be kept latent, as might a hidden truth behind appearances or a scandal dissimulated behind the smooth surface of things. Here the scandal of an entirely different force is surely that nothing is ever dissimulated or liable to dissimulation. However intensely it examines faces, Rossellini's microscope forbids itself from discerning anything that an attentive gaze would not perceive on its own. (179)

In a sweeping gesture Rancière takes leave both of André Bazin, for whom Rossellini's films become a "patient quest given to discovering the secret of beings and things," and Gilles Deleuze, who finds in the cinema "disconnected spaces and purely optical and sonorous situations" (166).

The surface on which nothing can be concealed is paradoxically, so it seems, a lamination of two planes where a cartography of locational control adheres to another of control through dissimulation. Rancière sees two different Rossellinis working in the strange confines of the Gestapo headquarters. In the torture chamber the resistance fighters "cry too much and speak not enough," while the adjacent salon or officers' club is "decorated with mirrors and paintings, furnished with a piano, a studio décor for a Hollywood film of Lili Marlene [Dietrich]'s Berlin" (168). On the one side is "Ingrid," who directs the actors and actresses and organizes the images that will, on the other side, under the jurisdiction of "Bergmann," extort truth from those who have fallen under their spell.[4] Rancière writes of a mapping tendency that gives definition, depth, and amplitude to the tiny milieu where they work:

> Bergmann, the head of the Gestapo, and Ingrid, his associate, have thus divided the sides and roles. Bergmann draws a map of the places, orders sequences and gives commands to the sound crew—to put it plainly, to the torturers—in the room to the left. Ingrid is confided with the direction of actresses and the organization of images that, on the other side, are to produce the desired words of the confession. Her art is that of trapping in their image, in the drug of mirrors, these "actresses" who identify their talent with the cosmetic art of making up their reflection in the mirror of dressing table—this mirror where we see the reflected gaze of Ingrid contemplating her prey, the sudden surprise in her discovery of the photograph of Marina and Manfredi, an immobilized picture on the stage, a little trap in the greater trap. And we understand that Rossellini seeks not to be oversubtle either with the act of denunciation or with Marina's motivations. The drug with which she is rewarded is merely the slight sum of her impoverished desire, of her great fear of the Unknown. (171)

Bergmann orders and plots the space where his enemy's secrets will be revealed. Ingrid, a stage manager of sorts, attends to a filmic "theater of operations." The former uses cartography, guile, and a blowtorch to extract the information he needs from his victims, and the latter exploits the fineries and remainders of classical cinema, its art of simulation and dissimulation, to bring her victims to the interrogation room. According to this reading two kinds of cinematic cartography are in play, the one inherited from logistics and from the art of espionage, the other from classical cinema. The "maps" that belong to the former tradition blend into cinema itself.[5]

Inspection of the kind that Rancière equates with the eye of Rossellini's camera lens reveals a variety of maps decorating the walls of different rooms in the film. They are related to the mirrors of truth and dissimulation at once of the film as film, to the spaces it invents, and to the traditions in which it is made. The first map occupies the entire screen. It determines the nature of the space of the room in which it is later seen in partial views, confirming the meaning of the title-credits seen less than five minutes before. The voice-off of the interrogator

(Bergmann, played by the dancer Harry Feist) states, "La città sarà divisa" (into fourteen sectors). His words respond to the title credits seen minutes ago. An ichnographic map of Rome and its environs, of a fairly small scale and of a size and aspect-ratio almost identical to the screen, fades into view after three SS troops have inspected the rooftop of an apartment building from which Manfredi, a member of the Italian resistance, has just escaped.

A Map Room

What happens before the map appears determines how it is tied to the articulation of everything seen and heard throughout the film. The Germans are aware of the proximity of Manfredi (Marcello Pagliero), the resistance fighter. Marina (Maria Michi), his lady friend, calls him from a telephone at her bedside. A bilingual member of the SS crew answers the phone, first making the mistake of revealing his German identity ("Allo," he utters, before correcting himself, stating, "Pronto"), a slip that Marina does not quite grasp because she states that she would like to speak to Manfredi. The telephone call gives the Germans further cause to search the apartment. After rummaging a vacant room the soldiers open a door and climb a set of stairs leading to a terrace in daylight. One soldier, seen in medium close-up and from a countertilt that captures the textured wall and chimney of the roof under a grey sky, looks outward and over the camera.[6] His gaze, focused on the horizon in the distance, does not seem to discern much of anything. A very fast pano-tilt drops down from the horizon to a maze of tiled roofs and a garden (where three chimneys are visible next to the branches and leaves of a small tree) in the complex of living space that would be below the German's eyes (shot 27). The camera stops there but yields clues neither to the German nor the viewer. The film cuts back to the German who begins to turn about-face.

In what appears to be a false or clumsy edit, a *faux-raccord,* the film cuts to a medium view of the man in the middle of his turn. He stops. Standing above two old Italian women to his left and right, and in front of two parallel western towers of a church seen in the first shot of the film, he is flanked by a soldier in the background to the right and, in the foreground to the left, another soldier who also wears the helmet of the Wehrmacht. He utters dryly, in fairly fluent Italian, "Chi abita là?" (Who lives there?). In the space of a second his speech betrays the reason why the former shot held on the living space of the building. The woman to his left responds, "C'è l'ambasciata di Spagna [it's the Spanish Embassy]," to which, miffed, he responds, turning back, "Ah . . ." (shot 29). The men have no inkling about where they are in the city they occupy. The German soldier looks toward the horizon before the map of the following shot dissolves into view. What the soldier could not see from the rooftop is not exactly what the map shows. The question concerning how to look at the city as a city and as a map is put forward in the minuscule divide between the end of the sequence of the search and the first takes in the Nazi inquisitor's office.

The map of the city is apportioned into fourteen zones that turn about an unmarked circle at center from whose line of circumference an arrow points upward to the border (north) of the map. The metallic voice, off, of a man who speaks perfect, clear, and pedagogically impeccable Italian, describes the map. The voice itself is doubled by a right hand that holds a lighted cigarette that seems to draw itself over the map as might a teacher's wand in a classroom. The camera pulls back enough to elicit a comparison between its own frame and that of the map in order to show, entering the frame directly in front of the camera, the back and head of the uniformed officer (epaulettes decorate the shoulders of his tightly tailored jacket). He is next to a less sartorially elegant civilian, seen in three-quarter view, who gazes at the map. The camera pulls back rapidly and decisively from the figure of the hand (wearing a chain bracelet) holding the cigarette and pulling its burning tip over the space that the voice (off) describes and that is reproduced in subtitle: "The city will be divided into fourteen sectors. The Schröder plan, which we have already applied in several European cities, allows us, using the minimum effort, to comb scientifically through large masses of people."

A first viewing of the shot, especially in the three or four seconds between its emergence into view and the entry of the two men in frame, has the effect of a *map that speaks*.[7] The voice, momentarily that of the map itself, recalls the tradition of power and godlike authority that administrators and engineers had ascribed to maps when they were first used both in arenas of monarchic control that gave way to democratic process. In the tradition of the *theatrum mundi* the image of a map could virtually speak in the name of the subjects inhabiting the space it represented. As the shot pulls back, the Italian police commissioner comes into view from the left. His aspect is in strong contrast with the svelte officer in frighteningly meticulous and formal control of the Italian idiom. The Italian does not speak. In the shot he is, as the editor of the screenplay describes, "listening deferentially" (Roncoroni 1973, 11). Two views on the map are offered in the same shot. One is from the standpoint of those in power over the *urbs* and the other from that of life lived by those born into the language and space of the *civitas*.[8]

As the camera pulls farther back to show that it is the brutally arrogant Nazi who speaks (with his left arm bent and cocked to thrust his elbow into the rotund Italian's chest and the thumb of his left hand pushing so hard on his side that it cannot fail to anticipate the presence of a thumbscrew) the police commissioner takes a black handkerchief from his jacket and nervously wipes what his gesture indicates to be a supremely aquiline—and therefore generically "Italian"—nose. The officer brandishes his lit cigarette over the map, literally burning the land as a torturer might put a hot poker to the flesh of the victim he interrogates. In response to the German's description of the Schröder plan and burning effect of

his cigarette the Italian nervously utters "Ah." The timorous vocative forces recall the perplexed "Ah" of the SS soldier who could not fathom how a Spanish
embassy can be situated below the tiled roofs of an Italian cityscape. As hinge
between the two sequences, the map unsettles both the city and its representation.
    The effect of a disembodied space is immediately amplified on the sound-
track. As the two men look at the map, and as the officer ends his sentence with
a tonic accent on *minima di fòrza* (the map will have *maximum* effect with a *minimum* of force), three theatrical taps are sounded. The officer raises his head and
puts into profile a look of ruthless contempt. A door opens and an assistant,
Krammer (Eduardo Passarelli), enters, passing by a set of files on which are posed
an officer's hat, upside down, bearing the ensign of an eagle.[9] The three beats
announce that a play will begin. The tapping and abrupt entry of Bergmann's aide
is a repetition of the entrance of the German police force in the first episode of the
film (shots 3–4 and 10). After a pan to the right that follows a small truck crossing a piazza and screeching to an abrupt halt, a long shot registers five German
soldiers jumping out of their vehicle: a ringleader runs to a doorway. In the far
distance he begins to knock loudly. All of a sudden, during the tapping on the
door, the film cuts to a view of a balcony, its balustrade to the left and on the right

Figure 11. *Roma, città aperta* (1945): Bergmann informs the chief of police of the
"Schröder" plan that uses maps to capture members of the Resistance.

a row of windows covered by wooden shutters. The transition is so abrupt—the noise is equally resonant in both areas—that continuity is strained. The closed shutters, like the map, begin to speak. In the midst of the din, in a second volley of banging, the voice (off) of a radio broadcaster announces in two languages, "London calling Italy, La voce di Londre." One set of shutters opens, but instead of an embodiment of the "voice of London" there appears an elderly woman, Nannina (Amalia Pelegrini) who leans and out and looks down. Suddenly again, now in a shot from her point of view, the camera cuts to an extreme downward tilt to the truck that displays on its roof what seems to be a red cross (shot 5). It no sooner cuts back to Nannina who looks skyward and wails, "O Jèsu," before she closes the door. From the outset Rome is "open" but its windows are "closed." An ambulance carries not medics but the phalanx of Nazi thugs. A theater of fear and confusion is announced. Like the map seen at the beginning of the thirtieth shot, the wall, the shutters, and the doors seem to be seeing and speaking from two simultaneous and opposite points of view. One is that of Italy and the Resistance, and the other the German occupiers who enter and control the space. In both sequences a door, a shutter, or a threshold opens onto spaces of inexorable violence.

Thus when the maps are first seen (in shots 32 and 34) reference is made to a theater of operations that fits a pattern of paradoxically expanding closure. With a telling flick of his fingers—that mixes condescension, sadism, homophilia, and homophobia—Bergmann orders his aide to leave. The film cuts back to record his exit and the strange décor of the bureau, dossiers, and inverted cap (shot 35). The camera returns to the commissioner and the inquisitor in front of their maps before it begins a quick pan that follows Bergmann as he passes by a third map, now of the world (the right edge cuts down through the middle of Africa), on the wall adjacent to where the two views of Rome and its environs had just been seen. Bergmann briskly walks to his desk, seen in three-quarter view, on which is posed a bright reading lamp. The three maps infer that a spatial progression is being registered in the career of the panoramic that begins with a small-scale view of Rome and passes by the world at large.

The office has the look of a map room or even of a perversely constructed counterpart to the tradition of mural maps, inaugurated in Renaissance Italy, that include the nearby Galleria delle Carte Geografiche in the Vatican.[10] If in the sequence passing reference is made to the model of the Italian *studiolo*, Bergmann's brisk promenade from the wall map to the desk follows to a certain degree the plan of the gallery in the Vatican, in which the person who walks through the space takes part in a spatial narrative and a process of illumination. He rehearses the principles of the "spatial narrative," a term coined by Michel de Certeau, in which *maps* that describe the plan or layout of an inhabited place are contrasted to *tours,* or existential itineraries that turn the mapped places into living spaces.[11] But Bergmann's tour is anything but existential. Simulated, it is an artificial form of experience. His words reiterate those of the designers of atlases, for whom the viewer looking at the images or turning the pages of the atlas would never need to travel outside of the simulated space of the maps and their texts.[12] The Italian commissioner marvels like a child over Bergmann's ingenuity in locating the resistance fighter's whereabouts from shards of photographic evidence. Bergmann proudly replies that he is a cartographic traveler. He has met Manfredi "right here, on this desk [*questo tavolo*]. Every afternoon I take a long walks through the streets of Rome, but without stepping out of my office" (shot 43). Seen in medium close-up at his desk, fondling the pictures and suggesting that they need to be coordinated with the maps—inasmuch as the image of Manfredi and Marina was taken in front the Spanish steps, at whose piazza the film begins—Bergmann adds that he is "extremely fond of this type of photograph, which takes people almost by surprise" (shot 43). In this inverted world it is the person who is betrayed or "taken" by the picture, and not the other way around.

The map room is an antechamber placed between a torture chamber and an officers' club. The studiolo, that had ideally been designed to "mirror the sum of wisdom attained by humankind" (Schulz 1987, 99), is transformed into an intermediary zone. As of this sequence (shots 30–48) the camera attends to action around the desk and the doorways that lead to and from the salon to the torture chamber. Rife with allegorical innuendo, the spatial component plots a neo-Freudian psychopathology of the Nazi world, in which an insufferable "superego" inhabits the officers' club furnished with a piano, heavy sculpture, and ornately framed paintings while the "id," its loathsome opposite, lives in a room filled with forceps, torches, and thumbscrews. Between them, in the antechamber containing the maps, would be the "ego" that owes its shifting and unstable character to the proximities of refinement and sadism.

Italy Wallpapered: A Map in an Apartment

A map identical to that of the Roman region on the wall in front of Bergmann's desk appears in Pina's apartment in the sequence leading to Manfredi's meeting with Don Pietro. The narrative builds on the spatial and cartographic allegory seen several minutes earlier. Pina has just returned from the local bakery where she has purchased some bread and generously given several loaves to a sacristan. Pregnant, she trundles upstairs to Francesco's apartment, in front of which she encounters Manfredi and gladly learns that he does not belong to the secret police. She summons her son, Marcello, who is playing with one-legged Romoletto, by the rooftop, where the boys are up to no good. She enters Francesco's apartment. In a strange spatial articulation the camera pans right to follow her movement (from left to right) into a crowded room where, on the wall to the left, appears the corner of a map behind a pendant lampshade.

Pina says that Don Pietro will soon return and that she and other women had laid siege to a local bakery. Manfredi speaks, voice-off, as if he were an officer interrogating her about the women who took part in the raid. Shrugging her shoulders, she turns about to avow that some of the women are committed to a good cause: the camera cuts, in the middle of her sentence, to a brief but startling view of Manfredi (shot 85). Isolated, in medium close-up, he stands in front of a closed window that opens onto a cloudy sky through a gridded barrier that had been applied to protect home dwellers from being hit by shattering glass in the event of explosions. A configuration of Xs is enhanced by a shadow that is cast on the jamb just to the left of Manfredi's right temple. By virtue of the lines radiating from his temple, as if his portrait were imitating an icon of the pantocrator or a divine inquisitor, his stare is relentless and penetrating. In the preceding shot nothing signals the presence of the window or announces the pose he now takes.

The image—sudden, radiant, unsettling, and ominous—complements two shots that follow in the space of two seconds where Manfredi suddenly appears, now in another area of the room, in front of the map of Rome and its vicinity. Between the one take and the other, in a countershot (in medium close-up) Pina looks directly at the camera (and thus Manfredi), finishing the sentence she had begun, in which she tells him that most of the women in the raid merely wished to steal as many loaves as they could, and that someone stole a pair of shoes and a scale, which prompts Laura (Carla Revere), who later will be revealed to be Pina's "bad" sister, to add, voice-off, "I'd like to know who stole . . ." (shot 86). Suddenly, again without rhyme or reason, Manfredi stands in front of the map and turns left to look in the direction of the origin of the other voice. The space of the apartment is shown flattened by what is given to be a diametrical opposition of the window to the map.

It cannot be said that a "good" map is set in counterpoint to its "bad" companion, just as the virtuous Pina is not quite the opposite of her decadent (in Pina's words, "stupid") sister, Laura. The antithesis is suggested in order to be called in question. A relation of adjacency replaces one of opposition, thus complicating the values that would be assigned both to the maps and the personages. The editing of the rest of the sequence makes this clear: in a plan-séquence of fairly long duration (shot 97, almost 38 seconds), in a dialogue given to the geography of Marina's early years, after Pina explains that Marina was the daughter of a concierge in the Via Tiburtina, where she and Laura were raised by their father who had owned a tinsmith's shop, the film cuts to Manfredi in profile in medium close-up, in front of the map. Behind his back the pendant lampshade, which seems to be a displaced tabernacle or baldachin, stands in front of its left side. The viewer is invited to look for the Via Tiburtina on a map where it cannot be found.[13]

Manfredi confesses that he is no longer "seeing" Marina, and that their relationship has gone on for too long. Pina exits toward the camera, leaving Manfredi to look down, not without regret or melancholy, to light a cigarette as he recalls, in momentary soliloquy, the places where he had known her. The map now "speaks" with nostalgia. A narrative worthy of flashbacks in the style of *Casablanca* shines through his words. He had just come to Rome, he met her at a restaurant near the Piazza di Spagna, and after the air-raid siren had sounded, the couple hunkered down at the restaurant when others ran for their lives. The map behind Manfredi becomes a stark contrast to the affective spaces he wrings out of the past when he mentions the Piazza di Spagna. His movement makes visible the map, that now would be a Carte du Tendre, which stands between him and Pina both as a document and a piece of wallpaper. Manfredi (at the end of shot 97) turns away from the window and looks right, toward Pina (off frame), who confesses that a woman can change when she is in love. The shot itself changes. Pina is seen for an instant, frontally, in the next shot, her last word, *innamorata,* in lip-synch. The film suddenly cuts to Manfredi who walks toward her, across the room, and while in front of the map asks her of the authenticity of her love. In moving toward her, his cigarette, dangling from his mouth, points at places on the map. Uncannily the cigarette that Bergmann had sadistically applied to the city-view (shot 14) now seems to burn a path over the topography around the Tiber to the north of Rome. Manfredi asks her if it is true that she and Francesco will be married.

Figure 12. *Roma, città aperta:* Manfredi, under a lampshade, speaks with Pina in her apartment. The regional map is identical to one of the maps in the interrogation chamber in the previous illustration.

Rubbing her hands on her belly as Manfredi puts the cup of coffee to his lips, she gladly affirms that she is pregnant by her friend and will soon be married. Manfredi looks across the space occupied by the map to Pina's belly. The composition of the woman and the map suggests that from the partial view a new body—a child and a nation—might be born.

In sum, the map in Francesco's apartment becomes an allegorical point of reference in the geography of *Roma, città aperta.* Manfredi and the map of Italy are abandoned and no sooner retrieved. In the long take the protagonists virtually "become the map," not only because they hide in closed rooms that bear the promise of a greater geography, but also because in the same space the men have planned a raid at the Tiburtina Bridge (not shown on the map) at six o'clock in the evening (as elaborated in shot 136).[14] But the hero is also "mapped" when he wonders, facing Francesco over the bowl of soup, how the Germans ever "found me out." The answer had been seen in the use, first, made of smaller-scale projections and then in the double-dealings with Marina, who put on the edge of a mirror a photographic memento of herself and Manfredi standing together on the steps of the Piazza di Spagna (shot 156).

A Theater of Torture

From this point the cartographic decoration in the domestic space disappears. Much of what follows takes place in Bergmann's antechamber, the salon, and the torture room. In the famously excruciating sequences (shots 466–624, roughly of a duration of eighteen minutes) that articulate the interrogation of Manfredi, and then his torture and murder in view of Don Pietro (and, later, Ingrid, Hartmann, and Marina) the film exposes a theory and a practice of torture. It is a theater of cruelty that includes the *dramatis personae,* the principal players in the film, along with their implicit counterparts, the spectators in the movie theater. The two sequences are riddled with maps that seem familiar but that also emerge from nowhere. For the first time the camera aims from a point to the front and left of Bergmann's desk toward a corner where his assistant Krammer sits by a typewriter. To his left, on the wall to the left of the doorway opening onto the torture chamber, is a fifth wall map, now a narrow view of Italy and Europe that is behind a bookcase on which sit four files (shot 470). The map becomes a sighting point and a visual legend to the torture. After a match cut from Bergmann to Manfredi that cues the former lighting a cigarette he gives to the latter, the camera pulls back to show Manfredi and Krammer walking toward the camera that, we soon discover, is at the threshold of the torture chamber. The Mercator projection is in the background (shot 477), directly behind Manfredi's head.

After Bergmann subpoenas Don Pietro to appear before him a volley of shots places the inquisitor in front of the wall map between Krammer's desk and the doorway that opens onto the torture chamber.[15] Bergmann stands in medium close-up while the map constitutes a flat and unremitting background behind him. But it is adjacent to the deeper and terrible field of view of the torture just to the right. As in the cinematography of Renoir, the decoration emphasizes a contrast of depth and flatness and of two forms of abstraction, one of the utter invisibility of pain and the other of a fake representation—seen from the standpoint of God—of the world.[16] The camera correlates, too, the power Bergmann exercises with the map by following him as he impatiently fixes himself in front of it (shot 509), at the very moment, ironically, when Pietro (voice-off) drones, "the paths of the Lord are infinite." In front of the map Bergmann impels his interlocutor to save his friend from pain that he cannot—voice-off—"imagine," just as the image-track focuses on the blind assurance printed on Don Pietro's face (shot 512).

The cartography prompts a viewer to wonder how the scene can be seen. The visibility of torture, itself a ritual that requires the presence of a spectator, is implicitly summoned by the way the map is placed in relation to Bergmann and the scene itself. A final confirmation of the visual power of the map is given in an uncanny moment when, exasperated by Manfredi's stubborn refusal to yield secrets, Bergmann makes a final plea (shots 557, 559, 561) to his victim. Bergmann's assistants revive Manfredi with an injection. In close-up, and in low-key lighting, Bergmann watches in the torture room that displays on the wall behind him (and later behind Don Pietro), in chiaroscuro, a strange shadow that seems to be "of a large torture instrument, like a wine press."[17] Whatever shadow it casts—of a printing press, a thumbscrew, a cruciform shape—it suddenly gives way to the image of another (possibly a sixth) wall map in the place where it ought to appear in the rhetoric of shot-and-countershot of Bergmann and Manfredi (shot 562). The film jump-cuts to a more pronounced close-up, now in less chiaroscuro, of Bergmann who is in front of a portion of the wall map of the Roman region that had been seen in both the antechamber and Francesco's apartment. Its upper-right portion is in shadow as Bergmann accuses Manfredi of being a Communist allied with reactionary political parties. It is logically the very space where the strange and powerfully abstract shape had been just four seconds ago. And suddenly again, in the same sequence (shot 565), the camera returns to the view of Bergmann in front of the abstraction. Even if this sequence was cobbled together from disparate fragments of film the relation between the uncanny power of an abstract symbol and a map is made glaringly clear.[18]

Wiped Surfaces

The lapse in continuity that confuses a wall map with a projection convoking myriad fantasies of torture would be an infelicitous mistake were it not repeated in other ways in the creases, gaps, and transitions in the film. Here the cartography opens onto a perspective where "realism," dissimulation, and power are equated to be of a measure reaching far beyond the context of Italy in 1945. In the early 1970s, upon the publication of the screenplays of his war trilogy, Rossellini noted that contemporary cinema treated only three or four subjects, and that in the instance of the misguided war in Vietnam (and it could be added, today, in the events we witness in the Middle East) war was being seen through a filter of "Freud, sex, [and] violence." No vision of the phenomenon was available for reason of "a paucity of cinematic themes," of "empty virtuosity, schematization, and oversimplification" of anguishing situations. [19] No treatment of visible and discursive formations—to borrow the idiolect of Michel Foucault—of war was possible, perhaps because images could not testify to the phenomenon itself. The latter had to be approached, he suggested, through a greater degree of abstraction.

The abstraction is seen in the ways that the maps belong now to an Italian cause and then to the power and torture led by the coalition of Nazis and Fascists. Rossellini's maps are signs of visibility that open, penetrate, and create spaces while at the same time they are exasperatingly occlusive, without clear symbolic or allegorical charge. For the sake of closer analysis it can be argued that they are to the field of the image in *Roma, città aperta* what a classical transitional device, the wipe, is to the narrative of the film. By 1945 the wipe had become something of an anachronism. Its role in Movietone News was parodied in the opening sequence of *Citizen Kane* (1941), in which it went in all four directions (left, right, up, and down) when the camera followed conveyer belts of newspapers delivering their pulp to the four corners of the frame. Surely by the end of the Second World War the wipe would have been a reminder of the effects of propaganda in newsreels taken before the filming of the concentration camps.[20]

It is often said that Rossellini's cinema owes much of its force to straight cuts of uncompromising violence and even discontinuity. The wipe appears in the film fifteen times, most often with deftness that often makes it either invisible or accords it a premium of action and movement.[21] The itineraries of characters are hastened when the wipe follows the direction of their steps and brings them to their destination. In accord with the narrative and spatial logic of the screenplay the wipe is present where people are on the move, in the streets and along the avenues of Rome, but not where they are incarcerated, interrogated, and tortured. Quite often straight cuts across doorways, especially those that separate the officers' salon from the "studiolo" and the latter from the torture room have a wipe-effect that speedily taxies the viewer from one space to another. Yet from its first instance the wipe is taken almost literally, as a progressive effacement of one plane of action adjacent to the inscription of another. When the first wipe (between shots 6 and 7) follows Nannina closing the shutter of her window from left to right the movement draws attention to the closing of slatted apertures. When brought forward by the action of the wipe the shutters, icons of the cinematic mechanism, suggest that when the film opens, it also closes. When the line of divide between the sixth and seventh shot reaches the middle of the frame, a

strange temporality is given: the space that gives way to another in chronologi-
cal time is situated to the right and *not* to the left. What has yet to take place
in the trajectory of the shot ought to follow the way an alphabetic sentence is
read. What is coming is felt as "past" because it is on the left. In these shots
one surface of panels with shutters gives way to a wall and, suddenly, to a terrace and a door from which Manfredi emerges and runs off in the direction of the
cityscape beneath the sky in the background. The wipe causes the film to close,
open, close, and open itself again. The wipe gives a literal sense to the shutters,
the terrace door, and the *oscuro,* if not the *chiaroscuro,* of apprehension and
escape, and of simultaneous closure and aperture. It leads from a viewpoint on
the Piazza di Spagna to that of the partial horizon of Rome.

The wipe is used both strategically and tactically. It draws the texture of editing into the drama and serves as a hinge or a line dividing viewpoints and places.
The cartographic effect of the wipe—or what the maps do to draw attention to
its virtue—is especially made manifest in two places. In the first, between shots
156 and 157, Ingrid has just entered Marina's dressing room in the cabaret where

Figure 13. *Roma, città aperta:* Ingrid studies a photograph of Marina and Manfredi at
the Piazza di Spagna. In the wipe the mirror on the left reveals the books (on a desk)
that figure in a plan to attack the German occupants. Ingrid sees both the photograph
and the space revealed by the wipe.

she works with Laura. A brazen vampire or a raven with a widow's peak, Ingrid has emerged from behind the door Laura opened upon hearing a gentle knocking in the thick of the music of the cabaret. The camera follows her in medium close-up as she moves, in profile, to Marina's mirror, on which is placed a photo of the actress standing with Manfredi in front of the Piazza di Spagna. Having turned to both sides to display the left and right sides of her face in profile, Ingrid moves toward the image and inspects it as might the spectator the film itself. But what she sees is—or is not—what we see: she looks at the picture but becomes doubled, turned into a split-representation of herself that she might behold at the same time she gazes upon the photograph. A symbolic magic seems to result from the image that suddenly turns the narrative into a historical and anthropological fact.[22]

The shot becomes the ground of a wipe before the wipe begins to move from left to right. When it splits the field of the image into two equal parts Ingrid suddenly gazes both at the picture of Marina and Manfredi and at three books in front of a stove that appear in three-quarter view before the shot gives way to a scene of Agostino (Nando Bruno) tending to the fire. For an instant Ingrid is omnivoyant. She sees her own reflection and the hideaway where Pina will appear. She sees and reads in the same gaze. All of a sudden the wipe confirms—doubles—the doubling of the shot and suggests a coextension of opposing visual planes and places. It reproduces much of the uncanny effect seen in the map of Rome and its regions decorating two antithetical spaces.[23] In its liminal and fugacious passage the wipe underscores how the film is producing a spatial unconscious in which opposing forces are both melded and kept at bay.

In the second instance, in the gap between shots 384 and 385, the partisans of two opposing ideologies, genders, and affective spaces gaze upon each other. The Gestapo on their heels after Pina's murder, Francesco and Manfredi take refuge in Marina's apartment to bide time before they can accede to the sanctuary of a monastery. The two men occupy the living room while Marina and Laura undress together in the bedroom. Fraught with grief, Francesco needs aspirin (the counterpart to Marina's cocaine) to assuage the pain of a splitting headache. Seen in profile, rolling a cigarette while Francesco lies on a couch to the left, Manfredi plots their future after the disasters and triumphs of the day. Marina, in the background behind an illuminated lampshade placed between the two men in the middle ground, furtively opens the door, eavesdrops, and closes it before she exits. She returns to the men's room with the aspirin and bids good night to them while Manfredi, self-contained (even though he cannot find a match to light his cigarette), does not turn around to acknowledge her words. He remains seated, looking down while Francesco, supine on the couch, remains in his field of view.

Suddenly the film wipes to the right, effacing Francesco and replacing him with a supine Laura, in almost the same pose, in Marina's bedroom. Between the two rooms is the lamp that could belong to either. For an instant Manfredi, eyes shut, seems omnivoyant in what he might be seeing on the inner surface of his eyelids. Through the spectator he sees the women who are in their space while he stays in the room he occupies with Francesco. An uncanny violence is contained in the two coextensive surfaces that are seen to be at once vigilant and somnolent, active and passive, male and female, resistant and compliant. As the shot is completed, Marina sits where the illuminated lampshade disappears. She sits in front of the bed that has the radiant design of a peacock tail (or an anticipation of the NBC logo) and then is adjacent to a shaded lamp on a dressing table next to an ashtray and a telephone. Manfredi's petrifying aspect gives way to its opposite. Each side is structured by way of its decorative surface of signs that turn the depth and volume of the rooms into affectively charged surfaces. Such, too, is the condition the maps have embodied elsewhere in the film.

This chapter began with reflections on cartographic consciousness as a pertinent trait of the auteur. Shared by Renoir and Rossellini, it is made manifest in the allusive but decisive presence of maps that speak in and through the narrative images of their features. The chapter began, too, with Jacques Rancière's reading of the suspension and then the collapse of images of meaning in Rossellini's

Figure 14. *Roma, città aperta:* Manfredi, in vigil, looks at Marina's sister, in another room, in the space of the wipe that moves between the living room (where the men are in hiding) and the bedroom (where the women sleep comfortably).

cinema from the neorealistic phase to postwar films that include *Voyage to Italy*. For Rancière a determining trait in the director's signature is found in the simultaneously active and passive virtues of the mise-en-scène, its shooting, and the editing. The camera submits to the director's active will, but it also elicits a passive and quasi-conscious viewing of what can be seen and read in and about the frame. After a close study of the maps it might be said that the cartographic impulse in *Roma, città aperta* also belongs to both the active and passive registers of the film. It binds the opening, which begins with a topographic view of the city at the Piazza di Spagna in twilight, to the end, where a slow pan follows the children and future of Rome who leave the scene of Pietro's sacrifice at the rifle range at Fort Bravetta. They descend to the Rome that, for a first and only time, is seen as an "open" city under a daylit horizon. Surely the theater of cruelty made visible in the film has found analogues in Abu Ghraib and other places. The relation, not central to the cartographic mechanisms, is nonetheless worthy of reflection.

4

A Desperate Journey:
From *Casablanca* to *Indiana Jones*

We have seen that the impact of *Roma, città aperta* depends in part upon its affiliation with classical cinema. Upon cursory glance the maps in the antechamber seem to be there as by nature or else by virtue of the realistic effects they bring to the décor. Rossellini's cinema is generally crafted from classical models that it tends to fracture or sublate into a style and form of its own. To see better how maps figure in the style Bazin affirmed retrospectively, in the postwar years, that had in 1939 "reached what geographers calls the profile of equilibrium of a river" (1999 [1975], 71), indeed a transparency and a smooth flow of sound and image, we might do well to look back to cartography in films that mold both the tradition out of which Rossellini's images emerge and that which might be called a postclassical cinema, a cinema that has become a model for entertainment and global appeal.

This chapter will take as a point of departure the axiom that journey or adventure constitutes a "classic" plot for which maps are crucial elements. In this kind of film, characters are on the move; circumstance and destiny require them to go somewhere, and often in desperation and with dispatch. One kind of classical cinema might be called that of the "desperate journey." Four films will be treated through study of interwoven connections. *High Sierra* (directed by Raoul Walsh, 1941) is a masterpiece in which cartography figures in both the montage and the areas where the film makes clear its own relation with its modes and ends of production. Emplotting a desperate journey the feature informs a celebrated avatar, Steven Spielberg's *Indiana Jones and the Raiders of the Lost Ark* (1982). Yet that film taps into another and no less crucial feature of cartographic cinema,

Walsh's *Desperate Journey* (1942), a film that informs Spielberg's work along lines similar to *Casablanca* (1942), Michael Curtiz's classic film that is also, to an equally marked degree, a variant of the desperate journey and its cartographic impulse.

Crashing In and Crashing Out

"Roy, I'm givin' it to you straight. You're just stickin' your neck out. You may catch lead at any minute. . . . What you need is a fast-steppin' young filly you can keep up with. Remember what Johnny Dillinger said about guys like you and him? He said you were just rushin' toward death, yeah, that's it, rushin' toward death."[1] Thus, in *High Sierra,* spoke old "Doc" Banton (Henry Hull), to his aging bandit friend Roy Earle (Humphrey Bogart) in a process shot in which the two men face the windshield and drive forward. The film documents his rush to death from the beginning where, as a inmate for life in the Mossmoor Prison, he receives a "pardon" from an unnamed authority in the office of the governor of an unnamed state.[2] As soon as he is released, incarcerated in the world at large, Earle begins a desperate journey.

The geography of the film meshes with its cartography. The credits scroll upward and over three views, each dissolving into the other, of the face of Mount Whitney. A first shot aims skyward toward the summit and ridge bathed in clouds; they soon obscure the peak and give way to a mesa below before the film dissolves into a new view of the crest in a deeper field of view. The film dissolves to a shot of a cleft and valley between two peaks after the names of the players, scrolling upward, have dissolved into the sky. Destiny is shown in the gap between the vast space of the mountain range under the name and credits of "High Sierra" and the shots taken of the prison. The open space in the credits is contrasted to the closed milieu of the penitentiary that incarcerates both the guards and the population of inmates. Within seconds the credits and initial montage have anticipated and summed up the spatial play of the film. The film is construed to be a field of illusory depth and a "map" or webbing of figures, signs, letters, and forms of a framed composition that can be read spatially and syntactically.[3] The tragedy is affiliated with its cartography of destiny.

Classical films tend to become maps of themselves when the images and words in the credit-sequences recur in the narrative. The latter "responds" to the former in both spatial and discursive ways, as if a contractual obligation were requiring the narrative to defend and illustrate, or to explicate and make clear the enigma of the title (Derrida 1982, 5–22). *High Sierra* is no exception. When Earle drives from the Midwest en route to the first meeting point in the Sierras he realizes the dream, of every motorized American tourist of the 1930s, to cross the United States by car. In the film, however, he returns to the space of the credits seen only minutes before.

The landscapes that had appeared to lie beneath or behind the title and scrolled words now emerge in an effectively natural state. They seem to belong as much to the inner geography of the film as the topography and geology of Southern California. There comes into view what the screenplay (Gomery 1979) describes as a long shot of the mountain, "[a]n overwhelming giant with pointed rocky turrets for a summit. Lordly and mighty it rises over the surrounding mountains" (shot 27, 48–49). Beyond the escarpment is a clear sky, pocked with clouds, that causes the atmosphere to be literally breathtaking. In the credits the same view had been static; now, however, the camera slowly pans right to record the jagged outline of the peaks below the sky before it stops and ever so slightly tilts down to draw attention to a dirt road at the bottom of the frame that leads toward the camera's point of view. A team of riders on horseback is discernible before the camera continues its career to the right and then tilts down again to the road on which (from the right) Earle enters in his car in medium view. A sublime landscape is seen, and so also is the entry of a strange and ill-fitting element—Earle at the wheel of his Buick coupe—along the road.

The mobility of the camera is shown to be greater than that of the riders or the driver. It anticipates what will become the expression of its ocular power through

Figure 15. *High Sierra* (1941): In his coupe, Roy Earle passes by men on horses (and the Western film) and drives into the landscape first seen in the title credits.

a haptic sensuality. The lens caresses the relief of the landscape at the same time it discovers a space riddled with contradiction. The car belongs to one age and the team of horses to another. Earle stops to look at what the viewer has just seen (what would be shot 34 in the screenplay). Dazzled by the light, he peers out of the window in which we see him incarcerated. Two economies pass by each other, one the gangster and his getaway car, and the other the cowboy and his horse. In the flash of an instant extensive reflection is afforded about the displacement of one style of itinerary, that of the urban hoodlum on a desperate journey into a world he knows only in the movies in which he figures, into another, that of the western trail where time slows down and where history blends with cinematic myth.[4] The shot might be likened to a cartouche in a greater cartography of destiny that the film will bring to a tragic finale.

A Map in a Montage

Much of the narrative is constructed around the preparation for a holdup of a hotel in Palm Springs. A secondary thread follows the hero from his puppy love for a club-footed sweetheart to the strong-willed woman who swears to stand by him. The holdup is botched, and in the getaway Earle and Marie (Ida Lupino) witness the grisly crash in which their hapless companions are burned alive. After Earle's murder of Jack Kranmer (Barton MacLane), a crooked fence, his discovery that he has been enamored of the "bad" good girl, and his realization that a dragnet is closing in upon him, Earle takes to the road.

His desperate journey begins. He puts Marie on a bus and drives off in search of cash en route to meeting her on the other side of the mountains where they will begin a new life together. Excised from the screenplay, an insert (shot 236, 163) of a road map shows Earle's finger tracing the route he will take to Cajon Pass (far to the south of Mount Whitney, suggesting that a broad topography of southeastern California is being filmed). Earle robs a general store and pistol-whips a customer while making his getaway.[5] After his departure a uniformed trooper inspects the scene and learns of the identity of the criminal who has just left the scene. "If it's Earle he's headed back over the pass," announces the officer. Grabbing a telephone receiver, he barks, "Operator, give me 420."[6]

A Vorkapich montage pulls the narrative from the scene of the drugstore to the chase that will lead the prey and his hunters up the side of the mountain. In it are inserted maps that combine geographies of reality and of tragedy. At a police station a report tells of the car being seen at High Bridge Road. A pan follows a policeman in a leather jacket (in a medium shot) running to a large topographic map hanging on the wall ("Good! We'll have him bottled up in about an hour!") next to another, of smaller size and scale of the state of California. The film cuts to a close-up of the map where thumbtacks are set adjacent to dots by place names. "Independence" is north of "Manazar," below which a hand pushes another tack while an iris closes on the space and the shot of a car on the road replaces the rest of the map. The shot dissolves to a detailed view of "Olancha" to the south of "Cartago" and "Monanch" (adjacent to "Owens Lake") while a hand puts a tack on a road that heads west to the mountain range. In the dissolve some head-lamps of the cars blend with the dots and tacks on the map before an iris closes the scene and gives way to a parade of the vehicles driving forward. A direct relation is established with the tack and dot that locate the victim on the map and the pairs of headlights aimed to "look for" their quarry.

In the montage, a tour de force of locational imaging, the film dissolves again to the greater wall map, seen in three-quarter profile, as a hand continues to push pins into new spots while the iris gives way to a squadron of cars and motor-cycles. The last and crowning map image is of "Lone Pine." Five tacks are placed on all roads and junctions, except for one that leads toward the mountain range. Superimposed on the map is a moving image of the police climbing on their motorcycles; the action recedes from view while, in a third layer of the same dissolve, the car driving down the road—the shot that had inaugurated the mon-tage—comes forward. The camera trucks in on the toponym of Lone Pine while the image dissolves to a shot of Earle's car driving down the main street of the town named by the map.

Figure 16. *High Sierra:* The police pursue Roy Earle. The montage sequence of a roadblock dissolves into an iris of a map of southern California.

Both the map and its territory are seen in the single and same image. So also are the totally arbitrary qualities and geographic reality of the toponyms and, now and again, their allegorical resonance. Earle has been seeking to find "Independence" after completing his heist, facing every kind of obstacle, and eluding authorities of both the law and its underside. His car now drives through "Lone Pine," a place that signals to what degree he is alone, an isolated and solitary hero enclosed in his car and sealed by fate. In the sequence that follows the blare and wail of sirens seem to be confused with a personified landscape. Present in the sublime beauty of the area that humans are sullying are the laments of the goddesses of Nature and Fortune who "pine" for the soul caught in the skein of history and destiny. "Lone Pine" crystallizes and locates the elegiac moment in the life of a victim of the gods, police, and gangsters who control him. The map on the wall is affiliated with the force of fate.[7]

The landscape quickly takes precedence over the humans within it. The narrative comes to an orphic conclusion when the hero turns back. Earle exits from his lair where he makes himself visible enough for a sharpshooter on a ridge far above to shoot him in the back. At the sight of the falling body Marie shrieks in anguish. The episode mythifies the location by bringing Orpheus and Eurydice into a composite shape in which landscape, pathos, and filmic consciousness are drawn together.[8] The end seems crafted to blend the freedom of journey with the closure of fate. Marie accedes to the vision of "being free." As she realizes that Earle has crashed out, or is "free," the right hand of an officer grasps her shoulder and holds her captive. The camera follows her gaze, which looks blindly and aimlessly upward while the genital area of the policeman's body figures in the background. The final tracking shot recedes as she advances, her arms cuddling the dog, toward the camera before she exits right as the face of Mount Whitney comes into view, now serving as a threshold for the end-credits that literally scroll up the side of the mountain with the accompaniment of background music that shifts from tones of pathos to lighter fare. To be free, it is implied, is to leave the theater at the conclusion of the film. *High Sierra,* like the series of maps seen in the Vorkapich montage sequence, becomes a territory of itself. And the maps are part of the language of the cruel gods who turn a touristic site into one of geographically and historically grounded tragedy.

In *High Sierra* the landscape and its cartographic depiction become synonymous with the powers of fate and of cinema. In the passage of over sixty years since its production, the film has become a familiar name in every gazetteer of cinema. Billed as the feature in which Humphrey Bogart has his first lead role—film historians tirelessly belabor the point—the film uses maps to situate and enclose the tragic hero. It posits a "diagram" of the greater idiolect of Warner Brothers and, too, a geography that belongs both to the director's work and a cinematic production of space. It suffices to look at *Desperate Journey* (1942), a feature of the same studio and same director that is also driven by a cartographic impulse.

Desperate Journey

Completed in 1942 to lend impetus to the effort of the Allies against what then was an indomitable Axis that had only recently lost the air war over Great Britain, *Desperate Journey* is a wish but also a piece in the signature of its director-auteur. A group of men is selected to perform a dangerous mission. They travel to their objective and execute their task with impeccable success, but then face the cruel task of having to return home, across hostile territories, by any and every possible means. Most are lost along the way. The storyline varies on the form of a "toponymic tale," a pilgrimage of sorts, whose itinerary moves from one episode to another in a series of close encounters at given places that situate and often mythify the events.[9]

Desperate Journey begins when anti-German resistance fighters blow up a railway near Schneidemühl, a town (now Szcecin) said to be located near the border of Poland and the northern coast of Germany. Before a Nazi guard kills him, one of the fighters rushes from the scene of his sabotage (he has dynamited

Figure 17. *High Sierra:* Roy Earle drives to his destiny. In this montage, a perspectival view of Earle in his car on the highway blends into a view of the main street of Lone Pine (where the film is shot on location) that is also indicated on a map. The circle frames Earle at the wheel in his car.

the railway) to an aviary from where he releases a carrier pigeon that flies off and across Europe and the Channel to bring news of the success of the raid to the British command post. The pigeon flies to its destination and is welcomed by a soldier who removes the information from a capsule attached to its leg. Officers at headquarters study the material and determine that one more intersection needs to be bombed in order to cripple the Nazis.

A group of soldiers, which includes veterans and a greenhorn, as well as Americans, an Englishman, and an Australian—all seasoned Warner Brothers actors—is chosen to fly a B-17 over the North Sea to finish the destruction of the site and to return. They take off, find their altitude, meet cloud cover, do battle with a Messerschmitt, and get rocked by flak before they fly low, drop the payload, and crash into a thick forest. Two soldiers are immolated when the captain is required to set the wreckage afire. The five remaining are captured and then interrogated by a Nazi captain (Raymond Massey). When one of them (Ronald Reagan) is called into the captain's office, through a side window he sights the movement of a convoy of strange planes. He tricks his interrogator and brings his companions into the room where they knock the officer silly. They jump out of the window and succeed, against all odds, in evading the guards. They slog their way through swamps, reach a bridge, and kill the Nazi sentinels who are on patrol. They exchange uniforms. In travesty as German soldiers, they board a train traveling west where they occupy a car reserved for Hermann Goering. An officer (Sig Ruman, known synchronously for his role as "Concentration Camp Charlie" in Ernst Lubitsch's *To Be or Not to Be*) discovers them and throws them off the train before Massey can apprehend them at the Berlin *Bahnhof*. The men hole up in an unoccupied building, knock sentries down, and decide to indulge "in a spot of sabotage" by blowing up a nearby chemical factory that manufactures incendiary bombs. The youngest of the group of survivors is severely wounded.

They encounter a woman who leads them to a doctor who cannot mend their comrade. Overhearing them speaking English, a patient tips off the secret police, whom the group outwits and kills. The men head east, by Braunschweig and Wolfenbüttel en route to Munster where some of the woman's relatives reside. But the men are tricked. They find themselves in the home of a warm and welcoming elderly couple who are in fact Nazis dissimulating the roles of Allied partisans. A narrow escape ensues. Kirk (Alan Hale), the comic character of the group, is shot and felled when the men must leap over a rooftop.[10] There follows a breakneck race of the three survivors in a car pursued by Massey and his posse in of a squadron of motorcycles. They drive across the flatlands of Holland before they reach a Nazi cache near the shores of the North Sea. They discover a plane hidden under a fluttering tissue of camouflage bearing British insignia that the Nazis are preparing for a bombing mission over the British Isles. They storm the craft, engage combat with the German soldiers, and manage to fly off and away, back to safety. As the film ends the pilot (Errol Flynn) turns to his crew (and to the viewer), smiling, "Now for Australia and a crack at those Japs."

Camouflage

Desperate Journey is rife with maps. At the beginning the Warner Brothers shield dissolves into a relief map of Germany, western Poland, and southern Denmark, a map resembling the accomplished depictions of Europe in the 1940s, often drawn in bird's-eye depiction and from an uncharacteristic point of view.[11] The camera closes in, moving north and east, as the shadows of three, and then five, flying aircraft are cast over the map. The view is slightly occluded when the names of the two leads, Errol Flynn and Ronald Reagan, dissolve into the mapped image. They disappear when "Desperate Journey" covers the map. The camera continues its approach as if the scene were being viewed from the belly of the cockpit of one of the bombers when its shadow is cast upon the projection below. The credits continue and disappear after the name of the director gives way to the city-view on the map near the mouth of the River Oder. The map, the simulation of the city and country, becomes the stage on which the first dramatic event takes place. An iris-wipe opens from the city-view in close-up, and all of a sudden a gridded construction, illuminated in the shadows, emerges into view. A German guard walks across the platform, his boots in close-up as the camera tilts down slightly to catch the face of a civilian covered with a network of crisscrossed lines of shadows cast by leaves and branches. He inches backward and down as the camera reverses the course it followed as the man moved into view.

The entire narrative is anticipated and duplicated in the first images and their montage that encapsulates and indeed "plots" much of the film. The civilian saboteur escapes to a shed from which he extracts a box. He opens its lid, removes a pigeon (as if taking a rabbit out of a hat), attaches a capsule with a message, and goes to an open window where he is shot by a German sentry. The bird flutters off, evading a final rifle shot. A fade to an ocean view shows the bird fighting the winds on its way (right to left) westward, where it will soon land at a bird coop at which a soldier, looking skyward, awaits its landing. The shot tracks left (the camera in relentless movement in the film) as the soldier enters the building and then tracks right before closing in on the man behind a grid of chicken wire.

The mesh screen becomes a first sign of camouflage. A see-through fabric of metal wire, indeed a moiré or translucent curtain, the hexagonal chicken wire becomes synonymous with the motif of maps and mapping in *Desperate Journey*. Through the mesh we see the soldier grasp the bird and attend to the capsule attached to its leg. A Vorkapich montage sequence begins with the camera closing in on an opaque glass wall on which is written "Intelligence Room/Decoding Section." The words cede to a hand writing a report on a desk on front of which are two inkwells. The camera pulls back to reveal a man passing a note to his messenger. They stand in front of a topographic wall map of contours and sur-faces—clearly a product of aerial "intelligence" before the camera moves in on the briefcase in which the note is inserted. It then dissolves into another close-up of photographs and a contour map that, as the camera pulls back, are seen being studied by two men and an assistant at a telephone who is adjacent to a frame wall map in the background. As they compare the map and photography (in medium close-up) the finger of the one crisscrosses the pencil held by the other.

The sequence seems to be uttering, "Objective: Schneidemühl."[12] The exam-ination and presentation of the maps comprise two successive stages revealing and masking the making of the war movie. Images are gathered and studied, and then they are brought forward to their audience. The film about the war *screens* the war it purports to represent. Yet the conclusion (a sequence that will be re-worked in *Indiana Jones*) shows how the cartography and the logistics of the war movie are alloyed. The survivors of the mission have crossed Western Europe and reached a point near the western border of Holland. The car comes to a halt and the men descend. At a loss about how to proceed, the trio soon wanders about and happens upon what first seems to be a painting or a moiré sculpture fashioned from patches of silken fabric hanging from a mesh network of wires extending across the top of a gigantic trellis. "What's that?" whispers Flynn. We and the three men behold three images, if not three surfaces, that appear super-imposed over each other. One is the airplane, aiming forward in the camouflage of the protective setting, while another is the entire abstraction that seems to be a pure work of art. The third is the composite figure of the aircraft and the design itself that turn the scene into a "map" that complements the many abstractions that were given at the beginning: the relief map in the credits, the crisscrossed beams of the railroad bridge, the lines of branches on the Polish resistor's face, the mesh of chicken wire through which the carrier pigeon was first glimpsed, and the aerial views of Schneidemühl and Northern Europe projected on the screen in the briefing room. The camera cuts into a medium shot of Germans beneath and within the camouflage—what seems to be an optical painting—loading a bomb into the belly of the craft that Reagan, voice-in, notes as being "one of ours."[13] In the midst of a narrative, unfolding at a breakneck pace, a grand illu-sion—a cartographic construction and a strange object—is placed before eyes of both the spectator and the protagonists.

The artifice within the film draws attention to the scene being made; it shows that the film itself, in all of its extraordinarily backlit and angled decors, is its own amplification and work of artful dissimulation,[14] which, in a spatial register, is accomplished in the last and celebrated line that Flynn utters after a cutaway shot displays the sight of the coasts of Dover through the forward cockpit: "Now for Australia and a crack at those Japs." The remark refers to Flynn's own coun-try of birth (Hobart, Tasmania), to his famous predilection for the female sex, and to a theater of operations on another hemisphere. The displacement that goes from the sight of Dover to the idea of Australia affirms that, although propaganda, in its spatial and cartographic dimensions the film is also a prayer. Shot at the threshold of America's involvement in the Second World War, *Desperate Journey* identifies cinema as camouflage, as a theory and practice of the application of a "masked law," that is, of the relation it establishes between itself—as a cartographic diagram and as a document of contemporary history and fiction— and the fictitious events it creates and the real ones that it wishes it would bring about.[15]

A Map Dissolve: *Casablanca*

Like *Desperate Journey* of the same vintage, *Casablanca* is a network of mappings that move between dissimulation and prayer. The maps that move from the front credits to the first matte shot of the city are set in a montage that tells the story of thousands of desperate journeys taken by displaced persons and refugees from the Pacific rim westward through Europe and across the Mediterranean and North Africa to Casablanca. In the credits that bleed into the background of the narrative a variety of maps are configured as emblems or, roughly, as moving combinations of textual and graphic matter. The shield in which is enclosed the WB of Warner Brothers is surrounded by a circular banderole on which

Figure 18. *Desperate Journey* (1942): Under a moiré curtain German soldiers prepare an Allied plane for takeoff.

the name of the studio is spelled out in uppercase letters in relief. The name of Jack L. Warner, the executive producer, is held in the lower corner of the spherical triangle. The logo dissolves into and is momentarily confused with a map of Africa.

As the logo recedes, the map (from an equipollent projection, striated with lines of latitude and longitude, which bears a decorative wind rose in the lower-right corner) emerges into view. The northern coast of Algeria and the Cape of Good Hope are cropped away, no doubt in order to offer the aspect of a continent-as-triangle, with three masses pointing in as many directions—French West Africa, Egypt and Arabia, and the southern peninsula—over which the names of the three leading players, Humphrey Bogart, Ingrid Bergman, and Paul Henreid, are respectively placed. They quickly dissolve into the map and the title that is vectored along the angle of an ecliptic band. Before it serves as the background on which the remaining names of the cast and crew dissolve in and out of the image, the map of Africa is confused with the romantic triangle given in the relation of the three protagonists. By the time (exactly one minute) "Music by

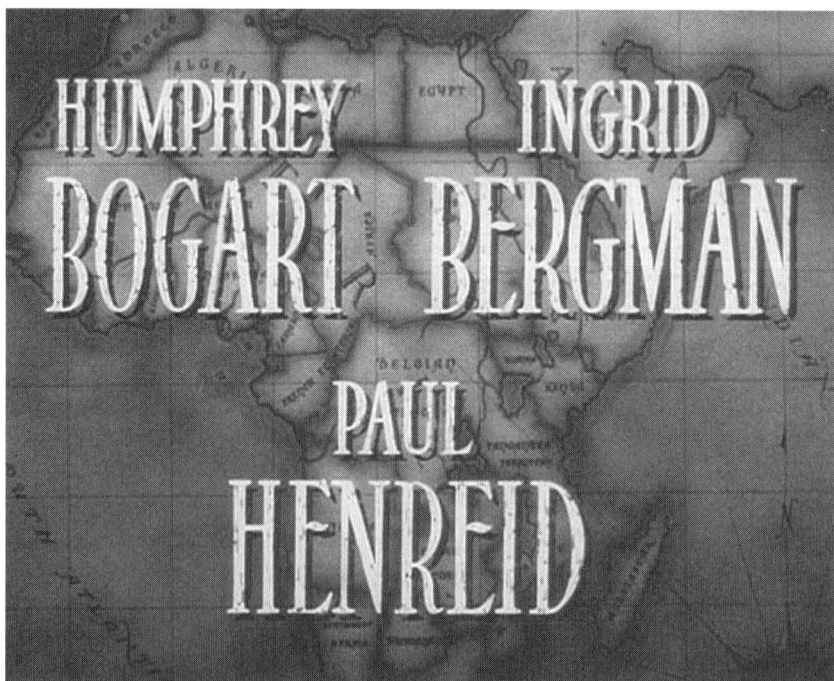

Figure 19. *Casablanca* (1942): Title credits display three leads in a triangle (anticipating a triangle of love) placed over the triangle of Africa. The dot designating the city of Casablanca in the upper left will bear its name only in the end credits.

Max Steiner" is placed in the credits the first bars of the "Marseillaise," a sound cue for an absent map of France, intervene with the name of director Michael Curtiz.

In the fade the sight of the map displaces the spectator. Where are we? The loss of grounding precedes a fade-in to a turning globe that sits somewhat uncharacteristically on a bed of cumulous clouds, and not in an eternity of outer space. Beginning with a view of what is designated to be the North Pacific Ocean, the globe is drawn in relief and in the style and from a perspective reminiscent of Richard Edes Harrison's spherical world maps.[16] At the outset the globe bears only one place-name, that of the Hawaiian Islands, which stands in subtle contrast to all other unnamed continental masses and islands, including Australia, Borneo, and the coasts of China. A newscaster's pebbly voice intones, "With the coming of the Second World War . . ." It is suggested that the history of the film begins in the minuscule setting of Hawaii and Pearl Harbor.

Confusion emerges from the relation of the voice-off to the turning globe. The broadcaster continues, "many eyes in imprisoned Europe turned hopefully, or desperately," as the camera closes in on the turning globe that shows Indonesia, Burma, China, and India. Some place-names are faintly inscribed into the lands

Figure 20. *Casablanca:* First shot of initial montage displays a globe in the sky. Only the Hawaiian Islands are named.

they designate, but by and large the earth is what turns and not "eyes in impris-oned Europe." The camera continues to close in, now to India, the Middle East, and Eastern Africa, while the voice utters, "toward the freedom of the Americas." The voice mentions, "Lisbon became the great embarkation point," without the globe turning toward Portugal. "But, not everybody could get to Lisbon directly, and so a tortuous, roundabout refugee trail sprang up." The globe revolves and the camera centers on France before the image dissolves to a topographic view of Paris marked by a large circle enclosing a five-sided star set upon a spot to the left of the confluence of the Rivers Seine and Marne.

A "route-enhancing" map begins to move. A broad line grows out of the bottom of the circle. Then begins a superimposition of maps and newsreel shots of the gripping historical montage. The line continues its path southward, toward Troyes, while the voice utters, "from Paris to Marseilles," and a stock shot—an extreme long shot of a port, a dock, and an industrial landscape behind—of lines of people who seem to await departure. The map has not reached the areas the voice is designating. Suddenly the view pulls back to a standard view of France as the ribbon designating the route of refugees winds down the Rhône valley en

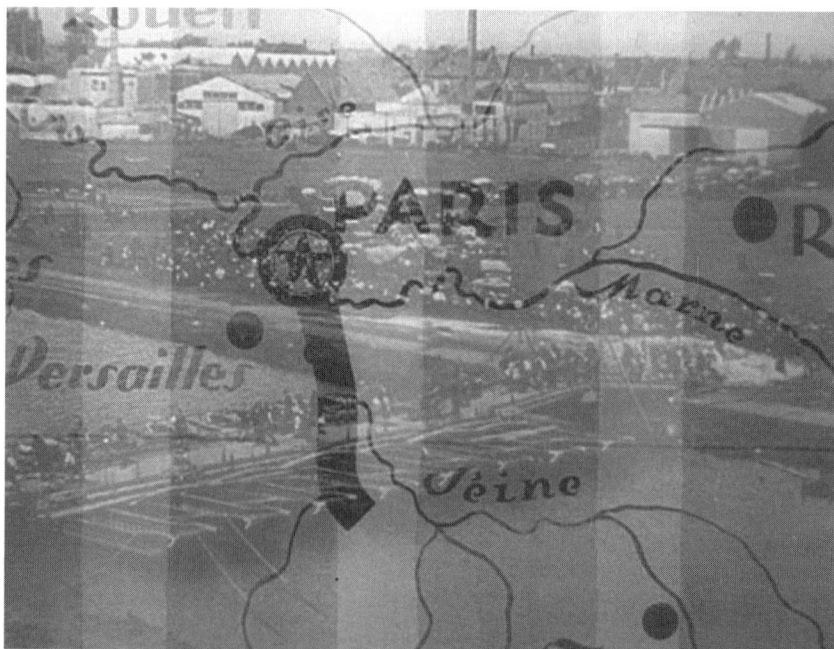

Figure 21. *Casablanca:* A map moves in a montage: refugees crossing a pontoon bridge are below a map of France in close-up, with a black line leading southward to Marseilles.

route to Marseilles. A medium shot shows women and men carrying their children and belongings melds into the map, and another a line of refugees amassed beside horse-drawn carts. The line drawn on the map approaches the southern port and continues, now dashed, into the dark area of the sea placed over an image of a ship sailing on calm waters. The voice continues, "across the Mediterranean to Oran," while three more shots of moving ships are placed in the maritime areas of the map before the dashed line reaches the city-name, just mentioned, that is on the map.

The next segment of the montage is devoted to overland travel. "Then, by train, or auto, or by foot across the rim of Africa," intones the voice, while the camera closes in on the coast of Morocco stretching from the place-names of Malitta to Tetuan and down to Rabat north and east of Casablanca, over a montage of four stock shots of refugees carrying their valises on foot, being carried on wagons and, finally, in a line of people, cars, and bicycles that figures under a view of the line reaching Casablanca.[17] The camera finally closes in on the circle and the name of the city that the voice-off identifies as the sentence ends, "to Casablanca . . . in French Morocco." When the close-up on the map occludes the image, the voice begins again, "Here, the fortunate ones, through money . . ." The map dissolves into a city-view to the right where a muezzin looks out from the upper terrace of a North African tower.

The style, tone, tenor, and story of the film are determined by what might be called its "map-dissolves," by a cavalcade of maps dissolving in and out of stock footage that conveys in seconds the burden of a relentless voyage across the world. It begins from a blank space in the Pacific where an origin of the history behind the film is concealed in the toponym of the Hawaiian Islands and leads to a non-place, to Casablanca, that stands in for the original site.[18] The desperate journey recounted in the sequence of a duration of 83 seconds uses maps and newsreel footage to elide history and a fiction based on previous cinema.[19] The dark voice of destiny carries the narrative from the world at large to a site of anxious transience, of uncertainty and closure, that may indeed have been the ambiance of movie theaters in the early years of the Second World War.

From Historical Geography to Melodrama

The most memorable and melodramatic sequence of *Casablanca* may be the five-minute flashback in which, in close-up and chiaroscuro, Rick (Humphrey Bogart) recalls his romantic idyll in Paris. At about one-third of the way into the film (in the thirty-ninth of 140 minutes), the flashback is inspired by notes of music after Rick makes implicit reference to the globe seen after the credits. "Sam," he mutters, staring blankly toward the spectators and over a glass of whiskey, "if it's December 1941 in Casablanca what time is it in New York?" The camera cuts to a close-up of the pianist, his black face barely visible in the dark, "Um, aah, my watch stopped." Cut back to Rick: "I bet they're asleep in New York. I bet they're asleep all over America." The time of the film is synchronized with the bombing of Pearl Harbor, the first site that was allusively named on the globe in the beginning. All of a sudden "As time goes by . . . ," the song of 1931 resurrected to be the catalyst of affective memory in this film, is heard in conjunction with the first image of the continuous revolution of the world.

The film indicates it is taking place far from the history in which it enters. In an almost unconscious register Rick's flashback to his days in Paris in June 1940 is elicited as much by the pressure of history marked on the initial map as it is by unrequited love. The allusion to December 1941 also refers both to the very first visual cue and to a world of spectators, like the film itself, at a sleepy remove from its historical cause. When Rick mopes, "in all the gin-joints in all the towns in all the world, she walks into mine," the arrival of the memory is confused with the fall into a new time, that of the American declaration of war on Japan and Germany.

The style of the montage in the flashback makes clear the relation of the first cartographic images to the romance. A long dolly-in to Rick's despondent face,

Figure 22. *Casablanca:* Flashback: Rick and Ilsa embrace while the arrows in a stock shot show that they will go in different directions.

his eyes bathed with light reflecting from a swell of tears on his pupils and his face clouded by cigarette smoke, dissolves into a three-quarter view of the Arc de Triomphe and the Champs-Elysées in winter or in early spring (the trees along the avenue are pruned and without leaves). The shot dissolves to a medium close-up of Rick at the wheel of a convertible where, to his left, sits Ilsa (Ingrid Bergman). Their hair wafts in the breeze as they drive away from the monument that recedes into soft focus before the background turns into a country road winding through woodlands. True to the elegiac tradition of pastoral poetry, they get lost in the landscape before the film dissolves back to the couple at the stern of a boat on the Seine, not far from the Pont Mirabeau in the immediate background where, in the distance, a section of the Eiffel Tower is visible.

A Place Named

The longstanding technique that collapses heterogeneous space and time inflects the geography of the "desperate journey" brought forward at the very end of the film. The journey recounted on the map at the beginning, arrested in the middle and mobilized in a backward motion in the sequence in Paris, recurs at the end. Rick has obtained and given the letters of transit required for Victor (Paul Henreid) and Ilsa's passage to Lisbon. At the end the screenplay taps into the tradition of the spatial story, in which place-names are tied to emotive "sites" that define subjectivity. The toponyms negotiate further the contradiction of the atopia of cinema and the histories, real and imaginary, that *Casablanca* both creates and evades. In the last gazes they share Rick tells Ilsa that they will "always have Paris," in other words, that they (and we) will always have a flashback whose affective charge will be driven by mellifluous song and sumptuous lap-dissolves. They will have their own atlas of emotion that, if good fortune holds in 1942, will be eternized a future library of film memories. Hence the paradox in the appeal to historical time and space that sets adrift the specificity of the moment. Surely in the final shots the close-ups of airplane engines revving and spinning their propellers cannot fail to allegorize the "motor of history"—the film that keeps its viewers "occupied"   that will promise the victory that the aptly named freedom fighter (Victor) assures will be theirs. The misty décor of the final shot in which Captain Raynaud (Claude Rains) and Rick share the pleasure of contemplating a new chapter in the history of the friendship refers back to the cloudy surround of the globe at the beginning. The world, in the balance of things, has become one of many points of light, of astral *dots,* of unnamed place-names that fade into black just before the end-credit returns to the map of Africa that had been seen in the front credits. The map calls into question the fluffy cosmogony in which the film would dissolve, and so also do the bars of the "Marseillaise," the anthem that earlier had been a call to action over and against the German occupiers of Casablanca.

Something strange takes place on the map at the terminus of *Casablanca*. In the front-credits a dot on the western coast of Morocco is not accompanied by a name to indicate the place it designates. In the end-credits "Casablanca" appears adjacent to the spot, near the upper-left corner of the frame. The film has become the agent that has "named" the city and finally put it on the map when, earlier, it had merely hovered over it. No other city on the continent is indicated, the inference being that Casablanca is a synecdoche for all of Africa. It would not be an interpretive leap, because the geographical signs would have to be supplied by the viewers having lived through the years 1940–42, to esteem that the space of North Africa in prominence to the right of the toponym also refers to the vast area where the Anglo-American African campaign had just won over Erwin Rommel's Afrika Corps. The sense of a desperate historical journey from a fiction of the past to real events in contemporary time figures implicitly in the map.

Indiana Jones

Indiana Jones and the Raiders of the Lost Ark is a cartographical film par excellence. The narrative leads to a map room, to a site of secrets, before it ends in an archive, another map room in guise of a vault in which is concealed all the memory of the movies of the world. To a significant degree it is about the mapping of cinema in the wake of the classical treatments of adventure and of desperate journeys, the genres it takes care to cite and to exploit. Two sequences are crucial for a comparative treatment of the maps in the movie. One, that is said to take place in Cairo, draws immediately on the memory of *Casablanca* while another, the episode of an attempt to steal an enemy plane, seems to refer directly to the pyrotechnic finish of *Desperate Journey*.

In a crisp appreciation that followed the French premiere of *Indiana Jones and the Raiders of the Lost Ark* in 1981, Olivier Assayas remarked how Steven Spielberg constructed his films to appeal to a public weaned on television and comic books.[20] He sought, argued the critic writing for *Cahiers du cinéma,* to make the most of a gold mine instead of sifting the stones of a riverbed in search of a nugget. George Lucas, he added, caught a "wave" on which he could ride with popular taste and be carried away with it. It was not quite a *nouvelle vague* but one that brought the producer to realize that he could turn the industry of cinema into a seamless art. It may have been a wave that had rolled forward in the wake of the new French cinema of the later 1950s and early 1960s in which a tactics of filmic citation became part of a diagram or a new mode of cinematic mapping. New films had to be mosaic forms in which reflections and refractions of earlier and other films shot through their images.

The adventure film was a privileged landscape to be redrawn. It could be easily industrialized on the basis of nostalgia, the form having "been stabilized for well over thirty years." As a result, adds Assayas, *Raiders* refers "not to an adventure as such, nor to the dreams of a generation for which the explorer or the arche-ologist were modern heroes, but rather to the warehouse of accessories of its cinematographic tradition" (2001, 141). Neither an adventure nor a desperate journey, *Raiders* appealed less to the hero's voyage and its perils than to the rules of navigation and the historical cartography that made possible its special—or, Assayas might say, specious—effects.[21] When the adventure film had been a possibility, perhaps in the era of what Deleuze called the movement-image, the freedom it gave to the imagination made it attractive for "the greatest cineasts who used it as a vehicle for their own preoccupations. In that way they were *auteurs*" (142). When the reproduction of the genre becomes the aim of the film, little place is left either for the signature or a style (*une écriture*). The action film becomes a hyperaction film, and the journey an itinerary where peril is constructed *not* to inspire reflection about time, space, and destiny. Today it can be said that *Raiders* establishes paradigms for the ways that cartographic effects, like jour-nalists in recent battlefields that are the testing grounds of new media reporting, have become embedded in the narratives they serve.

The film, a product of Paramount Studios, begins in the very aura of the com-posite mountain of its logo, a mix of a Mount Whitney, a Zermatt, a Grand Teton, and an Everest. The mountain of the celebrated logo fades into a great black peak, the blue skies on which cirrus clouds blow across turn into the storm and mist over a rain forest, and the arc of stars and words—the "A" at the apex of the peak denoting "A Paramount Picture" over "A Gulf + Western Company"—fade away. The year, indicated by the first intertitle tipped into the image, is 1936. The future hero of the film walks in the shadow of the emblem: thus begins a narrative born not from a departure but a logo.[22] The Paramount peak gives way to its silhou-ette in the first shot of the narrative. The phrase, "Paramount Pictures Present,"

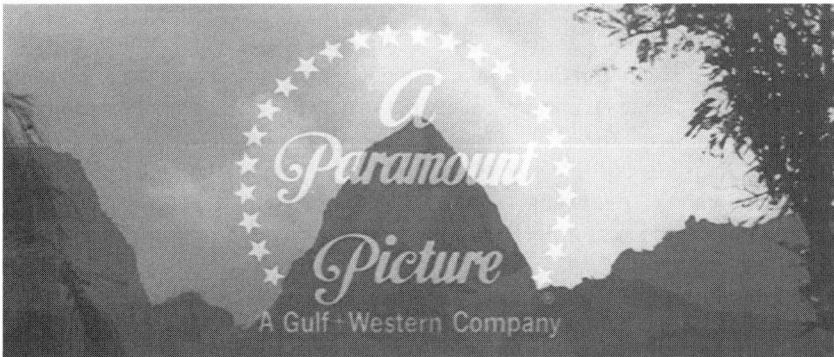

Figure 23. *Indiana Jones and the Raiders of the Lost Ark* (1982): The mountain of the Paramount logo gives way to the mountain in the setting of the first of Jones's treasure hunts.

stretches across the screen that fades into black when a silhouette of a person walks in front of the camera.[23] The background becomes that of a masked inter-title on which "A Lucasfilm Ltd. Production" is scripted. The silhouette of the man in front of the camera moves into the landscape, occluding the mountain whose shape his body resembles. Over it is written "A Steven Spielberg Film" that identifies the character, who does not yet bear the name either of Indiana Jones or Harrison Ford, with the director.

The front-credits are superimposed on shots that convey the impression of an adventure in a jungle, of a film in the mold of *Tarzan's Secret Treasure* (1941) or the 1950s television series, *Ramar of the Jungle*. They are rolled into the action of desperate pursuit in a rainforest before the hero, now recognizably Harrison Ford, emerges into view in close-up. He faces the camera, which records a cas-cade and a river pool in the depth of field behind his back. He enters a cave (not that of Plato's *Republic,* but possibly that of an originary movie theater) in which a broad arc of light is projected from a circular aperture in the earth above. He finds a golden statue resting on a plinth in the middle of an atrium overgrown with hanging vines. It clearly resembles both votive object and an Oscar. He fails to rescue (or pilfer) it and, after several harrowing encounters and pursuit by a tribe of bloodthirsty natives armed with blowguns and poison-tipped arrows, he reaches the open cockpit of a seaplane that carries him off.

The film cuts to a university setting and a classroom where, dressed in tweed, he glosses "Neo . . . lithic" on a blackboard behind a desk. Between the shots of Jones (now a meek and bespectacled young professor) at the blackboard and the lecture hall (bevies of pupils at their desks follow him with their eyes to make known the collective crush they bear upon him) is a globe, a venerable icon of the "classroom" known since *Zero for Conduct* and *The 400 Blows*.[24] It displays Africa when a colleague enters the room, stops to listen to the professor, and pro-ceeds to speak with him. In countershot, from Jones's point of view—for some inexplicable reason—the same globe also displays Africa and Europe. Has the earth made a revolution in the gap between shot and the countershot? Does the globe turn while the characters exchange words? No matter what the reason may be, the aquamarine tint of the globe's oceans and the burnt-beige surface of its steppes of Asia recall the map that had served as the background to the trailers and memorabilia advertising the film.

Behind the teacher, in three-quarter view, is a topographic map and on the adjacent blackboard is an ichnography of an ancient site. In its second sequence the film presents a visual recitation of its own historical geography. Archaeolo-gist Indiana Jones is forever on the track of secret objects and signs he can bring back to a civilized world. He learns that Germans are also in the hunt for magi-cal antiquities. In light of what archaeologists of cinema know of Fritz Lang and Joseph Goebbels, these objects can only be the powers of the medium. The "staff" on which the magic statue had been placed, the professor (standing next to several scrolled maps) soon tells two servants of the Allies, is to be found in a map room. The arc from the Ark is, he adds, "fire, lighting, the power of God, or something." And Jones's colleague adds, the "army that carries the arc before it is invincible," thus echoing the theory that war is waged with cinema and the media *before* real combat takes place (Virilio 1982, 36–37). Jones takes "M*arc*us," an aptly named colleague, to his home where another globe sits on his desk in the background. Upon learning that they will be paid to seek the Ark (or that the studio has approved the budget of their film), they toast to future success. The moment, Jones utters, itching with archive fever, "definitely represents everything we got into *arc*haeology for in the first place." The first overtly mapped form of the film is the background on which a red line is drawn under the image of a Pan American overseas cruiser that soars toward the depressed arc of the Golden Gate Bridge. The stripe of the itinerary is drawn over the lines of latitude and longitude of a Mercator projection as the plane emerges from clouds blending into the image of the Pacific Ocean. The map-effect is slick and smooth, the images pellucid and without blur or fuzz. The film will implicitly engage a historical cartography of the images that have been the stock and stuff of adventure since the era of the silent film and comic books in the tradition of Milton Caniff.[25]

Indiana Jones taps into a tradition of antiquated adventure films with which it establishes an implicit dialogue. One of its chapters (twenty-two) in the recently minted DVD edition is titled "The Flying Wing." In this episode Jones and his lady friend Marion (Karen Allen) attempt to wrest the Ark from the Nazis and steal away by getting away in a strange aircraft that seems to be a composite mix of a Messerschmitt 262, an American "flying wing" of the 1950s, and a stealth bomber. The nacelles of its two propeller-driven engines are aimed backwards

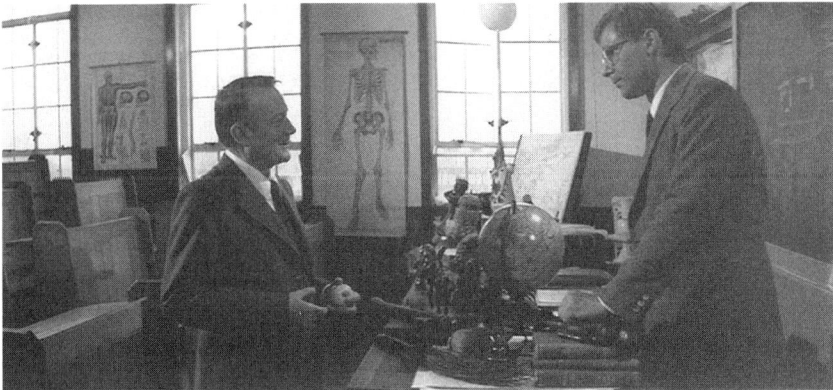

Figure 24. *Indiana Jones and the Raiders of the Lost Ark:* Prelude to the map room in the classroom: a globe and an apple, wall maps and scrolled maps are adjacent to Vesalian skeletons.

and its cockpit, at the origin of the dihedral of the wing, points directly forward. A ball-turret equipped with a machine gun is atop on the rear of the fuselage. The sequence begins when the hero pushes a gigantic perpend from the wall of a squat tower piercing a hillock in the desert. From a window opened onto what seems to be the studio set of the film, Jones peers onto scene before he and Marion climb over the threshold and descend a slope en route to the aircraft. Jones overcomes a couple of guards and engages an Aryan behemoth. Marion removes the chocks from under the wheels of the landing gear and uses them as a blunt instrument to knock one of the soldiers on the head. She climbs into the cockpit and quickly retreats to the turret where she opens fire on oncoming squadrons of troops. Because the plane is unmoored and its twin engines are idling, Marion finds herself turning about a 360-degree axis. Riddled with stray bullets, barrels of gasoline spurt their contents all over the area. As the plane turns about, the Aryan strong man, on the verge of overwhelming Jones, backs into the turning propeller where (implied by two cutaway shots displaying blood spattering all over the stabilizer and windshield), he is cut to shreds. The gasoline explodes as Jones and Marion make their getaway to hide in a tent where a native informant tells them that the Ark has been loaded on a truck. A new chapter follows.

The model for the sequence is found in the crowning episode in *Desperate Journey*. The cartographic implications of the sequence both in Walsh's film and others of the same ilk in the Warner Brothers studio show by a strange turn of paradox that the allusion to *Desperate Journey* summons the ideological contours of Spielberg's production of 1981. We have seen that in Walsh's film, attention was drawn to the way that both the film and its maps were agents, on the one hand, of dissimulation while, on the other, they held forth the promise and the prayer for a rewriting of history. The film was a "diagram" anticipating and programming

Figure 25. *Indiana Jones and the Raiders of the Lost Ark:* Theft of the "flying wing," a remake (or theft) of the ending of *Desperate Journey.*

change in the course of the Second World War. And, too, *High Sierra* was a toponymical tale showing that its mythic frame was light-years away from the events of its own time. In *Indiana Jones* the same "classical" films become the "archive" for the "arc" and "ark" or archway of the production. The film seamlessly cites the spatial rhetoric of the earlier films to the point where the montage-images of the Warner Brothers' features are turned into the smooth substance of an adventure without lapse, lull, or the slightest modulation. The film is an adventure and a journey that, as it were, digitalizes the cartographies of classical cinema. Various paradigms of displacement are found in *High Sierra, Desperate Journey, Casablanca,* and *Raiders of the Lost Ark.* The adventure film and the romantic epic on which they are based belong not only to an antique cinema but also to cognitive maps and diagrams of wishes and dreams. They appeal to the vitality of a child's imagination of the world and its conflicts. If only for comparative reasons it may now be productive to see how adolescence, romance, and cartography are configured in postwar cinema on the other side of the Atlantic.

5

Juvenile Geographies: *Les Mistons*

In his copious *Cosmographie universelle* (1575), a work of textual compilation, city-views, and local maps of the world at large, François de Belleforest carefully describes the topography and ancient monuments of southern France. He includes a double-fold image of the Pont du Gard, a great Roman aqueduct that arches over the limpid waters of the River Gard that flows from the Cévennes into the Rhône south of Avignon. On either side abrupt escarpments of rock anchor the bridge that counts three superimposed arcades of six, eleven, and thirty-three rounded arches. A few perpends of the upper cornice are chinked; stones in the lower columns are nicked or pocked with crevices; out of a cleft in the archivolts on the upper level pushes the trunk of a stout and healthy tree. Below the parapets of the upper bridge, two humans pass along the road paved on the middle level of the bridge. One, standing in a wagon, brandishes a whip to drive his modest team of horses. The other, a man walking ahead, carries a staff over his right shoulder. Both men, unimpressed by the décor, are unaware that their minuscule proportion lends a sublime grandeur to the scene. The image suggests that the bridge, displaying its age with pride, attests to the genius of Roman engineering.

In its time the woodcut was well known.[1] It figures in a body of works that mix chronicles of France and its regions with a growing number of woodcut maps and city-views. The image of the Pont du Gard was drawn to attest to the authenticity of France, a nation of a genealogy made clear by Greek and Roman monuments piercing the surface of its soil. Local officials hired archeologists to discover, classify, and herald antiquities that would assure the region of the depth and wealth of its greater Gallic heritage.

The Pont du Gard is shown in the same way in François Truffaut's first short feature, *Les Mistons* (1957). The monument might well be a first emblem of the personal and national geographies that mark the early cinema both of the director and of the early New Wave.[2] For the writer and polemicist of the 1950s the task of the director entailed melding a love of literature, a love of things French, and a love of cinema *tout court*. For Truffaut autobiographical cinema was to engage life conceived as an itinerary, in brief, as an affective plotting, mapping, and apprenticeship of life.

> In my view the film of the future seems even more personal than a novel, individual and autobiographical as a confession or as an intimate journal. Young film makers will express themselves in the first person and will tell us about what has happened to them: it can be the story of their first or most recent love, their consciousness about politics, a travel narrative, a sickness, their military service, their marriage, their last vacation. And it will be almost ineluctably appealing because it will be true and new. Tomorrow's film . . . will be made by artists for whom the shooting of a film is a marvelous and exalting adventure.

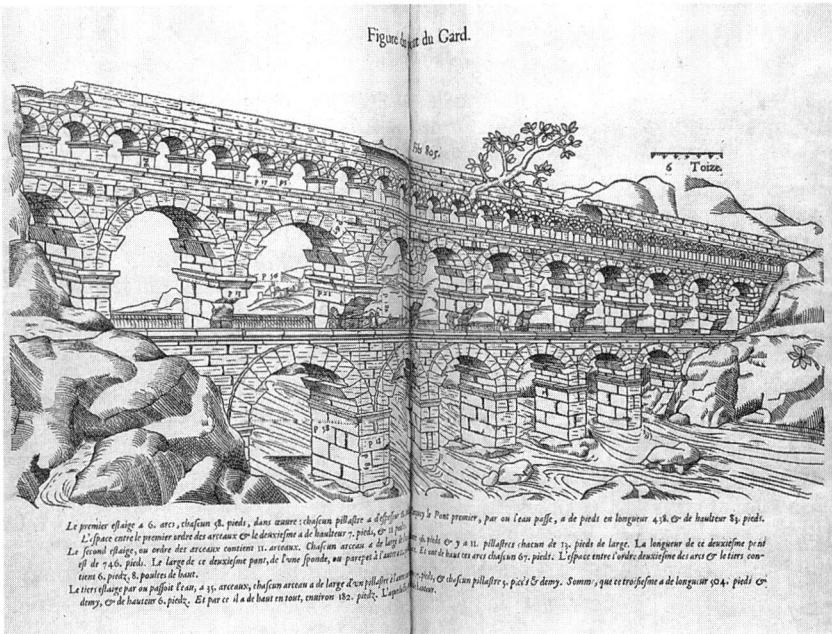

Figure 26. A woodcut image of the Pont du Gard of the 1560s, found in François de Belleforest, *Cosmographie universelle* (1575) and other works of early modern cartography.

Thus only "adventurers will make films," and their films will bear witness to "an act of love."[3] His adventure is grounded in geography and affective cartography. Film will trace the itineraries of new and unforeseen voyages, and it will draw bold lines of divide between what he calls listless cinemas of tradition or *qualité* and those of new wit and invention. The director will plot the itinerary of his adventure on a topography that includes the tradition of French cinema he admonishes. At the time Truffaut waxes romantically about new cinema he also writes polemical articles castigating the films of his infancy and childhood. They constitute a vital backdrop for a cinematic geography that the director fashions in the name of *la politique des auteurs* and first realizes in *Les Mistons*.

A Story Plotted into Film

Most viewers of *Les Mistons* remember the unsettlingly sensuous shot, taken in staccato slow motion, of a child lurching his face toward a bicycle seat from which a beautiful woman has just descended to take a swim in the limpid waters of the river. A prepubescent boy bathes his nose in a musky aroma smelling of everything he desires and fears. The scene would be what psychoanalysts call the *relation d'inconnu,* the relation with the unknown that drives subjectivity and is felt in the unending "mirror stages" that are lived from birth until death (Rosolato 1993, 153–69). As a moment in cinema it would be film crystallized in its purest state: the camera, in long tracking shots taken from a moving car, follows the woman pedaling from the streets of Nîmes, beginning from the Roman Maison-Carré in the background, along a serpentine road leading to the country, bending and passing over the Pont du Gard, winding to a grove where she stops, descends from her bicycle, and stoops to arrange her billowing skirt, ruffled by the wind, which is sticking to the seat. She pirouettes and bobs her way to the river. Suddenly, as in every classical eclogue, a band of satyrs runs and jumps out of the forest in fierce pursuit of the nymph.

Where, in classical literature, beasts had danced on their cloven hoofs and played flutes to entice their prey, now five boys crash into the clearing from the woods where they had been waiting to ambush the beauty. One seeks the bicycle, and the others a glimpse of the woman swimming in the water. In its close-up and extreme slow motion, transgressing the continuity of a classical film, the shot bears a juvenile fragility and exudes a new sense of style. The reader of Maurice Pons's story of the same title gathered in *Virginales* (1955) discovers that the episode of the bicycle seat is the very first image inaugurating the narrative. Thus begins the written text of "Les Mistons" that makes no reference to a geographical setting:

> La soeur de Jouve était trop belle. Nous ne le supportions pas. Lorsqu'elle se rendait au bain de rivière, elle laissait sa bicyclette cadenassée devant l'entrée. Comme elle roulait toujours jupe flottante, et assurément sans jupon, il arrivait, les journées

chaudes, que la selle de sa machine s'en trouvât tout humide. De semaines en semaines, il s'y traçait plus apparemment de pâles auréoles. Nous tournions, fascinés,
autour de cette fleur de cuir bouilli, as de coeur haut perché dont nous envions les
voyages. Il n'était pas rare que l'un de nous, n'y tenant plus, se détachât de notre
groupe et sans forfanterie ni fausse honte, allât poser un instant son visage sur cette
selle, confidente de quel mystère? (97)

Jouve's sister was too beautiful. We couldn't stand her. When she went to bathe in
the river she used to leave her bicycle padlocked in front of the entry. As she always
rode with her skirt billowing in the air and without a slip, on hot days it happened
that her bicycle seat was moist all over. From week to week on it were traced
pale halos. Fascinated, we turned around and about this flower of boiled leather, an
ace of hearts perched high and for whose voyages we were envious. It was not uncommon for one of us, unable to stand it any longer, to stray from the group and
without boast or false shame went to set his face for an instant upon this saddle, a
confidante of who knows what mystery?

Truffaut's film casts the narrative along an itinerary that *literally*—topograph-
ically—departs from Pons's minuscule novella. The first shot that follows the
scroll of credits records Bernadette (Bernadette Lafont) pedaling away from
Nîmes (that does not figure in the story) along the Pont du Gard (not in the story
either) and past a group of older people promenading on the bridge with their
dog. She rides toward the camera that recedes as she advances, moving through
the arcs of shadow cast by the upper arcade of the structure. She traverses blocks
of light and shade that suddenly resemble the photograms of a strip of film passing through the gate of a projector.

A straight cut gives way to a broad view of the architecture as it had been
remembered for ages before the camera swish-pans left, along a career of 90
degrees, across the lush landscape of the Gard. The lens arrests on the faces (in
medium close-up) of two boys who seem to gaze upon the aqueduct the viewer
has just seen. In voiceover the first sentence of the story is uttered when the profile is seen of two youthful faces that are almost mirrored images of each other:
"La soeur de Jouve était trop belle." What are they looking at? Is it the aqueduct
or the woman? The voice-off of an adult speaks in the indefinite past of what
will become a tale of intolerable exasperation that cuts through children in their
prepubescent years. His spoken words suggest that the adult is in the child. The
former speaks over a gap of time that could be located either before or after the
construction of the bridge (before A.D. 400). In the indirect discourse the children
may be contemplating the adult that they have not yet become. Yet, as we hear
the voice of the older man, he is of an arrogance enabling him to tell us who they
were. It is as if an absent and possibly moribund adult is speaking from a time
immemorial as that of the Roman aqueduct.

The exasperation, we soon learn, belongs to language and to the force of Eros. The children feel for a ravishing young woman desires exceeding what they could ever temper with their own words or actions. A long tracking shot follows a straight cut. The woman rides her bicycle toward an invisible moving vehicle on which the camera is mounted. Bathed in bright light as she pedals along a road bordered by flat shrubbery, she turns downward into a grove bathed in dappled light. Her descent is accompanied by the second sentence of the story that is slightly altered. "Elle roulait toujours jupe flottante et assurément sans jupon. Bernadette était pour nous la découverte prestigieuse de tant de rêves obscures et de nos imaginations cachées [the shot holds Bernadette in dark shadow when the voice utters *cachées*]. Elle était notre éveil et ouvrait en nous les sources d'une sensualité lumineuse [She always rode with a billowing skirt and of course without a slip. For us Bernadette was the prestigious discovery of so many obscure memories of our concealed imaginations. She awakened and opened us onto the springs of a luminous sensuality]" (98). The text draws the eye toward the play of light and shadow while the shot continues its backward track. The young woman pedals swiftly down a straight stretch of the road before it bends and dips to the left. She turns slightly and releases her hand from one of the handlebars to keep her skirt in place. A straight cut to a long shot of the road and woods begins a lengthy pan (of almost 300 degrees) left of Bernadette as she rides through patches of light and darkness as she had along the aqueduct. The film rejoins the beginning of Pons's story. A sudden take in slow motion rewrites the effect the text had obtained through the metaphor of an ace of hearts and the halo of rings of musky sweat and vaginal juice accreted in the vellum of "boiled leather."

Correspondence and Rewriting

It might be said that Truffaut's cinematic cartography begins here. The camera breaks all rules of verisimilitude by changing its speed *in medias res* and without plausible explanation. A sensuous eros frees the film from both censure and prurience. In a broader way the shot brings forward what Truffaut, like his *mistons,* could not quite put into words in the letters he wrote to friends and colleagues when he conceived the film. Truffaut first mentions the idea of adapting Pons's story in a letter he sent to the writer on April 4, 1957. He wishes to meet the young writer and to explain how he will go about financing the film. In order to show how good cinema is made from very short stories Truffaut invites Pons to accompany him to see Max Ophüls's *Le Plaisir,* a feature based on three of Guy de Maupassant's novellas.[4] In May, without mentioning his project, he writes to Chares Bitsch from Cannes to say that Nîmes, the city where *Les Mistons* will be shot, "est très bien et aussi la campagne [is very good and the countryside too]" (128). In August he writes to Bitsch again about the progress of *Les Mistons.*

Some initial glimpses of its vision begin to take form in the description of the way he goes about filming.

I shoot very quickly, almost without any rehearsing, in a single take, sometimes two. That (for me) is the best system, because I'm clear only during the projection and with freedom to rebegin and to reshoot three days later. It'll be a very uneven film with some terribly sore spots but also with some really odd happenings; taking advantage of a real train in a little station in Montpellier, I shot six minutes of film (three takes of two minutes each) in twenty minutes (between the arrival of the train and its departure). Gerard really did leave on the train, Bernadette returning toward the camera crying like a baby: cut! (1988, 129)

Truffaut lets chance and improvisation win over careful repetition on the script; without admitting that at the Montpellier station he is rehearsing Lumière's "Arrivée d'un train à la gare de La Ciotat" (1895), the director brags about getting six minutes of the final takes in the space of twenty minutes. Bernadette cries "like a *madeleine,*" as she might be indeed a refugee from Proust's world in which memory flows when the narrator, tasting a spongy pastry dipped in warm liquid, releases a torrent of memory-images from the landscape.

In the same letter Truffaut takes coy pleasure in noting the embarrassment (or even slight timidity) of the two adult leads, Gérard (Gérard Blin) and Bernadette, when they work together. He complains that his cameraman (Jean Malige)

has no taste, he is maniacal and works "for the sake of quality"; his photography is an eternal compromise between what he likes . . . and what I like. Result: once again, uneven, very good under a grey sky and when I say, "So what, we'll shoot nonetheless" (the station), pretty feeble when the sun shines bright (the tennis match). . . . In truth, an odd film, an odd reel and and odd ambiance) (30)

The cameraman is of the "tradition of quality" that holds to the text of the story and seeks an aura of classical elegance, in strong contrast to the director who prefers invention and chance. Truffaut adds that where a graffito on a wall in the street was scribbled "Votez Poujade" (a politician of the far right) he and his team wrote "Votez Rivette" (Jacques Rivette, the fellow cineast of the New Wave Pléiade). Finally, he adds that in the film will be an homage to Lumière, Vigo, Hulot (Jacques Tati), Ford, Dario Moreno, and Rossellini. He does not say, however, that he will have the children tear a poster advertising Jean Delannoy's *Chiens perdus sans collier* (1955) from a bulletin board by a local theater. The viewer gets a glimpse of the way that the film will be "written" by way of inscription and allusion.

A critical edge is born in the report and in the relation the director is gaining with the film. In a more formal letter to Maurice Pons in autumn of the same year (dated October 2, 1957), he invites the writer to work with him on the mixing in order to conserve the original tone. Truffaut is anxious about showing him a film not entirely faithful to the story. He finally admits that he has contradicted Pons's style, declaring that the filmmaker's temperament is at the antipodes of his author, and indeed the very images from the text that were most striking count among those that Pons will never recognize when he sees the finished work. To be *adapted* is to be *betrayed*. Truffaut defends himself before Pons as if he might have been a child having either transgressed the edicts of an imaginary father or surreptitiously denounced the writer in order to foment panic and scandal.

Scenes of Writing

As of the credits—the first shot—the story is entirely rewritten and redrawn. The tracking shot on which the credits scroll upward pulls backward. The viewer is invited to look through the writing at the woman on the bicycle but also to take note of the words and names that move upward on the visual field. A viewer of 1957 might have wondered if the inscription of the producer, Truffaut's intimate friend "Robert Lachenay," is an invention of the filmmaker insofar the name rhymes with Robert de La Chesnaye, the protagonist of Renoir's *La Règle du jeu*.[5] And the voiceover by a man named "Michel François" is especially "French" in the way the timber and grain of the calm and assured diction bears an Alexandrine measure.

Suspicions are confirmed in a brief shot inserted between the tracking shots leading from Nîmes to the countryside and the first take on the Pont du Gard. For an instant the moving camera meets and gives way to an American car—a 1955 Mercury convertible—that turns onto the roadway of the aqueduct. The car appears out of place in the décor of Provence and surely too long and wide for the road on which it is being driven. Yet the Mercury (an emblem of protean metamorphosis or of ruse and enterprise?) is seen beneath the name of the production company, "Les Films du Carrosse [Coach Films]." The *carrosse* refers both to a regal and classical conveyance and a metaphor—literally, a "mode of transport"— that belongs to old Europe, while the "Merc" beneath the writing indicates that a new or other world is present. Brief though it may be, the shot offers a telling allegory of the coextension of two traditions, two continents, and two cinemas. A classical geographical allegory of two ages of the world inheres in the shot.

The mix of writing and cinema in the credits pervades the film and becomes the key to many of its secrets. If Renoir's name is transmuted in "Robert Lachenay" and possibly the name of his late feature, *Le Carrosse d'or* (The Golden Coach, 1953) in "Les Films du Carrosse," the director's images recur in a sequence that gives way to what, following Freud and Jacques Derrida, might be called *a scene of writing*.[6] The boys have just been ogling at Gérard and Bernadette who leave a *mas* or stone-clad country house set behind a rocky wall.[7] The wall dissolves into an order of five neoclassical balusters that support the cornice of a wall enclosing a terrace to which the four boys accede from a point deep in the background. They reach the balustrade on the left, their movement punctuated by the four cupped areas that catch them assembling in the space beyond the barrier. They look away and off to the left. They finally squeeze into one of the frames and seem to mold themselves to its form, their legs pushing down toward the ground at the spectator's eye line and the rump of one boy and the upper bodies of all filling the open space above.

They are clearly defined by an architectural surround that has a somewhat unsettling effect—the children seem to be living caryatids in a type of frame or even a bas-relief—related to the Pont du Gard. The balusters are washed in the light of day and so brightly illuminated that they resemble gigantic lamp-chimneys, their squat and bulbous bottoms curving into elegant stems that support their lintel. The brightness occludes the somewhat darker background in the sunlit space into which the children have gathered. They are raw material for thematic and even psychoanalytical interpretation: the position of the spectator duplicates that of the children who had peered across the stone wall in the preceding shot that has dissolved into this sequence, thus implying that we too are prepubescent youth who are observing the *mistons* in the same way that the mistons set their

Figure 27. *Les Mistons* (1956): The rascals seen through a screen of balusters in a park. The architecture resembles that of *La Règle du jeu* (see chapter 2, Figures 9 and 10).

eyes on the aqueduct and, in the lap dissolve, on the couple that exited from the doorway of the stone house. In this way a primal scene, what theorists often call the very condition of cinema that the New Wave made clear to its public, would be shown, in the space of one or two seconds, in the form of a diptych.

On one side would be the preadolescent re-enactment of the *scène primitive*, the lovers standing in for the parents who embrace in the classical Freudian scenario in which subjectivity and growth depend on the way that the child copes with its discovery that it is a *persona non grata* in the familial unit from which it finds itself separated. On the other panel, and in a gentle comic reversal, the spectator would now be the parent who gazes upon the children, but with a consciousness that rivals that of the child or that at the very least seeks to regain the children's proclivities. Spectators would have purchase on the scene because they can hear the voiceover of the adult where the children cannot. It would mesh with the point of view that discerns the children *through* the parapet or balustrade. The optical and architectural composition of the scene causes the adult who looks through and across a classical form to wonder if the shot is merely given to inspire reflection on the *topos* of the child as the father of man by way of the man in empathy with the child: look as we may across the barrier, we cannot quite become the children we want to be. Our desire would mirror that of the children wishing to cross the line demarcating the child from the adult or the confused eros of the youth fathoming forever forbidden and unknown genital pleasures in the images they concoct for themselves of Gérard and Bernadette. In this reading a first primal scene, a scene reiterated time and again in the film, dissolves into another in which the spectator looks backward, as if it were through a glass or a stone barrier darkly, to see in the children the fresh and untrammeled force of eros, translated into the visual delight of gazing upon a world before it is named, striated, and mapped. The vision of the children mirrors that of the viewer.

The sensuousness owes less to childish innocence than to a relation with cinematic form. The voiceover of the adult who recalls his childish past is matched by a direct allusion to Renoir. A balustrade of the same style was both a theme and, as we have seen earlier, a spatial and even cartographic marker in *La Règle du jeu*. Renoir used the terrace of the château to keynote the thresholds of day and night, of public and private spaces, of dreams of love and of the nightmares of history, and of pre-Revolutionary France and the eve of the Second World War. The balustrade and the globes on its posts were an oblique frame that cut into the deep field of view in which Corneille, Schumacher, the Marquis, Jurieux, Christine, and Lisette crossed (as we have seen in chapter 2) when they mounted the alluvial stairwell. Sometimes it was seen in daylight and at others under ominous clouds. It gathered a play of light in *contrejour* when Octave (Jean Renoir), in the role of a music critic, mimed the movements of Christine's father, a musical conductor before his symphony, in the silent darkness of a cold night in early spring (Curchod 1998, 218–19, 223–24). The balustrade became the décor for the most complex articulation of theater, cinematic form, pathos, and fantasy in the final sequence of the film (269–70) where the La Chesnaye calms his audience after the murder of the aviator Jurieux with parting words of sympathy and affection before he invites his public to return to the confines of the château and, by extension, to those of the film.

In this sequence of *Les Mistons* the architectural décor opens onto both new and familiar spaces of cinematic memory. The effect of occlusion, by which we perceive the children through or across physical and temporal barriers, is enhanced by the memory of other films embedded in the same image. Icons drawn from a history of film become the substance of an implied dialogue or even an allegory in which the dramatic, psychic, and cinematic stakes of *La Règle du jeu* are read through Truffaut's short film and vice-versa. A multivalent sense of history is obtained when the present film affects that of Renoir. The fluid lateral movement of Truffaut's camera, like Renoir's in much of *La Règle du jeu,* does not allow time enough for an allegory (of the Quarrel of the Ancients and Moderns) to settle into the frame. Unlike the tradition of the "cinéma de qualité" that Truffaut took to task for its visual stasis and turgid treatment of written material, the sequence draws attention to its own penchant to create a form of cinematic writing inscribed on the surface of a filmic unconscious. The camera moves as soon as it sets the children into the inner frame in the shot. It pans right as the voice-off calmly recalls,

C'est à cette époque que s'ouvrirent les hostilités. Sur les palissades, les troncs d'arbres, les parapets et des ponts, sur tous les murs de la ville de Gérard et de Bernadette nous annonçâmes les fiançailles à grands coup de coeur transpercé. Car nous étions à l'âge où on ne distingue pas encore les fiançailles de l'amour.

It was at this moment when hostilities began. On the palissades, the tree trunks, on all the walls of the city we announced the betrothal of Gérard and Bernadette with a stricken heart. For we were of an age where celebration is not distinguished from love.

When the narration ends with a slightly tonic accent on *amour* the camera begins a swish-pan to the right that sets the balusters in a blur between the horizontal line of the lintel and floor. The shot moves past a rectangular cartouche in the parapet as the one of the children casts a quick glance at the camera that follows him leading the three others off to the right. The four boys hustle en route to a place, revealed in a quick lap-dissolve, to be a brick wall and another cartouche bearing on its surface an illegible inscription. In the passage the blur of the pan suggests that the balustrade is a strip of film, and an architectural décor, like that of the Pont du Gard, a site fraught with history.

The classical appearance of the balustrade is matched by the limpid articulation of the voice in the setting of the shot that begins with the children running onto the terrace, crowding together, and then sprinting off to the right. As the children begin to run and as the camera begins its pan the voice declares in the preterit tense that "[o]n the parapets, the tree trunks, on all the walls of the city we announced the betrothal of Gérard and Bernadette with a stricken heart." The parapet is the given space, *in*, of the shot, while the trees and walls are those, contiguous and off, that belong to the aura of the Midi. And the stricken heart, the emblem of a valentine, arches back to the figure of the bicycle seat that the writer had compared to an *as de coeur*, an ace of hearts that, when glossed in English, names the part of Bernadette's body that obsesses the children. On the walls of the city they draw an emblem of the part of a magnificent rump that bore a cordiform imprint on the bicycle seat. It becomes their affective map, their version of a *Carte du pays de Tendre*.

The relation of the voice to the image suggests that the camera is endowed with mystical force. The narrator's speech is conjuring an image that immediately becomes incarnate. "[L]es murs de la ville," what would belong to a cavalcade of local images, emerges into view by seemingly being metamorphosed into what it is from what preceded its name and what was seen (including the name of the author Pons) in "les parapets et les ponts." In the moving image the lap-dissolve accomplishes what enumeration in the sentence of the narrative could only approximate. In the shot that concretizes the textual allusion to the *murs de la ville* a delay is discerned between the vocal and visual signs. The film causes the wall (and the shot itself) to become a surface on which inscriptions will be drawn or carved.

The boys write their announcement on the brick surface as if it were a blackboard or even a palimpsest. On the cartouche reserved for the engraving of a street-name (just above the boys' eye line) are marks of graffiti. The space that they reach upward to chalk with words is of two textures. One surface is riddled with lines and embeds a textual inscription, the other an unadorned surface on which an icon (or a nonlinguistic sign [a sign that does not transcribe a vocable into an alphabetic character]) is drawn. In the area to the left a text is *drawn* while on the right-hand side an image is *written*. The shot takes care to reproduce the parallel and correlative acts of writing and drawing in a single take. As "gerard et bernadette" is inscribed so also are the arcs of the heart soon pierced by a line indicating an arrow. The two hands of the boys on the left and on the right work as if in synchrony. When the boy on the right draws the shaft piercing the field of the heart, his companion on the left begins a new line of text in the area below, on the next level of bricks where the viewer awaits the inscription of predicate of the plural subject, and where "son" is drawn before one of the boys raises his right hand to indicate that the letter *t* has been omitted. "gerard et bernadette son . . . t [gerard and bernadette ar . . . e]."

All of a sudden the writing calls attention the economic virtue of cinema. The misspelled plural of "to be" (*sont*) indicates the nominal *son* or sound traduced in the silence of the flashback where no voice reiterates what is being written. The second boy raises his index finger to indicate that the consonant is needed for the graffito to make sense. He rehearses the same gesture in Poussin's "Et in Arcadia Ego" (1647), known to anyone who has strolled through the Louvre, possibly the greatest of all classical paintings in seventeenth-century France, in which a group of heroic but apparently analphabetic shepherds gather about a tomb and trace with their fingers the inscription of the morbid device that tells them they are suspended in a timeless space. In *Les Mistons* an "Arcadian" or even a pastoral world, prior or outside of that of writing and of history, is suggested by the gesture. It is repeated when the second boy in the middle raises his hand to gloss the inscription. In Poussin's painting the enigma about the character of writing in the medium of painting finds a cinematic correlative in Truffaut's film. The boys feel to the quick a confusion of envy and jealousy; they have no language or symbolic agency to explain or to mollify the intensities of their emotions. They can only "learn to curse" by writing graffiti, a form of glossalia, that acts out their feelings instead of representing or translating them.[8] The image or icon on one side is a complete and visually arresting translation of the graphic formula to its left.

The composition of the shot appears crafted to be superimposed on the next, a long shot that in a pan to the right and then left follows Bernadette on her bicycle as she rides along the zigzag of a road on the slope of a hill in a landscape typical

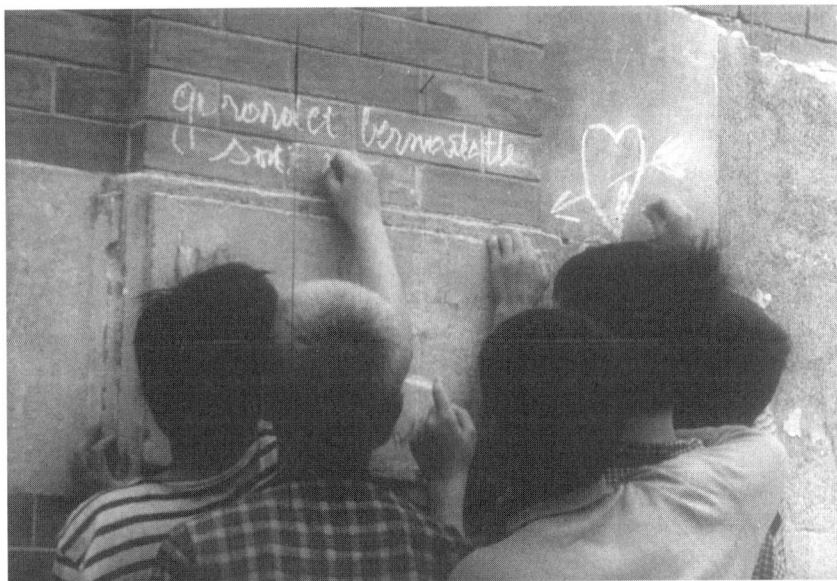

Figure 28. *Les Mistons:* The rascals inaugurate a scene of writing on a wall in Nîmes. (See chapter 7, Figure 32).

of the Vaucluse. In the dissolve the dark background formed by the shrubs on the top of the hillside make visible the children's writing that both emerges from and remains inscribed on the landscape. The act and movement of writing inaugurated in the preceding shot dissolves into the gentle course of the bicycle that Bernadette, her skirt billowing in the air and displaying her shapely legs, guides down the hill, from left to right, before she turns and follows the slope in the opposite direction. She literally continues the movement of the writing both of the text and of the inscriptive instrument—the arrow or pen—seen in the icon of the *coeur transpercé*.

The montage of images interprets the words of the text in order to defy the author's—Pons's—control of his story. The bicycle that emerges from the scene of the boys scrawling graffiti becomes a new and different writing instrument, an instrument of mobility, visual aura, and of erotic appeal. It becomes at once language and landscape replacing and supplementing what the children seek to put into words and icons. It seems as if the origins of cinema, indeed a film by the Lumière Brothers, are residually present in an allusion to one of the plans-séquences of their oeuvre prior to 1900, in which a man rides a bicycle as if to signal mobility and even torsion that will inspire the camera to take to the road and enter the landscape. The bicycle is also at once a textual reference that extends laterally and almost synchronically from Lumière to Marcel Proust's glimpses of young women riding bicycles in light that stipples the paths of *A l'ombre de jeunes filles en fleurs*. The landscape that flickers across the screen turns the "enemy" in the direction of an attraction both to the mysteries of Bernadette and to a richer and broader context of cinema and literature in which the children are at stake, and where their *jeux,* like those of Jean Renoir, cannot go without their rules. Crucial to the sequence—because it has been determined by the children's graffiti—are the visual points in the frame where the speech seems to congeal and then vanish. Speculation about the nature of love turns into a celebration of movement that caresses signs of death and mortality, exactly where Bernadette is identified with the atmosphere, aroma, and light of southern France.

Much of what Truffaut makes explicit in his later work is glimpsed in the sequences that lead toward and issue from the children's scene of writing. It is repeated three more times and in contexts that vary on the relation of the symbolic magic of graphic inscription to cinema. The children intensify their offensive against the lovers by agglutinating their enemies' names into "gerardette" within the graffito of another heart. They spy upon and then disrupt the couple's idyll in a sequence clearly referring to the episode of Henri and Henriette making love in Renoir's *Une partie de campagne* (1936). They mock the lovers who steal kisses in a movie theater which begins, in a *mise en abyme*, with a take of Jean-Claude Brialy leading his blonde prey to a couch. Running out of the dark room and into the daylit street, they tear a movie poster—advertising Jean Delannoy's *Chiens perdus sans collier* (1955)—from a wall adjacent to the theater from which they exit, literally "unwriting" their earlier inscription by removing a text and image emblazoning the film they decided not to see in its entirety. Ultimate revenge is enacted on Bernadette through a risqué postcard, on whose back they scribble their defaming words and then send to her domicile where she awaits the return of Gérard from an expedition to the mountains.

The postcard episode is foregrounded by a sequence in the railway station beginning with allusion to Lumière's *Entrée d'un train en gare*. Gérard has just slapped one of the children who has interrupted the couple in the landscape and has yelled, "Sale petit miston," just before the shriek of the train whistle signals the arrival of the locomotive as it had arrived in the film of 1895. Before this moment some snippets of *Boudu sauvé des eaux, Une partie de campagne,* and *La Bête humaine* (1938) have appeared. A medium close-up records Gérard and Bernadette waiting for the train to stop and open its doors. Gérard climbs aboard and Bernadette follows him. He caresses her and then blows kisses with his hands, uttering, "Sois sage, tu m'écriras, et rentre vite car il va pleuvoir [Be good, you'll write me, and come home soon because it's going to rain]." She responds, "Tu m'écriras? [Will you write me?]" before he answers, disappearing in the perspective in the blast of steam and the noise of the chugging locomotive, "oui." They will write but at the same time they are literally written by scenes of writing that have shaped the character of their attraction.

As the Crow Flies

When the two lovers beg to write each other—in other words, to inscribe or mark each other, and not write *to* each other—their fate is named and sealed. Their destiny reveals an unnamed relation with another film of destiny, Henri-Georges Clouzot's *Le Corbeau* (1943). The mosaic allusion tells much about the greater cartography of *Les Mistons*. The sequence that follows the arrival of the train in the station and the final separation of Gérard from Bernadette portrays the children demonizing Bernadette by sending her an anonymous *carte postale*. The camera attends to them composing their note that mocks the solitary woman in the name of "Les Mistons." *Sale petit miston,* the word Gérard first uttered in swearing at the children, is now pluralized and signed in the name of an anonymous band of juvenile terrorists. Immediately after the postcard is mailed news follows that Gérard has died in an accident in the mountains. Close-ups of the text and photographs of reports in the newspaper tell of the mishap. In the greater texture of the film they are both the aftermath and the continuation of the initial scenes of writing. The parataxis or "impersonal enunciation" of the film suggests that the children's writing and mailing of the postcard might have been the cause of the accident, and that so also would have been the decision the couple had taken, in the thick of the cinematic imbroglios that were scripting their words and actions, to write each other, that is, to objectify each other in fixed and immobile shapes.

Clouzot's film of the Occupation comes forward under the name of the "mistons" who signed the fateful text on the verso side of the postcard mailed to Bernadette. *Le Corbeau* takes place in a provincial town that seems timeless and of a timeless character like the décor of Truffaut's Nîmes. In its dark plot a town is tyrannized and terrorized by the mailing of letters that vilipend those to whom they are written. The letters exploit gossip and innuendo to play members of the community off and against one another. The image of a "crow" serves as the signatory autograph. It is eventually revealed that an aging doctor, the rival of a younger and progressive physician (Pierre Fresnay) who most resembles a hero, is the author of the notes. The would-be hero makes clear his beliefs by encouraging the women's right to abortion and by affirming that he does not believe either in God or in pious ceremonies that invoke a superior deity or idea for self-serving ends. Having had a brief affair with a young woman who is the object of the affections of the old doctor's spouse, despite his precarious status in the town, he remains resolute and calm in the midst of accusations and slander.

At one point the older doctor, a person taken to be a local sage, imposes a "writing lesson" on the suspected authors of the letters. Gathering them into a classroom and having them transcribe *dictées* in the spurious style of the letters as they have been gathered, he strives to find a victim who, under the stress of the exercise, will succumb to contrition and madness. The young doctor's mistress, pregnant and of frail disposition, faints. For an instant she is scapegoated. Like others who are singled out for abuse, she wilts under false accusation. Ultimately the older doctor's domestic, after noting the traces of his hand on the blotter in his office, plunges a knife into the villain's back. The very man who engineered the dictation is the author of the letters. The last shots of the film are taken from the point of view of the younger doctor who visits the scene of the crime. He first beholds the head and shoulders of the cadaver arched over a desk on which the fateful blotter, stained with images of crows, absorbs the fresh blood flowing from the wound in his neck. Then he goes to the window opening onto a sunny street where, in solitude, the woman dressed in black walks away before the end-credits bring the film to a close.

In *Le Corbeau* the circulation of letters written to damage the community are anticipations of death notes. They belong to a symbolic magic of writing, on the one hand, but on the other, they also refer to the sorry history of letters that circulated abundantly in French towns under the Occupation for the sake of their authors' vendetta. The German occupants exploited tipoffs and gossip to snare unwanted citizens, political dissidents, Jews, and whomever they felt were deviant. In 1957 Truffaut's film would seem to be light-years distant from France of 1943; yet the last shot of *Les Mistons,* in which Bernadette Lafont, dressed in black, approaches the camera that backtracks as she moves forward, affirms that Clouzot's film is being cited.

The children were crows in the name of rascals. Their antics were possible cause for an unwarranted murder and revenge taken on a woman whom they feared and adulated. Where *Le Corbeau* ends with a woman in black who ambles away, *Les Mistons* finishes with the children gazing across a stone barrier at the woman in profile whom the spectator sees frontally. Clouzot's film is an admirable study of the mechanism of the scapegoat and view of the travails of life in France under Nazi surveillance. Shot in conditions of extreme censure, its latent allegory underwrites a political virtue of the first magnitude: although the town being represented seems outside of history, the events are local, contingent, and specific to the Occupation.

Would Truffaut's film betray a politics through its latent affiliation with Clouzot, a director for whom his feelings were complicated and difficult? The answer would be affirmative if the cause of Gérard's death is taken to be a sign of the relation that *Les Mistons* holds with history. In 1957 a strapping young man would leave a provincial town less to estivate than to complete military service in the Algerian War. Were he to die, he would die in the midst of the indelibly bleak affair of the tyranny that goes with the imposition of Western democracy upon people of beliefs other than those of the occupants. Truffaut tells of the relation of his film to contemporary events through the unlikely cause of Gérard's death. The accident can be the result of the mechanisms of writing—graphic and filmic—that mime what prevails in *Le Corbeau;* it may be an affirmation that an aesthetic cartography, a politique des auteurs, stands in the place of the tactics of survival and vindication in the postwar years and the as yet unfelt trauma of the Algerian War, or, too, it may be engaging in an *écriture de l'histoire* by which its politics are gleaned through the unnamed relation that the film is holding with *Le Corbeau*. In this way the spectator discerns a politics in an undercurrent that flows back to a traumatizing moment of collective and personal history. One film is folded into another. The effect brings forward a deeper political stake in what would seem otherwise to be a representation of prepubescent fantasy or a new mode of cinema.[9]

With coy or unconscious allusion to *Le Corbeau* we discern a film that writes a history of cinema within the geography of its narrative. The history tends to be originary by treating it on the same register as the origins of perception and the origins of the seventh art. In the narrative, the drama of the awakening of a child's erotic drives in the present time of the story is matched by retrospective flashes to cinema when it became conscious of its own visibility.

Old Films and New Worlds: An Allegory

The film thus reconceives human space and time by means of a technology that Truffaut, as shown in his words about his dialogue with Jean Malige, wishes to "liberate" from the grasp of the tradition of textual quality and artistic elegance.

The voiceover of an older narrator, clearly a writer of an established tradition, tells of a nascent, indeed "virginal" eros where the image-track "writes" a visual text of its own signature with volleys of tracking shots and swish-pans which appear to be of a time and space beyond what the voice can describe. Something immediate and vibrant is brought forward. A major undercurrent of the film and of the time of *Les Mistons* is the flow and character of its writing, a writing inscribed upon a latent map of the French nation. The film engages a program of a new esperanto, a *ciné-écriture* crafted from a multitude of sources. By way of control and of chance it accedes to a hieroglyphics, to a new "language of the gods" by means of the art of adaptation, a grafting of allusions to and a staging of other films, in which unforeseen connections are made and a cinematic—but visually and linguistically French—synesthesia is born. From another angle it can be said that *Les Mistons* is crafted to have secrets circulate in its visual and aural texture. These enigmas or riddles constitute not only the delphic matter of the film, its mystery and symbolic magic, but also the reverie of children and their childhood. They are at once witness and blind to the hieroglyphics of which they are analphabetic or even arcadian readers.

From its very first shots *Les Mistons* betrays a new sense of cartography through the marriage of mapping to cinema. A geographical space is plotted and espoused in the narrative in which children seem to be orphans of the world they inhabit. Where the children are bereft of familial ties (they never return home and, if they have parents, they are Gérard and Bernadette), they belong to a national space marked through monuments, landscapes, and postcard images. Such is the role of the Pont du Gard in the political geography of Truffaut's film, in which the aqueduct figures in the décor of the film in a manner comparable to the way it had in early modern cosmographies and atlases. The monument becomes a character, even a vestige of bygone ancestors and parents, which pulls both the children and the film into a project of identification with a national tradition. The film exhumes the past by revisiting old edifices; the movement of the camera, following Bernadette who could be a prosopopy of France or even an avatar of *La Marianne,* turns an inherited place into a living space. She re-draws a topography with the tracks she traces with her bicycle on the landscape of the Midi.

The geography tends to alter some of our received ideas about the politique des auteurs. For Truffaut the short film may have been both an experiment and a total, autonomous work, what he had proclaimed to be an "act of love" projected through the children and their fetish-objects. If politics are defined as the "art of the possible," the film invites its readers to fathom a cinema rejuvenated through new modes of writing. On the one hand, the narration of *Les Mistons* attests to what Truffaut stated five years later. "In fact, I believe that a film ought not to innovate everywhere at once. In a new film there needs to be something that ties it to classical cinema: the simplicity or the force of the subject, the presence of a star or other things. You get the feeling that many films were shot in a kind of unconsciousness."[10] *Les Mistons* counts among those films shot "in a kind of unconsciousness." On the other hand, the same state of being is a politics of revision and erasure which, like *film noir* not long before, had been put forward as a virtue: the fate that befalls Gérard is caused by what is *written* of him in a newspaper and, indirectly by the black magic of the children's writing. The death is an accident lacking an obvious historical cause but mantled in the secret of another, namely, through allusion to *Le Corbeau,* the relation of the eternal children and youth of the film to the German occupation of France. The film mystically erases is own erasure by alluding to what it cannot make explicit or else makes clear in presenting juveniles oblivious to what they are acting out.

The children are unaware of a future that might conscript them to battle not with a mysterious female but with Algerian nationals in a sordid colonial war. The magical erasure of collective history is paralleled by that of the perplexity over the nation, its past, and events in which the filmmaker was born. In demolishing a *cinema de qualité* Truffaut, wearing the hat of a critic, taps into broader disquiet about an aesthetics of fascism coloring his cinephilia. Prior to shooting *Les Mistons,* Truffaut had pitted himself against the proponents of the *film à these.* His detractors, defenders of "traditional" cinema, denounced him in the name of art for art's sake and egocentrism running contrary to the collective task of the Liberation to clean France of the mess of the war years. The author of "A Certain Tendency of French Cinema" had praised pro-Nazi Robert Brasillach for having died for principles that led him to be executed. And Lucien Rébatet, virulent anti-Semite, film critic, and author, lauded Truffaut's review in the right-wing *Arts* (November 4, 1955) that had recently torpedoed Jean Delannoy's *Chiens perdus sans collier.* Truffaut's independence of spirit made him comparable to the "hussards" of the French right, some of whom had been executed by firing squads while others had gone underground.

In *Les Mistons* the contradictions of a fascistic "liberation" of and by cinema are shown after the children act out their fears of the unknown in the local movie theater. As members of what would be at once a modern gang of prepubescent storm troopers and a traditional French charivari society they rail Gérard and Bernadette for exchanging kisses in the dark room where the public watches the projection of a love story that stars Jean-Claude Brialy. They exit merrily, regain the light of day, and rip from a kiosk the poster advertising Delannoy's feature. The defilement would be a cinematic analogue to the words Truffaut had written in his review.[11] In the space of the film their gesture is more complex than the words in newsprint. The children fetishize the film by "writing" it, that is, by ripping it off—in other words, also ripping off it—in a manner close to what is felt through the mute presence of Henri-Georges Clouzot.

Here and elsewhere double-edged actions of inscription and effacement belong to a deeper or "thicker" tradition that has origins in early modern topography.

The setting of *Les Mistons* is that where the French right has been strongest. From the start the camera uses emblematic monuments of the region to enhance children's virginal conflicts of anger and fear over the attractive menace of a divine female. A Roman coliseum and an aqueduct become the sites of daring cinematic experiment. They also stand for the triumph of *Gallia,* of France, and of French cinema from the ruins of a gloriously checkered history. The Pont du Gard is effective for the way, as Bernadette Lafont rides on its path, it leads the viewer to imagine a bridge extending between two worlds. One, that is old, is that of France itself and its tradition of architectural quality. The other, new, would be that of a juvenile cinema and future renewal through the Americas.

The allegory is cartographic. It belongs on the one hand to the *Querelle des anciens et des modernes* in which Truffaut is an active player, while on the other it reaches back to a geography of apocalypse that saw an older hemisphere giving way to a newer one. Montaigne, one of the sacred authors of the New Wave, had remarked in his essay on "Coaches" (1962, 886–87) that his world has just discovered another,

> si nouveau et si enfant qu'on luy aprend encore son a, b, c; il n'y a pas cinquante ans qu'il ne sçavoit ny lettres, ny pois, ny mesure, ny vestements, ny bleds, ny vignes. Il estoit encore tout nud au giron, et ne vivoit que des moyens de sa mere nourrice. Si nous concluons bien de notre fin . . ., cet autre monde ne faira qu'entrer en lumiere quand le nostre en sortira. L'univers tombera en paralisie; l'un membre sera perclus, l'autre en vigueur.

> so new and so childish that it is still being taught its a, b, c: barely fifty years ago it knew neither letters, weights, measures, clothing, wheat, nor wine. It was completely nude in the lap of its nourishing mother nature and lived only by her means. If we conclude well about our end . . ., this other world will only enter into light when ours will disappear. The universe will fall into paralysis; one member will be shriveled, the other in vigor.

Truffaut's juvenile geography is of the same allegorical imprint: it must relegate its own past, in which are found wartime memories of a markedly French cinema that seemed to be outside of historical time and space, to shadows while it celebrates the entry into the light of day of another cinema, nourished by the breasts of mother France and soon, those of a Marilynian America.

The Pont du Gard, a cherished monument in French atlases and their gazetteers, is cited to advance the cause for a new French cinema. In *Les Mistons* it figures, too, in a tender map, a pubescent cartography of affect of a tradition that reaches back to the French classical age. Before seeing how Truffaut builds on the material of his first film we are behooved to see how *La Carte du pays du Tendre* figures with modern maps in Louis Malle's *Les Amants.*

6

Michelin *Tendre:*
Les Amants

The road movie, as shown by the films studied in the name of the desperate journey in the fourth chapter, is a genre made for geography. Certainly the "tender
mapping" that Truffaut presents in his first film bears little resemblance to anything an American director would have conceived at the same time. And surely
Louis Malle's *Les Amants* (1958) would also be an unlikely candidate for inclusion in a gallery of road movies and roadmaps. In a peculiar way that viewers
might attribute to French cinematic traditions reaching back to Renoir and, before
him, Lumière and other directors who emphasize the plan-séquence, the two-
shot, and reduced montage for the sake of dialogue, the feature of 1958 might
be an inverse classic of the convention. Movement and hurried travel do not
mark *Les Amants* as they do the celebrated features that put starstruck lovers,
like the crazed couple of *Gun Crazy* (1949), on the road. To the contrary, a soft
and mellow tenor, enhanced by repeated quotations of Brahms heard both in and
out of frame, prevails. In this chapter the stake entails study of the cartography
of a movie inaugurating a sentimental journey in which affective images play a
decisive role in the narrative and spatial design of the feature.

Viewers and critics are correct to note that *Les Amants* is plotted through a relation it holds with the spatial and narrative articulations of *La Règle du jeu*. Much
of the film takes place within the rooms and corridors of a château that bears
resemblance to the residence in Solognes owned by the Marquis de la Chesnaye.
Malle continually uses deep focus to depict characters moving in and through hall-
ways or vestibules. The camera slowly pans across the space of drawing rooms,
a salon, and a broad spiral stairway in a fashion that almost requires spectators

to compare what they are seeing with memories of camera movements in the classic feature of 1939. That Gaston Modot, the polished actor who had played Schumacher, the Marquis's gamekeeper in *La Règle du jeu,* appears as the butler and domestic in the château of Malle's film, invites greater comparison of the one and the other. Both films treat of characters confined to closed spaces— social, amorous, historical, and even geographical—from which exit is impossible. In each the protagonists seek an aperture of escape, a *point de fuite,* from which no evasion is possible, where *il n'y a point de fuite.* In both films the mores of contemporary times are seen through the filter of pre-Revolutionary France. Renoir wrote his screenplay in homage to Beaumarchais's *Mariage de Figaro,* a play that anticipated and to a degree explained the events of 1789, perhaps in order to have *La Règle du jeu* uncannily embody the Sitzkrieg and convey a Maginot mentality that anticipates the coming of the Second World War.

A Book and a Movie

In *Les Amants* director Louis Malle obtains the collaboration of Louise de Vilmorin to redraw the narrative of a short tale that Vivant Denon wrote in the pre-Revolutionary years under the title *Point de lendemain* (roughly translated as "No Tomorrow on the Horizon").[1] It, too, deals with vanishing points in its representation of triangulated love and female subjectivity in postwar France. In Malle's adaptation Jeanne (Jeanne Moreau), the somewhat cloistered wife of Henri (Alain Cuny), a well-to-do publisher in Dijon, the owner of a château and a surrounding estate, finds solace in trips she takes to Paris to spend weekends with her friend Maggie (Judith Magre). She is seduced by the elegant world of polo, where she meets the elegant and sportive Raoul (J. L. de Villalonga), the man who, as the husband quickly discerns, becomes her lover. The husband casts his wife in the webbing of a scheme that will catch them unaware. He arranges a fishing party to which Maggie and Raoul are invited. They speed from Paris to Burgundy in a Jaguar while Jeanne, dissimulating her designs, drives alone from Paris to the château in her Peugeot 203. The vehicle breaks down along a road that runs along a canal. She flags a man driving a modest vehicle, a "people's" car— a Citroën 2CV or "Deux chevaux"—driven by a young man, Bernard (Jean-Marc Bory), who happens to be a student of philosophy driving to Burgundy to leave some books with his mentor. Bernard picks up Jeanne, who is impatient and fidgety, no doubt about being unable to play out a scheme that would allow her to spend time with Raoul under her husband's nose. Jeanne is literally beside herself when he takes a detour to his mentor's home in a small town in the Yonne or Auxerrois. Bernard finally delivers Jeanne to the château where the husband, bearing the manners of the country gentleman that he is, invites the stranger to have dinner and spend the night with them. Bernard occupies a solitary room. Jeanne refuses to see Raoul. She gathers herself by going downstairs to get water.

She passes by Bernard's room where he has been listening to a recording of Brahms. She goes out into the moonlight, back inside again, where she meets Bernard once again. They spend the wee hours of the morning in ecstasy. In the moonlight Bernard opens the fish cages by a dam at one end of the pond where a morning of fishing was scheduled to take place.

Having decided to leave with Bernard for good, Jeanne returns to the château to get a few belongings. She first encounters Maggie inside the château, and then her husband just on the outside, before she takes off with Bernard. They putter off in the 2CV (the slow whir of its transmission having affective charge in the memory of drivers having driven the popular vehicle) as Jeanne's voice speaks in the past tense, off, of the doubts and fears precipitated by the decision she has taken. Just before the end they stop to have a cup of coffee inside a roadside café where, unfolding what appears to be a Michelin roadmap, they plot their future itinerary. The couple returns to the car that the camera records slowly moving forward on a country road and away from the environs of the lives they had been living. The music of Brahms that had inaugurated the film in the sequence of credits, heard at capital points throughout the narrative, now turns the conclusion toward a new and uncertain future.

Maps enter the film at three distinct junctures. First and most famously, the title and credits, in white characters, dissolve into one another over an image of Mademoiselle de Scudéry's *Carte du pays de Tendre;* the celebrated allegorical map had accompanied *Clélie,* the ample novel of her signature that had been a bible for the Précieux in the early and middle years of the seventeenth century.[2] It had been conceivably drawn in opposition to the military cartography, inaugurated by neo-Cartesian engineers under kings from Henry IV up to Louis XIV. Named *ingénieurs du roi,* these cartographers, as we noted in chapter 2, set about redrawing the defensive lines of the nation and the design of fortresses in a period when new modes of artillery were changing the ways of waging war (Buisseret 1964). Mademoiselle de Scudéry's *Carte du pays de Tendre* of 1654 brings the viewer back to the world of the *salon* and a space that women had crafted for themselves, quite possibly in opposition to the masculine world of the engineer and soldier.[3] For viewers nourished on French literature the very map, reminiscent of Molière's groundbreaking one-act satire, *Les Précieuses ridicules* (1659) in which men play a trick on two women who mime the language of sentiment, becomes something other than that for which it stood.[4] In *Les Amants* the Carte du Tendre is anything but a comical object. With an uncanny affective valence the map melds into the music of Brahms (Opus 18, String Sextet 1 in B-flat Major) and comes forward to pervade the visual field in much of the film.

The presence of the map of the Pays du Tendre in the film stands in strong contrast to two other principal cartographic moments. One takes place when Jeanne, confused and in turmoil, descends in the middle of the night to drink some water. Hearing Brahms being played on the turntable—the same that accompanied the image of the map in the credits—in the room where Bernard is reading, she leaves her bedroom. As if both seduced and bothered by what she hears, Jeanne crosses the space of a room crammed with objects—a sort of *Wunderkammer*—in which a folio atlas is opened. She moves by, closing it, as if signaling that the duplication of one spatial depiction of a small scale within the closed confines of the room and the château might be too much to bear: better, it is implied, that the monumental projects of classical France, such as Guillaume Blaeu's *Grand Atlas* (1647), a hefty tome of the kind that seems to be what she closes, be forgotten.

The other sequence is of two parts. In a first section Bernard and Jeanne are in the 2CV en route to the château. The couple needs to consult a map in order to find their way to Dijon and Henri's regal residence. The map is unfolded but not really heeded or studied in the heat of the moment. At the end of the film the couple pours over the same roadmap that they unfold on the table of a café where they stop to get their bearings after having taken leave of the château.

"Attention au départ"

Because of its association with the music of Brahms the "Carte du Tendre" seems omnipresent. It provides multiple views of the roads that will be taken, and it also infuses the uncommon spatial texture of the film in general. More radically, the music brings a cartographic presence to the way the camera records the landscape. One moment, early in the film, is crucial. Jeanne has just returned to the château from one of her first trips to Paris. She enters the vestibule of the château (much as had Christine in walking on a floor paved with black-and-white tiles in *La Règle du jeu* [Curchod 1998, 106–15]), where she meets the maid who brings forward Jeanne's young daughter. The mother salutes her daughter and their keeper before entering into a living room where Henri is seated, pensive, looking at a fire that crackles in the fireplace. Happy to see her, but reserved and somewhat suspicious, he follows her movements in the way that the camera pans from left to right (and she enters) and then right to left (as she moves toward the fireplace behind the sofa where he husband is seated. The camera takes note of a fairly diminutive landscape painting in which a road cuts over a field to the right and by a wooded space to the left. The painting becomes visible as the camera holds on the couple in a plan-séquence in which Henri inspects his wife with his eyes, remarking by way of what might be a crocodile's compliment, "Tu deviens tendre" (the English subtitle reads, "You're affectionate," but Henri's words are slurred enough to confuse "tu deviens tendre" [you are becoming affectionate] with "tu viens tendre" [you come or arrive with an affectionate or tender air]). Jeanne makes no definitive answer, ostensibly ruminating on what he might mean or on the rhetoric of a ruse that would be one step ahead of one of her own.

All of a sudden "Tendre," the word that the map had called to every viewer's mind in the credits, is folded both into the narrative and the field of the image.

In Henri's voice it is a tender trap. Jeanne is discovering tenderness in a new and amorous longing for a man whose identity Henri will seek to discern, but the adverb resounding in the inner ear of the protagonist turns into the very landscape of the painting that hangs on the wall. The landscape becomes a variant of the *précieux* map that in itself had been a landscape, an estate map, or a map destined to foster commerce and trade in the tradition of Georg Braun and Franz Hogenburg.[5] The painting that we are almost unconsciously asked to associate with the map becomes a point of attraction and of vanishment in the shot itself. The camera keeps the picture in view long enough for the wandering eye to associate the "Inclination fleuve" that cuts a deep furrow through the center of Mademoiselle de Scudéry's map to the road on the landscape. Viewers familiar with the details of the credits usually note that the itinerary of the map tends to go from a town, "Tendre sur In[clination]," whose buildings erected on both sides of the river are connected by an arched bridge, to another, at the bottom, slightly larger but of similar aspect, called "Nouvelle Amitié" (New friendship). They might be tempted to see in the landscape the road replacing the river that leads from one agglomeration to another.

If not, at least the connection is obvious enough to blur the line of divide between the credits and the field of the image. The picture is placed in the frame in order to spot a vanishing space that refuses to vanish. *Point de lendemain, point de fuite:* the picture is placed at the center of the shot much as "Tendre sur Inclination" is placed at a point where sightlines converge on Scudéry's creation.[6] Yet the picture cues an *optical itinerary* by which spectators can see themselves wandering about the shot itself, moving left and right with Jeanne Moreau, and into and through the words as they are spoken and heard both tenderly and strategically. The camera seems to be refashioning Renoir's tendency to shoot partial views of greater wholes that cannot be discerned. The depth of field that had been Renoir's signature is also Malle's, but now the picture-as-map, seen in the broad horizon of cinemascope, flattens the image and requires the eye to "unfold" its constituent surfaces as it might a roadmap that is being opened and extended in full view.

The film is composed of closed spaces whose implicit totalities are defined by allusion to those in Renoir and other classical films. The episodes of the narrative are determined by spatial closures out of which the protagonist and the film itself seek an exit. How to find a way out of Renoir's world is an issue doubled by that of the protagonist in the repeated instances where she would like to "drive" (but not "crash") out of a tender prison. Jeanne spends an evening in Paris with Raoul. They consume the first hours amusing themselves in an amusement park. Raoul takes her to the shooting gallery where she hits the bull's eye after the paramour had shown her how to aim and fire. Allusion to the hunting sequence of *La Règle du jeu* is clear, but less obvious is the way the sequence dissolves into the couple's entry into the flying car of a newly fashioned merry-go-round.

The device is a wheel whose spokes carry miniature cars that levitate and descend up and down as the mechanism turns counter-clockwise. In a medium shot Raoul gallantly places Jeanne in one of the two seats of the miniature vehicle before he climbs in and sits next to her. She adjusts a veil over her head while Raoul, sporting his bow-tie and tuxedo as the voice-off, heard from a megaphone, intones, "Attention au départ." The departure and takeoff are effortless. The six ensuing shots crosscut three medium close-ups of the couple in the driver's seat, looking about the flicker of moving lights and gently clasping and fondling each other, with long shots of the mechanical motion of merry-go-round from the "takeoff" to the "landing." At one point the camera, set on Raoul and Jeanne, drops slightly to show the headlights of the car, implying that they are in a toy-version of the vehicle that will later be cause for everyone's change in fortune. As the sequence unfolds, the characters are not seen descending or exiting but, in the smooth transitions of the editing, they dissolve into the following sequence in a dance hall where they bob up and down to the rhythm of a mechanical mambo.

The sequence moves too quickly to allude to the claustrophobic ending of Julien Duvivier's *Panique* (1946), in which two ill-fated and evil lovers seek exit from the crimes by taking refuge on a merry-go-round. No indication of is made of an exit from the machine. But in the midst of the music lingers the voice-off, "Attention au depart." A call is made on the part of the film to the spectator and the characters to take heed or be careful in watching the film from the beginning. Malle elides the caution with the words Raoul whispers into Jeanne's eyes in the sequence that follows. "Je voudrais tellement te rendre heureuse [I so much want to make you happy]" barely drifts over the music while Jeanne, voice-in but also ostensibly off, says calmly that she is happy, to which Raoul responds with an unconscious explanation of the spatial and temporal construction of the film. "Notre vie n'est faite que de moments . . . c'est toute une vie avec toi que je voudrais [Our life is made only of moments . . . I want a whole life with you]." If Raoul's words have any weight in the midst of the levitation, he wants their lives to conform to the definition of an *image* or of an *event* in the manner that André Bazin had defined them: an epiphany, a momentary but totalizing grasp of one's space and place in the world in which the relation of the individual to a broader geography is felt in the duration of an instant.

Attention au départ: After Henri imposes the plan in which he will bring the suspected players of the tryst to his domain for a weekend of fishing, an establishing shot (that immediately recalls the first shot of the film) puts Raoul on his dark horse in the middle ground. He rides in a circle before Jeanne arrives in a white car, deep in the background. The camera cuts to Jeanne stopping her car, opening the door, exiting, coming forward to meet Raoul on horseback, and announcing, "Je pars . . . je m'en vais [I'm leaving, I'm off]." A remarkable dissolve ends the sequence when Jeanne, her head posed against Raoul's thigh, his right hand holding the end of the polo club and two reins drawn behind her, looks off and away (in exactly the way that Geneviève de Marrast had done in *La Règle du jeu* [Curchod 1998, 161]). She contemplates love with Raoul as a perilous venture at the very instant her face blends into a roadscape: doubled for a flash in the same shot, she is in the foreground, in close-up, but also in the distance, speeding toward the camera as it recedes along the way. The two straps of Raoul's club seem to be white lines painted on the edge of the road that runs parallel, we discover as it unwinds, to a canal.

The "departure" leads, of course, to the breakdown that becomes a new point of departure. The car rolls into what seems to be a map-like picture of the bend of the road and the canal whose sides are decorated with pylons of trees, bar-like shapes reflected in the calm water to lend a loosely gridded aspect to the frame and bring forward memories of similar shapes in the first shot, but also another film shot along inner waterways, in the closed spaces of Jean Vigo's *L'Atalante* (1934). The shot becomes a tableau-sequence when it laterally reframes itself, moving left to display the road and hillside behind Jeanne's face, which registers disbelief when a jalopy (filled with locals of a lower class) goes by, waving but not stopping to help her. Car and Carte du Tendre begin to mesh in the long take that follows, in which Jeanne fidgets and tosses a cigarette in the water (as had Henri at the end of Renoir's *Une partie de campagne,* 1936) before another jalopy—a 2CV, a *deux chevaux*—comes into frame from an area behind the bend in the road and canal, thus beginning a new departure.

The Gleaner and the Grease Monkey

After the student has driven Jeanne to a local garage Jeanne enters into the strange space of a garage, the fiefdom of a mechanic and his grease monkey. A man repairing a bicycle wheel (from an angle that is identical to the gigantic water wheel by which the lovers will walk later in the night) is deaf to her entreaties while the boss, speaking in a thick Burgundian accent, tells her that her words cannot be heard. He asks her what kind of car she has, and she responds that her Peugeot 203 "is not for him." As he informs her that his is a "Renault" garage, the student enters the frame with a map in his hands, asking her if she doesn't need his assistance any more (the deaf mechanic tells her where she can find a telephone). In the background he stares down at the guidebook. He opens it and lets his hand point both at the page and, in the greater space of the shot, at Jeanne's body, in the foreground, which his index finger almost caresses. The camera pans right to follow Jeanne en route to the telephone on the wall. The young man's voice utters (as Jeanne approaches the phone, occluding him and thus, in the unconscious register of the film, uttering in her thoughts what he says, now off, to the Burgundian repairman who is occupied with repairing the tow truck): "Quelle est la meilleure route pour aller à Montbard d'ici? [What is the best way to get to Montbard from here?]" As she dials and asks for "Dijon 413" the Burgundian is in the background, his rotund back facing the viewer while muttering some directions, arched over a grille, he plumbs the depths of the motor of a Renault. The camera reframes the space of the garage in the plan-séquence. Jeanne's rescuer remains in the background before he takes leave, kindly thanking the boss for the directions, while Jeanne awaits word from the receiver that she holds in her left hand. She annuls the call, hangs up, and runs to catch the young man who has just entered a sunlit area where his car is parked. In the next shot (taken from an angle perpendicular to the view of the inside of the garage), Jeanne trots toward the Citroën, seen from the back, on whose corrugated bonnet the young man consults his map and his guide. As they depart he announces that he must stop in Montbard to deliver books to a former professor. The shot, taken from the back of the car (the camera no doubt mounted on a tripod in the open trunk), registers the forward movement before it dissolves to a classic take of the couple looking forward from behind the windshield as the space in the background now slowly recedes. When Jeanne examines herself with a pocket mirror, it is clear that a play of reflections underscores the ambiguity of a movement backward countered by a movement forward in the physical and affective space. A first sign of a real departure is given when the sign of the place-name of the village (seen on the right) recedes while the car advances. The couple seems to be moving into a new world underlined by the memory of the map seen in the credits, especially insofar, in view of Jeanne's self-involved presence, as the young man's defensively ironic demeanor seems to be anything but *tender*.

They drive into the countryside. The road they take surely reproduces the central conduit of the Carte du Tendre, except now the car is seen moving on a landscape that is indeed a map whose elements of force and doubt are shown in the slight reversal or shifts in itinerary. In these takes the memory of the map in the countryside turns what would be nothing more than the shot of a car-driving-down-a-country-road into a far more complex relation of sensibility and perception of a path or itinerary.[7]

Pleats and Folds

Spaces open and close much in the way that the roads move back and ahead. They are illuminated and darkened, walked and driven through, and sometimes discovered as *terrae incognitae*. The interlude with Bernard that brings Jeanne out of the château and into the night seems to be an entry into a painting of Magritte or Delvaux. As Jeanne and Bernard cross fields and hedgerows bathed in moonlight (or day-for-night) and disappear into wooded lairs, they retrace the paths taken by starstruck lovers not only in Denon's pre-Revolutionary fiction but also along the shores of the Lignon in Honoré de D'Urfé's *L'Astrée* and in the thick foliage of the paintings of Poussin.[8] "Est-ce un pays que vous avez inventé [Is it a country that you've invented]," Jeanne asks while swaying in her lover's arms, before she asserts, "pour que je m'y perde [so that I'll get lost in it]." The landscape in which she loses her bearings needs to be situated. She does not wish to go off the map but to find new and other places within the territories it represents.[9]

They soon climb into a skiff that embraces their enlaced bodies and drift downstream to the outstretched trunk of a weeping willow where they moor the craft before descending to the *terra firma*. The exit from the boat is enveloped in the memory of the final sequences of *Une partie de campagne,* in which Henri and Henriette first descended from a skiff moored by a willow tree in broad daylight to find the imaginary "home" in the woods in which they furtively lost themselves in love—before, on a second trip to the same spot, the forlorn lover opened a melancholic wound in revisiting the place to which Henriette had just repaired with her hapless husband in order to dream of her discovery of love with Henri. The pathos of Renoir's film comes forward as if to mark the delicate urgency of the instant and to describe a space of another film in which the lovers have become unmoored. The fragility of the idyll is enhanced by the allusion to Renoir's short feature; yet, at the same time, Jeanne and her paramour put their feet on the ground and move forward. They steer their way through the memory of Renoir's rewriting of Guy de Maupassant's tale. When the lovers return to the land, they regress to reminiscence of the château de Solognes in *La Règle du jeu* from whose interior, in Renoir, any egress (except for that of the director in the role of Octave) was shown to be impossible (Curchod 1998, 266–67). By the walls of the edifice, adjacent to the mottled bark of the flaky trunk of a plane tree and the black spots on the hide of a white Dalmatian that guards the periphery— the patches of wood and the dog resembling islands and hills of a topographic map—Bernard utters, as if he were remembering the stakes of Renoir's closed spaces, "Je ne veux pas monter dans le château. Allons-nous en [I don't want to go back into the castle. Let's get out of here]."

How to find a way out of an overly plotted territory of film, love, and idyll becomes the stake of the final sequences. A map helps the lovers in their quest to find new and other spaces, but only after a tender geography of love intervenes. Brahms accompanies the couple in their act of love. The bars of music continue to cue memory-images of the Carte du Tendre as the camera contrasts Jeanne supine, her bare flesh and head in profile against a background of crumpled sheets. The camera tilts down along her arm and stops to display her open hand against a line of dots sewn into the bedspread. A broken line of imaginary places on the bed leads to the lifeline in the palm of her hand, the wrinkles suddenly melding with those of the sheet on which it is posed. Soon she rolls over and with an index finger writes a text or the lines of an itinerary on the back of her lover. They clothe themselves in bathrobes and put towels over their faces in order both to refer to Magritte's paintings of lovers "wrapped" in cloth and, it seems, to distinguish between faces and folds of fabric that would be molded to the hills and valleys of their faces.

Their play with towels and diaphanous scarves is capped at the point where the departure is suddenly realized. In profile, in a medium close-up Jeanne adjusts a veil about her head as the camera holds on a fan framed on the wall behind and between the couple who stare at each other. She has just walked by a bed whose elevated stead is decorated with diapered folds of fabric erected from a false baldachin. Its bends contrast the pleats of the fan, flattened to emphasize a painted floral pattern that in turn draws attention to the bends and twists of the scarf she plies about her neck. Its paisley pattern rhymes, as it were, with the floral design of the wallpaper in the room she has just exited (and to which she will soon return). The husband enters from the right, mocks Jeanne in repeating her own words in a whisper, "dépêche-toi [hurry up]," as the camera follows her exit into the next room where Bernard arranges himself in front of a mirror. She arrives and looks into it: the mirror image shows Jeanne's face in its beauty, while the backside is an amorphous mass of folded fabric. In the allegory of the film it would be said that one side is the uncertain "map" produced from the contact of the fabric on the contour of the heroine's head and the other the face and gaze that look anxiously both backward and ahead.

The fan—an *éventail,* the word accreted in the image for French viewers—and its flattened folds announce an "event" of the departure, the virtual unfolding of the space of the film from an allusion to Mallarmé's poetry of folds that constitute vital and fugacious *events.*[10] The sequence, punctuated by the words, "il faut partir [we've got to go]," "sortons d'ici [let's get out of here]," "partons [let's leave]," is now and again shot in a mirror, in total reflection that draws attention not only to infinite specularity—to something totally imaginary—but also to the possibility of real spaces out of frame.[11] The latter are reflected on the front of the windshield of the 2CV as it leaves the château in view of the four characters— Maggie, Raoul, Coudray (Modot), and the husband—who, all immobile, watch it drive away. A long take (no doubt a matte shot) in medium close-up of the couple, in profile, looking right, at the windshield and what lies beyond, but also at the right side of the frame, registers the fear, doubt, and pleasure the lovers evince at a moment resembling any of many scenes of departure—Rinaldo and Armida of Ariosto's *Orlando furioso* among others—in elegiac literature. Jeanne's headdress wafts in the air in a way that makes the wind and breeze an element of the event of departure and commencement. "Où allons-nous? [Where are we going?]," utters Bernard who looks ahead and quickly turns his head toward and away from Jeanne, who responds, "Allons n'importe où . . . j'irai partout avec toi [Let's go anywhere, I'll go everywhere with you]."

A contrary movement on the image track no sooner counters her words and the drift of her voice affirming that they go forward. After she speaks, the direction of their movement reverses. She raises her right hand to look in the mirror in such a way that it is impossible to know whether she looks at herself (as she would have in the early stages of the film, at the moment of her defensively narcissistic plenitude in respect to her husband and their insufferable marriage) or at the landscape that would be receding in the distance (so that doubts and second thoughts about the departure would come forward while the landscape disappears). In all events the raised hand is sign of a continuity that links this shot to what follows: the shot turns on its axis by 180 degrees by displaying the couple in profile from the window of the door on the driver's side. Her left hand is now poised on the opposite side of the frame and such that the cut is shown to be at once visible and seamless.[12]

They now look from right to left, apparently toward a future that had just been "past" on the left side of the frame. Jeanne puts her hand to her mouth as if to silence the words just uttered or to turn the film into an emblem or a "mute speaker" in which what is seen "speaks" as much as what is heard.[13] Bernard raises his hand to embrace hers (her wedding ring shines) that holds the mirror, and he pulls it to his cheek to affirm his affection while she closes her eyelids and covers her left eye with her hand in a hieroglyphic gesture that signifies the

Figure 29. *Les Amants* (1959): In place of a Carte du Tendre, the lovers plot their departure to unknown places over a Michelin roadmap. The distortion is due to the anamorphic lens through which the film was shot.

grief of inward vision, which Bernard underlines when he states that he would like to see her (while he must keep his eyes glued to the road ahead). The visual dialectic holds until the car (and the lateral movement of the landscape that passes from left to right) goes by the countryside while a rooster crows three times (the biblical innuendo clearly marked in the insistent resonance of the cockle-doodle-doo) before the vehicle comes to a halt in front of what seems to be a blank space or a wall. Three signs (one a restaurateur's license and the other a panel of a telephone booth) indicate they have arrived at a roadside café. Jeanne, still coiffed in her silken scarf, responds to Bernard's words, "J'ai faim. On s'arrête? [I'm hungry. Shall we stop?]." She looks left and right, her nose almost caressing a small poster in the background, beyond the frame of the window of the car door, placed on a windowpane, that advertises "Gitane" [Gypsy] cigarettes. In a small blue rectangle the silhouette of a gyrating woman in a still image serves as a legend to the shot and its implicit narration. Has Jeanne become a gypsy after leaving her husband and their daughter? Is she now a rootless nomad or any of the few figures from the third world glimpsed now and again in the film? Or does the emblem merely tie a text or a title and an image to the silent narration of the shot, thus conferring upon it a tension of image and language that may not have been so visible up to now? If the answer to the question is affirmative, the cartographic impulse of the camera is clear.

The Michelin Map after *La Carte du Tendre*

In a barely noticeable but uncharacteristic gesture Bernard exits from her side of the car, no doubt in order not to bump into the camera that peers through the window on his side and to keep the image of the dancing gypsy between them as they exit and enter the café. A dissolve brings the couple to a table. In the overlapping of the two shots the side window of the car draws a frame around the pair seated at a table, a cup of coffee before them, and what is surely, because of its oblong format, a regional Michelin map (perhaps of northwestern Burgundy) extended over its surface as if it were a tablecloth. They look down while, in the space of the dissolve, the three signs are retinally suspended in the image: the "cabine télé-phonique" is set over a barkeep in the background, the restaurateur's license over Jeanne's face, and the Gitanes poster to her left. It melds into a mirror that reflects the horizontal line of the zinc surface of the bar and the backside of her head as she smiles, seated next to Bernard who gazes down at the map. A local character wearing a beret passes in front of them from right to left. The camera dollies forward into medium close-up to register Jeanne's doubt and lingering perplexity— as well as her own beauty—as she looks at herself in the mirror before looking back at the map, and at Bernard, before he notices the presence of sunshine. The light prompts another departure now begun after the couple has studied the map.

The last sequence of the film is bound to the image of the Carte du Tendre.

When the couple is again seated in the car and looks ahead through the windshield (seen from a three-quarter angle) the music of Brahms returns. Jeanne's voice-off throws the time of the episode into limbo: "Ils partaient pour un long voyage dont ils connaissaient les incertitudes [They were leaving on a long journey of whose uncertainties they were well aware]." The voice-off continues as the car rolls. "Déja à l'heure dangereuse du petit matin, Jeanne avait douté d'elle. Elle avait peur, mais elle ne regrettait rien [Already, at the dangerous hour of dawn Jeanne had doubts about herself. She was afraid but held no regrets]." The camera pulls away from the car as she reconstructs in the third person the ambivalence and doubt of that moment in her life. Emerging into view is a landscape under a partly cloudy sky that is marked by a sign on the roadside (to the right) indicating "Vandenesse," the little burg where they had stopped to sip a cup of coffee and get their bearings. It is the first of several signs that pass by. After it recedes, the car passes a stout white horse, a farm animal that would draw a plow, inattentive to the passing vehicle, which calmly grazes by the roadside. It disappears and to the left emerges the tower of a church piercing the broad expanse of the sky. The camera slowly pulls farther away and directly in front of the moving car. The long take of the shot recovers a landscape divided by the road but now marked by a visual trajectory that moves from the converging lines of the road to the church and upwards along those of its spire. Where the eyes of the personages look forward and are doubled by the headlights the viewer is tempted look into the landscape that recalls the bird's-eye view of the map.

The ambivalence of the moment is conveyed in a spatial dynamic by which the pull to go forward wins over the view that would be led into the picturesque background. Yet the lingering figures of the road sign, horse, and church cannot fail to bring forward another relation, no less dynamic, through allusion to the end of Robert Bresson's *Journal d'un curé de campagne* (1950), a film literally framed by two road signs. It begins with a tracking shot from a vehicle that enters a country town called "Ambricourt" (in the Boulonnais) and ends, after the excruciatingly painful death of the young priest (who succumbs to stomach cancer) with a shot that passes by the road sign indicating that the traveler is exiting the town. On the sign is printed "Ambricourt," but now, in the longstanding tradition of semaphores on French roads and highways, the toponym indicates that the traveler is leaving the place whose name is struck through by a red diagonal line. Ambricourt is put "sous rature" or under erasure. In Bresson's adaptation of Georges Bernanos's novel, what would have been a priest's written representation of the life and times of the inhabitants of the little village as he encountered and gave himself—thus bringing salvation—to them is called in question. The project for a representation both of the contents of the novel and the film as unmediated or virginal image is subverted.

At the conclusion of Malle's film it is clear that we are both *in* and *outside* of a religious curfew or pallor cast over the narrative and geographic space of

Denon's tale. The church in the background, its presence announced by the three crows of the rooster less than a minute before, recedes even though it is part of a configuration of vanishing points that persist in the image and in the story (aptly titled *Point de lendemain*). The church seems present to underscore the dangers of the itinerary made on the map. A transgression is made and is not made. Jeanne cuts through the barriers of an unwanted situation, but she is also simply on the road that leads ahead. The couple drives on a secular path of the kind, as any good edition of the *Michelin vert* would indicate, engineers in pre-Revolutionary France had built throughout the French provinces.[14]

The dialogue with Bresson leads further because in *Les Amants* the road sign marked "Vandenesse" is not barred by a line indicating exit, termination, or departure. The town disappears, but it is not stricken from the map of the movie. The name is left open and seems to dissolve into the landscape and clouds above. André Bazin astutely observed that in Bresson's version of the *Journal,* textual matter, such as a geographic marker, is seen not in order to lend credibility to the film, but to call it in question.

Figure 30. *Les Amants:* The lovers depart in a Deux Chevaux (2CV) down a road from Vandenesse in a Burgundian landscape drawn over the memory of the Carte du Tendre.

The most moving moments of the film are rightly those in which the text is supposed to say exactly the same thing as the image, but because it says so in a different way. In fact the sound is never present to complete the event seen: it reinforces it and multiplies it as does a violin's resonating box the vibrations of its cords. And even this metaphor is wanting in dialectics because it is less a resonance than the mind perceiving a gap like that of a color which is not superimposed on a drawing. And in this fringe the event liberates its meaning. It is because the film is entirely built over this relation that the image, especially toward the end, reaches such a degree of emotional power. (1999, 123)

In the final sequence of *Les Amants* "Vandenesse" disappears into the past but does not become oblivion. An ambiguous marker, like the figure of the gypsy on the Gitanes poster or the itinerary to and from "Tendre" and "Nouvelle Amitié" on the Carte du Tendre, the toponym signals movement that can be taken in various directions. In its name the viewer is tempted to hear Brahms's violins by way of the metaphor Bazin coins to describe the end of *Journal d'un curé de campagne*. Malle literalizes the critic's metaphor through the music accompanying the tracking shot of the car as it drives forward along the Burgundian road. The emotive power of Malle's film is heard in the resonant notes of the violin, to be sure, but also in the automotive whir, a sort of white noise, of the little engine that powers Bernard's "deux chevaux." The car containing the two lovers literally doubles or passes the single horse grazing by the shoulder of the road.

The film becomes what in the introduction was called a cartographic "diagram" because it does not lead to a terminus or sum up a state of things past. Malle chooses not to let the end-credit, "Fin," emerge from the landscape in a dissolve. The word that would be a vanishing point is not in the field of the image for the reason perhaps that it would otherwise not have allowed the road sign, the horse, or the church to bear the allusive meanings that they might seem to have. Against a black background, the white letters of the last word of the film occlude any converging lines of perspective. The ending reverses, too, the excruciating effects of closure that Bresson brought to the *Journal*. Bresson's film terminates with the image of an indeterminate black cross on a white field. It becomes Bazin's clearest manifestation of the reality of pure cinema: "Just as Mallarmé's white page or Rimbaud's silence is a supreme state of language, the screen void of images and rendered to literature here marks the triumph of cinematic realism. On the white cloth of the screen the black cross, maladroit as that of a death-notice, the only visible trace left by the Assumption of the image, attests to what its reality merely stood for" (1999, 124).[15] Malle puts his word in white in smaller uppercase letters upon a black background that refuses to release any sign of development or closure. It is as matte and opaque as the map of the front-credits and of an enigma that a return to the Carte du Tendre would have severely obviated.

The viewer of Scudéry's map in both *Clélie* and *Les Amants* is led to wonder how it figures in the dialectic of city and country or Paris and province. Paris does not figure anywhere on the Carte du Tendre, nor are any of its memorable places ever seen in Malle's feature. Yet both the map and the film would have been most intensely seen and read in the capital. Would the effect have been one that displaces the country into the city? Would the sensuous landscapes and tracking shots along the roads of inner France, "la France profonde," have the impact of a new discovery or an unforeseen rural encounter? If we displace the ambiance of the pre-Revolutionary era as it is felt in Denon's tale into the landscape of *Les Amants* a new cartography comes into view. During much of the Enlightenment new roads were built to radiate, like spokes of a wheel, from the hub of Paris. A colonial mission was felt to inhere in roadbuilding, but at the same time there developed an "erotics of space," the discovery, rapt, and rape of what was taken to be a landscape of pleasure, novelty, and also of fear, that in order to be controlled was quickly taken to personify the feminine character of the nation (Certeau, Julia, and Revel 1975, 158).

Malle's camera rehearses the dialectic in plotting unforeseen itineraries through a countryside bristling with life. Accompanying the hum of Bernard's 2CV are warbling birds and a distant buzz of cicadas. Living and palpitating, the landscape is discovered in all of its tender vitality as the personages make their way through it. And so does the camera when it takes to the road and discovers what topographers and writers had found when they ventured, like new lovers, at once within and out of the confines of their cities and châteaus. If the nation is mapped as might the geography of the comely body of "France" the viewer wonders if indeed the navel would be Paris and the torso and appendages the provinces. In order to test the validity of such an unlikely allegory and prosopopoeia we can return to Truffaut, the director whose early cinema willfully confused its origins with the capital city, mother, and nation.

7

Paris Underground:
Les 400 coups

One of the first great maps of the Paris Métro is the "Nouveau Paris monumental: Itinéraire pratique de l'étranger dans Paris [New Monumental Paris: Practical Itinerary for the Foreigner in Paris]." An edition of 1903, published three years after the inauguration of the subway, offers in the same field a bird's-eye view of the city—set in verdant environs that lead to an undulating horizon under a blue sky that seems to stretch into Normandy and to the English channel on the horizon—and an ichnographic perspective of the streets and boulevards on which are traced, in red ink, bold and dashed lines of the network as it was either recently completed or under construction. The orientation resembles what is given on thousands of practical city-maps that have followed: the north, at the top, is capped by the Sacré-Coeur; the station at the Porte d'Orléans marks a southern limit; to the west the maze of alleys in the Bois de Boulogne offers fantasy of infinite promenades under leafy trees; to the east, at the Place de la Triomphe de la République, is found a sculpture celebrating secular France, that is protected by the moat-like circle of a subway line. A railway inside of a circular, crenelated wall of medieval aspect surrounds much of the city. Blocks of pink, denoting the inner space in the city, are cut by a broad swath of white lines indicating the width and length of Baron Haussmann's creation of boulevards. The Seine, colored in blue, bends its way through Paris, dividing the Right Bank (above) from a lesser mass of the Left Bank (below). The major monuments of the city are finely drawn and situated at their proper places. Yet their scale, of far greater proportion than that of the map itself, makes clear that the city is an assemblage of enduring monuments. Especially striking is the Eiffel Tower, seen in a bird's-eye perspective that towers over the city's churches, its Hôtel de Ville, and even the Arc de Triomphe. The map has been shown figuring in the iconography that accompanies René Clair's *Paris qui dort,* where it bears graphic testimony to the strategies deployed in touristic literature at the turn of the twentieth century. Monuments everywhere in the air and flesh of the city are a stone's throw or a few blocks from any of the new or projected stations. The effects of Haussmann's arteries of boulevards are shown in an ideal state, white and clean, without any congestion of traffic. Following the vision of the engineer Fulgence Bienvenüe, the layout also shows the viewer that subway riders exiting their stations are likely to be no more than 400 meters from a memorable site (or another subway station) in proximity. The treasures of Paris above the ground are linked to a mycelium of rails below. But above all, the subway map is made to correlate the new mode of public transport to the Eiffel Tower. The Tower had been a main attraction of the Exposition of 1889 and now, more recently, after the Exposition of 1900, the monument and the metro share the same measure.[1] The former, reaching into the sky, is countered by the latter, which burrows safely through the sewers and lower depths.

The "Quarrel"

This map serves as epigraph for a treatment of François Truffaut's first feature film, and not only because it presents the subway and the antiquities of Paris as myth, history, or ideology, but also, more immediately, because avatars of the same map are visible almost everywhere, it seems, in the travels of Antoine Doinel in and about Paris in *Les 400 coups.* Few cities and few films are riddled with maps as much as Paris in Truffaut's first full-length feature. Map and monuments appear wherever the pedestrian and the viewer happen to take stock of where they are. Their ubiquity at once seems to betray and confirm the design of the feature. From the opening shots Truffaut reaches back to the memories of 1889 and 1900 in which city-planners constructed the blueprint of a new, modern Paris, a city that would literally turn its past, its urban "tradition of quality" into the sublime ruins of history.

The ideal of a city Enlightened, of a city illuminated in eternal day belonged to the dreams of the Revolution and to the "moderns."[2] As René Clair made clear in *Paris qui dort,* the Eiffel Tower was a photogenic maze of girders buttressing a metallic illusion of infinite progress. In 1924 the director showed how much the monument delivered on its promise to be a beacon of the future in the everyday life of the present. When he shot images of humans scurrying through the maze or perching in the hard folds of the I-beams, we have seen that the Tower bore the trappings of a society of controlled incarceration. It had become at once a map on or from which any number of subjects could be located and, like the city at large, a prison in which they could be confined.

Perhaps because *Paris qui dort* sets forward much of what is inferred about the city, Truffaut makes no immediate reference to the early masterpiece. Yet the Tower is the first monument seen in the film. A series of eight tracking shots, each from the perspective of a different street on which the car rolls with its camera, displays what seems to be a cinematic cubism that rivals Robert Delaunay's many paintings of the structure. Because Truffaut had been known for his polemical pen before he began his directing career, the allusion to painting seems more immediate than to querulous literature and poetry. Apollinaire wrote at the beginning of "Zone" (in *Alcools,* 1913),

A la fin tu es las de ce monde ancien

After all you're tired of this old world

The *incipit* is an awakening, an admission of fatigue lingering from the nocturne of an earlier age and the onset of a new century, new expression, and new artistic experiment. Apollinaire turns the Tower into an emblem of a present instant anticipating an uncertain future or even, as the reader notes at the end, bodily dismemberment at the end of the day and of human time.[3] He inserts it into the tradition of the *Querelle des anciens et des modernes* in such a way that an allusion to Louis Blériot's feat of flying over the English Channel (in 1909) in a monoplane, taken to be an X drawn by the crossing of a wing and a fuselage, is made to resemble the Tower's chiastic design of crisscrossed beams. With Pope Pius X (the most Christian of Christians who had recently blessed the building), Blériot and Eiffel count among "moderns" who look forward and ahead. "Zone," Truffaut had no doubt intuited, mapped out some of the poetics that would inform his own cinema. It declared that poetry was everywhere, but especially in the street, in posters, newsprint, advertising, and paper ephemera of every kind. In paratactic lines without punctuation marks,

Tu lis les prospectus les catalogues les affiches qui chantent tout haut
Voilà la poésie ce matin et pour la prose il y a les journaux

You read ads catalogues posters that sing on a highest line
That's poetry this morning for prose the newspaper is fine

Poetry is born of writing *seen* in the texture of everyday life, of streams of impressions taken in the haptics of walking and ambulating in the world at large:

Les inscriptions des enseignes et des murailles
Les plaques les avis à la façon des perroquets criaillent

Inscriptions of signboards and on every wall
Posters plaques like parrots peck and call[4]

It may be that Truffaut plots his relation with the "moderns" in the ongoing *Querelle* through Apollinaire all the while the Tower serves as an icon or a memory-image of a style that puts writing into motion and exploits retinal suspension of graphic material in fields of images. The Tower also belongs to an adolescent geography very much related to what Truffaut had initiated in *Les Mistons* when he developed a style of filming landscapes and monuments in the province that in *Les 400 coups* he now exploits in an urban way.

Credits

Seen independently of the credits written over it, the initial shots of the Tower suggest that what follows may be a "monument" on a miniature scale that rivals with the one it records; that the iconic weight of the Tower sustains, like Atlas, the politics and polemics of Truffaut as critic and auteur; that, too, it belongs to a tradition of tourism, in which "seeing and visiting" a sacred building are comparable to that of movie-going. The Tower might also be taken to be, in the same glance, a figure on a literal and metaphorical map, at once a plan of Paris and that of the director's cinematic and quasi-autobiographical *Bildungsroman* and a "writing instrument" drawing and plotting the maps in and of the movie itself. It is arched skyward, its tip inking the sky in the way that, in the first shots of the narrative that follows the credits, the children in the classroom write the words of a dictée in paper pamphlets. In *Les Mistons* we saw that the children's confusion about their world—their attractions and hostilities—had been expressed through scenes of writing locating where they were in their own pubescence. Much of the same prevails in *Les 400 Coups,* but with the difference that the feature produces more and other maps that the director finds wherever writing becomes a function of its ambient social space.

Nine tracking shots of the Tower (in 158 seconds) include in the words of the first Anglo-American edition of the screenplay, "a variety of Parisian architecture" that "appears in the foreground" as the chords of strings and violins of the musical theme "continue throughout the sequence."[5] A straight cut separates the shots that bear, respectively, the title, leads, the secondary players (including many children), and the crew. The title is drawn in bold characters across the first shot that approaches the tower from a street (possibly the Rue Saint-Dominique) in the seventh *arrondissement* while the name of the director appears, also in white characters, in the groins of the four great metallic legs, below the dark underside of the first floor of the Tower when the car mounted with the camera drives along the Avenue Eiffel. The fifth shot, following a long track in which only the top of the Tower is glimpsed over warehouses and industrial buildings, catches the spire from the western shore of the Seine. The car moves from the Rue Franklin and by the Place du Trocadéro en route to the Avenue du Président-Wilson.

The smooth stone mass of the western wall of the new Trocadéro Palace momentarily eclipses the view of the Tower: the camera virtually caresses the site occupied by the Cinémathèque française since its inauguration (by Henri Langlois) in 1954. Suddenly the Tower is glimpsed through a network of branches of trees in the grey setting of winter. The median shot in the credit-sequence thus becomes a palimpsest of various "maps": those of Paris from all sides of the Tower, the perspectives on the Tower itself, the names of players known (Jean-Claude Brialy and Jeanne Moreau) and unknown (Jean-Pierre Léaud in his first film and bevies of children in their first and last) or of secret valence who might be known to cinephiles (Georges Flamand and Guy Decomble).[6] Other than in the pointed reference to the Cinémathèque, the city and the monument of the credits seem suspended in a timeless space. Even with the final intertitle dedicating the film to the memory of André Bazin, no narrative or historical tag (such as that of a car parked along an avenue) is tendered to indicate where the film is coming from or what exactly might follow.

Class Room and Map Room

The first interior shot, a tour-de-force of 56 seconds, moves from a medium close-up of a boy writing in a notebook on the wooden surface of a pupil's desk (with a sunken inkwell and a groove to hold pencils and pens) to a medium-long shot of the front of a classroom where a stern and dutiful teacher (Guy Decomble)—a modern Gradgrind—presides. The shot begins by recording the tracing of letters on paper. After the child lifts the cover of the desk to extract a Vargas-style pinup on a calendar, the camera follows the object as it passes surreptitiously (forward and right to left) through the hands of four boys before it reaches the future protagonist, Antoine Doinel (Jean-Pierre Léaud), who turns it about in order to draw black marks on the woman's face. A voice-off (of the teacher) summons (or interpellates) Doinel. The voice, now *in,* associated with the austere face of the teacher who has just been turning one sheet of paper over another, his glasses resting on the desk in front of him, demands that the boy come forward. In a swish the camera follows his movement forward as he surrenders the pinup to the teacher.

Suddenly the shot becomes a maze of maps. Above and behind the teacher (whom the children will call "Petite-Feuille" or "Little-Sheet") is the lower edge of a large topological map of the Mediterranean coast of France, the island of Corsica piercing the bottom of the frame near the right hand corner. In front of the left-hand corner is posed a globe whose visible surface displays the Indian Ocean below the Middle East and lower Asia, and between them is a faintly drawn map, possibly of the Cotentin and the western coast of Normandy. To the right of the desk stands a blackboard set on a wall where patches of paint and plaster have flaked away, suggesting that they are islands of an archipelago of decay and decrepitude. Doinel's head fills the screen before he moves forward and hands over his dubious treasure. Petite-Feuille exclaims, "Ah, c'est joli! [Oh! That's pretty!]." Then he tells the boy to go (to the right) to a corner. The camera tracks movement as Doinel disappears behind a blackboard set on an easel posed in front of the corner of the classroom. To the upper left is an anatomical "map" of a man's torso, revealing the muscles of the back and the buttocks. On the wall to the right is the lower portion of a large map of France with cities framed in a lower border and toponyms listed along the right side. Doinel peeks out from behind the blackboard and winks at the students (whom we assume are both students and a viewing public). The camera swish-pans to the left, back to the teacher, who demands silence after the children begin to howl.

The shot ends: a straight cut follows and, abruptly, a diametrically opposed perspective of the classroom is given as Petite-Feuille had seen it, except now he marches down the central aisle before the camera pans left to register his movement toward the door at the back of the room. On the upper wall in the back of the room stands the lower edge of another map. When the camera pans left it almost disappears before another map of France is seen (from an oblique angle, suggesting a play of anamorphosis) on the wall to the left. Petite-Feuille goes forward toward the camera, having strutted from one end of the classroom to the other in the space of thirty-four seconds.

By now it is clear that maps are on all four walls of the classroom. The impression is confirmed in the fourth shot when the teacher stands in front of the easel and the map in collecting the students' written papers and then walks to the right (the camera panning to follow him), dismissing the class and then arresting

Figure 31. *Les 400 coups* (1959): Petite-Feuille surveys the classroom. Three maps are behind him: lower France and Corsica, a globe displaying Africa (two "recalcitrant" areas, Corsica and Africa), and what appears to be an antique map of Europe and North America. The peelings of paint on the wall to his left resemble a strange island map.

Doinel. Doinel stops in his tracks next to the map on the right-hand wall; Petite-Feuille walks by and exits; the camera holds on Doinel next to the map of France. The camera is fixed on the boy, caught in bitter reflection, who stands by the map (bearing the topographical names of antique Gaul) for which he seems to be a personification. He then walks left, back to the easel, where the other maps—of France and of the male body—stand in the background as he tosses an eraser into the air, catches it, and moves behind the blackboard.

After a straight cut, a long shot of the playground (of four seconds)—where children romp in a modern version of Bruegel's "Children's Games"—records Petite-Feuille whispering words to "Monsieur le Directeur" about the sorry state of a mother and her child. A cigarette dangles from the lips of the interlocutor who wears a hat that identifies him not as a principal but an avatar of the intendent of *Zéro de conduite* who had championed the boys' revolution. A medium shot of the kids playing, pushing, and shoving each other ensues before the next shot, a close-up (shot 8, of four seconds) records Doinel scratching on the wall, in a gesture recalling those of the children of *Les Mistons* exorcising the lovers they admired and hated, a commemorative graffito. As in the film of 1957, the scene of writing is composite: the left hand side of the greyish wall is the white surface on which the words, fitting for incision on a tombstone or a commemorative plague, are written; to the right are the corners of two maps, one the southwest coast of France that runs from the Bordelais to the northwest corner of Spain, the other an inset map of Charlemagne's France at the time of the signing of the Strasbourg oaths, the official date of the "beginning of French literature."[7]

The ironies in the shot are many. It rehearses what Truffaut had already exploited in *Les Mistons,* thus establishing a scene of citation promulgating the cause of citation in the name of an "author," who here is Doinel writing for the second time in the film. He acts out the originary moment in the birth of all things French in the contrast of his inscription to the map-memory of the heritage of Charlemagne, known to children less as an emperor than as a name associated with the first written document in French. The sea, which will be the end-point of the film, is denoted by the shoreline on the map above. Doinel *reads* aloud what he *writes,* thus drawing attention to the autonomy of the sound in respect to the image-track. When the shot (of four seconds) cuts to the schoolyard where Petite-Feuille collars two children by their necks and pushes them forward, Doinel's voice continues to utter the words he inscribes. The boy writes (in the preterit!) that he suffered for "un pin-up" fallen from the sky. It had circulated in the class in the first shot and is now virtually seen in the somewhat strange and borrowed word that might be as American as one of the "pinup girls" whose entomology André Bazin had recently studied in an article in *Cahiers du cinema.*[8] And the shot anticipates and duplicates the "dictée" that Petite-Feuille will soon administer as collective punishment to the class in the wake of Doinel's writing.

An inscription of an autobiographical tenor is countered by another belonging to the aura of classical French literature. Petite-Feuille chalks the innocuous Alexandrines of "Le Lièvre" on the easel as the children copy his speech (shots 18 to 35). As Petite-Feuille writes, Doinel erases. The teacher copying the "Lièvre" at the blackboard stands in front of the boy who is behind the easel, removing his graffiti from the wall with soap and water (shot 20). But before the opposition is made clear, a close-up (shot 16) shows Petite-Feuille behind his desk, barking to Doinel to copy in three tenses—but not the preterit—"je déface les murs de la classe et malmène la prosodie française [I deface the classroom walls and botch French prosody]." In speaking, and in repeating "française," he stands next to the globe that in the first shot had displayed the Indian Ocean. Now it is turned to display the African continent when the adjective "French" is heard.

Would a viewer be accused of overinterpretation if the uttered insistence on the national treasure—French, after its prosody—were compared to the continent of Africa seen on the map? The positions on the globe have turned. Where Petite-Feuille imposes the authority of French the globe suddenly makes visible a colonial heritage and a world of unspoken "others," especially Algeria, the nation with which France was then at war. As in *Les Mistons* a politics bearing on the colonial heritage of the nation is folded into that of cineasts and auteurs. The globe offers a view of the continent where a majority of French colonies were still located. The suggestion of colonial tension is underscored in shot 18, a close-up of the teacher that pans right when he stands and moves to the blackboard, announcing "Le Lièvre," once again displays Africa on the globe to the left and Corsica on the wall map behind him.

Figure 32. *Les 400 coups:* Next to a map illustrating the origins of France (to the lower right is the division of the Carolingian Empire at the time of the Strasbourg Oaths, the first document written in French), Doinel scribbles words expressing misery and defiance. (See chapter 5, Figure 28.)

In a coda to the sequence of the dictée and the pandemonium it causes, standing at the head of the class in the depth of a long shot, Petite-Feuille ironically—and prophetically—exclaims that he pities France in ten years (shot 39) before he goes to the desk and angrily tosses a book on the floor. The shot cuts to the full-frame of a sculpted lintel displaying an allegory of post-Revolutionary France (shot 40): a portly Mother France extends her arms to five children, three to her right, one between her legs, and one to the left. The older child to her left writes on a sheet of paper that he holds in his left hand. The camera tilts down from the subscriptive words Liberty, Fraternity, Equality, before it records a mother in flesh and blood seen from behind, her head hidden by a leopard scarf, who awaits her child among those who are exiting the gates of the school. Doinel has just smudged the walls of a room matched by the dirt and soot caked on the statue of the Mother country.

Mother and Mother France

The first forty shots determine much of the economy of space in the film. The classroom places maps everywhere in its visual field. Wall maps convey a silent authority of the country and a sanitized tableau of its history. They are crowned by the maternal figure of the "nation" sculpted in the style of the secular ideals of the Third Republic. Time and again the children leave the classroom and return to it. The images blend into broader configuration of hieroglyphic images in which textual inscriptions, maps, and other legible matter are confused with spoken words. The former cause the latter to be visualized and to figure, in turn, in a more extensive—but no less constricting—narrative space.

Figure 33. *Les 400 coups:* Petite-Feuille, prohibiting Doinel from recess, seems to indicate that the boy is a map of France.

In the celebrated sequence of the "English lesson" (shots 168–75) the stuttering teacher begins by asking René to repeat after him, "Where is the father?" (168). Where is he? Where, it is inferred, does he figure in a broader psychogeography? In the center of the shot is the familiar globe that displays Africa; to the right, behind René, is a list of words in English that includes the name of the father. René can't find where he must put his tongue in order to get the lisp needed to pronounce the last syllable of the word (he utters "pha-zehr" and not "pha-there"). Instead of asking of the whereabouts of the mother (since Doinel had already spotted her with a lover in broad daylight), the instructor queries, "Where is the girl?" (shot 170). Where is she? The curly-haired boy who had made a mess of his notebook during the dictation answers in compressed words, "Zeegirlisatzeebeach" (shot 171). The viewer hears *biche* for beach, a familiar term designating a cute girl, but also the *bitch,* the English for "La chienne," the title of Renoir's first sound film, the feature in which Georges Flamand, René's very father in *Les 400 coups,* had played the role of Dédé twenty-six years before. "Bitch" also has personal resonance insofar as it might be a name whispered to refer to Truffaut's close friend, Charles Bitsch. To obviate the innuendo and immediate counter meaning the teacher diphthongizes the word ("bee-each," shot 172), but the boy persists in speaking with a French accent.

At the end of the film Doinel goes to the beach. He realizes a childhood dream—a dream he had avowed to his friend René (shot 228)—when he escapes from the detention center and runs tirelessly to the sandy bank at the edge of the sea (shots 390–92).[9] The *beach* that could not be properly uttered becomes the vanishing point where the child is finally (or provisionally, at least in Truffaut's greater narrative saga of Antoine Doinel that includes two sequel features) immobilized in a freeze-frame. The maps in the classroom configure coastlines and edges between land and sea. The dialogue shifts between a figure of a menacing mother—a *mère* who is a *bitch*—and a dream-object of oceanic proportion—*la mer*—that would be as boundless as the imagination of an infinitely smooth space of the greater world in which the child floats effortlessly.[10]

In the history of the reception of *Les 400 coups* the final sequence quickly became an emblem of the politics surrounding the "New Wave." Doinel, every viewer recalls, dips his feet in the splashing waves of the cold sea. He seems to experience something new and other before he is frozen in the frame. The sequence was taken to mark a moment of liberation from the worlds of confinement, incarceration, punishment, and surveillance in which the child had been living. Doinel, noted one critic, had found himself in "classrooms, the queues, the locks and bars of prisons, all the *apparat* of social confinement" before he "runs away from the reform school and rushes to the sea he has always wanted to look upon."[11] For this critic and others who take the film at its token value narrative themes—the trials and apprenticeship of an unloved child—have precedence in their form and its laminations of life, contemporary space, and cinema.

"In this last of a series of a long series of regressions from city to country to primeval amniotic sea, the picture turns into a still as though the camera itself had given up motion." The film reaches its terminus and so is taken to be a case-history, an autobiography, not a work of art, but an "extreme of vagueness that even *la nouvelle vague* can scarcely tolerate" (1960, 249). Trying to rise to the level of Truffaut's word-play, the critic labors a pun conflating English and French meanings of *vague* to show where *Les 400 coups* stands in the context of film history.

In Truffaut's juvenile geography equally at stake is the presence of various films that displace and even fracture the thematic treatment that is so often made of them. Already *Zéro de conduite* had been alluded to at least three times. When Doinel contemplates his fate while in solitary confinement he may be thinking of the prisoner Fontaine in Bresson's *Un condamné à mort s'est échappé* (1956). Certainly Doinel's apartment is shot as Renoir had represented the exiguities of the Lestingois household in *Boudu sauvé des eaux*. Now, in this sequence, in the shot in which Doinel hides under a bridge to evade the police, there is reproduced a sequence in the Scottish highlands in Hitchcock's *39 Steps* (1935). But Jean Vigo's *L'Atalante* (1934) is surely one of many intertexts that determines the shape of the film's ending. When Captain Jean (Jean Dasté) and his mate Jules (Michel Simon), the two pilots of the barge, reach Le Havre, the end of the voyage, a short sequence records Jean, maddened and blinded by the loss of Juliette (Dita Parlo), his newlywed spouse, looking for salvation and calm in the image of the sea. He runs along a seawall, then descends (in an extreme countertilt that cameraman Boris Kaufman uses to slice the frame diagonally to contrast atmosphere and stone or pavement). A shot taken with a wide-angle lens begins with Jean running directly away from the camera, toward the line where air and sea meet on the distant horizon. A countershot, taken from a diametrically opposite angle (on an axis of 180 degrees), from a point toward which Jean is sprinting, records him moving toward the camera before it pans right and tilts downward to show his footsteps and bring into view an unshaven, distraught, and bedraggled face that sees only disillusion and despair.

The end of *Les 400 coups* is in a spatial and historical dialogue with this sequence of *L'Atalante*. For Vigo (as also, for Fritz Lang of the same period) the effect on the same axis of the shot and countershot of Jean running away from and toward the camera betrays a condition where space, the condition of possibility of life, is reduced almost to nothing. On the beach Truffaut does not copy Kaufman's treatment of the nonescape of the protagonist in Vigo's film; rather, he keeps it in a comparative context. Doinel also leaves footprints in the sand and turns about after having looked outward and down at the water. For Truffaut the freeze-frame executes in its own way what the shot-countershot had done in *L'Atalante*. Vigo's unremitting political commentary, a caustic critique of the state of things in France during the Depression, is a backdrop to Truffaut's autobiography or "case history" of a boy who was never weaned from his mother. Allusion to Vigo brings to the mother *mer* of the last sequence a taste that would be bitter, *une douceur amère,* a sequence bearing a trace of sweetness in the wit and invention that meld language and cinema.

If the attractive but depressive maternal figure in the film is the mother (Claire Maurier) who fills the cinemascope frame with grouper-like lips that extend from one side to the other (shots 48, 180, 381, 383), then cinema, a "good" mother, is his likely counterpart. Like the "bad" mother in the narration, film—the benevolent figure who occupies the space of cinematic citation in the feature—is also not without contradiction. She is "France" insofar as she belongs to a tradition of French cinema, but a highly selective tradition that belongs to directors and films, such as those of Renoir and Vigo, that were banned or who expatriated themselves from the country. Throughout the film a war is waged between the nation and its "authors" who, by way of citation, expand the limits of the geographical space depicted in the film.

The initial sequence of the film stands in dialogue with the warring forces of maternity capped at the end by the wash of waves. In the faultline between the first and second shot Truffaut sets his camera on a sightline of 180 degrees, as had Vigo at the end of *L'Atalante,* to indicate, with an effect similar to the maps seen on all the walls of the classroom, that no symbolic space is available for anyone in French institutional systems. The sight of Africa on the globe points to a genealogy of France that is different from that of the pedigree of French that Petite-Feuille imposes on students of different social classes and geographical origins. Conflict in the space of the class matches that of recent French history.

A Child's Map

From a standpoint of the ways that a history of cartography is inscribed throughout *Les 400 coups* greater and deeper contradictions come forward. A good deal of the film takes place in the classroom where the maps seem to make the surroundings shrink like the wild ass's skin of Balzac's *La Peau de chagrin.* When René and Antoine embark on their ventures in the streets of Paris they pass by subway maps that sempiternally tell viewers and pedestrians (shot 95 and others) "where they are." In the sequence in which Antoine and René pilfer a typewriter—a writing instrument of a double inflection, that both liberates and incarcerates—from the office of a parent, the boys descend into the metro to go from the Champs-Elysées back to the Place Clichy. In shot 279, adjacent to the ticketbooth, in the depth of field are seen an older person and a child toying with an electronic metro-map that shows its user (who pushes on the button by the place-name of the appropriate destination) the best itinerary available. Like an electronic toy, it allows the older man and the boy to take a virtual voyage by following the illuminated dots of a broken zigzag of lights. When Doinel is thrown into jail and meets an Algerian who has been incarcerated for no good reason (shot 312) he stares out and sees two cops who idly play a version of Parcheesi (shot 313) in front of a map of Paris tacked to the wall. Doinel's father, who plots future solace on maps he studies in planning trips driving outside of the city (shot 111a), can never find his *Guide Michelin*.[12] It is implied that in the last shot of the film, in its inherently free indirect discourse, the boy wonders about how he has been "mapped" and, from the standpoint of where he is, how he can ever get out of the world in which he has been born and raised.

A greater history of the genealogy of the nation that maps impose in the classroom is given in the first sequence. By a turn of irony Petite-Feuille has the children copy "Le Lièvre," a poem in Alexandrines that begins, "Au temps où les buissons flambent de fleurs vermeilles . . . [In the time when the bushes burn with vermilion flowers . . .]": the flaming "bushes" would be a sylvan setting in autumn that promises an illusion of escape from the grime of the classroom and the soot of the city. The substantive also figures in Truffaut's associative style where words and their referents perpetually ramify and where names scratched everywhere on the surface of the city sometimes reveal unforeseen secrets. It suffices to recall the celebrated episode of the "athletic lesson," in which students flake away from a line that a whistle-blowing gym teacher leads in the streets of Paris, jogging and flexing his arms without heeding the children behind him (shots 195–97). The camera, set above an intersection, pans and catches for an instant the scribble on a wall of the unlikely name, "Giraudoux" (shot 196). Reference is, of course, to Truffaut's avowed past master of la politique des auteurs, Jean Giraudoux, who reputedly stated that "there are no more works, but only authors."[13]

In a similar way "buissons," the word marking the hemistich of the Alexandrine, refers to a uncanny cartographic history informing the space of the classroom. In the heyday of the Third Republic, Ferdinand Buisson authored two ample studies that bore influence on the use of maps in French secondary schools. In two works (1878 and 1882) the architect of the secular classroom in the regime of Jules Ferry fashioned a form of "mute map" from waxed canvas on which students in the primary schools were asked to inscribe place-names and draw the lines of rivers. The surface on which they wrote was intended to be the analogue of that on which the mind's memory would be shaped. He wished students to be able to draw maps from memory. "The map," he said, "is to the teaching of geography what the collection of images is to the study of natural history. . . . It is not only a means of representing objects to be studied, it is also the only means of acquiring a basic notion about them, the condition without which one would forever have only words in one's memory, and not ideas in one's head."[14] Buisson had learned his lesson from the defeat of the French in the War of 1870. At the time of the mobilization, German students, he reported, had been more geographically informed than the French because educators had been putting large and very general mural maps in the classrooms of their secondary schools.

The mapped space in which Doinel is first seen in *Les 400 coups* bears the signs of pedagogical wars of the nineteenth century and their aftermath. Literature is papered over geography, and over geography circulate both pinup girls and "memory-maps" from pedagogical films of French heritage ranging from *Zéro de conduite* to Marie Epstein's *La Maternelle*. In this sense, as in *Les Mistons,* the film attests not just to an autobiography or to a sentimental education by way of film (a sort of *Bildungscinema*) but, more tellingly, at once to a writing of history and to the writing of ways—scriptural, cinematic, cartographic—by which personal and national histories are written. In the sequences shot in and about the avenues of Paris are seen the city and its underground. The buildings, statues, and streets that mark the children's passages are mute objects bearing names and titles that would be included in a gazetteer of events and their memories.[15]

On the walls of the classroom is defiled a history of pedagogy over which Doinel rehearses and repeats a scene of writing. The space seems to be diurnal, but it is bathed in a grey texture that could qualify it in the underground realm of memory, a time both timeless and a time dated and marked by the Parisian milieu. *Les 400 coups* is partially a chronicle of a child's life in 1958. It is a film that, too, in the confusion of day and night and the ground above and below the city, alludes to the Second World War, less by direct account of the invasions (by Germany and by American and British troops) than through the evasions of a generation born in the immediate aftermath (children who fled to the cinema or into the subway in order to stay alive or retain a semblance of sanity). Truffaut recalled that during the Occupation the subway was a sanctuary and the schoolroom "a machine for the manufacture of lies."[16] That is precisely what constitutes a pedagogical map, a history of past time which an author writes in order to cope indirectly with unnamable issues in the present (Certeau 1975, 101–9). The maps in—and of—Truffaut's film are a mute and eloquent testimony to broader relations with the machineries of film, the medium that it shows writing beautifully mendacious histories of itself and of its authors.

The wars refracted by the maps of *Les 400 coups* include Gaul and the *gaulois* in the time of the Roman Occupation, the struggles in the aftermath of the Carolingian dynasty, the Franco-Prussian War, and France in the years of the German occupation. They are set in counterpoint to the affective journey in a city that is the stage for the difficult labor of psychogenesis.[17] It might be said that Truffaut films maps at once to counter (and to celebrate) the antiquities on the walls of the classroom and to summon inherited schemas, mostly of Freudian origin, of repression and castration. The new maps take the form of citations of literature and cinema, on the one hand and, on the other, they are displayed in the practice of writing, a writing that can be taken, as it had been for Gilles Deleuze in his study of Michel Foucault (1985b, 51), at once as becoming, struggling, and mapping. In an essay (1993, 81–88) on children and childhood that he places between two others on Walt Whitman and Herman Melville, the same critic praises the ways that the infant—who could be pubescent or adolescent—is always exploring places along dynamic paths of its own creation. Children make maps of their trials, errors, and tribulations. Parents are "themselves a milieu that the child moves through, and for whose qualities and powers he or she draws a map" (82). In its growth a child's libido undergoes monumental metamorphoses as it charts "historico-worldwide trajectories" (83). In this cartography imaginary and real places are fused, sometimes juxtaposed, and at others laminated upon one another.

And this is where, Deleuze goes on to note, a cartographic conception of psychogenesis is very different from the archeological model we usually associate with Freud. For Freud the analytical vector moved backward and downward, into commemorative or monumental places. But when the child's maps are overlaid upon each other we no longer are witness to "the search for an origin, but of an evaluation of *displacements*. Each map is a redistribution of impasses and entries, of thresholds and closures that naturally go from the bottom to the top." The unconscious is no longer something to be commemorated; rather, it enables movement and ever-shifting itineraries and new discoveries. For that reason the analyst ought not interpret symptoms but instead get a glimpse of patterns and vectors that subjects trace among and through images, letters, words, and things. Thus maps are not to be understood in terms of their extension, not only "in respect to a constituted space of trajectories," but also to mappings of intensity, density, that are taken up with what fills space, what sub-tends the trajectory" (83–84).

The sequences devoted to Antoine and René's movements through Paris when they play hooky (to what in French is called "l'école buissonnière," as if wishing to evade Ferdinand Buisson's cartographic schemes), or else steal and return a typewriter—one of the many writing instruments that figure as contraband—from one end of Paris to another can be read as mappings of this kind. The film begins with the most familiar icons and monuments on the Parisian horizon before it tells of spatial itineraries of another order, of the child's underground world, of discoveries and adventures that turn the city into a site that unfolds new surfaces and plots unforeseen and unpredictable displacements. As Balzac had done in his cartographies of the city in *La Comédie humaine,* Paris becomes a site of adventure and of apprenticeship (Balzac 1922–29). The city and its children are filmed in the manner of a stratigraphy, with many layers and levels of intensity that the actors and their milieu make manifest through their travels. In this light *Les 400 coups* could be taken to be a film of voyage and adventure. But if, like *Les Mistons,* the a film has an underside with untold memories of war and occupation or if, like *La Règle du jeu,* it anticipates an unwished future, it might be fitting to look at films done after the New Wave retracted and receded and, perhaps, came back and forward again.

8

A Roadmap for a Road Movie:
Thelma and Louise

We have seen how *Les Amants* turns a desperate journey into a tale of tender travel, and how *Les 400 coups* tells about how children cope with the maps that objectify them. Both films would seem to be at a far remove from Ridley Scott's cult classic, *Thelma and Louise* (1991). In this film maps, but not exactly the traditional Rand-Mcnally motorist's map, have an engaging and unsettling presence. Road movies quickly remind us that *itineraria* and their maps played crucial roles in the classical past. Soldiers used them for the expansion and defense of the Roman Empire not long before pilgrims of the early Christian era carried maps in their travels to and from sacred shrines (Dilke 1987, 234–42). The great Peutinger *tabula*, a roadmap of early Christian times, is well over six meters long and a little more than a foot wide. A thirteenth-century copy of an earlier map, it is what historians call an *itinerarium pictum*, a painted or pictured itinerary drawn to show principal routes and places along the way or in areas beyond the their immediate path. Major cities are personified as noble women; stopovers that take the shape of ideograms tell much about little-known places that travelers might encounter in the course of their voyages. Matthew Paris (ca. 1200–1259), a Benedictine monk, drew itinerary maps that go from London to southern Italy and Sicily, structuring them "as a journey, with stations a day's travel apart," reflecting the "restless curiosity" of a traveler who saw what he described (Edson 1997, 121).

Of more recent vintage, the automotive map belongs to the same tradition. It often betrays a rhetoric telling its reader of places and things unknown. In North America, after the western frontier had disappeared, the roadmap became a site where charts telling the traveler how to get there fueled the fantasy of finding alluring and strange places. Drivers equipped with maps could think of themselves as reincarnations of Lewis and Clark, but unlike the pioneers they could be reasonably sure they would safely reach their destination. By the 1920s the design of maps had transformed adventure into a theater of dreams, into what James Akerman aptly calls the effect of "blazing a well-worn path" (1993a, 10–20).[1] It might be said that the road movie, a genre that took shape in the 1930s, began as a complement to the mapping designs of the automotive industry. Like a folding map purchased at a gas station, a road movie could generate a desire to get on the road, to travel errantly, and to engage adventure. Adventure, as we have seen in *High Sierra,* came through identification with heroes driving to their destiny.

The aim of this chapter is to bring the rich and variegated tradition of roadmaps and guidebooks into the context of the "road movie" of both classical and more recent vintage. Immediately recalled are Fritz Lang's *You Only Live Once* (1937), Edgar G. Ulmer's *Detour* (1946), Ida Lupino's *The Hitchhiker* (1953), Godard's *A bout de souffle* (1960) and *Pierrot le fou* (1964), and Arthur Penn's *Bonnie and Clyde* (1967).[2] Ephemeral maps, especially those sold in gasoline stations or in tourist bureaus, would be the *vademecum* for the desperate hero and heroine evading the net that an intrepid police casts over the territories they speed across. An unlikely sequence in Ridley Scott's feature reveals that the Michelin or Rand-McNally roadmap does not always appear where it would be expected. Other and different kinds of maps bring unforeseen itineraries into the tradition.

Geography and Gentility

Over a decade after being seen in movie theaters and cineplexes, the film now belongs to the geography of nonplaces, in the aisles in shopping malls and outlets such as K-Mart, Wal-Mart, or Target Stores where row after row of action movies and contemporary "classics" (including *Casablanca* and *Thelma and Louise*) are on display. A browsing customer in these spaces is wont to wonder if the two heroines will turn up at the checkout register. The plot might have led them either there or in the setting of the feature. To find brief relief from both oppressive or browbeating mates, and to be freed for a few hours from household and workaday drudgery, two women set off together to spend a weekend of fishing in the mountains (presumably the Ozarks). In the time-tested role of a cynical waitress who works in a local diner, Louise (Susan Sarandon) is shown knowing how to handle demanding clientele.[3] She drives her Ford Thunderbird convertible (circa 1966) to pick up her younger friend, Thelma (Geena Davis), a confused (and abused) spouse married to a egomaniac (Christopher McDonald) who drives to work in a Corvette that sports a personalized license plate bearing the title "The-1." Thelma packs loads of clothing into the trunk of the car. By chance she takes along a revolver she has placed in a plastic bag. Worried about Thelma's own fear of the weapon, Louise stashes the gun into her purse.

They drive off in glee and find that the open road is congested with traffic. They no sooner stop in a roadside saloon to have a drink before they find themselves invited to dance: a charmingly disingenuous skirt-chaser addresses Thelma with seductive words and leads her to the dance floor. A hayseed under a black cowboy hat beckons Louise to take a turn with him. The skirt-chaser pursues Thelma, inebriated, who finds herself in a parking lot where he accosts and begins to rape her. Louise emerges from a crowded ladies' room and walks into a parking lot where she discovers Thelma in distress. She suddenly aims the revolver at the man who refuses to apologize for what he has begun to do. When he crassly insults Louise ("I shoulda fucked her," he snipes, before inviting Louise to "suck my cock"), she cocks the hammer and pulls the trigger. He dies almost instantly. Shocked at what they have wrought, the two women speed into the night aimlessly before they stop to take stock of themselves and get their bearings.

They decide to head for Mexico but encounter a variety of obstacles in a meander of misadventure. Along the way they meet a seductively vagrant hitchhiker (Brad Pitt) who teaches Thelma lessons in love and petty larceny. For a third time they pass a gasoline truck, driven by a crude and lascivious driver, who has repeatedly made obscene gestures to them from his cab. The women park their car and, like the sirens of *The Odyssey,* invite him to share their charms. Tricked, he watches them set his truck ablaze with bullets. They get away but soon discover that they are driving toward the Grand Canyon and are being pursued by an expeditionary force of police cars. They reach a high plateau where the forces of law—a battalion of policemen armed with telescopic rifles—are behind them while the depths of the canyon stand in front of their eyes. They go "rushin' toward death," driving their car over the edge of the canyon. The film ends in a freeze-frame, their car suspended in mid-air, at the zenith of the trajectory that will soon turn to a free fall into the abyss of the canyon.

One of the geographies on which their adventures is plotted belongs to the allegorical tradition of the gentle "Carte du Tendre," that reaches, as we have seen earlier in Louis Malle's *Les Amants,* back to the map that accompanied the publication of Mademoiselle de Scudéry's *Clélie.* In *Thelma and Louise* feminism and gentility are vectored, it seems, from forces that come out of the past, from the women's experience with men and the sentimental education they gain as they travel across America. We later learn that the sight of Thelma on the verge of being raped in the parking lot forces Louise to recall a similarly traumatic—and defining—episode earlier in her life. The vagrant youth whom the women meet on a mesa, a male prostitute who has a flair for preciosity, shows Thelma the Ovidean *ars amandi* (in the words of Louise, the pleasures of "a good lay") while, at the same time, he teaches her how charming and decent words ("please," "thank you," "if you will," and so on) can assist the basest of thieves.

After watching his rehearsal in the bedroom (he wields a hairdryer as if it were an automatic pistol) Thelma performs a successful holdup of a roadside convenience store.

Jimmy (Michael Madsen), Louise's male friend, who had first been uncouth with her upon learning about the ladies' escapade, tries to understand their differences and allow her, in deference to Virginia Woolf, to find a space of her own.[4] The "good cop" (Harvey Keitel) who works amid a bunch of uncouth males—more interested in masturbating over pulpy magazines than understanding the women—tries to tell Thelma's husband that he ought not to browbeat her. The encounter with the trooper (Jason Beghe) is an episode of mirrored civilities. The policeman assumes a vigorous and gentle expression of authority when he apprehends them; they return the same words to him before incarcerating him in the trunk of his car that they have aerated after firing two shots into its hood. They enact a costly lesson in civility upon the truck driver who had made rude and lascivious gestures in transit. Thus, considered together, the meetings with the men engage lessons in tenderness. Assailed by at least five different males, they seek respite and kindness but find no such space outside of the nacelle of the Thunderbird. Tenderness, they discover, is hard to find on the arid and dusty badlands of the American Southwest.

Cinematic Diagrams

The affective cartography is embedded in another, one in which a welter of allusions, citations, and references blend past cinema into the geology of the landscapes of Arizona and Utah. Various genres and styles of cinema inform the film. As in the work of French directors, many of the episodes of *Thelma and Louise* seem to be sedimentations of many films directly or allusively cited in dialogue, action, and the framing of the images. If we cannot exactly tell where we are, for some reason we know we have often been there before. Louise stashes in her purse the revolver that Thelma had packed with the rest of her things. Recall is immediate of the opening episodes of *A bout de souffle*, in which a hooligan, Michel Poiccard (Jean-Paul Belmondo) discovers a gun in the glove compartment of the Oldsmobile he has stolen and is driving across the French countryside. He plays at shooting oncoming cars before the instrument determines his fate. Allusion to Godard ramifies to a similar episode in *Taxi Driver* that in turn informs *La Haine*.

When the ladies begin to dance to country music many conventional scenes of paroxysm come forward which determine the fate of dubious heroes and heroines of film noir. Behind the country music played in the Silver Bullet Lounge is recalled the piano music in the private club where pianist Lou Tingle hit the notes that made Burt Lancaster fall for Ava Gardner in *The Killers* (1946); the nightclub episode in *D.O.A.* (1949), in which Edmund O'Brien was fed a fateful drink powdered with luminous toxin that caused him to live only as long as the remainder of the movie that followed; the hallucinating dance that linked Burt Lancaster with Yvonne de Carlo to the rumba beat of Ezy Morales's orchestra in *Criss Cross* (1949). Thelma, mollified by music and alcohol, falls prey to the evil of men. The grounding patterns of many films noir suggest that a desperate journey will shortly ensue. The pursuit itself seems to be fashioned from a number of classical Hollywood films. In *High Sierra*, as we have seen in chapter 4, the deep space of the desert and great vistas of the high Sierras cause the inexorable destiny of the hero to be played out, ironically, in a breathtaking setting under a sheltering sky. The couple in *Thelma and Louise* discovers endless horizons and thousands of "points of light" in the celestial vault over Monument Valley and the Grand Canyon.

Citations of other films begin to multiply. When the two women stuff the state trooper into the trunk of his car they reveal that they are far less sadistic than Cody Jarrett (James Cagney) of *White Heat* (1949), the crazed criminal, strutting and munching on the drumstick of a fried chicken, who tosses a stoolpigeon into the trunk of an old Packard. He slams down the hood and, hearing the man begging for ventilation, shoots two bullets into it. In Ridley Scott's variant on the scene a black bicyclist examines the car, hears the policeman thumping and begging to be freed, and blows cigarette smoke into the bullet hole. At the end of Raoul Walsh's film Cody Jarrett blows up the world when he sets ablaze the Hortonsphere on which he is perched. The great globe explodes and a mushroom cloud, clearly an allusion to the effects of an atomic bomb, goes skyward: as does that of the tank truck (one had also figured in *White Heat*) in *Thelma and Louise* that the two women ignite and leave in a conflagration.

The explosion recalls, no less, the episode of *North by Northwest* (1959) in which the crash of a cropduster into a tank truck ignites a conflagration on the badlands of the Dakotas. Prior to that allusion the women, singing merrily, are rushing off toward Oklahoma City. They wave at a cropduster that buzzes overhead and leaves a mist of spray in their midst before turning about and upward. The memory of *North by Northwest* inheres in the film, but with a new twist, and not merely because the women are traveling south by southwest: the sequence ends with a view from the airplane that flies over a highway that runs parallel to endless swaths of green fields of soybeans. The shot has no point of view that would be related to anyone in the film, unless it were that of fate itself, or a baroque perspective related to cartography that approximates a God-like point of origin. If it is understood as such, then the shot exceeds its allusion to Hitchcock by making point of view itself its own issue because for the baroque imagination point of view is not a matter of relativity, "not the variation of truth according to the subject, but the condition under which a subject perceives the truth of a variation."[5] By reference to Hitchcock a panoptic and controlling viewpoint, generally coded in terms of gender, is implicitly theorized. Through its diacritical relation with *North by Northwest* and other postwar films, two contrastive "spheres" of reference are given, and as a result no stable point of reference is ever apparent. Surely the setting of Monument Valley ceaselessly refers to *Stagecoach* (1939), the western that produces the effect of a *huis-clos* in the wagon that transports its passengers across the expanse of northern Arizona and southern Utah. It is tempting to see how the two women find a monad, a capsule of happiness and security, in the vintage Thunderbird—whose emblem and name were a souvenir of Amerindian mythology in the package of what was, in 1991, an automotive fetish.[6] The paradox of intimate enclosure and intolerable social constriction ties the spatial articulations of *Thelma and Louise* to these classical films. Constant and almost nagging reminders, the allusions configure a geography that seems to be plotted on a historical map of cinema. At the same time the allusions suggest that, like the characters in the narratives of their destiny, the viewer can never get off the map of cinematic citation.

A Map Room and a Baroque Motel

After shooting the rapist, Thelma and Louise fall into a state of shock. They take to the road in the traffic of semi-trailers rolling onto interstate highways. Thelma, her lips bloodied by her assailant, gets behind the wheel of the car and drives away, swerving and spinning in every direction. They eventually stop in a diner for a cup of coffee and respite enough to find their bearings. In a two-shot in medium depth, in profile, they face each other from the opposite sides of a booth by a window—sliced by long horizontal lines of Venetian blinds—in front of a parking lot where a couple of pickup trucks seem to be lingering. The camera tracks in on the couple as Louise, sucking on her cigarette and blowing whorls

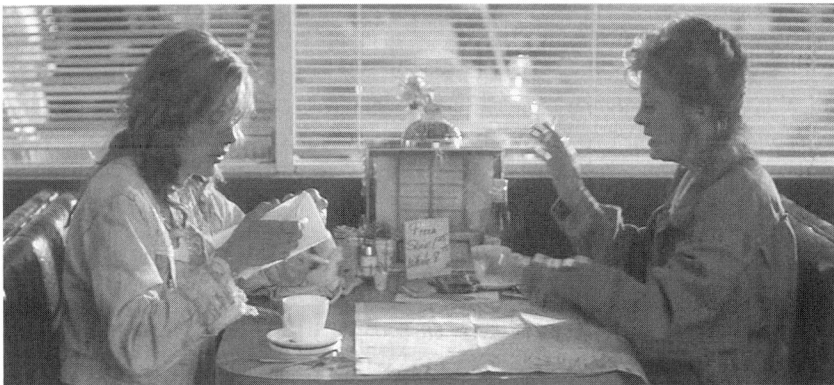

Figure 34. *Thelma and Louise* (1991): The two heroines, after leaving the scene of the crime at the Silver Bullet, consult a map to see where they might escape.

of smoke in the air, utters, both to herself and Thelma, "Now's not the time to panic, if we panic now, we're done for. Nobody saw it . . . nobody knows the results. We're still okay . . . we just have to figure out . . . what we're gonna do next . . . we just have [Louise now looks more intently on the map while the blue smoke from the cigarettes whirls in the air] to figure out what we're gonna do." Thelma, disheveled and in tears, has no inkling about where they are, what they are doing, or which moral or literal road they might follow.

The roadmap does not offer an exit from their dilemma. Nor do three other maps, of a very different tradition, that appear in a motel room where the two women seek repose enough to find their bearings. A sequence crucial to the cartography of much of the entire film takes place in the room of a motel, adjacent to an interstate highway, in which are found three baroque wall maps. The montage and composition of the shots make little distinction between the road and the motel. A straight cut moves from a close-up of Louise facing the windshield as she drives ("We're gonna need more money") to another of Thelma, in a negligee, in front of checkered curtains ("Whaddayagonna do? Why'yall unpackin'? I thought ya said wez just gonna take a nap") by a window. The film cuts to Louise in medium close-up, wrapped in a towel, standing in front of a mirror in a black frame and to the left of a beige lampshade. She comes forward, for an instant displaying in the mirror the reflection of her backside ("I'm tryin' to figure out what to do").

As she advances, a straight cut gives way to an establishing shot of the space of the motel room. The lampshade is on the left, adjacent to a television set whose screen is at an oblique angle, standing in front of the bulbous base of the lamp, its glass checkered with crisscrossed lines. On the wall behind both the shade and a pendant cylindrical lamp with a net-like design hangs a large planisphere of the New and Old Worlds. Each roundel holds a large cartouche. At the border of a glass door-window, open and to the left, stands a frame of eight vignettes behind its reflective surface. Louise stands in medium close-up, facing right, while a reflection of Thelma's body and face in profile, seemingly attached to Louise's back, is all that is visible of her until she moves right to grab a piece of dark clothing from the top of a bed. Then Thelma is seen, her body reflected on the pane of the door in front of the right border of the map and almost molded to the lines of Louise's back.

She stands behind a small round table and in front of the outdoors behind the open threshold of the window. In view is a roadside landscape, bathed in bright hazy light, foregrounded by a frugal iron barrier at the cusp of a mountainous landscape of desert cut by a bridge and an interstate highway. The window-door on the right is opened at the same angle as the one on the left, its glass reflecting what seems to be the shrubbery of a landscape on the outside. The door stands to the left of a square frame that reflects light and has the shimmer of Plexiglas. Louise pirouettes, and Thelma moves right, emphasizing how each body, like the binocular spheres of the map on the left, seems to be the Siamese twin of the other. Louise, dressed in a white skirt and a shoulderless blouse (of a "Southern belle") is reflected on the map to the left and in the window to the right.

Louise moves to sit down on the bed, her body seen through the diaphanous texture of her blouse as Thelma turns left and fidgets with her clothing. The camera pans slightly to the right as Thelma lies down. Her body supine, her head rests on a pillow and is framed by the dark line of the bedstead. Two pictures are on the wall behind her, their images reflecting ambient light and fluttering leaves or branches of trees, outside of the room, that shimmer on their surfaces. As Louise moves toward Thelma who lies on the bed as might a funerary sculpture of a dead queen on her tomb, a fifty-three-foot semitrailer rolls past in the background from left to right. As in the two-shot in the diner, the women take stock of their dilemma in a plan-séquence, As she lies down, Thelma jibes, "When y'all figure it out, just wake me up," and Louise retorts, "What the hell's wrong with you?" Thelma: "What's that supposed to mean?"

Louise is now isolated in close-up against the beige-white wall. She looks down (presumably, at Thelma, in an expression of perplexity and fear). "Like what? How'm I supposed to act," cries Thelma. The camera moves upward, holding on Thelma as she now sits upright and is haloed by the spherical map. To her right, the lens now reveals, is the edge of another baroque map that is partially occluded by the glass door. Thelma moves her head to the left and right, holding her legs in her arms, and exclaims, "Excuse me for not knowin' how to act when you blow someone away."

As she speaks the map becomes discernible. It is a framed copy of a map of the New World by Michael Mercator (circa 1620), in which North and South America occupy a large central sphere. Visible in the spandrels on the right side

Figure 35. *Thelma and Louise:* In a roadside motel, Thelma wears the halo of Michael Mercator's map of the "New World" (1620).

of the frame are inserts in circular frames of the Island of Cuba (above) and the title and attribution.[7] The arcs that curve upward and downward of the Tropics of Cancer and Capricorn on both sides of a median axis drawn by the Equator, along with the floral design in the left and right borders (of a texture that rhymes with the curls of Thelma's slightly unkempt hair), emphasize the distortion of a curved or even bulbous surface of the globe on a flat plane.[8] The map includes the extensive lands that the women will later cross. The American Southwest extends far and wide across the upper left of the map, above Thelma's head, and thus seems to reflect in its composition a vast presence of unknown and un-marked spaces that go westward.

The sequence includes five shots and countershots in which Louise convinces Thelma to go outside to the pool (and it happens to be one of two aquamarine sites in the film, the other also an adjunct to a second roadside motel). A sixth shot, now of the landscape seen from the right, captures the desert and highway (another large semi with "Zip" printed on its trailer speeds along the road) by the sign of the "Motor Inn" on two pylons. The camera pans down by the iron balustrade and, in the lower distance, a parasol and an ice machine by the pool. We hear, voice-off, Louise, who is telephoning, "Jimmy, Hello, this is Louise, ya know, I've been tryin' to call you," as the "Zip" goes by.[9] Louise enters into the frame from the point of view of the camera. She holds a telephone as we hear Jimmy answer (voice-off), "Louise, hey baby, where the hell are you at? Yallright?" and Louise responds (voice-off, her head above the upper edge of the frame as Thelma's head is visible by the poolside below), "Yeah, long time no see."

As she turns about, the camera cuts to an establishing shot of the space about the pool. Another semi drives by right in the background ("Freymiller" is printed on the trailer) while Thelma walks left, around the edge of the pool, pulling her valise, below the "Motor Inn" sign and the red, white, and blue chevrons of a marquee in the sky above). The conversation continues, off, Louise telling Jimmy that she is in "deep shit. Deep Shit, Arkansas." The camera cuts to Jimmy, in a weightlifter's t-shirt, speaking into the phone in the clutter of a room illuminated with two spotlights to the left. The next three shots are queued to the words, uttered in lip-synch, of each interlocutor before the camera suddenly frames Louise, in a medium close-up, between the mirror and lamp.

Louise has been speaking with her friend from the telephone. She sits between a large lamp and a television set on which is poised the bottle of Miller Lite (the label is in full view). Her back is against the wall (as the camera is now to the left of the window, giving onto a swimming pool below and an interstate high-way in the middle ground in front of a mountainous horizon). Louise seems to be split in two: the shadow of her head and shoulders cuts across the lower cor-ner of a Dutch mirror identified by its ample ebony frame. The dark silhouette of her head partially a reflection in the mirror, and partially a shadow on the frame and the wall), shoulders, and right arm behind her seems to be a Siamese twin of her human form. But at the same time the camera catches the left-hand border of a great wall map. A cut to Jimmy shows him in front of a punching bag, a sort of pear-like globe, that is the counterpart to the pendant lamp that, as the camera laterally reframes the setting, is set on an axis that is to the left of the area where the two spheres of the wall map intersect and seem, in their own way, to be two hemispheres attached to each other as might be Louise and her shadow. The camera holds with greater emphasis on this map than it had in the instance of Mercator's "America sive India nova." We now clearly see Claes Jansz Visscher's "World in Two Hemispheres" (1617), a unique world map of the baroque age.[10] Its lower orb of the lamp that hangs in front of the planisphere occludes the view of South America. The pendant is, literally, a *cul-de-lampe* that doubles the central spandrel between the two spheres of Visscher's map.

Two shots later the camera pulls back to re-establish the composition. Visscher's double sphere is in the background, framed by vignettes of scenes of the seasons of everyday life in early modern Europe. The pendant lamp stands in contrast to the beer bottle, on the television set, whose neck and tip are near Louise's mouth. A plan-séquence, the shot ends when (to the sound of country music in the background), Louise, whimpering, murmurs into the receiver, "Do you love me?" She grabs the beer bottle when she hears Jimmy hesitate in his response to her question. She wants to know if he loves her enough to forward cash; he seeks to locate her. Louise indicates that the money can be forwarded to Oklahoma City, the mere mention of the place-name telling us that it has absolutely no correlate on the wall map. The sequence ends when the camera cuts to a medium shot, exterior, of recumbent Thelma on a deck chair by the pool in the foreground while Louise parks the Thunderbird in the background.

Figure 36. *Thelma and Louise:* Louise telephones Jimmy and sips a bottle of Miller Lite while Thelma sits by an outdoor pool. The planisphere map on the wall is by Claes Visscher (1617).

"Long time no see": when Louise's words are uttered neither of the women is in full view. The speech underscores the crushing irony of the woman trying blindly to gather her bearings in an unlikely map room. Visscher's map, like Louise and her Siamese shadow, has a binocular effect that draws attention to the stakes of looking all over the depth and surface of both geographical and visual fields. It stands in elegant contrast to Mercator's single sphere, or possibly monocular map, of the New World and its undiscovered regions. A tension is established between flat and curvilinear space on the one hand, while on the other the camera invents a paradoxically spaceless space in the room where the map bears promise of new and unknown worlds in an age anterior to the present.

An unconscious attraction to the map is shown where the tip of the bottle, the virtual nipple of the lamp, and the vaginal shape of the central spandrels (between the two spheres) are brought forward (the connection is made clearer after a close-up, in the first shot of the next sequence, taken between Thelma's legs before she turns to cover the view by pulling her suitcase of front of her crotch). The intersecting circles depicting the new and old worlds have visual analogues in the myriad shots of characters wearing sunglasses, of hubcaps, of droplets of water on the windshield, of breasts pushing against the women's blouses, and especially of medium takes of buttocks.[11] An itinerary comes to Louise's mind in the next sequence. Behind the steering wheel, she looks ahead, plotting their trip to the "Vagabond Motel" in Oklahoma City, where they "gotta haul ass." Two sequences later, as they await the passage of a freight train crossing their path, Louise tells Thelma to look at her roadmap in order to find all the "secondary roads that take us from Oklahoma City to Mexico. I think we should stay off the Interstate."

Reflectors and Benders

The maps are part of a visual shimmer and play of reflecting surfaces that cause the women's dilemma of being on the run to extend to that of being in the world. The many shots where Thelma and Louise look in mirrors—in ladies' rooms and in the Thunderbird—have counterparts in the reflections of themselves on the glass surfaces of telephone booths, on fenders or automotive chrome. Their specularity implies that, as in Visscher's map, an allegory prevails. When seen in what seems to be far more real than traditional process shots of people driving cars (as seen in *High Sierra* and *Casablanca*) the protagonists draw attention to the splashes of light on the bent windshield of the Thunderbird. They look forward and through the glass as the landscape recedes. Because the windshield wipers have cleaned the dust in their semicircular path, Thelma and Louise are framed in another planisphere such that their faces resemble the "continents" of the new and old world visible on Visscher's projection. Rings of dust cast a blur on the area of the windshield untouched by the wipers that melds into the clouds on the horizon in the background. The ocular traits of the baroque world map find an analogue on the curved surface of the safety glass.

A double effect of forward movement ("there's no goin' back") and regression is given when the rearview mirror occupies the center of the frame. The movement reflected on its glass runs opposite—and hence negates—that of the car that speeds ahead. The effect is "classical" insofar as it had been the trademark of a confined space in earlier road movies. In Scott's film the effect becomes "baroque" through its obsessive reference to these films on the one hand, while on the other oblique and angled views supplement their classical style of representation.[12] In the midst of the melee the ladies turn left in a plume of dust and aim the car toward a rocky butte that seems both to be a landscape and a locus coming out of the distant past of the film. The convertible turns, the camera pans, and dust rises: behind the powdery mist extends the horizon that had been the background to the front credits, seen earlier as a topographical view, that now recurs. In an extreme long shot a minuscule car, leaving a trail of dust in its path, drives across the ledge of a great bluff.

As the car moves right the camera reframes itself laterally, then dips to display a helicopter that flies below and to the left, in pursuit. The camera zooms to bring the metallic bird into close-up, and then tilts up into the blinding light of the sky before the film cuts straight to a long shot picturing the cavernous reaches of the Grand Canyon. The helicopter now descends from above and over the camera. Following the extreme long shots in which the women drive across a landscape of an expanse beyond their ken, they screech to a halt at the edge of a cliff. A two-shot records them staring through the arcs of the windshield cleaned by the wipers. Thelma utters, not in obvious lip-synch (the women's voices seem to be elsewhere than where their bodies are), "What in the hell is this?" The film cuts to an extreme long shot of the blue sky over vast patches of cumulous clouds that hang over a lower edge, near the bottom of the frame, of two great buttes. The image appears to respond to the question when it slowly pans to the right, as the voice of Louise, virtually emanating from the space on the screen that her speech identifies, utters, "Uh huh, I dunno . . . uh, I think it's the goddamned Grand Canyon?" Then, voice-off, in the same panoramic that now displays the sky above two rocky towers, Thelma's voice responds, "Isn't it beautiful?"

Orpheus Rewritten

The women are already disembodied, their speech momentarily located *in* the sky and the landscape they are naming.[13] When the film immediately cuts back to the two-shot of the women staring forward and toward the spectators, they have just seen themselves in a mystical incarnation *in* the landscape prior to the final of the film moment when they drive over the cliff. Before they make their leap, Hal, the "good cop," seen in medium depth in front of a rock formation that seems to have the mute faces of a classical chorus sculpted in the red-ochre stone, argues with his cohorts in order not to let the women be murdered: nonetheless, the posse cocks their rifles and aims them at their prey. Where the good cop, enjoining the women to return, runs after the car that speeds toward the precipice of the Grand Canyon, the Orphic theme of the film comes forward. In *High Sierra* and in other features that varied on the same ending,[14] the hero seals his fate when he turns back. Duped and destined to die as he does, the Orphic hero reenacts a moment of mythic pathos. So too do Thelma and Louise, but in a way that would open the cinema to dialogue about feminine agency and its own "tender geography." In Scott's film the women do not turn back. "Let's keep goin'," cries Thelma.

A suicide of affirmation: many of the debates about the feminism of the feature have centered on this sequence. Did the women participate in a mystical voyage where they remain suspended, in a freeze-frame, their car just past the zenith of an arc, beginning to plummet into the Colorado River thousands of feet below? The question can be addressed through reference, first, to the "media event" that had been staged to document the Orphic moment in *High Sierra* and, second, to the toponymic character of Scott's road movie. The film ends as the tale of a strange occurrence by a cliff of the Grand Canyon. *Thelma and Louise* masks the presence of the industry producing its effects of pathos and terror where the earlier feature did not. But in a less direct but more enduring way the finale belongs to a literary and cartographic tradition that one critic calls "the toponymic tale," and another the "hagiographical variant" (Lestringant 1993, 109–27; Certeau 1975, 274–88). Thelma and Louise drive off into a myth, a new version of Orpheus, which they write by taking a high road to oblivion. In doing so they inflect the Grand Canyon, a glorious commonplace on roadmaps and touristic guides, with a tale that virtually baptizes the area in the name of the canyon of Thelma and Louise.

Thelma and Louise becomes a feminist hagiography based on a mythic voyage. It plots a variant of the Carte du Tendre in which two women are led from sites of "New Friendship" and "Tender-on-Inclination" across the "Dangerous Seas" of desert sands to self-affirmation in view of destiny. The end-credits recuperate the myth by replaying key moments of the story beneath the names of the players that scroll upward: the two women taking a picture of themselves, freezing themselves in a frame identical to that in which they have just been frozen; the sequence in the motel where Thelma reveals to Louise her bliss at having experienced eros as it ought to be; the moment when they map their getaway to Mexico; the ladies waving at the cropduster that buzzes by them as they drive across the green prairies; Louise awaiting Thelma at the curbside; the couple smiling from the cockpit of the Thunderbird. In the indirect discourse of the film all these memory-flashes, coupled with the Orphic gaze into the rear-view mirror—that had marked *High Sierra, Gun Crazy, Les Amants,* and especially

Jean Cocteau's *Orphée*—would be equivalent to the fabled instants of the totality of a life that we are supposed to see before our eyes at the point of our death.

The Map in the Picture

Much of what happens at the end of the film is anticipated in the motel in which the two women seek their bearings. The long take of Louise sitting beside a Dutch mirror to the left of Visscher's world map is clearly a variant on any of Vermeer's paintings in which maps are set adjacent to women who seem to reflect on light, life, history, and time. The film begins to philosophize at the point where allusion is made to the Dutch artist. The tableau vivant in the unlikely setting of a non-place, or an "any place whatsoever," affords further reflection on art, cartography, and cinema. To find Visscher and Vermeer in a roadside motel would be both likely and uncanny: likely, because early modern world maps are the stuff and substance of calendars and reproductions offering quaintly attractive images of the world for a general public. A traveler's motel would be tastefully decorated with pictures depicting the discoveries of new lands in the western world. It is uncanny because of the size of each reproduction, especially that of Visscher, which makes obvious the unsolicited connection both with Vermeer and the stakes of finding strange beauty in areas that would seem to bear little visual attraction.[15]

An extended analogy is made between a mapping impulse and landscape as they are shown in deep-focus cinema. In a pathbreaking study of cartography in Vermeer's paintings Svetlana Alpers (1987, 72) argues that the Dutch artist belongs to a properly northern tradition in which landscapes and maps are of the same texture. Both the canvas and the copperplate were surfaces on which the world was engraved. The panoramic view of the world resembled a "mapped landscape view" while the cityscape pertained to a topographical city view. Both the cartographer and the painter sought to *describe,* that is, to draw the world, to capture "on a surface a great range of knowledge and information," and to create works compiling material seen not from a single point of view (as in Italian art), but in such a way that both map and canvas were surfaces" on which was laid out "an assemblage of the world." Alpers insists that mapped landscapes were created by artists who traveled "on the road, looking, artists who were not staying at home listening to travelers' accounts" (59, 81).

Vermeer used Visscher the elder's work in the construction of masterpieces that include "The Soldier and the Young Girl Smiling" (1657–58), "Woman at the Window" (1662), "Woman in Blue Reading a Letter" (1662–64), and above all, "The Art of Painting" (or "Ars pictoria," 1667).[16] In the background of that picture ten city-views comprise the decorative compartments that border a map of Belgium. Its resemblance to Visscher is so striking that the viewer of the film sees both the allusion to the Dutch artist's complex reflection on mapping and painting and the presence of strips of celluloid, of photograms that bear strong likeness to the city-views in the paintings to which allusion is made. The shot that portrays Louise next to Visscher's map begs us to look at the relation of cartography and cinema as a supplement to that which Vermeer extends from graphic to painted media. For the draftsman and the artist, maps and pictures "describe" the world in literally graphic ways. The window that looks onto the highway over the blue mirror of a swimming pool outside the room is not seen in the shot, but it is present in reflection on the mirror and in the light that enters the frame from the right. "Light" is seen on one side and is named and written on the other, in "Lite" printed on the label of the beer bottle adjacent to Louise, which in her words with Jimmy she will clasp in her left hand and bring to her mouth to drink as she looks directly outward at the sunlit space outside. As the shot pulls back, the pendant lamp is seen lit only by a bar of light reflected on the right side of its gridded cylinder and the brass of the pendant boss on its bottom. As a reflector and an erotic shape it occludes and draws attention to Visscher's wall map, showing that the decorative panel on the right side is extended in reflection on the glass door opened in front of it, its jamb on exactly the same axis as the right-hand border of the map. The lamp, itself gridded as a map, also stands in counterpoint to the neck of the beer bottle that Louise brings to her lips. The object is clearly, too, an uncanny avatar of the unlit chandelier in "Ars pictoria," which also reflects light that emanates from a source hidden by the folded drapery in the foreground.[17]

Both the lamp and the beer bottle draw attention to the difference between the flat surface of the wall map and the curvature of the television screen. Her legs crossed, Louise pushes her right knee in front of the left side of the television set in order, it seems, to underscore a visual parallel between the black frame of the Dutch mirror and the black box and oblong surround of the television console. The attractive contour of her bare knee and calf, their outline illuminated on the right side, calls attention to an anamorphic image on the screen. On the curve of the screen there seems to be the reflection of the window off-frame, but it is a bent window that also reflects the knee (in the same way that the mirror above completes the shadow of Louise's head, and the vertical span of the beer bottle is extended in the penumbral shadow it casts on the wall).[18] Indiscernible, the anamorphic image of the television screen comes not from inside the set but from the window beyond (or even emanates from both areas at once). The detail calls attention to our own desire either to identify what would be emitted or, if the set is off, to glimpse the moving reflection of a technician or a cameraman who would break the spell of the illusion.[19]

The women in Vermeer—whether Clio, the woman in blue who reads a letter, the woman at the window who holds a pitcher, the lady hooded in white cloth who hears gallant words from a man dressed in a red coat—seem to live in full cognizance of the greater space and light infusing them with sensuous grace. They turn the places where they are into matrix-like space whose defining surfaces promise depiction of greater worlds to come. Their rooms are pregnant with potential of growth and inner travel. By contrast, in the film the motel room becomes an intimacy in which the women become victims of both agoraphobia and claustrophobia. Open space of the road in front of the window is the object of Louise's gaze in a primal moment (she suckles the nipple of the beer bottle) as she hears Jimmy affirm that she is in Oklahoma. A new Orpheus, she cannot look back.

Women Plotted

In *Thelma and Louise* the question concerning the displacement of women into roles usually granted to men is inflected by the cartographic image and its relation with Vermeer. In a lengthy take that immediately follows Louise's last words in front of Visscher's world map, we see a medium close-up of Thelma in a blue bikini. Supine, on an aluminum deck chair, as she had been on the bed inside the motel room, she holds a Walkman in her hands while, eyes closed, she seems suspended in a trance. She is plugged into a pair of yellow earphones and might or might not be listening to the music, off, that throughout the sequence plays in the background. The words, "I can feel it when I hear that lonesome highway" accompany the outdoor shot. They belong to an indirect discourse. When they become resonant they lead us to believe that Louise is led to press her head painfully with her right arm, the music apparently whetting a painful desire to be where she is not or simply being the cause of a migraine headache.

From the left the Thunderbird enters, its horn honking, Louise yelling, "Thelllma!" Louise jumps out of the car, runs forward in the deep space, and touches her partner. Startling each other, in vaudeville antics they jump while the music drones on, "So many miles to go before I die," in view of semi-trailers rolling on the interstate on a line parallel to the cyclone fence between the poolside and the car. Louise runs back to the car, and Thelma jumps forward to get something—it will be her suitcase—in the foreground. The vocals continue, "We can never know about tomorrow," just as she brings her belly and thighs forward enough to establish a sightline that run through her legs and below her crotch before she pulls the valise into view. When she raises the suitcase the sightline is blocked, occluding any viewer's desire to see the road across the divide of Thelma's thighs. The shot closes in on the gateway in following Thelma lugging the bag, tossing it into the back seat of the car, and jumping in while the music continues, "Still we have to choose which way to go." As the line ends Thelma's buttocks become the point where her movement is queued below a truck that passes by above her head. She has just clambered over the door and plopped into the seat as the car takes off and turns right ("You and I are standing at the crossroads . . .").

Do Visscher's map and the setting to which it drew attention plot two forms of spatial desire? Could one be said to be projective and the other introjective? Inside the motel room Louise looks with fear at a space that will not fulfill her or ever be bathed in pregnant luminosity. Outside, by the pool, the spectator's point of view is one that gazes on an attractive body whose position compares with the nudes of Titian, Velasquez, and Tintoretto. Thus the response to the questions posed above is affirmative, in part because the cartography of the sequence begs the viewer to wonder who looks and who speaks. We see in the shot binocular forms—Thelma's bilateral symmetry and the hubcaps of the Thunderbird—that resemble the composition of the world map. The area inside the motel is projected outward, but it remains unconscious, hence of a vaguely projective identifica- tion: what to look at, how to act, and where to go become questions that sum up the women's plight. Point of view has become so unmoored and visual desire so mixed that we wonder if they are men playing women or women playing men.[20] The confusion may be part and parcel of the road movie and its geographies.

Gender in *Thelma and Louise* seems to be as unsettling as a baroque map in a roadside motel. The film tells much about what it means to get lost on the Amer- ican road. The heroines never accede to an interstate highway where they would not be lost, nor do they take advantage of "welcome centers" at rest stops that would afford them free maps of the states (Texas excepted) in which they drive. The fact that they don't know where they are going affords us, in turn, thanks to the story of their demise, to act out fantasies of getting lost in a world where cinema figures in a growing network of roads that foster illusions of boundless- ness. In a brief, telling, and strange way Visscher and Mercator provide maps for that illusion.

9

Cronos, Cosmos, and *Polis:*
La Haine

In *Thelma and Louise* we have seen that a mapping impulse motivates an industrial cinema that exploits politically and a esthetically viable forms to target a broad and often international public. Even if Ridley Scott is an auteur who maps and plots his films with spatial devices in a manner of his own, his films have a polished and seamless appearance that their maps call into question or, failing that, open onto broader theoretical horizons. *Thelma and Louise* draws much from classical and New Wave cinemas and indicates its debt to the legacies that have been the topic of the earlier chapters. In this chapter and the next the task will entail seeing how mappings in French and American cinema of the postwar era inform and return to films that sought to shape new agendas and alternate spaces. May 1968 has been called "the month of 44 days," in which students and workers, alarmed by rampant social contradiction, brought the French nation to a temporary standstill. It was a touchstone that capped the dire prediction Truffaut's teacher made about the future of the country in the opening sequences of *Les 400 coups:* "I pity France in ten years!"[1] Long after its events May 1968 became a signboard that begged viewers to make comparisons between a time when it was felt that the world could be changed and another, of the present, when few signs of promise were visible on the horizon. Truffaut anticipated a crisis and, since then, other directors have looked back to it in search of new ways of approaching the future. It might be said that directors have returned to the halcyon days of the New Wave and the utopian tenor of events of 1968 in order to address and to exorcise ills of the present.[2]

In an equally equivocal way so also returned, accompanying the memories of

1968, the images of the Earth that had been taken from the capsule orbiting the moon during the mission of *Apollo 8*. These pictures were the first empirical views of what Ptolemy and classical cosmographers had previously only imagined. Two were noteworthy, one of which figures prominently in Mathieu Kassovitz's *La Haine* (1995). "Earthrise, 1968," displayed the planet Earth emerging from the galactic depths of outer space over the barren landscape of the moon. The other, an untitled picture from *Apollo 17* (coded as NASA AS17-22727), is a full view of the earth. A cloudy mass of swirls in the Southern Hemisphere and bright ochre displays earthen patches of northeastern Africa and Saudi Arabia. The two images, notes Denis Cosgrove (2001, 263) have been reproduced more than others from the same program. "They remain in wide circulation today, used for an array of purposes from commercial advertising, book illustration [that includes the title page of Cosgrove's book], emblems, and symbols of 'global' educational, humanitarian, and ecological issues." A call to change the deplorable state of the *oikos* came with the speech and clamor of May 1968. With the images taken by the cosmonauts in the Apollo missions emerged a strange and eerie feeling, common to what is found on celestial maps, of the fragile beauty of the planet.

In *La Haine* Kassovitz returns to these memories in order to plot two "diagrams" or mobile cartographies that situate the specific politics of his film within a broader frame of the histories both of cinema and of local struggle and dissent. Images from the Apollo mission allow the topography of the film, the locale of the housing projects on the outskirts of Paris, to ally with a "cosmography," understood here as a strain of metaphysics in which the situations in the narrative constantly beg the personages to wonder where they are in the world. The metaphysics belongs to a mix of Pascal's *Pensées* as they are remembered from quotations gleaned from school manuals and the lyrics of hip-hop music. Two sequences of the film are of strong cartographic and cinematic resonance.

Children of France

The film tells of three youths who are outsiders in the sordid milieu in which they live. The protagonists are trapped in a squalid *banlieue* of Paris at a moment prior to the general strikes that disabled the nation in the winter of 1995. Perhaps the unsparing photography and the mix of reggae and hip-hop music on the sound track impelled Jody Foster to claim that *La Haine* would "rock" whoever saw it. Despite its graphic depiction of the freefall of three adolescent boys into primal chaos, the maps in the film bear witness to a classical metaphysics of space. The latter is shown in what its first and last words tell the viewer to consider: the society in which we live, likened to a person having jumped from the fiftieth floor of an immense skyscraper, blithely falls through the air until he or she crashes onto the asphalt below. In the literature surrounding the film, metaphysics is set in tandem with the epigraph the published scenario draws from

Le Rouge et le noir. The narrator, up to his ears in social conflict, cites Stendhal: "'J'ai assez vécu pour voir que la différence engendre la haine [I've lived long enough to see that difference engenders hate]" (Favier and Kassovitz 1995, 5).[3] Hate can also be thought of in terms of its geography, in the mix of imaginary and real spaces that the film constructs from its descriptions of the suburbs and city of Paris.

To ascertain how the reflective apparatus of *La Haine* figures in a broader literary, geographical, and philosophical dimension it suffices to recall the quatrain François Villon was said to have uttered as a parting shot just after his executioner tightened a noose around his neck and before he was dropped to his death:

Je suis François dont ce me poise
Né de Paris empres Ponthoise
Or d'une corde d'une toise
Mon cou saura que mon cul poise.

Here goes François, child of France
To swing into his final dance.
His neck at last shall have the chance
To weigh the tonnage of his pants.[4]

In this parting shot the criminal inverts the world by displacing the center into its suburban periphery. Hailing from Paris "near Ponthoise," the poet bears the heavy task ("dont ce me poise") of thinking about what his identity may be: he is *François,* but he is also French (*François*). He is tagged by both a proper and a common noun that describes him, and thus he might be given to reflect upon what it means to be French in a "globalized" world or to worry about the push and pull of "competing" national, international traits defining his character before he will swing from a patibulary gibet erected on the outskirts of Paris. His thoughts anticipate what his neck will discover when his bottom is pulled down and away, earthward, from its habitual environs. The foresight of death after a life of criminal behavior and unjust treatment at the hands of authorities (the narrative line of Villon's *Testament*) is staged as a cosmic comedy.

Villon's rhymes can be taken as a strangely appropriate epigraph to a film that draws upon the story of a person, falling from the fiftieth story of a building (because of its size certainly not in the suburbs), his eyes squeezed shut, repeating in a voice loud enough for the inhabitants at every floor to hear him uttering, "Jusqu'ici tout va bien, jusqu'ici tout va bien . . . [Up to here everything's okay, up to here, everything's okay]" (Favier and Kassovitz 1995, 8). Of import, concludes Kassovitz, is less the fall than the landing. For Villon anticipation of the drop reveals how the lower depths of the body think and speak with admirable wit. For the rogue poet the weight of the buttocks will be a healthy—if summary—

jolt, an affirmation, that will correct and resolve the poet's metaphysical bent in the upper half of the same quatrain. So too, we might say, the freefall of three youths from the suburbs of Paris and back marks a geography of social contradiction plotting that of the very *difference* that Kassovitz, thanks to Stendhal, attributes to an inexorable and universal condition of hate.

Kassovitz's preface to the screenplay maps out two areas of difference that bind the real and allegorical spaces of the scenario that follows. It relates that in 1992 during an interrogation a policeman clubbed to death a youth named Makoum. The event raised the question about how the handcuffed victim, strapped to a chair, could so madden an officer assigned to interrogate him. Did a lack of respect for public order inspire an uncontrolled reaction? Did the policeman blow his fuse because of the endlessly heated confrontations, occurring day after day, hour upon hour, in the suburbs between delinquent children and the police? The same questions could be asked of youths who find themselves gratuitously cuffed and kicked by the hands and feet of agents of the law in the dull routine of their identity checks. Failing to own a symbolic language that might mediate that of their peers, they can only reproduce the violence that is imposed upon them.[5]

Kassovitz describes the situation as a vicious circle that requires a perspective of contemplation that would modify—rather than incite—violence overtaking the suburbs in the 1990s. Surely the simple plotline of the film attests to a vicious geometry: riots break out at Les Muguets, a housing development bearing the unfortunate name of the aromatic flower of community that workers give to each other on the first of May, the French Labor Day. Televised news reports that a young *beur* named Abdel was grievously injured and transported to a hospital where he lies in coma. His friends, a triumvirate of *boulevardiers* (chosen allegorically to personify the mixed demography of French youth), include a Black, an Arab, and a white Jew whose cropped hair resembles either an inmate from a concentration camp or a skinhead, a white Neo-Nazi of extremist leanings. Abdel, seen only in televised images in the film, carries the weight of the near-cognate name of the brother, the "Cain" who would be the police, who are implicitly asked, nonetheless, to be their brother's keeper in a world driven by hate.

Events Crosscut

The narrative hinges on two events that follow the inaugural sequence in which (beneath the overlay of the credits) a televisual documentary records an outbreak of war in the suburban streets. The scenes of violence are accompanied by Bob Marley's lyrics about a world consumed in flames. Damage is done in the housing settlements. A school has been trashed and its gymnasium ransacked. The youths, who may or may not have been responsible, want to visit their hospitalized friend. The police firmly but in cognizance of the law deny them access to his bedside. The action prompts Vinz (Vincent Cassel), the crazed and almost psychotic member of the trio, to swear that in the name of his brother's keeper, should Abdel succumb, he will avenge him by murdering a policeman.

Exclusion from access to a space of exchange or sociality epitomizes other episodes in the film. Earlier, the males of one of the buildings in the development at Les Muguets cook *merguez* sausages and watch television on its rooftop. Sayid, the beur (Saïd Taghmaoui), steals a merguez in partial response to the privilege that Hubert, the Black (Hubert Kounde), gains when the cook at the makeshift grill offers the latter a free sample for the simple reason that he too belongs to the housing complex. Sayid hides under the shadow of his brother Nordine who pays for the sausage. Violence is averted, but a news report reveals that a policeman lost a gun in the melee of battle at night (11, 30). Officers arrive at the scene, one in uniform, another in plainclothes. One is identified by his jacket, on which one shoulder has a shamrock sewn emblematizing the "Fighting Irish," and the letters on the back spell "Notre Dame." The cop is "nicked" by a name that hovers between allusion to the *métier* that identifies the Irish in America, whether footballers or police (Officers Finnerty, Kane, McKenna . . .), and to Catholic devotion given by the name of the cathedral and Holy Mother at the center of Paris.

In the initial sequence the policeman from Notre Dame and his cohort gently ask the crowd to "descend" (but not fall freely) from the roof. Nordine begs them to realize that in the community no harm is being done. The aptly named Chef Toit ("Captain Roof," who is on the roof, but also "Captain You," in the familiar) retorts, varying on Kassovitz's formula heard in the credits, "c'est pas l'histoire de faire quoi que ce soit, c'est l'histoire qu'il faut descendre [it's not about doing anything whatsoever, it's about having to go down]" (11, 49). In the confused perspective of the dialogue, the elemental story concerns a descent from the roof that will be a double murder, a *descente* (a suicidal fall from a position of community and communication) and a story that itself will include a victim of a homicide (in "it's the story that has to be shot"), *descendre* a pun on "going" and "shooting" down. Two primal groups affront one another. An attempt to negotiate and mediate is offered, and in lieu of a scenario in which "conflict gives way to exchange," aborted negotiation gives way to conflict.[6] Each time the youths attempt to cross a barrier a confrontation results and violence erupts. In the apartment building in Paris, when Hubert, Sayid, and Vinz want to find "Astérix" (translated as "Snoopy"), they are the butt of ridicule or admonished by the voices transmitted over the intercom (42, 117–18). They crash an opening in an art gallery, are shown to have come from "dehors," and thus are deemed out of place. Where do they come from? "Je veux dire de quelle banlieue [I mean, like, from what suburb]," one of the party-goers asks of Hubert (55, 149) before the trio is pushed out of the space in which they have crashed.

The episode in the apartment building is cause enough for the police to apprehend Sayid and Hubert. An officer begins his interrogation with false gentility, uttering, "Bonjour, messieurs, Police. Alors, il paraît que vous faites du grabuge?

[Good morning, gentlemen. Police here. Now it appears that you've made a ruckus?]" (45, 122). Vinz, who exits while the two friends are accosted, escapes by virtue of wit and strong legs. A bifurcated sequence follows in which two simultaneous events are crosscut. Vinz is seen inside a movie theater identified by a neon exit sign ("sortie") over a door. As if a refugee from a French New Wave film, Vince enters a movie theater where he either sees or is oblivious to images that speak to the situation and context of his state of being.[7]

For directors of the 1960s the inside of the theater was a site of exchange and of citation, a *locus amoenus* for personages who could escape *into* the prisons of American and French cinema. Here the citation merely inspires and mirrors the brutality of everyday life. We (as Vince may or may not) hear the voice-off of Clint Eastwood, Sylvester Stallone, and a Walt Disney film. These quotations prompt Vinz to rehearse the "point-and-shoot" gesture he has learned from *A bout de souffle* and *Taxi Driver* to aim at, in a degraded citation of *The Deer Hunter,* what is implied to be an animated cartoon of Bambi (46, 123–34).

Meanwhile, in the police headquarters Sayid and Hubert are shown in deep focus, in a *plan américain,* handcuffed and chained to two chairs (44, 124–25). They submit to scorn and loathsome torture at the hands of two interrogating officers. The victims are hazed and cuffed to a point where many spectators, if we recall the torture scenes of *Roma, città aperta,* can only be revulsed by the sadism. The sight of a third officer who assumes the spectator's point of view matches the viewer's gaze. Being trained by his henchmen, he cannot bear to see what takes place before his eyes. The close-ups of his face and eyes are set in counterpoint to those of Vinz in the adjacent sequence. A paradoxical sense of distance and immediacy is given by the style of the interrogation. It rehearses many of the scenarios in the television show *Law and Order,* the film *Mystic River,* or, in real life, Abu Ghraib in which armed forces isolate their suspects in a room and haze or torture them. In *La Haine* recall of *Roma, città aperta* cannot be avoided nor can in another way, *Les Maîtres fous* (Jean Rouch, 1955), in which a scene of frenzied ritual exorcism of colonial masters takes place in a remote spot outside of Accra in Ghana.[8] In the precinct the observing recruit is shown preferring to close his eyes and forget that he belongs to an order of organized sadism and a longstanding "theater of cruelty."[9] As the didascalia of the screenplay emphasize, "Seul dans son coin, le civil 3 ne participe pas à la fête, il ne dit rien, mais on peut voir que dans la situation présente, il a honte d'être flic [Alone in his corner, the third policeman does not take part in the festivities; he says nothing, but we can see that in the present circumstances he is ashamed of being a cop]" (47, 125).

This sequence may indeed be the most excruciating of many in a film that is patently difficult to watch. It obviously reenacts the memory of the murder that Kassovitz invokes in the first sentence of *Jusqu'ici tout va bien . . . :* "En 1992, à Paris, un jeune homme de dix-huit ans du nom de Makome a été abattu à bout portant par un inspecteur dans un commissariat [In Paris in 1992 a young man of eighteen named Majome was beaten point blank by an inspector in a precinct]" (7). By contiguity with Vinz's synchronous descent into the labyrinth of Hollywood violence the episode in the commissioner's office, graphically and unremittingly displaying the physical pain endured by subjects submitting to the torture of interrogation, is matched by its counterpart in the movie theater. The mindless violence of contemporary American films seems to be the fantasied obverse of the projected violence that was aimed at the bodies of Sayid and Hubert. The sequence in the theater where American cruelty is heard off is shot in the prevailing style of televised advertising, in extreme close-ups of Vinz's face. He is pushed up against a wide-angle lens as if to rewrite and redefine Gilles Deleuze's concept of the *image-affection* that turns the view of a face into a quasi-total world of sensation in synergy with the topography of the character (1983, 105–20). Implied is that the greater film owes its own effects to the thousands of stupid American films put before Vinz's eyes. Thus it theorizes itself and, paradoxically, gains a distance on its own violence by collapsing the geography of the world of Paris and the suburbs onto that of American (and hence, aggressively international or globalized) cinema. The dialogue of the two sequences opens a reflection on the space of conflict exactly where there would be an identity of the physical and mental worlds held within what Kassovitz calls a "vicious circle."

The Lower Depths

The two sequences on which the film turns—when the denial of access to Abdel's bedside precipitates Vinz's threat to use the gun he found to shoot an officer (17, 60–62), and the torture in the police headquarters (47, 124–25), along with its obverse episode when Vinz hides in the movie theater—concretize the project Kassovitz announces in his preface to the scenario. They also reiterate what becomes ruthlessly redundant and, at the end of the film, a pummeling resolved only by the crash of ritual murder. Vinz is "he who must die" because he has internalized the difference to a point of crazed frenzy. He is shot in the head in close-up when the officer, his automatic pistol thrust against his temple, pulls the trigger. The gun cracks, Vinz expires, and a spent brass casing, ejected from the chamber of the gun, clicks and rolls on the asphalt where the victim soon collapses (70, 179–81). Chef Toit, the plainclothes officer seen earlier on the rooftop and identified by his Notre Dame jacket, is held responsible for igniting the passion. Before shooting him he hazes his victim, pressing the barrel of his pistol against Vinz's cheek, uttering, "Regardez comme il chie dans son f . . . [Look how he's shitting in his f . . .]" (70, 181). The executioner, incited by the violence of his own words, goads *himself* into applying pressure to the trigger.

The raw speech localizes the sadism that runs rampant throughout the film. Vinz dies in a communion of unmitigated dejection. For this reason the geography of

violence in the film, if projected upon a bodily surface, finds its most represen-
tative site in the vicinity of the rectum, an area of a transitional eros, where tenderness and pain are inextricably mixed. The metaphysical dimension of *La
Haine* projects the physical space of the *banlieue* and all its psychic depredation
onto this region of the body. Here, too, is where the film incarnates the social
practice of what Stendhal is said to call "difference" and Kassovitz "hate." The
director noted that his film tends to show sympathy for the youth who lack a
symbolic language of negotiation while trying to keep a necessary distance and
perspective in which a dialogue can be established between the warring parties.
"*La Haine* se situe clairement du côté des jeunes tout en essayant de conserver
la distance et le recul nécessaires [*Hate* clearly leans in the direction of the youth
while trying to conserve the necessary distance and hindsight]" (8). *Du cul et du
recul:* hindsight might be the perspectival object that continuously reiterates and
reframes the physical and bodily geography of the film. The two sequences and
the variants that mark the style and plot are set in strong contrast to two others
that do not quite belong to the tenor of baiting ending in conflict or to a stage
where cruelty prevails. Rather, two affective and strangely tender moments in the
film open a space in which all of a sudden animal instincts give way to a propen-
sity to reflect on the situation or to obtain distance or *recul*. Each episode with-
draws from the site of violence not by reflecting *on* or over the dilemma in a
metaphysical way, but, paradoxically, from *within* its bounds, that is, within the
limited scope of the topography of the film.

In sequence 39 (113–15) the triumvirate, after erring about in the streets of
Paris above the ground, pause to relieve themselves in the basement toilets of a

Figure 37. *La Haine* (1995): Vinz (*right*) and Hubert ponder the effects of hate (*haine*)
in the space of a men's room that displays a poster advertising Heineken.

bistrot. In a miniature hall of mirrors that vaguely recalls Christine's boudoir of *La Règle du jeu* or that of Tom Duncan's widow (Jeanette Nolan) in Fritz Lang's *The Big Heat* (1954), even the hall of mirrors where Arthur Bannister (Everett Sloane) and his wife, Elsa (Rita Hayworth), pursue each other at the conclusion to *The Lady from Shanghai,* the young men are splintered in the confined space. Sayid clasps a bottle of chocolate milk, appropriately named *Cacolac,* in his left hand, as he tries to punch a number on the digits of a pay telephone in the background. In the first shot, in medium close-up, Sayid holds the phone and brandishes his bottle of milk. To the left Vinz looks upward before it becomes clear that he is pissing into a urinal below. To Sayid's right is Hubert's back. Sayid turns left and right, offering a sip to either or both of his buddies.

The following shot, a plan américain, puts four figures in view: Vinz is to the left and is the mirror image of Sayid who places his telephone call to Astérix (a rich drug merchant) for the purpose of completing the sale. To the right Hubert is in a mirror and then, to his right, Sayid again appears. The third shot, in medium close-up, cues on Hubert's suggestion that Vinz forget about avenging the death of Abdel. The camera catches Vinz and Sayid in conflict over Hubert's words (the subtitles read "Yes!" and "No!"). The shot pans to the right, forcing recall of the fact that Vinz had already been in a mirror. He emerges in close-up, retorting that "my name's not Rodney King!" The camera follows his head left, back to the mirror, where Sayid, in full view, occludes Hubert.

The title of the film suddenly falls into the sequence. At the terminus of this long take (that lasts about 83 seconds) Hubert avows that Vinz should have stayed in school instead of taking to the streets. "Tu savais que s'il y a un truc que l'histoire nous a appris, c'est que la haine attire la haine [You know that if there's something history has taught us, it's that hate attracts hate]" (79, 114). Vinz upbraids Hubert for being on the side of cowards because he has learned the lessons of life directly ("t'es toujours du côté des enculés?! Moi je vis dans la rue [you're always on the side of the assholes who get shafted. Me, I live in the street]"). Vinz holds his head in his hands when all of a sudden a white mass enters the frame. It is a door that opens from a booth. From it emerges an old man who utters in a foreign accent tinged with a lisp, "Ça fait vraiment bien de chier un bon coup [It's really nice to take a good shit]." A countershot captures Vinz and Hubert staring back in astonishment when the man asks, "Vous croyez en Dieu? [Do you believe in God?]." The old man makes his way through the space, the back of his head, out of focus but following much of the frame as he advances. Still seen from behind, drawing attention to his act of cleansing his hands, he adds, "De toute façon il ne faut pas se demander si on croit en Dieu, mais si Dieu croit en nous [In any case we mustn't wonder if we believe in God but if God believes in us]."

He adduces the truth of the chiasmus by telling his story of his friend Grunalski who accompanied him on a train filled with forced laborers. The Russians had impressed the two men into service after the liberation of the German concentration camps. While en route from Dachau to Siberia the train made occasional stops to fill the boiler of its locomotive. During these short stopovers the prisoners habitually descended from the train to relieve themselves. Grunalski had the habit of defecating out of the sight of his companions. The man's timidity or refusal to abandon social graces, avows the storyteller, cost him his life when he could not both keep his pants pulled up and scurry to the accelerating train. The camera holds on the old man as he relates his story. When he tells of Grunalski coming out from behind a bush, the camera changes the perspective, catching the man's head, slightly out of focus, in the foreground, in front of a pair of swinging doors fashioned after those of a saloon in classical American Westerns. Behind them is a poster of a bottle of beer displaying a label that reads *Heinek*, the last two letters of "Heinek*en*" (graphing the vocable *N*) obfuscated by the wall in the middle ground. The man's white head in soft focus becomes the object of Hubert's gaze.

Baffled, Sayid (off) asks why the old man told the tale. The trio, somewhat astonished or unmoved by what they call the "depth" of the story, leave through the doors and exit right, each passing by the poster. The camera holds on the doors for three seconds, adding a Bressonian touch that implies the framing of the space is of a consequence exceeding that of the characters who have just departed. The style of the shot tells the viewer that it begs to be deciphered. Surely the *en* lopped off *Heineken* rhymes with *haine*, the word Hubert twice utters in the same space. The allusions to things *behind* the space and time of film recall the lower depths of the Holocaust and of hate in a past world of which the youths are unaware. The poster suggests that the presence of a brand name may qualify the film, as we have seen in the "life" spot in *Thelma and Louise*, to be of the dubious stuff and substance of advertising. No matter what is implied, the film is suddenly elevated to a tradition of *ciné-écriture*, where meanings are built and circulate through lexical allusions scattered by written shapes seen and read in the visual field. However ponderous or nuanced the innuendo, the sequence marks a rare instant when the characters pause long enough to consider their metaphysical condition. The cloacal depths become the space *par excellence* where the three characters begin to think abstractly. Sayid mutters a piece of speech that concretizes the brand-name: "*Hein*, pourquoi il nous a raconté cette histoire? [Uh, why did he tell us this story?]" (115). The site suddenly becomes a place where language and image are mixed, and where too a sense of *recul*—hindsight—is exactly what the inexperienced youths need to gather a sense of who and where they are.

Their perplexity is emphasized in the cut to the next sequence that takes place in the Parisian *métro*. The view in the train is seen in strong depth of field, the parallels of each side of the car converging toward a vanishing point at the doorway to the next wagon. The shot uses extensive depth of field to stress how spatial extension is foreclosed by the artifice of cinematic illusion. Closure and constriction are implied. Given the recent images of the toilets and the story of Grunalski running behind the train and paying dearly for his discretion, the itinerary in the subway moves from one depth of occlusion or blockage to another. A layered pattern of abysmal spaces runs from the nightmare of the gulags to the subway and its underground world of workers, travelers, and panhandlers in perpetual war with each other.

Wherever the métro and the R.E.R. are brought into the narrative so also is a heightened sense of social, physical, and mental geography.[10] In most likelihood the fortieth sequence (116) is apparently inserted to reiterate the exchange where confrontation and hate are summed up in a pattern of quid pro quos. Begging in the moving subway, a young Romanian woman tells the story of her plight that is matched by Sayid's cynically veracious account of his own situation. After he tells her off, she flips him her middle finger ("un doigt d'honneur") to indicate to him that he ought to get fucked. The gesture is connected to the cartographic dimension of the next sequence taking place at the Rue des Halles. Sayid, Vinz, and Hubert are lost in the city. Sayid asks a policeman for directions that will lead them to Astérix's apartment. The officer looks in his guide and shows the youth how to get to the address. A straight cut separates the sequence in the métro from that of the Rue des Halles. In broad daylight Sayid runs down the street and flags a policeman who responds by offering help and wishing him a good day, saluting the youth and uttering, "bonne fin de journée, m'sieu [have a good afternoon]." Sayid runs back toward the camera where, on either side of the frame, amble Vinz and Hubert. "Tu vois comme ils sont polis, les keuf ici. Il m'a carrément dit vous et tout [Hey, don't you see that they're polite, the police who're here? He squarely addressed me in the "vous" and all that]."

In Sayid's remark the metaphysical geography of *La Haine* is suddenly concretized. In the scenario, "T'as vu comme ils sont polis ici? [Have you seen how polished they are here?]" (41, 116) brings forward a confusion of world, government, social conduct, and violence: an agent or uniformed personification of *la police* carries his city-map and speaks with terse elegance. Sayid's words, "polis . . . ici"—both "polished" and "police" here—echo his observation about *policy*. The words also carry a suggestion of the art of governance and of domestic regulation. It resides in the broader historical definition of *police,* and by extension to the world at large as *polis,* the noun describing the city-state as a global locale. The theme of the film that poses the question about how best to go about regulating a world on the precipice of disaster is borne in the visible and aural dimensions of Sayid's pun. The three outsiders who are lost inside the city cannot decipher maps or realize where they are. For a moment, perhaps as an aftereffect of the old man's story, a threshold of communication is gained. Linked to an overarching effect of atopia and set in the context of trains that serve as a metaphor of spatial communication, the short sequence—in its abrupt transition from the underground to daylight or from violence to exchange—plots a metaphysical geography in the midst of conflict.

The World Is Ours

The relation that ties human conduct in a social topography (a *polis*) to the cosmic figure of the world floating in space is confirmed in what might be the most abstract sequence of the film (61, 155–57). Late in the night the trio has crashed an upscale opening at a gallery before finding some respite in the darkness of the night. They are seated on a rooftop that looks over Paris in the background. Soon entering the field of view are the illuminated outlines of the Eiffel Tower. A extreme close-up of a ring on Vinz's finger (that spells "Vinz" in bold characters) precedes the long shot on the roof accompanied by a piece of rap (whose air uncannily recalls Raymond Devos's voice in *Pierrot le fou,* chiming "Est-ce que vous m'aimez [Do you love me]," that here is turned as ". . . tu me connais? [(do) you know me?]." The question thresholds the view of the sky and stars that Hubert and Vinz contemplate, the backs of their bodies facing the camera on either side of the frame as they rebound a volley proverbs that end with "Liberté, égalité, fraternité." The words refer at once to the grounding contradiction of the film, to the bond the threesome share, and to the emblematic Tower of France.

In response Hubert's voice suddenly waxes metaphysical after Vinz reflects on the tale the old man had told in the men's room. In the script Hubert murmurs in response to Grunalski's parable, "Je sais pas, mais c'était profond [I don't know, but it was really deep]" (61, 156). In the final version he in fact appropriates what the old man had been scripted to say in his monologue. "Moi je pense qu'il croit en nous, car Dieu nous aide et fait pousser le caca, vous saviez ça? [As for me, I think he believes in us because God helps us, he pushes the shit out of us, did you know that?]" (39, 115). In the final version the words are given to Hubert who varies on the formula. He declares, "Si Dieu fait chier, c'est Dieu qui fait pousser le caca [If God is a pain in the ass God is he who pushes the shit]." The remark is made as Sayid, in the background, writes his name on the surface of the building with the can of spray paint. He moves toward the center of the frame in the middle ground and offers a poem (not in the published script) he reads from memory to the two seated figures in the foreground who seem to be "thinking." "Voici un poème" (the English subtitle translates "here's a poem" as "check out this shit"), he announces, before stating, "Le pénis de Le Pen à peine il se hisse [Le Pen's penis can barely get a hard-on]."

The wit elides with Hubert's remark reiterating what he had said, voice-off, in the first shot of the film, prior to the credits, that displayed a color image of the world as it had been photographed from the Apollo mission to the moon in

1969. Hubert asks Vinz if he knows the story of the man who falls from the building of fifty floors who repeated "jusqu'ici tout va bien. . . ." Vinz replies that he knew it from a rabbi. In the final version of the film, in a shot that displays the back of his head in extreme close-up to suggest that his skull assumes the form of a globe, Vinz suddenly begins to think along the lines of Pascal's remarks on interplanetary space in the concept of the *deux infinis*. Instead of putting himself in the place of the man falling from the apartment building, he avows in words uncharacteristically bereft of obscenity, "je me sens comme une petite fourmi perdue dans l'univers intergalactique [I feel as if I were a little ant lost in an intergalactic universe]." In the shot his head figures as a virtual planet amid an infinity of galaxies. Since an image of the globe is remembered from Hubert's first telling of the tale of the falling body, Vinz's skull, now seen as a human globe, is a counterpart to the memory-image of the terrestrial sphere first shown to the world from the *Apollo* rocket in 1968 and the aftereffects of May 1968.

The sequence in the toilets showed that when the film underscores a point the camera tends to hold on an image in order to promote reflection. Fixing on the space of the bathroom and the Heineken poster, it invites a gloss of the name in the context of the lower depths in which it is placed. The same effect recurs when the young men exit the frame. The camera remains centered on the Eiffel Tower in the distance. The bars of light that illuminate its sloped girders are extinguished from the bottom to the top. The boys had tried to coordinate the darkening of the Tower with a snap of their fingers, but they leave—admitting that synchronization works only in the movies and that for all they care they can plug carrots in their mothers' assholes—before the camera registers the disappearance. On first glance the Tower would be an icon ironized, like the slogan "Liberté, égalité, fraternité" adjacent to its surrounding obscenities in the dialogue uttered earlier in the same sequence. Like a meaningless slogan, it would be a carrot thrust into the night. But as the camera holds on the Tower and the onslaught of darkness heightened by the extinction of light from the base to the summit, the structure suddenly resembles a silent rocket that seems to ascend and evanesce in the night.

The camera is asking the viewer to "read" the effect of the Tower in view of the "writing" that Sayid has just sprayed along the edge of the building. In the first version of the script he was to rhapsodize, "Mon nom est écrit partout sur la façade, je suis un putain d'enculé de tagueur qui brûle la ville de son sigle . . . [My name is written everywhere on the façade; I'm a fucked-over scumbag of a graffiti-sprayer who burns the city with his initials]" (61, 156). A straight cut to a street in Paris (63, 157) returns to the poster, bearing the legend "Le monde est à vous," that displays in black and white the *imago mundi* first seen in color before the credits, and then glimpsed when the threesome were taking the R.E.R. from Les Muguets to Paris (35, 95). The scenario underscores the contrast between the battle zone of the intermediate areas glimpsed through the windows of the train en route from the housing area to Paris. The desolation becomes the object of Hubert's thoughts as he contemplates the landscape. For the viewer memories of *Les 400 coups* seem to inhabit the image so much that the three boys would seem to be disaffected and disowned sons of Antoine Doinel.

> Hubert thinks. Refusing to answer to Vinz's aggression, Hubert is immersed in his thoughts and looks at the landscape, or rather the city-spaces that parade before his eyes, sometimes with a few pieces of graffiti happens to color different spots, but in general everything is grey and sad. A bus stop shelter under which an old man is standing has been shattered and sprayed with graffiti, a luxury car, its wheels having been removed, is perched on the stone squares in a wasteland. Further off is glimpsed the poster with the planet first seen at the beginning of the film. We discover that the poster is an advertisement for a travel agency and that under the planet is written the following slogan: THE WORLD IS YOURS. (95)

The camera holds on the poster before a shot in vanishing perspective displays the trio before an esplanade that recedes into the immensity of Paris. The slogan is part of a tesselated construction of recurring mementoes that includes a graffito in the suburb which reads, "l'avenir est à nous" (15, 56) and a remark by the concierge in the apartment building. In a Portuguese accent she exclaims, "Vous êtes pas fou dé sonner chez tout le monde? Vous croyez que le monde est à vous? Dehors! [Aren't you out of your minds to buzz everyone. Do you think that the world is yours?]" (42, 118). In the sequence where it appears for the second time the poster displaying the *Apollo* image stands at a distance midway between the suburbs and the city.

By contrast, now, in the tiny gap between the two shots, between the evanescent penal shape of the Tower and the globe that follows, a metaphysical geography emerges. The date of the image shows that the hope felt in 1968 in the power of people to address the ills of the world in 1995 is dashed. It is clear that the poster is an interfilmic reference that allies *La Haine* with a number of other films.[11] "The World Is Yours" had been seen on the horizon of Howard Hawks' *Scarface* (1932). The French title alludes to Renoir's utopian experiment, *Le Vie est à nous* (1936), and surely the empyrean beyond the grasp of everyone in the film is invoked in the oblique reference to Jean Grémillon's patently idealistic scenario of a flyer in *Le Ciel est à vous* (1943). Within the field of allusion the poster displays an ironic commentary on the failure of the western powers to improve the human condition despite its development of an apparatus that brought humans to the moon. In the same light it can also be asked if the Eiffel Tower, seen in view of Sayid the *tagueur,* can be seen as a calamitous writing instrument that exhausts its illuminated ink as might a pen its fluid or an aerosol can its compressed paint.

An answer to the question is found in the long take fixed on the poster and the depth of the street in the sequence that follows the extinction of the Tower (63, 157). The film cuts suddenly from the bird's-eye view of Paris. Seen in deep focus and in a perspectival view of the street on the right side of the frame, the three boys walk toward the image from the *Apollo* mission that stands at the left. Sayid stops, pivots, and paints an *N* over the *V* of the "vous" at the end of the legend: "Le monde est à v (n) ous." The camera holds on the difference long enough to allow the viewer to gloss the words in myriad directions. It initially forces recall of the inaugural expression of graffiti in the film.

In his first scriptural gesture in the film Sayid is introduced to the spectator in a delay (3, 19). The camera pans right along a row of uniformed policemen standing listlessly by their vehicles. The felt tip of a marker is heard squiggling before the pan reveals Sayid penning his words on the backside of a van. The screenplay furnishes an interpretation of the gesture when it anthropomorphizes the vehicle: "Dans les cars blindés, des CRS dorment ou jouent aux cartes et personne ne remarque qu'à l'arrière, le jeune beur est en train de taguer discrètement le cul du bus [In the armored vehicles the riot police sleep or play cards, and no one is aware of that in the back the young *beur* is discreetly painting graffiti on the bus's ass]" (3, 19). Sayid, *à l'arrière,* decorates *le cul* of a bus bearing the emblem of the riot police. Sayid's name, drawn in imitation of Arabic or of an exotic alphabet, stands above the words, "Baise la police [Fuck the police]." It offers a calligrammatic figure of the Eiffel Tower in the letter *A*. The miniature ideogram anticipates the advent of the grandiose architecture that is drawn into the night enveloping the city at large.

Figure 38. *La Haine:* Sayid has just rewritten the legend to the image of the world seen from the moon. Spraying an *N* over the *V* of "Le monde est à vous," he changes "The world is yours" to "The world is ours."

Graffiti and Glossolalia

In both sequences the drawing of the signature would be a frustrated attempt to raise consciousness about the collective nature of a degraded *habitus,* or a call to arms to think globally (about marshaling energies misspent in the cursive art of cursing, or occulted frustration about a world at war) while acting locally (leaving a mark in and around Paris and defying police brutality). The drawing of the letter *N* would be a manifest sign of a metaphysics of squalor, or of what Kassovitz called a need to gain hindsight or *recul* on the world. In shorthand the letter *N* stands for *Haine,* the noun that had been glimpsed in the toilets heralding a bottle of "Heineken" after Sayid had drunk his modicum of "Cacolac." In the prevailing language of the film the world that is "à nous" would be a hypothetical world-anew and a world-anus. It would belong to a metaphysical order on which Pascal drew inspiration for his *deux infinis,* of a terrible human governance—or *police*—of things, in which Montaigne, the author inspiring Pascal's thoughts about the human condition wryly remarked that

> [l]a presomption est nostre maladie naturelle et originelle. La plus calamiteuse et fraile de toutes les creatures, c'est l'homme, et quant et quant la plus orgueilleuse. Elle se sent et se void logée icy, parmy la bourbe et le fient du monde, attachée et clouée à la pire, plus morte et croupie partie de l'univers, au dernier estage du logis et le plus esloigné de la voute celeste, avec les animaux de la pire condition des trois; et se va plantant par imagination au dessus du cercle de la Lune et ramenant le ciel soubs ses pieds (1962, 429)

> Presumption is our natural and originary malady. The most calamitous and frail of all creatures is man, and more often than not the most boastful. It feels and sees itself lodged here, in the mud and dung of the world, attached and nailed to the worst, the deadest, and the most stagnant part of the universe, at lowest floor of the building at the greatest remove from the celestial vault, with animals of the worst condition of the three; and with its imagination it goes planting itself above the circle of the Moon and bringing the heavens beneath its feet.

In this context the film folds an archaic cosmography, an aura of timelessness, in its representation of contemporary social space.

It is revealing to see how the metaphysical geography of *La Haine* is meshed with its craft of distribution. As much as it reflects or analyzes the social injustices it portrays *La Haine* figures in a broader invention of the *malheur des banlieues* in which the French left and right have played equally strong roles. Reception of the film is noteworthy. "One side reads the suburban youth culture as a 'culture of protest' and the other a 'culture of psychosis.' For the first, it is the society which is the problem and the emergency requires fighting exclusion. For the second, it is the kids who are the problem, and the emergency requires more police force and border patrol."[12] As it recedes from recent memory the film blends into a syndrome of frenzied opposition to civil chaos that runs from the memory of Rodney King to the O. J. Simpson trial and the idea of suburbs in perpetual disaster.[13] *La Haine,* notes Jenny Lefcourt (Lefcourt and Conley 1998), became a reference that soon figured in the mythology of the banlieue. At one point in the film the three boys sit under a televised map of a weather report in France. The meteorology is used to show that the film is a symptom of condition of violence of its time and that its mood conveys the atmospheric pressures in what Baudelaire had once called the "spiritual barometer" of the nation.

Returning to the persona invoked in Villon's parting words in his *Grand Testament,* we recall "François, the child of France" who remarks that his neck will be aware of the gravity of his buttocks when he hangs from a gallows located at the edge of Paris. His words seem lighter and more ethereal than Hubert's thrice-repeated fret about the man who will crash on the pavement after a fall from a building of fifty stories. Villon's figure philosophizes about the space of the world by refusing to entertain any extended meditation about time, the world, and social contradiction. Kassovitz predicts apocalypse in the space of a couple of seconds.

If film, like poetry, can be said to be a mechanism that philosophizes independently of its readers or consumers, *La Haine* tends to think in the areas where its sense of space exceeds its own intended objectives. That sense is not located in the suburbs, in Paris, or in the suspension of a body falling earthward from the moon or a skyscraper, but between its ideology (which includes both its conscious and unconscious relation to itself and its ambient modes of production, if we are to recall Louis Althusser at the time of the American mission to the moon) and other spaces that are opened within its forms of expression. The unmitigated *anality* of *La Haine* indicates that the film is above all a work that belongs to a classical French literature that goes back not just to the *fabliau* but also to the *salon* and the literature of the *précieuse,* to the world of elegantly oppositional practices that we have seen in Louis Malle's (and, indirectly, in Ridley Scott's) appeal to the Carte du Tendre. Where there is tenderness a space for metaphysics is possible. The tender map is one that belongs to euphemism and elegant idiolect. It constructs another world or a different way of living in the one that is given.

In *La Haine* the same language is omnipresent, but as in Villon, it is turned topsy-turvy. Swearing about failing to hitch wires that would allow the three young men to jump-start a car they have jimmied so that they can return home safely, Sayid curses, "Enculé de putain de fils de pute de bâtard de vérole de moine de merde de volant à la con!!! [Motherfucking asshole of a son of a bitch and a monk's buggered bastard at the goddamned wheel]" (58, 152). Alert reader that he is, Vinz, the youth with the foulest mouth, tells him to stop philosophizing and get the job done: "Arrête de philosopher et tire." We have seen that Sayid, armed with a marker or a spray can, was the writer and the chronicler of the forms of repression. In *La Haine* he was the artist of glossolalia, a language of intransitive expressiveness. Vinz, who responds to Sayid's outburst with gnomic curtness, here suggests, building on Montaigne once more, that to philosophize is *not* to learn how to die, but to euphemize—to euphemize upside down—where the bottom is celebrated residing in the place of the top. The distance that the film gains from its topic in its inversions, where its *recul* from itself identifies its site of pleasure and its festive underside becomes the sign of its appurtenance to a tradition that, as the fashion of an idiolect born of 1968 would have it, "deconstructs" its pretension to shock, alarm, disgruntle, or bait its viewer.

Three maps are made visible in *La Haine*. One, taken from the *Apollo* mission in 1968, is attached to the credits and recurs in the suburbs and in the city. The meteorological map of France under which the children place themselves for a moment indicates that the film is an allegory and that its meaning moves from *police* to *polis* and from *polis* to *cosmos*. One of the maps is less evident but ultimately the most memorable. Walking with his friends through the grounds of Les Muguets, Vinz turns about and sees a Holstein cow that looks for pasture in the midst of the asphalt. "O Téma," he utters in place of "O la vache!," an exclamation that would have called a holy cow a cow. For the viewers the bovine is not a memory of a laughing cow on a cellophane wrapper, a *vache qui rit,* but is more likely a totem of a *vacherie,* of a suburban cowshed where humans live in miserable compression. The splotches of black and white on the cow resemble a pattern of continents and oceans of a world map. A tradition of aesthetic cartography has turned Holstein cows into bearers of cartographic projections.[14] Artists on both sides of the Atlantic have painted "maps" onto their skin in order, perhaps, to have the viewer recall that the hide itself had been the *prima materia* of portulan charts, the medieval maps on parchment that sailors had formerly used to navigate their way about the Mediterranean. In a crazed way Vinz seems to imagine a world-map on the cow that his fantasies bring into the courtyard of the housing project. The map is one that figures in the metaphysics and underlying abstraction of Kassovitz's feature. If it belongs to antique and modern traditions, the projection and its material bring the viewer back to a greater history of cartography that figures in cinema. An added irony of *La Haine* is found in its own icon of France and of cinematic writing, the Eiffel Tower, which in chapter 1 we saw affiliated with the origins of the seventh art.

10

Ptolemy, *Gladiator,* and Empire

The design of the preceding chapters might resemble Visscher's planisphere in the roadside motel in *Thelma and Louise,* French cinema of the "old" world residing in the circle to the right and American films of the "new" world in the adjoining circle on the left. For viewers of *Thelma and Louise* or of *La Haine,* the geographies taken up in chapters 8 and 9 do not seem to belong to the one world or the other. The traits that signaled their national traditions seemed, if not motley and mixed, at least in a sustained dialogue with one another. In both features the protagonists find themselves in wastelands and non-places in which famous landmarks appear unexpectedly or incongruously. Nondescript motel rooms and diners of the road movie have as their counterparts the housing projects, subway cars, and street life in the docudrama. In one the two women see the Grand Canyon and then die, while in the other the three boys take a dim view of the Eiffel Tower before they plunge into violence. Far more than other films taken up so far, these two features suggest that they invent spaces that touch on global proportions. Thelma and Louise are in awe of the empyrean above the Canyon, and in the wee hours of the night a hoodlum feels that he is an ant lost in an intergalactic space. The mixed feelings the characters share about the compression or immensity of things might indeed be a sign of the ways that a good deal of contemporary cinema is plotted to appeal to universal issues, not for their own sake or that of pure contemplation but in order to be assured of economic success on screens all over the world.

It is a fact that the architects of early cinema sought to bring the medium into a frame of global distribution. Shortly after the turn of the twentieth century

Alexandre Promio wished to have Lumière's films capture the essence of the places in which they were shot before circulating them to theaters in every major city. Georges Méliès placed the logo-emblem of "Star Films" in the intertitles and credits of his films to confer international appeal on his commodity. A good deal of contemporary cinema makes clear the same ambitions in its use of cartographic matter. In the paragraphs that follow Ridley Scott's *Gladiator* (2000), another cult classic, will be studied with the aim of seeing how the map we see in the film translates these ambitions and how, at the same time, it tells us of a condition of cinema built at once upon geographical and historical illusion. The latter belongs to a ramifying network of special effects, effects in which cinema, cartography, advertising, and popular culture are of a same measure.

A Correspondence: *Empire* and *Gladiator*

The cartography of *Gladiator* is first seen in the northern reaches of the Roman Empire in its waning years. When Commodus (Joachim Phoenix) and Maximus (Russell Crowe) fight to their death a battle of Empire and Democracy is staged in a tragic mode much as Preston Sturges's struggle between Capital and Labor on the top of a speeding freight train at the beginning of *Sullivan's Travels* (1941) was made for farce. Fate is such that in a monumental study, *Empire,* published roughly synchronously with *Gladiator,* authors Toni Negri and Michael Hardt argue that the last decades of the twentieth century have witnessed one world overtaking another. A "society of control" is replacing a "society of discipline" that had prevailed up to the Second World War. The two authors propose that the laws which now regulate nations and economies in the global sphere no longer impose limits or geographical barriers. In disciplinary regimes, they note, in some homage to Michel Foucault, wrongdoers are punished for reason of violation and transgression of laws are understood to be permanent.[1] In a society of control a law is interpreted as a mean that allows for various degrees of deviation. By contrast, in the disciplinary society a law is formulated in order to invite its transgression. Its formulation incites a desire to do what is proscribed.[2] Our attraction to laws is due not to the fear and loathing they inspire, but to the ways we can deploy, move about, and reconfigure them. The global "empire" of democratic capitalism controls its subjects through the play and the give-and-take of its relations with law. Such, they say, are some of the pertinent traits of the global *empire* in which we live.

In the coda to their history of the formation of the contemporary world they advance an agenda of resistance and articulation that bears some of the trappings of the great left-wing movements of the nineteenth century. They assert that a global society is politicized when it confronts directly or unambiguously responds to the question concerning how the actions of a global multitude can become politicized. They assert—with enthusing fervor—that it must begin with "the central repressive operations of Empire. It is a matter of recognizing and engaging the imperial initiatives and not allowing them continually to reestablish order" (399). The reader hears a call for transgression in a system of controls where the act is difficult to discern or at least where an oppressive order is of global extension. Hardt and Negri imply that disenfranchised Goths, Vandals, and Visigoths of the second, third, and fourth worlds, from the Chiapas to Chechnya, need to break the chains of the optical cables that enslave them.

The reader of *Empire* who has seen *Gladiator* (2000) and indulged in its "peplum" style (a word the French use to describe the genre because of the short skirt-like flaps below the armor of soldiers of the empire) recalls that the film came to theaters on the spurs of the circulation of the book in stores and on Web sites. Parallels between the book and the movie are many. Both use the decline of the Roman Empire to inaugurate their narratives. *Gladiator* begins with the destruction of the last horde, the final remnant of the bestial infidel massacred before the empire decays from within it own ranks. *Empire* builds its history from the point where no worlds are left to conquer, and from where Polybius's vision of the three "good" forms of power in the Roman Empire—"monarchy, aristocracy, and democracy, embodied in the persons of the Emperor, the Senate, and the popular *comita*" (314)—have uncanny parallels in today's nation-states, "media-organizations, and other 'popular' organisms, . . . even though certainly its contents are very different from the social and political forces of the Roman Empire" (315). *Empire* and *Gladiator* are both done in an epic style, painted with broad historical strokes, either to legitimize civil disobedience or to warn against passive obedience to regimes that produce terror in the wars they declare on terror.

The edges of both the book and the film are gnawed at by a disaffection with the state of constructive dissonance known since 1968. The hero of *Gladiator* returns to Rome without quite realizing that his valor in Germania (projected in the style of Tacitus's *Annals*) was perfunctory, for a cause that many viewers might have associated with the traumatic effects endured among soldiers returning from the war America had lost in Vietnam. The emblematic image on the flyleaf of *Empire,* an image reminiscent of the pictures from the *Apollo 17* mission studied in the chapter above, is a satellite-photograph of an oceanic surface of the globe over which whirls a spiral of clouds. As we have seen in chapter 9, this type of picture reminds us that the first color pictures of the globe and its heavens came at a time of great civil protest against the American policy and, soon, with Watergate, the revelation of extensive corruption in Washington. Despite the clean and clear Icarian point of view of the emblematic photograph (the "map" suggestive of global empire), Negri and Hardt make a plea to the world to fight powers imposing the controls of corporate democracy.

They do so from the standpoint of a politics of modulation, that is, of immanence, of practice, and of invention that have affinities with the art of the everyday—indeed, with individual mappings and spatial stories—that are tools of the

politics of Michel de Certeau's "spatial stories." The authors propose that constructive dissent ought best work within networks of activities that strategic
orders cannot or have not yet co-opted. It appears that Ridley Scott's *Gladiator,*
an otherwise entirely strategic film telling its viewer to admire the handiwork of
its special effects, invites counterreadings or interpretive mappings that would
be far more mobile and of tactical merit than what it seems to represent.

A spectacle of imperial corruption is witnessed through the grisly gladiatorial
contests. The Roman games were corrupt, *Gladiator* suggests, and so, too, the
film seems to remark boastfully, are its own ambitions. In *Empire* the economic
history of the west is rehearsed in order to show that it can be rewritten otherwise, and not merely from the standpoint of capital. In *Gladiator* the spectacles
in the Coliseum stage the history of the conquests of Rome but are brought to
opposite conclusions through the astute logistics of battle, learned from the codes
of the Roman army, turned and aimed against the partisans of the empire. *Gladiator* ends with the hope for political change after the ritual death of two personi-
fications; Democracy, wounded and shafted by Empire, dies just as he impales
and kills his evil enemy. *Empire* depicts a degraded and polluted world order
that will only be cleansed, both politically and ecologically, with the revival of
the *militant,* "the fundamental actor of the 'long march' of the emancipation of
labor . . . , the creative singularity of the gigantic collective movement that was
working-class struggle" (412).

Coincidence of the timing of the book and the film and other parallels notwithstanding, the former advocates a cohering countermilitancy and the other displays
a willfully confused and spectacular history of strategies and tactics, of archives
and diagrams, within what might now be called a media-industrial-military complex. If the film succeeds in conveying a politics the latter is seen obliquely in its
inclusion within its own form of some of the guiding principles of Paul Virilio's
work (1982 and 1999) on the affinities of war *in* and *as* cinema. In *Logistique de
la perception,* we recall from the first chapter, he argued that the imagination of
armed combat in early cinema inflected not only the shape and style of future wars
(the First and Second World Wars) but also their very fact. Films produced a *perception* of war in order to anticipate and, by force of the imagination, even to con-
jure up its event.[3] Producers quickly realized that their films were not histories
or mimetic reconstructions of past events but, rather, *maps* that were setting into
the imagination spatialized images of the kinds of social order and control they
could wish to lock into a collective psyche.[4] When D. W. Griffith staged the waves
of Union and Confederate troops in attack and counterattack in *The Birth of a
Nation* (1915) the "archive" of an image of war waged exactly forty years before
the film was made was in essence a "map" of the territorial battle that would be
waged in the trenches of northern France immediately following its completion.

In *Gladiator* Scott and his team transpose the paradigm onto the arena of media
warfare. In the narrative they show that the disenfranchised senators belonging

to the former democratic regime—all appear impotent because they resemble grey-haired sexagenarians shrouded in bedsheets—correctly observe that gladiatorial combat lures the populace away from the hard thinking and labor required of an egalitarian regime. In the spectacle of its images the film shows that it also ("Et tu *Gladiator* . . .") is serving up the same ritual fare. Its titanic order, its own aspiration to be an empire of itself, is cast as a political lure. Its self-critical dimension, what Negri and Hardt would call its theory and practice, would be located in the way in its own form it reflects on the effects of its spectacle.

Ptolemy's *Italia*

The map in the movie bears on what might be, if not the theory and practice of *Gladiator,* the raw material with which the viewer can turn it into something different. The projection appears in the field of the image for the duration of not much more than half a second. The charismatic leader, Maximus, his centurions, and their soldiers win an electrifying battle over the hirsute German horde. He returns to a sumptuously furnished tent in which he confers with the aging and debilitated Roman leader, Marcus Aurelius (Richard Harris). Nearing death, Marcus Aurelius asks Maximus to be the next patron of the Roman people. By choosing Maximus on grounds of his merit and the unalloyed admiration he has gained by and from his countrymen, Marcus Aurelius oversteps a salic law that would require him to put his son, the malevolent Commodus on the throne. Marcus Aurelius commits an act of transgression in a world where he would wish a more flexible political system. His action also yields the consequence of drawing the narrative, up to then about combat, into the plot of a family romance.[5]

Figure 39. *Gladiator* (2002): The aging Marcus Aurelius asks Maximus to "look at this map." It is ostensibly a wall map in the style of Ptolemy of *Italia* and lands between the Adriatic and Black Seas.

In an amber chiaroscuro Marcus Aurelius avows to the hero of the day that the burdens of leadership have been and will continue to be heavy. He infers that the Romans may been overly ambitious in expanding the borders of their empire. In a brief but salient series of shots and reverse shots, turning about and pointing his arm backward and over his shoulder he asks Maximus to "look at this map." A cutaway shot shows, displayed, hidden among the curtains and objects in the darkened quarters—a burning candle to the left, the bust of a Caesar to the right—a wall map of Italy and the greater lands of Eastern Europe over and above the peninsula. It is hardly as svelte and boot-like as we know it on contemporary projections. A rugged and broad interior contained by a jagged coastal outline, the great mass of land on the bottom that thrusts into an aquamarine surrounding recalls the map of Italia in the *Geographia* of Ptolemy (ca. A.D. 145) (1991).

The rapid reference to the map is so offhanded—at once perfunctory and riveting—that it begs for interpretation. First, the map here does not quite play the same crucial role that it does in most classical military films. It is remote from the computer maps that sparkle on the screens in the briefing chambers at the outset of the same director's *Black Hawk Down* (2001). Yet it functions as it might in a war movie. In *Desperate Journey* we have seen how commanders and their subalterns pour over maps before they trace imaginary lines upon them with pointers and pencils. Maps are generally reserved for films of the First and Second World Wars, for Vietnam or Somalia, but not for Roman campaigns.

The map usually plots the imaginary space of the conflict and passage for what lies ahead.[6] In *Gladiator* the map of *Italia* does not include the entire Roman Empire of which Marcus Aurelius has spoken. The view is partial, indicating that the men are far from a circumscribed homeland. And as other elements of the cinematic rhetoric have shown (in the music of pathos, in the calm of fatigue following the battle, in the shift from clatter and noise to a somber mood), the map seems to indicate shrinkage and even decline. Rome is Rome, but Italia is a minor appendage of the continental body to the north, and the meager spoils the battle has yielded in the snowy realm have no place on the map. The map, anticipating the presence of the Eastern Roman empire as it would appear after A.D. 395, does little justice to the Mediterranean reaches of the Roman world. The projection is shown to bear the signs of historical fatigue that in surrounding close-ups (and there are many) are traced in the wrinkles furrowing Marcus Aurelius's face. The leader points to the map to remind the charismatic commander of the armies of the "big picture," of the dubious future of imperial administration. Set on a darkened wall that stands behind the old man, *Italia* is a painful reminder that overarching conquest of new space can lead to entropy in matters of jurisdiction. A project that seeks to globalize through conquest will result in decline. By *not* situating the hinterlands where the Romans had just beaten the Barbarians, the map betrays the locational signs spelled out in the first intertitle, set over the snowy landscape, indicating that the events are taking place in boreal climes on the northeastern fringes of the kingdom. It begins to call into question the time and space of the military operation and its relation to that of centers and peripheries.

The projection is, second, an initial sign of an intertextual component that motivates much of *Gladiator*. The map clearly refers to a cartographical sequence in a film on which the sequence of *Gladiator* is patterned. Anthony Mann's *The Fall of the Roman Empire* (1964) constitutes the model for the beginning of this film. In that feature the Romans are also in the north and are waging perilous combat with an enemy hidden in the hills beyond the Roman stronghold. The past glory of the empire is evoked when a parade of chariots passes before the aging Marcus Aurelius (Alec Guinness) and his great commander (Christopher Plummer). Each chariot stops; its driver, wearing a breastplate, a peplum skirt below his belt and a feathered helmet on his head, bears the ensign of each and every region of the kingdom. The geography is declined by the leader's vocal identification of each of the ten-odd chariots that pass in what seems an excruciatingly protracted review.

When Marcus Aurelius asks his general to take command of the empire he struts by an easel on which are mounted a number of great sheet-maps that otherwise confirm that the Roman territories are as vast as what had been indicated in the preceding military parade. Later in the same film, after poisoning his father, and now in a bind because enemy hordes are approaching the kingdom from all sides, Commodus (Stephen Boyd) acts out his decadent ways by strutting over a mosaic floor that depicts the Italian peninsula in the greater region of the Mediterranean, the Holy Land, Africa, Spain, and Europe to the north and east. Reproducing a *topos* common to imperial propaganda, Commodus virtually walks over and defiles what is rightfully his to command but that he has wrongfully obtained.

Viewers of *The Fall of the Roman Empire* are reminded of the construction of the reporting of the Gulf War in early 1991 when networks placed on the floors of their studios various maps of the Persian Gulf, Egypt, Saudi Arabia, Iraq, Israel, and the eastern Mediterranean that the anchoring newscasters trod upon in the course of their reports. The style of their gait and the pressure exerted by their massive wingtip shoes on the map attested to an aggressive domination of the Gulf as much by the media as the air attacks and the illusions of "surgical" bombing being reported. Anthony Mann's film clearly provided a source for this effect. That Ridley Scott chose not to use it in the analogous sequences in which Commodus struts about the senate could be sign that the implied contest of global arena, of a *theatrum mundi*, would be enhanced by eliminating allusions to the real setting of the Roman Empire. The map connotes the history of the composition of the film. Mann's work is clearly seen through that of Ridley Scott, and vice-versa.

The motley quality of *Gladiator* given through its allusion to *The Fall of the Roman Empire* is further enhanced, third, by the fortunes of the map seen on the wall. A historian of cartography would immediately discern that what Marcus Aurelius shows to Maximus belongs to the style of Ptolemy. But whose Ptolemy, and when and where? The Ptolemaic map of *Italia* figures among the twenty-three topographical views that follow the mappamundi and precede a detailed gazetteer of place-names and their location according to latitude and longitude. The maps were executed in the middle of the second century A.D., and rediscovered in the fourteenth century, when they were copied in manuscript and soon after published in handsome folio editions. In the latter the arts of woodcutting (in Strasbourg, but also in northern Italy) and copperplate etching (in Bologna and Rome) were developed and refined. As editions of Ptolemy were put to a test in view of experience and observation (perhaps because of the accuracy of portulan charts of the Mediterranean), two projections, one old and the other new, were included for each region.[7]

The map of *Italia* that we see in *Gladiator* belongs to a diacritical tradition peculiar to Ptolemy and to humanistic cartography, in which the history of the construction of the map is shown in the difference of an earlier and a later view. The veracity of the map is found in a field of differences, and not merely in the fact that the one projection replaces another. The map in *Gladiator* figures in this postmedieval context at the same time it marks a series of differences in respect to the sequence it draws from Anthony Mann's earlier feature. Seen as an "earlier" view of the Italian peninsula, the map figures in a history that locates the projection in its distance in respect to its recovery in the Renaissance, the time when such a map was made visible for a general public.

In light of the history of the map to which he draws Maximus's attention, Marcus Aurelius is oddly telling the warrior to heed an anachronism or to wonder what indeed may be the logistical power of cartography in future waging of war. When we locate ourselves both from Maximus's point of view and our own, the map that situates the old leader and the military commander at a distance from Rome also indicates *where* we must imagine ourselves in the epic narrative soon to follow. In the context of what would seem to be a historical reconstruction the anachronisms unhinge disbelief and promote a closer examination of the filmic space. We find ourselves not just in Rome at the beginning of its decline, but also in a late-medieval setting that imagines Italy through a lens underscoring its remoteness from present time and space.[8]

In these three functions the map informs us that from the outset we are being asked to engage the film in the style of a comparative exercise. We are baited into evaluating and enjoying the film as a potpourri of combat and logistics. It is hardly surprising that "serious" historians have castigated the opening sequence. The catapults that launched fireballs referred to war movies showing how howitzers or shelling from battleships "softened" the terrain before foot soldiers were sent forward to engage enemy. The thousands of flaming arrows launched by row upon row of archers resembled movies of the grist of *Ivanhoe* (1952) but also recalled the rocket-launchers seen in the newsreel footage of the Second World War. When Maximus rides forward, yelling, "Unleash Hell!," he is accompanied by a German shepherd that inspires recalls of the equestrian soldier in the guise of Albrecht Dürer's famous woodcut, "Knight, Death, and the Devil," in which a soldier in armor, his lance erect, puts his spurs to his stallion as his faithful canine runs beside them. The cumulative effect of the battle prompts comparison with the grisly beginning of *Saving Private Ryan* (1998), a film that might be its nearest rival or enemy brother. One wonders if the sequence was conceived to call in question the so-called authenticity of any Roman epic or other war movie by its own willful confusion of military codes.[9]

Map Effects and Special Effects

The cartographic material inflects the relation of cinema and history in other areas of the film, in shots that on cursory glance seem no less perfunctory than Marcus Aurelius's implicit nod to Ptolemy. Commodus, following his triumphant return to Rome, decides to make gladiatorial games the opiate of his people. He offers to the senate the plan of sating the public with a new stadium. A close-up of the edifice is shown. Bathed in dark grey, on first view the coliseum seems to be real; as the shot unwinds the stadium is slowly perceived to be a model whose proportion requires a comparative correlate. In respect to the architecture seen up to this point the arena seems grandiose, but only before a gigantic hand enters the frame from the right and sets into the middle a set of pegs to represent combatants on the field of play. The following shots reveal that the hand belongs to Commodus and that he is conceiving an architectural model for the new Coliseum. The shot of the *maquette* or miniature three-dimensional plan precedes an aerial (ichnographic) view of the finished stadium seemingly taken (at least for anyone who has watched professional football) from a Goodyear blimp that flies in the sky over the Eternal City. Thousands of dots, seeming throngs of people, mill about and around the site shown to be the realization of the emperor's wooden model. The sleight of the emperor's hand, toying with the wooden gladiators, reveals that the virtual character—the computer-generated imagery—of the architecture underscores how much a "Coliseum-effect" is built as much from simulation as from representation. The model avers to be the real thing because it is anchored in the regime of perception that the film is inventing and negotiating.

The shots that register the emperor's architectural fantasy and its realization sum up the narrative of special effects that accompanies the epic tale of the return and vindication of a soldier betrayed by his country. A simulated architectural form gives way to a computer-programmed monument offered to the eye not as a mimetic form that reconstructs an integral object from the remainders of a contemporary ruin but a simulacrum creating its own order of beauty. As a result, when Maximus and his band enter Rome and gaze at the Coliseum from the streets below and on the outside of the structure their expression of marvel does not come from a sense of disproportion about their own size against the enormity of the building (nor, either, if the plot is recalled, does Maximus exude a lingering narcissism of astonishment fueled by his having come from a ramshackle stadium to play in one of the seven wonders of the world). Rather, the gladiators seem to be in suspended admiration over the special nature of their own special effect. They are programmed to marvel at the effectiveness of themselves as computer-generated and, with their pectoral sinew, body-built simulations. In that way, in the role of optical intermediaries between the spectator and the spectacle, their gaze elicits a critical relation with the modes of production of the film. Their eyes engage in a play of perception of all that is virtual in the film's reality.[10]

In the DVD edition of *Gladiator* a good deal of the supplementary plastic disc is devoted to the ways that Ridley Scott and his crew "generated" the panoramic shots about and in the monument. In Malta they built a coliseum, no doubt from the same kind of maquette that fuels Commodus's imagination, but they left open more than one-fourth of the structure in order to allow light to enter the arena. For shots of the inside and outside, panels were constructed to mask the open areas and to extend the stands and the archivolts and cornices all about the inner and outer perimeters. When Maximus battled the greatest of living gladiators and, while fending off tigers released from cages below the playing field (a citation from Delmer Daves' *Demetrius and the Gladiators* [1954]), the dramatic effects came from programmers who moved the images of the felines closer to those of the hero wielding his sword.

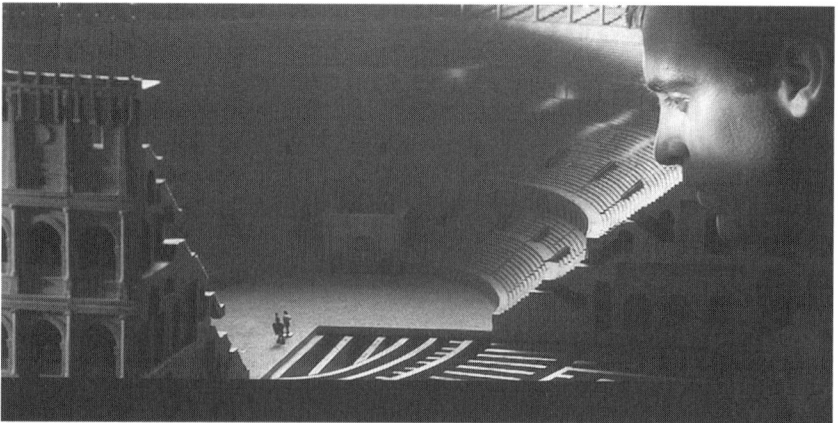

Figure 40. *Gladiator:* Commodus looks at toy gladiators in the model of a coliseum, which will be seen as a computer-generated image from an aerial view in the next shot.

The visual pleasure accrued in these areas of the film could be appreciated as genuinely bogus beauty. On one level the film plays into the world of publicity effects and advertising while on another it seems to be mapping them in ways that celebrate facticity not for itself but, as we have seen through the logistics of the map in the beginning, a relation of facticity to history that can, with adequate distance and alert appropriation, serve to militate in the direction of a cruel lucidity.[11] Somehow the circular image of the Coliseum, flat and deep as a hologram, resembles the shape and sheen of DVD diskettes.

It is here that these two "maps" in *Gladiator* can be taken in a sense consonant with the reflections of Negri and Hardt on empire, subjectivation, and control. The film is less an overt writing of history *Saving Private Ryan* or *Schindler's List* than a self-interested speculation on what indeed comprises a writing of history. In other words, the flatness of the depth of field yielded by the computerized images tells of the workings of an operation that evacuates the present from its discourse by *not* locating where it stands in actual time. The special effects speak to the present through another time that the film claims to resurrect from oblivion and, thus, to distort and exorcise inherited images of history by displacing them into the present (Certeau 1975, 100). *Gladiator* indicates that its simulation of a campaign that Tacitus had described in arresting detail in the *Annals* floats between one epoch and another, and that its military "look" can be drawn through any number of wars. In turn, its reconstruction of the gladiatorial system is overtly plotted through various sets of images. Some are historical, others cinematic, and still others sportive.

Super Bowls

One that is the intertextual complement to Anthony Mann's *Fall of the Roman Empire* is Stanley Kubrick's *Spartacus* (1960), a film that argues for constructive disobedience, after which much of the African and Roman sequences of Scott's film are patterned. Another complement, put forward in the supplementary material included in the DVD version, is professional sport, especially American football, which reigns in televisual media and newsprints from July of one year to February in the next. Throughout the film the spectator is invited to compare its gladiatorial battles (there are at least five) to sports events of our time. The staging of sports events in the televisual realm becomes exactly what *Gladiator* does not elide, but whose broader military connotations it leaves out of its frame.

The contours of the film are visible between the narrative reiterations and their interplay with the media-productions of professional football. Like the distinction between advertisements and the plays seen on a gridiron (a map), the lines distinguishing its history of gladiatorial combat from its relation with media are blurred. From that blur emerges a "logistics of perception." In the narrative Commodus has just strangled his father, Marcus Aurelius, after learning that not he but Maximus will inherit the task of leading the Roman people. He orders his henchmen to put the popular hero to death. Maximus is brought into the woods at daylight and thrown to the earth. Asking for a military death by having a sword plunged down his neck, Maximus, ruseful as Odysseus, is able to wrest himself free from his captors. He grabs the butcher's weapon and kills the executioner and the other members of the phalanx. He escapes after suffering a deep cut in his shoulder above the tattoo, "S.P.Q.R.," that seems to be the Roman equivalent of a marine's tattoo of a globe displaying the Americas and an anchor set above "Semper fi." Maximus finds a horse and, clasping his wounded shoulder, struggles to ride homeward. Along the journey over a lunar landscape he startles himself at the thought that Commodus will have sent centurions to massacre his wife and child at his villa. His intuition is correct. Maximus rides homeward and discovers their charred bodies hanging from a tree at the entry to his gated domain. The sight causes him to swoon. An itinerant band rescues him and takes him to a slave market in North Africa. A former gladiator buys him and puts him among a group that will play before a mixed public in a small arena on the edge of the empire. Maximus becomes a gladiator resembling a football player shipped to "NFL Africa."

His success and *esprit de corps* bring him fame in the minor leagues where the games are played at the edge of the kingdom (for reason of having been proscribed in Rome during the sagacious reign of Marcus Aurelius). After Commodus returns to Rome in the name of the new emperor (in a depiction clearly patterned to recall the arrival of Hitler in Nuremberg in *The Triumph of the Will*), the games are revived. They will, murmur the senators, be a panacea to the real contradictions of social injustice and a degenerate infrastructure. But as media events, politicians agree, the professional sport will nonetheless entertain an increasingly ignorant, mixed, and illiterate populace. And so they do. As armies of gladiators are needed to stage the spectacles Maximus and his friends finally return to the major league, to the newly built professional stadium in the Eternal City.

He first plays in a performance billed to be a re-enactment of the victory of the Romans over the Carthagians. When his valor, bloodthirstiness, and military know-how reverse the predictable conclusion—when he kills the Romans who had killed the North Africans—he rewrites history that has suddenly returned to the narrative fantasy. After other similar performances he soon becomes a revered figure. When Commodus learns that the "Spaniard" is indeed Maximus it becomes clear that the two will ultimately confront and murder each other in a sunburnt arena: which they do after Commodus has tilted in his favor by stabbing Maximus in the back. The death of the evil leader assures that a democracy will return to the senate, and that the stupendous waste of life and energy in the gladiatorial world might also soon be on the wane.

The virtual map of the film is located, on the one hand, between the parabola of several reversals of fortune in the diegesis (the general is turned into a slave before he overcomes his enemy brother; history is inverted in the events staged in the games in the Coliseum; Democracy cedes to Empire and Empire to a promise of Democracy) and, on the other, the intertextual parallels with the combat of militarized bodies of professional football players who now wear light but massive shoulder pads, are coiffed in bright and thick helmets with cage-like faceguards, run in shoes spiked to grip sod and dirt, their bodies clad in tight-fitting Lycra to display svelte sinew and fulsome thighs.

The parallel, however, is so obvious and so overplayed in the literature surrounding *Gladiator* that we wonder if it is tendered to be brought forward that so we can "admire" our critical faculties for making the connection; so that as a contemporary public we might possibly entertain a distanced view on the relation of opiation to the proliferation of televised sports. If so, the film exploits the fluid movement between advertising and the presentation of combat. It shows, in a commercial in which a forty-something quarterback throws a football at the bull's eye of a tire swinging at the end of a pendulum under a tree in his back yard, a mature man's need for more oomph (or Viagra) than he had in his earlier and more mythic days. It shows, too, that when a cap bursts from a bottle of Budweiser that beer is the imaginary aphrodisiac players drink when they squirt fluid from squeeze-bottles into their open mouths. The gladiators in Scott's film and their contemporary avatars "win" through mediated similitudes taking place in the flow between the event and its frame.

The advertisements seem to be cartouches and inserts blending into the map that is the game itself. As in classical cartography, the one inhabits and flows in and out of the space of the other. When the film and the sport to which it appeals make clear their relation with mediation they raise critical consciousness. Like Maximus in all but one of his battles, *Gladiator* would be said to "win" because it entertains a globalized public in accord with the prevailing modes of representation that it mildly historicizes.

In its blur, however, of frame and subject or cartouche and map are glimpsed obvious allusions to contemporary media. After Maximus and his cohorts rewrite the history of the Punic Wars the spectators award the fighters "two thumbs up" with so much approbation that Commodus is unable to have his enemy assassinated. In turn, when Maximus beats a famous gladiator into submission, out of ostensive frustration Commodus signals "thumbs down": refusing to exercise the death penalty, Maximus defies the emperor's orders. In the rhetoric of computerized images the play of events seen from afar (the sight of the great arena) against things very near (close-ups of thumbs that turn up and down) enhances the antitheses that mobilize the story. But they also refer to an emblem popularized by a pair of reviewers, Roger Ebert and the late Gene Siskel, syndicated by Chicago Newspapers, that has crept into the language of cinematic judgment. A film having the benediction of "two thumbs up" assuredly finds success when the sign is reported in newspapers and printed in movie-trailers. Thus *Gladiator* gives "thumbs up" to itself by having its own public exercise a power of decision otherwise reserved for an elite.[12] Other allegorical figures follow the same model. Loaves of bread thrown to the fans are not just historical record; they belong to strategies of publicity found in every stadium or arena, which uses every available parcel of visible surface that can be seen by a camera. The Roman past is given as one that has "not yet" succumbed to subliminal advertising for the reason that the film conveys as much in its own graphic style.

Aftereffects

Some of the aftereffects of *Gladiator* locate the economy of its perception and of its reception. At the National Football League Divisional Championship in January of 2001 at Giant Stadium in the New Jersey Meadowlands two great television screens stood over each end of the football field. On the giant monitors were shown, just prior to the official kick-off at 1:05 p.m., the opening shots of *Gladiator*.[13] "Unleash Hell!" Spectators were invited to compare the introduction of the players as they ran out of corridors issuing from the bowels of the stadium much in the way that Maximus reviewed his troops in the clank and clatter of the buckling of Roman military gear or emerged from the depths of the Coliseum into the bright arena. The raised fists and high-fives shared between Maximus and his fighters—like those of Mark McGwire and José Canseco of the Athletics shared with each other in the early 1990s—were the imaginary correlative to what was happening on the field. The beginning of one event was co-extensive with that of the other. *Gladiator* was served to incite combat and to sell perception (and the future DVD) through the comparisons being served up to the spectators.

Just prior to the game, when the Giants would battle another tribe of Goths from the north, the hoary Minnesota Vikings, a squad of Marines marched across the field, arms on their shoulders and with the gonfalon of the American flag in their midst. They stood immobile while the national anthem was played.[14] Three veteran paratroopers descended from the empyrean and guided their parachutes to the center of the field where they landed in a tumble, rolled up their paraphernalia, and were saluted to the applause of 78,000 spectators. *Gladiator* was the most immediate memory-image in a game that staged, more than any of the contests in the regular season, the analogy of American professional football to American military might.

What was implied in co-presence of armed forces, sequences from *Gladiator*, and football players became more pronounced in the fabled Super Bowl that took place just two weeks later. There, before the eyes of even more spectators, were multiplied many of the agencies producing perception. *Gladiator* was not played on the screens of the Raymond James Stadium in Tampa Bay, but its retinal persistence held strong. The same paratroopers descended on the field.

Minutes later, an American stealth bomber flew silently over the stadium. Then in a great blare a squadron of F-16s whooshed over the crowd and left gossamer contrails in their path. The military complex was felt ubiquitously *above* the stadium, in the persons of the aviators and skydivers who emblazoned the invincibility of American armies both in and outside of the arena. On the occasion of Super Bowl XXXV (Roman numerals strictly in uppercase) the pregame pageant featured a timely commemoration of Super Bowl XXV, in which exactly a decade ago the same Giants had beaten the Buffalo Bills. Super Bowl XXV had taken place at the same time war was unleashed in the Persian Gulf. In the introductory ceremonies in 2001 the heroic combatants of 1991 also emerged from the depths of the stadium and ran into the arena. Reinaugurated, along with the near-synchronous inauguration of George W. Bush, was that moment when George Bush Sr., then president, had enjoyed unparalleled popularity. The moment of the game was staged, it appeared, to celebrate the triumph of Americans over the Iraqis, the Infidels, Barbarians, or Carthaginians of modern times. With the real or implied presence of Norman Schwartzkopf and Colin Powell the game was staged to rehearse, six months before 9/11/01, the invasion of Iraq in 2003.

The construction of the perception of a military complex embedded in a space and architecture of entertainment did not stop with the implicit analogy of Super Bowl XXXV to gladiators replaying Roman battles won in the Punic Wars. Every seatholder at the contest was awarded a free plastic cushion to which was attached a pouch containing a radio with batteries and earphones, and a disposable flash camera in a box labeled "E Trade Super Bowl Halftime Show." The camera was thus thought on first sight to be a memory-machine supplied to everyone who would want to eternize the halftime spectacle by flashing pictures of friendly fans in and about the stands or aiming the camera and shooting directly at the theater on the field. The latter was organized around an immense floor over which stood great girders with lights and speakers. It recorded the calisthenics of Britney Spears and her furies while charge after charge of sky-rockets were blasted into the air, like antiaircraft cannons, or flaming arrows with exploding tips that shrouded the bowl of the stadium under immense clouds of smoke. The disposable snapshot devices given to each spectator had the function of recording the event in which they were playing a part. The devices (clearly antiques in contrast to the camcorders many fans brought to the stadium) were supplied en masse in order for the many cameras set all around the coliseum to record thousands of "points of light" flickering in the dark surround of the stands. Hundreds of thousands of flashes became the scintillating background to the spectacle available to viewers at home. Where they were producing memory-images of the game, the spectators were also participating in the construction of an aerial battle in the black of night. The flashes they made were conveyed on the airwaves as part of the overall dazzle that restaged and prolonged the military effects with which American aviators inaugurated the game.

In the context of a globalized network to which it alludes, *Gladiator* became a mobile map that moved toward contemporary genres of entertainment and an array of films past and present. It became part of an "empire" of cinematic control whose ultimate projection is one of a worldwide circulation of itself. A trajectory drawn from a glimpse of a map bearing some resemblance to Ptolemy's *Italia* to the spectacle of the coliseum reveals that a fragment of an archive figures in a broader cinematic diagram. *Gladiator* itself is meshed with other maps, mostly of strategic agencies of advertising and entertainment, but its cartographies open an interpretive space in which the ends of cinema, mapping, and globalization are shown interrelated. The film allows us to see how modes of control in popular culture are interwoven and reach beyond the confines of a coliseum, a television screen, or a movie theater. *Gladiator* ultimately seems to be light-years away from a modest feature such as *Paris qui dort,* the film chosen to inaugurate this study of cinema and cartography. Both films play on perception to a maximal degree in the idiolects and technologies of their time. Closer inspection shows that they share many of the same traits. It may be fitting to move to a broader conclusion in order to see how and why.

Conclusion

This project began from the impression that films often display maps in their visual field. From there it has been hypothesized that cartography and cinema share many of the same traits. A map, it was shown, requires complex modes of decipherment quite similar to those required for close and exacting making and study of cinema. Reading and seeing, that since the Renaissance have been assumed to be two different modes of intellection, are co-extensive in cinema and cartography. Printed language, topographic representation, relief, perspectival tension, depth of field, and decorative framing of the kind seen on manuscript and printed maps are found in movies. Building on masterworks that tell us what a map is and what is required to read it, I have sought to see what happens when we discern a map in a moving image.[1]

To lay a groundwork for applied analysis of a sampling of films' appeal has been made to what appears to be a "cartographic impulse" inspiring a good deal of film theory. A point of departure is found in the writings of André Bazin in which philosophy and criticism inform questions concerning the nature of filmic space. The question, "What is cinema?" has as its corollary "What is the *event* that we call cinema?" If an event is what causes us to perceive the conditions and actions of perception in what we are seeing and perceiving (and often, we discover, what sees and perceives us), it follows that the maps we discern in a movie often heighten our awareness about perception and subjectivity. A map in a movie prompts us to sense the "quiddity" (or, in the philosophical idiom of Gilles Deleuze, the "haeccity") of the medium. The visual textures, indeed the tactility of the image, give rise to sensations of a kind common to the physical and intellectual pleasures we experience in deciphering a map. The theory examined in the introduction confirms a point that as viewers we often feel displaced whenever we watch a film in a movie theater. The film uses any number of means to foster the illusion that "it is where it is." As soon as we become aware that the representation is only on the screen we tend—often on a psychogenetic plane that may or may not be related to what we are viewing—to harbor doubts about where and why we are looking at the moving image, or why, perhaps in order to let ourselves nestle into a state of passive pleasure, we want to suspend disbelief. These doubts bring forward issues of bilocation and multilocation: we need to feel ourselves in different places at once and, for our own health, not always to be where we are told we are. Broadly then, when a map appears in a movie a swarm of nagging questions arises about being, identity, space, and location. As a general rule a map in a movie can unsettle or displace the inferred contracts tendered at the beginning of every film about the conditions of viewing that follow.

The map can bring forward issues that cause it to become a point of departure for an interpretive itinerary. When a cartographic shape—be it a projection, a globe, an icon of the world, an atlas, a diagram, a bird's-eye view of a landscape, a city-view—is taken as a point of departure, it becomes a model, a patron, or even a road map from which transverse readings can be plotted. It lifts the viewer from the grip of the moving image and thus allows our gaze to mobilize its faculties. At times it looks into what might be assumed to be the unconscious register of cinema, a domain that, as we have seen through the attention Jacques Rancière brings to the areas of the image that the camera records passively, remains unbeknownst to the artist or technician who imposes an action or conscious control upon it. These spaces transmute into a "mobile geography" of cinema. In it voices and visual signs, moving about, tend not to be where they are always thought to be. Maps give shape to other forms that unsettle or make canny things uncanny; they even open onto dimensions of which the film, in the words of Melville's Bartleby, often "would prefer not to" speak.

The films made by the pioneers of cinema, directors who may belong to the regime of the "movement-image" and who realize the potentialities of the medium, are often cartographers. As auteurs they produce a vision of the world through the sum of their films. Yet their cartographic sense is so stirring that they are continually plotting their work when they fold maps into their images and narratives. Sometimes these directors construct itineraries of their own creation, while at others they use maps to inquire of and comment on the state of the world being shown. They insert cartographic material into their work in order, it appears, to build archives and diagrams that exert critical force upon the collective experience of both the films made and their viewers. The films made by the inheritors of cinema, perhaps directors or independent cineasts who live in the regime of the "time-image," establish more precarious and moving cartographies, Gilles Deleuze

(1985b) and others have argued, in which their maps are shown in deficit or excess in respect to the spaces and situations plotted and represented. But no matter whether a director belongs to one regime, to the other, or to both, he or she destabilizes the field of their images.

In the early chapters it has been suggested that certain genres have exceptional affinity for cartography. They would include the Western, in which space is the object and *modus vivendi* of narratives that tell of the founding of new political orders or claims staked to new lands; those of the war movie, in which maps are the precondition to the representation and execution of battle; the road movie, where narrative is written as a line drawn upon an ephemeral map; mysteries or thrillers in which secret places are encountered in the struggle between forces of order and disorder, in worlds where maps have strategic virtue for the proponents of both good and evil. They include, as we have seen by way of Truffaut and Kassovitz, the *Bildungscinema* in which tales of children and youth experiencing the world find themselves amid controlling maps that they cannot read or understand. And, in a less likely way, we have found that maps can also inhabit sentimental films where psychological and affective journeys take place, making of themselves what Giuliana Bruno (2002) calls an "atlas of emotion." They can include film noir, in which maps underscore how much everyone is lost and adrift in a world where neither ethical nor geographical bearings can be found in the chaos of war and confusion. Blockbuster films, too, often include maps in order to emphasize the enormity of control they wish to hold on national and frequently global scales.

The films studied in the chapters above, it is hoped, confirm and complicate the hypotheses tendered in the introduction. René Clair's *Paris qui dort,* a film about modern times and modern cinema, touches on areas of strategic control that would make cinema a medium patterning and channeling collective perception. Seen from a distance, *Paris qui dort* is a "diagram" that charms—but locates and fixes—the spectator in a world, at the threshold of the talkie, under its control. Its shape as a map anticipates the "global positioning" potential of cinema of which today we are abundantly aware. Comparative treatment of Jean Renoir's films from 1932 to 1939 disengages aesthetic issues that become increasingly politicized. The maps that form an innocuously casual background to *Boudu sauvé des eaux* cause the film to compress and dilate so visibly that it calls immediate attention to what will be the theme of atmospheric surface and depth prevailing in much of French cinema of the 1930s.[2] In *Le Crime de Monsieur Lange* a map of North America tells the viewer that we are *not* in a Western where space would expand and that, as a consequence, the social utopia that the characters in the film seek to inaugurate is impossible. The map in fact makes clear that the revolution engaged in the film belongs almost exclusively to the camera. Cued by the map, the circles that the lens describes run in a direction that might be contrary to the collective will on the part of a group that would invent a unaministic world in the miniature space in which it lives. In *La Grande Illusion* a military map summons the technology of military progress. The same film introduces a mosaic map that is likened to an imaginary museum of art that fuels the illusion vital to the lives of a community of prisoners of war. The stone spheres on the terrace of the Château de Solognes on which take place events crucial to the narrative of *La Règle du jeu* are at once globes and cannonballs on the verge of explosion. The globes elicit and refuse an allegory that would foretell the advent of the Second World War. In a different register the maps in Roberto Rossellini's *Roma, città aperta* belong to the struggle of forces that would either terrorize or unify the city and country in its darkest hours in modern times. Ostensibly decorative material, the same projections are found in the living and working spaces of both the "good" and "evil" forces, thus dashing the lines of divide in battles engaged in a milieu marked by the world-theater and a theater of cruelty.

In the name of the "desperate journey," what would be a genre or a convention, the relation of cartography to camouflage is discerned in the ways that maps foster illusions of displacement. The resilience of the genre is made manifest when, in *Raiders of the Lost Ark*, director Steven Spielberg cites earlier films in his construction of a seamless and utterly smooth treatment of adventure. Along the way the film makes clear its own power to be an archive and, too, a controlling diagram for a cinema of aura. By contrast, *Casablanca*, a classic map-film, figures in the tradition of the desperate journey where its maps are related to the immobility of a historical condition in which the narrative is begun. Important avatars of the desperate journey include two of Raoul Walsh's many films that follow the model. *High Sierra* folds maps of fate—of mythic destiny—assigned to characters caught within its webbing. *Desperate Journey,* by contrast, makes clear the illusion on which the authority of guiding maps is based. In its place is glimpsed an art of camouflage that becomes the very object and objective of the film.

Mapping is a pertinent trait of French New Wave cinemas. It is deployed to establish a national geography, indeed a layered landscape, conceived with and against the film theory of André Bazin as well as from classical cinemas of various origin. The New Wave writes obliquely of its relation with the Second World War, directly of its own inventive form, and immediately, too, of its dialogue with director-auteurs whom its adepts take to be the masters of the seventh art. Maps in New Wave films tell of that relation. We have seen that in *Les Mistons* appeal is made to topographic images of historical depth that reach back both to the history of Gallia in early Christian times and to classical cinema. In *Les 400 coups,* a map of a boy's life in Paris is placed over those of French history—including those locating the origins of French literature—in a classroom. Different events pock the road of Antoine Doinel's progress while others make manifest, as if he sees them through a glass darkly, an art of citation that verges on creative plagiarism. In a fashion not dissimilar to what is seen in the maps of subjectivity in Truffaut's cinema, Louis Malle, in *Les Amants,* tells a woman's tale of a dangerous departure toward unknown places. She and her lover take leave of a Burgundian landscape associated with Mademoiselle de Scudéry's Carte du Tendre of the middle years of the seventeenth century. The film crafts its sumptuous images of the milieu through the filter of an allegorical creation. If books and literary citations are part of the composite shape of French New Wave cinemas, so also, it can be concluded, are maps and mapping.

The final chapters constitute an essay on cartographies of what might be called post–New Wave films. In *La Haine* the maps that are seen remain in the heritage of the French directors of the postwar years. We have noted that the maps in *La Haine* pertain to an adolescent (but no less vital) cosmology or even a metaphysics. As an icon inserted to spur reflection on the state of the world, a satellite image of the planet Earth figures in a grid of cinematic sources and variants embedded, like iron rods in the reinforced concrete of low-cost housing in the Parisian suburbs, within the scope of the film. Bearing strong resemblance to *Les 400 coups, La Haine* tells of a subjectivity going in reverse.

In *Thelma and Louise* and *Gladiator* maps, belonging to an international and industrial mold, show that the features are conceived and plotted for broad distribution. The infrequent but decisive presence of maps in Ridley Scott's two features unlocks their stories and opens the films to broader speculation on how contemporary cinema crafts formulaic narratives that move across national borders. The effects of the maps show why. They also open perception onto deeper histories in which the films are meshed. The baroque maps found in the roadside motel in *Thelma and Louise* point to a neo-baroque articulation of what might seem to be a fairly traditional road movie. The quasi-Ptolemaic map seen at the outset of *Gladiator* indicates what the film is copying, much in the way that sequences in *Les Mistons* and *Les 400 coups* were a mix of citations: when we see the map we also discover a principal source of the film. Marcus Aurelius's words, "look at this map" directed at once to Maximus and ourselves, can be seen as an imperative to "look at another film in this film." It affords not only a diacritical reading with *The Fall of the Roman Empire,* first of all, but then, too, of the "peplum" genre that includes *Spartacus, Demetrius and the Gladiators, Ben-Hur,* and other films. The map shows that a critical perspective inheres in the otherwise strategic design.

Gladiator, it is well known, makes much of computer-generated images and digital process. Some of its shots refer to global positioning or to what in contemporary cartography goes by the name of locational imaging. Its special effects in respect to icarian perspectives are related to what we see in other media. Made manifest where great arenas are in question, the architectural shots of *Gladiator* remind us that other films theorized or even "invented" their power by linking cinematic form to mapping. One of them was *Les Mistons,* in which the empty coliseum of Nîmes is a stage for a battle between children and the couple whom they adulate and demonize. In the struggle the winner is cinema, for within the architectural frame extensive reflection on the history and power of the medium comes forward. Others films include *Paris qui dort, Les 400 coups,* and *La Haine,* in which the Eiffel Tower is a site seen as an originary plot of cinema. It is used to mark the distance gained or lost between its time of construction, given to be of Cartesian facture, and a world without a past, from which a new utopia becomes the harbinger of a dystopia, one in which cinema will be the medium marshaled to manage perception. The films studied in the final chapter return to the rela-tion that cartography and cinema share in the design of what one critic long ago (Jameson 1982) called "strategies of containment."

Since the films address the delicate and perplexing issue of perception, their mapping impulse can be associated with the relations of writing to space. The force of the former engenders perception (or even the creation) of the latter and, as cinema shows us, the latter tends to fissure the meaning of the former (Ropars-Wuilleumier 2003). The cinemas turn their places—themes or commonplaces, non-places, any-places-whatsoever, or the locations in which they are shot—into critical spaces. If indeed, as it was argued in the introduction, the perception of space, what can be qualified in the philosophical sense as an event, calls being into question. In this way reflection on perception also questions that of the perceiver who, in the instance of these pages, is taken to be an ordinary viewer of cinema. When a map unsettles the image in which it appears, it also conduces the spectator to wonder about his own or her own sense of location. When map in a film coyly asserts, "you are here," the spectator may respond interrogatively, murmuring, "Where am I?" If the concept of a "subject-position" in speech-act theory can be turned into a "viewer-position" in cinema studies, a map in a movie can prompt us to ask where we are in view of the film, and how and where our imagination negotiates different positions and places in the area between the cartography of the film, as it is seen, and the imagination as it moves about and deciphers the film. Thus fears about how the controlling and strategic agencies of cinema are deployed can be displaced by alternate uses of the car-tographies the medium mantles to establish its hold on perception. The readings of the films studied in the chapters above, it is hoped, have led critical labors in this direction.

Other films and other maps might be grist for continued inquiry along similar axes. Where are all the maps in Fritz Lang's cinema, from *M* (1931) to *Moonfleet* (1955)? Why do we find a glaring absence of a map in the same director's claus-trophobic Western, *Rancho Notorious* (1952)? Why not study Bonaparte's vision of a map of Italy on the face of Joséphine in the pyrotechnic finale of Abel Gance's *Napoléon* (1927)? What about the map of Hiroshima at the flashback at the begin-ning of Alain Resnais and Marguerite Duras's *Hiroshima, mon amour* (1959)? What has it to do with the map of the Ganges at the end of Duras's *India-Song*

(1975)? Why has nothing been said about the projection of North and South America on whose surface Cameron Diaz traces an itinerary with her finger in *Gangs of New York?* What does the harbor seen at the end of *Mystic River* have to do with its several maps of Massachusetts seen in the precincts of the city? Study of a map in a movie resembles an endless itinerary in an archipelago of films where we enjoy gaining and losing our bearings.

Notes

Introduction

1. Christian Metz's productive and open-ended speculations on the relation of language to cinema (1974 and 1991a) gain force when juxtaposed to François de Dainville's *Le langage des géographes* (1964), a rich encyclopedia, dictionary, and history of cartographic signs. For Dainville maps possess special idiolects that belong to deeply embedded visual and oral cultures that change over time. For Metz the comparison of film and language becomes a heuristic quest that goes from linguistics to psychoanalysis and back again to linguistics.

2. The term is pivotal and decisive in the historical parabola that David Buisseret draws in *The Mapmaker's Quest* (2003). The author argues that the advent of cartography in the early modern age brought with it a new sense of location and a sense of place in the world. It initially takes the shape of topography but is ultimately tied to those agencies—cinema included—that seek to locate their subjects in the places they represent for them.

3. "In that empire the Art of Cartography reached such Perfection that the Map of one Province alone took up the whole of a City and the map of the empire the whole of a Province. In time, these unconscionable Maps did not satisfy and the Colleges of Cartographers set up a map of the Empire which had the size of the Empire and coincided with it point by point. Less Addicted to the Study of Cartography, the succeeding Generations understood that this widespread Map was Useless and not without Impiety they abandoned it to the Inclemencies of the Sun and of the Winters. In the deserts of the West some decayed Ruins of the Map, lasted on, inhabited by Animals and Beggars, in the whole Country there are no other relics of the Disciplines of Geography" (Borges 1964, 90).

4. In a remark implying that cinema is of a cartographic order Michel de Certeau (1984) observed that the filmic image is of many layers and of different interpretations that inhabit its space. It "is a multiplication of texts and of their readings upon a single surface. From this point of view an intimate relation exists between the image and the landscape. A landscape is a stratification of texts that allows for a multiplicity of readings. . . . I believe that there can be no fundamental difference between an image and a text, a text having been for ages perceived as an image."

5. Jacques Rancière (2001) argues that cinema is a product of both *active* and *passive* agencies of creation. The artist or *auteur* imprints a style or signature upon a film, but the lens itself records elements that are not entirely under the director's control. A map in a film calls attention to the interrelation of these agencies.

6. In his compelling *Fate of Place* (1997) Edward Casey concludes that the experience of "being-in-place" ties sentience to geography (342 and passim). The point is made with graphic precision throughout *Representing Place* (2000), in which landscape, being, and spatiality are studied through the lens of the artist as philosopher.

7. "Where am I in fact when I look at a map and I say 'I am here?' It is worth recalling that in a statement of this kind the personal pronoun 'I' refers to the person who speaks, an empty form in which the enunciator invested. 'Here' is the linguistic designation of a particular position in space: it is defined in respect to the context of the enunciation, but also to the system of language and of lexicon and meaning." Here and elsewhere Christian Jacob (1992, 431; 2006, 341) synthesizes the act of reading a map with *deixis* as it is understood by Emile Benveniste (1966).

8. Many films and directors could be read transversally. If the work of a director-*auteur* can be fathomed as a cartography, it would be tempting, in Hitchcock's *The 39 Steps*, to link the map of Scotland that Robert Donat, the man who had asked Mr. Memory of the distance between Montreal and Winnipeg, extracted from a dead woman's hand to the Bridge of Forth at the northern border of England. There, where the hero escapes the clutches of the police, he defies the vertigo we feel when the camera peers downward from the upper reaches: the same feeling overwhelms the timorous hero of *Vertigo* near the Golden Gate Bridge, a structure transforming a touristic site into one of trauma. The bridge in turn has a miniature (and perhaps traumatizing) analogue on a smaller scale in the cantilever brassiere that his friend Midge has designed in her architectural studio. And the Golden Gate would figure in a map of monuments and what they commemorate or repress in the greater body of Hitchcock's oeuvre. Through its maps each film or body of films brings forth a different network of relations with space and time. Each requires study within the confines of its own cartographies.

9. Blache's impact on French schools is noted in Guiomar 1997.

10. Deleuze marks the relation of "prehension" and perception to events in *Le Pli: Leibniz et le Baroque* (1988, 103–12, esp. 103, a propos a "nexus of prehensions").

11. Ptolemy 1991, 25, col. 2. The full quotation is given in chap. 1, n. 14. Pieter Apian illustrates the analogy in his *Cosmographia* of 1521 and many subsequent editions up to 1550.

12. The history and taxonomy of the *isolario* or island-book is taken up in Lestringant 2003. It coincides with a moment when, in the development of oceanic travel, the expansion of the borders of the world led cartographers to compose atlases in which new information could "float" aside inherited knowledge. Deleuze himself was a philosopher of islands. One of his first writings is "Causes et raisons des îles désertes [Causes and Reasons of Desert Islands]" (in Deleuze 2002, 11–17). The article considers the geographer's distinction between continental and oceanic islands as a creative philosophical principle.

13. Bazin inaugurates his "Evolution of Film Language" with a quasi-ironic similitude yoking biblical typology to the history of cinema. "In fact, now that the use of sound has sufficiently demonstrated that it was not seeking to destroy the Old Testament of cinematography but to fulfill it, there is reason to wonder if the technical revolution coming with the sound track indeed corresponds to an aesthetic revolution, in other words, if the years 1928–30 are indeed those of the birth of a new cinema" (1999 [1975], 63).

14. Deleuze is probably thinking of *Hallelujah!* (1929). It will be shown in chapter 2 that in Renoir's *Le Crime de Monsieur Lange* (1936) the "collective and *unanimiste*" character of cinema is brought forward and, by way of virtual mapping, is severely called into question.

15. Perhaps one of the keenest moments where the cliché is summoned is found in Tay Garnett's comic masterpiece (laden, by the way, with maps), *Trade Winds* (1938), in which Frederic March and Joan Bennett "deconstruct" each other's amorous clichés.

16. In his typology Deleuze is not far from Jean-Luc Godard's aesthetic that argues for images that despite themselves must be resurrected from the ashes of Auschwitz in order to redeem over and again both cinema and the world. Deleuze calls them "time-images" through his affiliation with Bergson, while Godard juxtaposes old and new images in his *Histoire(s) du cinema* (1998), especially 1:134–35, that is the topic of close and productive analysis by Jacques Rancière (2001, 232–35).

17. The relation with the atlas is uncanny. Printed editions of Ptolemy in the wake of the Columbian discoveries were designed to include "old" and "new" projections such that a sense of history and typology could be gained by the juxtaposition of two maps of the same area, and not, in the name of progress, the removal of one in favor of the other (Goffart 2003, 14–15).

18. The cartographic latency of Deleuze can be found in Bogue 2003, Lacotte 2001, Château and Lageira 1996, and Fahle and Engel 1997. Rodowick 1997 remains a point of reference.

19. See especially Ropars-Wuilleumier 1997, 243–54, and Leutrat 1997, 407–19.

20. At stake here is Michel de Certeau's distinction between a *strategy*, taken as a general mode of control or even of hegemony, and a *tactic*, a local and specific practice that works otherwise or even against the control of strategists. In concert with much of Michel Foucault's work on discursive and visible formations, the distinction is crucial not only to Certeau's polemology but also, on a certain scale, to the analysis of film: how to use films—that most often are conceived on the grounds of strategic ends—for interpretive tactics has much to do with the study of maps and mapping of cinema. In *L'Invention du quotidien 1: Arts de faire* (1990) the pages on uses and tactics (57–69) and on the "arts of theory" (97–116) serve as a threshold to the cinematic and cartographic treatment of city spaces in a section titled "Spatial Practices" (139–93), in which the author shows how citizens map and correlate language and space in what the author calls the invention of everyday life.

21. Little wonder, as fairytales have shown since the dawn of time that a film bearing a rating of PG-13 is often of far more erotic force than those classified as NG-17. See Williams 1999, a work that shares much with the Foucaldian principle of the diagram.

22. Much of Paul Virilio's writing on the ways that cinema seeks to control perception in *Logistique de la perception: Guerre et cinema* (1982) has its conceptual grounding, it appears, in Foucault's work and may even bear impact on Deleuze's readings. In all events the convergence of Virilio and Foucault is felt in many of Godard's cinematic diagrams, especially those of the first hour of his *Histoire(s) du cinema* that blend words and images that are direct citations of Virilio's book: in, e.g., the juxtaposition of the logo of 20th Century Fox (whose beacons signal the presence of antiaircraft technology) to a clip from a bombing mission and images taken from Rembrandt and Goya (in the textual accompaniment to the videotape [1998, 1:100–105]).

23. Emphasizing the cartographic style of Foucault's investigations Deleuze draws attention to writing, understood in a Certallian sense, as a tactic. Foucault in reality was quoted as saying, "The use of a book [and here we can put in its place a film] is narrowly tied to the pleasure it affords, but I do not at all conceive of myself making a body of work, and I am shocked that one might be called a writer. I am dealing with instruments, I am a maker of recipes, I am someone who indicates objectives, a cartographer, a reader of surveys [*releveur de plans*], an arms maker" (1994 [1967], 725).

24. In *Maps and History: Constructing Images of the Past* (1997) Jeremy Black shows that since the advent of the Ortelian atlas (1570) cartography has been a taken to be a spatial representation of history. It figures in pedagogy where geography and chronicle are used both in texts and in the space of classrooms to mould citizens (the point will be developed below in chapter 7, in the classroom in Truffaut's *Les 400 coups*).

25. The film attests to "intelligence and the consciousness of means" that are in perfect equilibrium with "the sincerity of the story" (Bazin 1999 [1975], 235).

26. Giuliani 1986, 135. The film confirms what Thierry Jousse remarks in the context of a recent retrospective at the Cinémathèque de Paris: "For as much as the world of [Howard] Hawks is circumscribed, limited, and finished, Walsh's is vast, limitless, expansive. In Walsh's films the border is endlessly displaced and his characters never cease to go toward it" (2001, 65)

27. The sequence is taken up in greater detail in chapter 9 below.

28. "In the appreciation of a work of art or an art form," he reminds us, "consideration of the receiver never proves fruitful. Not only is any reference to a certain public or its representatives misleading, but even the concept of an 'ideal' receiver is detrimental in the theoretical consideration of art, since it posits the existence and nature of man as such. . . . No poem is intended for the reader, no picture for the beholder, no symphony for the listener" (Benjamin 1969, 69).

29. Marie-Claire Ropars-Wuilleumier has noted that Freud's writing is cinematographic (1981, 65–66). In his work on Freud, she observes, Derrida translates *Zusammensetzungen*, Freud's word describing lexical forms in which different figures reside in the same graphic sign, as *montage*. Samuel Weber makes a similar point about Freud's concept and practice of dream-writing in the name of *Bilderschriften* in his *Legend of Freud* (1982, 33–35). David Rodowick situates Freud's "montage" and "picture-writing" in the context of film theory in *Reading the Figural, or, Philosophy after the New Media* (2001, 91–92).

30. At the beginning of "The Uncanny" Freud writes geographically. Aesthetics, what he will take up in the essay not merely as the theory of beauty but as "the theory of the qualities of feeling," belong to a "remote" province usually overlooked by specialists. Freud admits that he must "plead guilty to a special obtuseness" on the topic of the uncanny and that, because it is distant from him, "he must start by translating himself into that state of feeling, by awakening in himself the possibility of experiencing it" (1955, 17:219–20). The small Italian city surely belongs to a remote province of the Uncanny; Freud's visual acuity might be seen in the 45-degree angle opened on the inner side of the letter *z* and his obtuseness in the 135-degree angle on the other.

31. The editors of the *Standard Edition* note that in a letter of May 12, 1919, to Ferenczi Freud had written of taking an old paper, possibly dating to 1913, out of a drawer and rewriting it. The story he told to his interlocutor betrays a repetition-compulsion at the same time it spatializes a traumatic history: the essay was begun around 1913, before the First World War, and then gestates until it is rewritten and published in 1919, a year whose doubled numerical sign attests to the uncanny. Both letters and numbers are reiterated: Freud published the text in his sixty-second year, the number he finds "uncanny" in the paragraph following the story of his promenade in the small Italian town (1955, 17:237).

32. This point is based on what Piera Aulagnier reports (1975) from clinical labors in psychoanalysis in which analysands need to construct mental maps that allow them to gain a bearing on their lives where otherwise their relation with the world would be devastatingly rootless. I have tried to set the findings in the context of mapping in *The Self-Made Map: Cartographic Writing in Early Modern France* (1996c, 7–18, 22).

33. The dyad of a local-and-global consciousness that Jameson puts forward in *The Geopolitical Aesthetic: Cinema and Space in the World System* (1992, 10), "how the local items of the present and the here-and-now can be made to express and to designate the absent, unrepresentable totality" might belong to a discursive formation, indeed a cartographic archive, that reaches back to Pieter Apian's *Cosmographia*—Latin edition, Antwerp, in 1529, and twenty-nine more editions in five languages over the next eighty-five years (Karrow 1993, 52–53)—in which the connections that tie humans at a local level to a cosmographic picture are implicitly shown to be tenuous. The new twist, as Colin McCabe makes clear in his preface to *The Geopolitical Aesthetic* (xiv–xv), is found in stress placed

on the politics of interpretation. A discussion of Apian's work, on mapping and painting and its implication for film, however anachronistic it may seem, is taken up in chapter 8 below.

34. In his discussion of cinematic deixis Christian Metz writes of the ways that characters in a film become landscapes (that voices become spaces) when speech is discerned to be impersonal (1991b, 34). A broader philosophical treatment of the same issues is Wolff 1997 (200–202), in which remarks are made on the invention of the world that takes place in the act of enunciation.

1. Icarian Cinema

1. Mercier 1999 [1770]. The text was first published by E. van Harrevelt in Amsterdam (either in 1770 or 1771), soon translated into English as *Astraea's Return ; Or, the Halcyon Days of France in the Year 2440 : A Dream.*

2. Alexander Moszkowski, *Conversations with Einstein,* cited by Michaelson 1979, 47 (emphasis added).

3. The Garnier "Nouveau Paris monumental" (1900–1903), titled "Itinéraire pratique de l'étranger dans Paris," featured the monuments of the city drawn on a scale larger than the map itself. The largest of all is the Tower. Clearly shown are the subway lines that make the buildings accessible to the tourist. A more detailed description of this map is found in the opening paragraph of my chapter 7.

4. Most modern atlases begin with descriptions of the creation of the planet or composition of the globe and its core, as does *The National Geographic Atlas of the World,* when it draws a broad time line starting with the formation of the earth (4.6 billion years ago) and ending with the Cenozoic period (Shupe et al., 1995, 1–2). The penchant for an atlas to tell of the history of things is taken up in Goffart (2003, 444–45 and passim).

5. Abel 1994, 406–7. The hero builds a pneumatic clock "that can accelerate time in his interest. After a quick text, in which the traffic on a Paris street goes into fast motion" (406), the film tells of the next twenty years of Onésime's life. Abel notes that the film was commonly taken to be a precursor.

6. In *Le Mystère René Clair* (1998) Pierre Billard argues that Clair had wished to have the memory of Durand's film present in order to mark his own originality. Clair's "escape into a farcical fantasy is solidly rooted in the concrete reality of Paris at the time" of the filming (80).

7. The digest version is appended to René Clair, *Under the Roofs of Paris/Sous les toits de Paris.* The longer version is distributed by Timeless Video (Hollywood Select Video, North Hollywood, 1993). This version carries intertitles, in English, that are decorated with a globe in the shape of a human face that smiles or grimaces according to the sentiment expressed in the words adjacent to it.

8. Ptolemy 1991, 25–26. The importance of this distinction cannot be underestimated in the history of cartography, studies in spatial theory, and even film theory. Its importance in terms of language and image is taken up in Nuti 1995, 53–70, esp. 55.

9. The re-edited version does not include this shot. It cuts to a panoramic (also in the earlier version) that tilts downward to capture the École militaire at the end of the Champ de Mars. In the foreground are two supporting wires that appear to be attached to struts above and below the man who appears in the lower area of the shot as it tilts downward. Very clear, especially in the restored version of the film, is the movement of cars along the Avenue de la Motte-Piquet between the garden and the military school.

10. In the edited version the take of the Invalides dissolves back to the eastern view of Paris that had been seen in the first takes of the earlier version. No dissolve is apparent in the latter, immobility being emphasized.

11. The film confirms J. Brian Harley's hypotheses that draw in part on Michel Foucault, in which

cartography is seen in a historical field as an agent of control and of power. Cartography is traditionally a teleological discourse that reifies power, which itself is "enforced, reproduced, reinforced, and stereotyped" by conscious and unconscious processes of domination. Harley argues that they provide hidden rules of cartographic discourse "whose contours can be traced in the subliminal geometries, the silences, and the representational hierarchies of maps" (1988, 302–3).

12. The spiral staircase has more than panoptic virtue in the revolution of point of view that the watchman gains as he descends. From the Middle Ages it belongs to a rich tradition of perspectivism and of anamorphosis, as shown in Guillaume 1985, 24–47.

13. The shot is very similar in its articulation to abutting triangles of water and of pavement in much of the photography of Jean Vigo's *L'Atalante* (1934). In that film photographer Boris Kaufman concretizes an overbearing social contradiction in which implacable stone—the street and asphalt that are home to the homeless—is offset by atmospheric illusion. Here also Clair does the same. The abstraction of a fluid area is in strong contrast to the city, which Gilles Deleuze calls "a geometrical configuration of combined parts that superimpose or transform movements in homogenous space" (1983, 63). Clair gives it its keenest expression by conferring life upon "geometric abstractions in a homogenous, luminous and grey, depthless space" (ibid.). I have tried to make a cartographic reading of Vigo's feature, with allusion to Clair (2006, 253–72, esp. 264, 269).

14. The intertitle of the later version is less interpretive (or psychoanalytic) in tenor: "Tout s'est immobilisé cette nuit" [Everything came to a standstill last night]. The words appear to be the voice of an absent prestidigitator from earlier cinema.

15. In the earlier version of the episode of the arrival the plane is aligned with the voices of the six persons who regroup themselves around the first car. The events are literally spoken for by the characters (a cutaway shot to the top of the Tower is enough to establish where the watchman had been the night before), which the arrangement of intertitles and cutaway shots continue to make clear: after they arrive at the apartment where one of the passengers seeks to find his mistress, everyone regroups by their cars to confer about what to do. They deduce that an event took place at 3:25 a.m., which is confirmed by two cutaway shots (in daylight) to a clock, and another to a speeding plane in the air. The title-cards indicate that they will take refuge at the top of the Tower *before* they enter the mistress's apartment.

16. The battle on the cornice of the Tower, the stuff of silent cinema, is interrupted by sound cues that the early version of the film had put into the narrative *prior* to the sequence devoted to the inhabitants' ennui and the violence they enact on each other. Albert and the woman repair to the bedroom where a wireless, attached to a megaphone, is said (by virtue of an intertitle) to emit a faint voice. The later version elides the episode announcing the presence of a voice. The men interrupt their combat and run to the room containing the wireless *after* having beaten and run after each other in the maze of girders, and just before an intertitle states, "'Si quelqu'un m'entend'" ["'If anyone hears me . . .'"]. The "coming of sound" is coded into the first version and effaced—perhaps for reason of the reduced number of intertitles—and entirely lost in the second.

17. André Chastel sketches the background of the sign in *Le Geste dans l'art* (2001, esp. 68–70).

18. Certeau 1985, 873–78. The work can be read productively adjacent to his "Les revenants de la ville" (1987). A similar mystical voyage and fable inspire René Clair's *Le Voyage imaginaire* (1925), a film that uses panoptic takes from the top of Notre-Dame-de-Paris.

19. Courcelles 2003. The author calls mystics creatures of experiment, seekers of new and other truths who gather in the life about them a vital sense of alterity (41–42). They speak and write in a way that their words are laced with images and figures of absence. Language and image are both present and absent.

20. Paul Virilio (1982, 31 and figure 13) makes the connection between the RKO pylon and the Eiffel Tower. He adds that the beacons surrounding the megalith that bears the name of 20th Century

Fox belong to the apparatus of antiaircraft detection and thus figure in the emblem to remind the viewer unconsciously of the power invested in the medium. Following Virilio, in the text of his *Histoire(s) du cinema* (1998) Jean-Luc Godard places the Fox logo, replete with beacons flashing in every direction, adjacent to footage of a bombing raid Goya's "Night of the First of May" (1:101–5). The printed words of the voiceover read, "de naissance d'une nation/de l'espoir/de Rome ville ouverte/le cinématographe n'a jamais voulu faire/un événement/mais d'abord une vision" [from birth of a nation, from hope, from Rome, open city, the cinematographer never wanted to make an event, but first of all a vision]. Godard replaces Virilio *perception* with *vision* in order, it appears, to redeem actuality as a document of art. Surely René Clair's work is at the origin of the issue. See also the Introduction.

21. Richard Terdiman (1992, 106–47) studies the poem in view of the changing demography and topography of the city "(la forme d'une ville/Change plus vite que le coeur d'un mortel)" (ll. 7–8). The politics of Terdiman's reading are of a tenor similar to Clair's.

22. Guy Rosolato defines the perspectival object as a sign of a representation of the unknown, or a figure of a lack that the viewing subject perceives in a visual field, in, first, *Eléments de l'interprétation* (1985, 123–32); and, second: "L'Objet de perspective dans ses assises visuelles" (1987, 151ff.). Its relation with the unknown is developed in his *La Portée du désir ou la psychanalyse même* (1996, 167–68).

23. Clair's film makes manifest, it seems, the "spiritual automaton," a concept that Deleuze (1985a, 203–5) relates to a possibility that film communicates in a "common power of what prompts thinking and of what thinks" (204) when images of movement are perceived. The spiritual automaton, he continues (214), quickly becomes the subject under fascist control. Andrew and Ungar (2005, 194) reach a similar conclusion. Clair "polishes everything to a smooth surface without mystery or depth, so that all elements can interact according to a rhythm."

24. Jean Starobinski (1973) documents the dream of a world where night will never fall. In *L'Ecriture de l'histoire* (1975) Michel de Certeau shows how the Freudian dream of "enlightenment" amounts to an articulation based on "things effaced or lost and that cause the text to be the deceptive sign of past events" (296). In *Une politique de la langue* (1975) he and authors Dominique Julia and Jacques Revel show how the emblems of a land (that might include, it can be added, the Eiffel Tower) and its language are built to turn an unconscious sense of things—a darkness—into the constructive effect of a political mission, a figure of the "Nation" (165). Ousselin (1999) offers a strong reading of the Tower through close analysis.

2. Jean Renoir

1. In "Le Cinéaste de la vie moderne: Paris as Map in Film" (1996b, 71–84) I tried to assert that *Boudu sauvé des eaux* inaugurates a "geographic unconscious" in which the film maps out embedded layers of spatial and historical relations. Paris is shown to be a site of conflict. The remarks that follow on *Boudu* intend to be more specific in addressing the presence of maps in the image-field of the film.

2. Without the maps in the field of view it would be difficult to obtain the effects that Alexander Sesonske, à propos Boudu as a vagrant and a disenfranchised *flâneur,* calls the "flatness of the space" in which he moves (1980, 131). Sesonske notes that the shots of the figures in the water are "rather like a cinema version of Brueghel's *Icarus*" (125).

3. David Woodward (1990, 109–22) distinguishes between route-enhancing, center-enhancing, and "equipollent" maps. In the latter, an innovation of Roger Bacon, equal value is ascribed to all points on the map itself. The same can be said of the deep-focus shot in Renoir's cinema.

4. The text itself is crystalline. *Plan* can be read to mean a plane, a shot (within a shot), a map,

and even a way of organizing an image. In an exhaustive treatment of Deleuze Ronald Bogue generalizes the discussion of multiple framings to include "the world-as-reflection, as infinite mirrorings, stagings, performances, spectacles, rites, and ceremonies" (2003, 133).

5. For admirers of *Les Fleurs du Mal* the sites might include "La vie antérieure" in the first section, "Spleen et Idéal," or in the Dutch landscapes and map-pictures of Vermeer alluded to in "Invitation au voyage"; the prose poems about the noise and agitation of Paris, in which he tipped into one of his pieces the English slogan, "Anywhere out of this world"; and of course, "Le Voyage," the final poem that begins by invoking the child who travels in admiring prints and maps of different origins.

6. Christian Jacob (1992, 106–9) notes that the Baroque atlas has a cinematic disposition in the way that the movement from a world map to local views makes the "reading" of the pages inspire "the pleasures of the imaginary voyage, of the voyage of the mind. The atlas thus pertains to a global curiosity for foreign countries" (109). At this moment in *Boudu* Baudelaire meets the Baroque atlas.

7. Christopher Faulkner notes that the shot is "of an internal montage that seems to signify the final irreconcilability of established values with the world of the clochard" (1986, 38). Faulkner argues that for Renoir an individual's social action cannot lead to political change. (My thanks to Margaret Flinn for taking note of this passage.)

8. *Orthographe* is used in the architectural context known to the word in the Renaissance. "Orthography" had meant both the art of spelling and of the disposition of a well-ordered façade of a book and of a building. In the introduction to his works of 1544 Clément Marot writes that that "every building that is not well arranged [*sans sa disposition*] makes its orthography less comely, no matter how it is plotted [*cymettriée*]" (Defaux 1993, 3).

9. In Renoir's cinema culinary cartography is everywhere. Boudu refuses to eat bread with fresh butter from Normandy and cannot stand the white wine so different from the taste of the water in which he has been swimming. In *Toni* (1934), Albert, the principal antagonist and stranger to the property that he owns in southern France, despises *ratatouille*. Personages tend to estrange or even to call in question what Renoir perhaps somewhat disingenuously called the total social fact of human "belonging" to the locales in which they were born. " [E]ven more than race," man "is tributary to the soil that nourishes him, to the conditions of life that shape his body and mind, to the landscapes that through the entire day are shown before his eyes," "Souvenirs de Jean Renoir" (in *Le Point,* 1938), reprinted in Bazin 1989, 146.

10. In the first chapter of his *Theory of Film Practice* (1981), Noël Burch demonstrates that offscreen space, openings, and closures of windows and door mark Renoir as of his *Nana* in 1927. It is surely given greater force in *Boudu* and becomes a hallmark of Renoir's style up to *La Règle du jeu*.

11. The soft focus implies that his body is as infantile and sensitive, like unprotected protoplasm, in contrast to the view of Batala who is in crisp and even crystalline focus in the background and who is seen in totality as he approaches Lange.

12. Bazin 1989, 42. His map of the site is printed on page 41.

13. Alexander Sesonske uses the same passage to emphasize further in *Lange* a "feeling of unity in diversity" (1980, 216) that the displacement of the map calls into question. For Sesonske Renoir's camera has the redemptive virtue of holding in its shots and editing a "coherence" through the "overlapping, enclosing, opposing relations" that circles and circular movements bring to the staging. He sees a "vitality of the life of the court" in the "success of the recurrent cyclical forms in achieving completion and closure" (217). The map itself, a *pan de mur décoré,* indicates that neither it nor its surroundings encloses anything at all. The point is made clear where Andrew and Ungar (2005, 217) contrast the making of a film-in-the-film to Lange and Valentine staring at one another in front of the map in the garret. The line that connects their heads is the Mexican-American border running from Arizona to Texas.

14. Isabella Pezzini (1996, 63–65) argues that utopian maps are often the ground plans or even the very sites of fiction. Maps are made to effect transformation from an initial projection, an image of things created by words. Her treatment of More's *Utopia*, drawing on Marin 1973, could apply to *Le Crime de Monsieur Lange*.

15. A propos *La Règle du jeu* Bazin (1989, 76) wrote, with obvious affinity for Baudelaire's fourth sonnet of *Les Fleurs du Mal*, that "the film is only an interlace of reminders, allusions, correspondences [*correspondances*], a carousel of themes in which reality and the moral idea answer each other [*se répondent*] without lacking meaning and rhythm, tonality and melody." Throughout *Cinéma 1: L'Image-mouvement* Gilles Deleuze (1983, 65–66, 114–16) establishes a distinction between liquid and concentrated mass. In French cinema of the 1930s the one is always set in contrast to the other, as in the separation of water and pavement between a diagonal line in Vigo's *L'Atalante* or even the shimmer of water behind the letters that spell the name "Boudu" in the title-shot of *Boudu*. Here, too, the distinction is made but with political and spatial inflection.

16. "Traitement provisoire de *La Grande Illusion*," in Bazin 1989, 169.

17. Some of their maps are of uncommon clarity and detail, as shown by Buisseret 1964, 13–84. The quality of the cartography is made clear in the facsimiles in Dainville 1968. See also Buisseret (forthcoming) and Hale (forthcoming).

18. *La Grande Illusion* (1971, 76), Criterion, in the DVD edition of the film at chapter 11, at 58:19 in the film). In a recent assessment of the episode John Hamilton (2003, 43) notes that the teacher, donating his life to Pindar, "suffers a radical expropriation. . . . In preserving the life of Pindar's poetry, Demolder literally must bury himself in his books and suffer a kind of scholarly interment." Hamilton notes that Demolder says little in the film and that, both visually and thematically he "is somehow in the way, obstructing Boëldieu's important cartographic investigations" (42). Hamilton's misreading of Boëldieu (and of playing cards, *cartes,* that he assumes to be "regional" thematic maps related to diseases) in fact attests to a broader cartographic dimension in the sequence. Playing cards, checkered towels, posters, and a map are all in proximity.

19. The backcloth belongs to an art and practice of folding and of unfolding in the production of portative charts. Military maps, bicycle maps, touristic maps, and road maps follow patterns of folding that bear on perception. In Jacob 1992, 115–19, and 2006, 82–86.

20. The words do not figure in the script (Renoir 1971, 76), nor does any description of the pictures.

21. Which, of course, they are: medieval maps affirmed a "moralized cartography" that scientific procedures set aside. See Schulz 1978, 425–35, and Peters 2004, introduction and conclusion.

22. Chapter 17, at 1:51.30 in the DVD copy.

23. It is tempting to think that Rosenthal's words anticipate Gilles Deleuze and Félix Guattari's concept of "smooth" space that contrasts its "striated" counterpart. Smooth space would be oceanic, without borders, undifferentiated, totalizing, and of open possibility, while striated space would be that of distinctions, frontiers, lines of demarcation, class differences, and divisions among first, second, third, and fourth worlds. In Deleuze and Guattari 1980, 592–625.

24. Huizenga 1955 draws extensive attention to illusion and in-play, an element that a map in a film almost invariably elicits. Stanley Cavell ends *The World Viewed: Reflections on the Ontology of Film* (1979, 230) with a treatment of *La Règle du jeu*. The film "unsettles the illusions by means of which civilized people conduct themselves," and it is by means of a "loving brutality" that "Renoir declares film's possession of the power of art."

25. Shot 70 of the film, translated from Olivier Curchod's meticulous critical edition, *Jean Renoir "La Règle du jeu": Nouveau découpage integral* (1998, 86–87). See also McGrath and Teitelbaum 1971, 57. Primary reference is made to Curchod, whose descriptions of the shots and their movements are thorough and informed.

26. The contradiction is enhanced by an implicit visual joke, a latent rebus, seen in the folding walking stick that La Chesnaye carries with him. In popular French *mener une vie de bâton de chaise* is an idiom describing people who live by the seat of their pants. Vagrants or errant souls, they are classless and homeless. The film is riddled with visual and verbal contradictions so doubly bound that the meaning of what is seen is undone by what is said or heard and vice-versa. Some of the consequences are taken up in my "Laws of the Game" (1996a, 95–117).

27. "[I]n his *Cosmography*," notes Samuel Edgerton Jr., Ptolemy insisted "that the mapmaker first view that part of the world to be mapped as if it were connected at its center to the center of the viewer's eye by a 'visual axis'" (1987, 14).

28. In a cartographic moment in "Les Mistons" François Truffaut shoots the protagonists of his film through the very same style of balustrade. See chapter 5.

29. See Pelletier 1998 and 2001; Jacob 1992, 410–12.

30. Such is the frontispiece to Jean Le Clerc, *Le Théâtre géographique du royaume de France* (Paris, 1631), in which Henry IV is seen as Hercules, holding a club in his right hand with which he crushes the Catholic hydra below his feet, and in his left a globe that is both the world and a cannon ball. Illustrated in Pastoureau 1984, 533, figure 44. See also Hale 1964. Renoir himself bore knowledge in pre-Revolutionary artillery. He writes in 1937 of Lieutenant-General Vallière who "rendered to artillery the greatest service that could be done" in having the king sign a decree requiring an examination for every officer enrolled in the division of artillery. "It was the only arm where a commander did not need to be a nobleman, but where nonetheless knowledge needed to be imparted" (1974, 127). Vallière was responsible, he adds, for the superiority of French artillery over that of the Prussians.

31. Cavell adds that the absence of Octave (Renoir) from the *mise-en-scène* identifies the director as "both cause and casualty": of the murder and therefore, too, as an artist who poaches and who is poached (1979, 230).

3. Maps and Theaters of Torture

1. Skelton 1964, vii–viii. Karrow (1993) offers a telling and concise treatment of the impact of Ortelius on the European horizon.

2. Among other authors, the "theater of cruelty" is taken up in Lestringant 1996, 147–98, and Conley 1990, 1–6.

3. Rancière's allusion to comedy prompts recall of the opening shots of Preston Sturges's *Palm Beach Story* (1941), a film whose effects of spatial doubling and mirroring merit extensive comparison with *Romà, città aperta*. Peter Brunette (1987, 41–60) offers a balanced view of the making of the film and, too, a careful study that accounts for the resistance it poses to critical assessment.

4. A reader wonders if the names themselves are so obvious that they reveal amorous secrets on the part of the director, who reputedly was then or soon to be in love with Ingrid Bergman. If so, then a rupture or a division was inscribed in the division of the name into male and female units.

5. Paul Virilio (1982, 34–36, and figures 7–9) tirelessly makes the point that the war movie is decorated with maps but also determines how they are used in the reality of war. In a study of *Objective, Burma* (Raoul Walsh, 1945) I have tried to show how the map is tied to the decipherment of cinema and an eroticization of the field of the image (Conley 1991, 71–101, esp. 86–87).

6. It is shot 26 and is of a duration of 2 and 15/24 seconds: reference is made to Roncoroni 1973. Further reference to specific shots will be made to the numbers provided in this edition.

7. In a study of Elizabethan cartography and literature Richard Helgerson (1992, 133) writes of the way that "the land speaks" in a topographic and chorographic tenor. Works such as Michael Drayton's *Poly-Olbion* and the atlases of John Speed and Christopher Saxon were designed to

chronicle the power of monarchs and the spaces they owned, but the increasing attention that they paid to localities indicated that they were speaking for their inhabitants. "Service to the country alone—with all the ambiguous meaning the word *country* then had; kingdom, nation, county, locality, countryside—was displacing service to king *and* country, just as the latter had displaced service to God and his church or service to one's liege lord regardless of country. The emergence of the country as a single, if variously significant, term for the focal point of allegiance parallels the emergence of the description, survey, or chorography as an autonomous and widely practiced genre." The shift of emphasis in cartographic representation from lands of the king to the lands known by and for the population in England merits comparison with the more embedded historical process in Rossellini's cinema. His films (especially when they are superimposed upon one another) deal with national unification: how, in the midst of war and military apparatus, such as maps, that propel subjugation, can the difference of nation and locale be addressed?

8. Richard Kagan (1998, 76–77) makes a vital distinction that pertains to this context. A chorographic image of a city is a topography made available to cartographers and engineers. In these views *urbs* "served mainly as a screen," but the act of peering through it "afforded a glimpse of the city's inner self, the city as *civitas*" (103). Chorographic views, like tourist maps, were made for people living outside of the city, while "communocentric views served a home audience that was presumably already endowed with a 'public image' of their city or town" (103–4), intending to solidify a sense of a community and its individuality. The tension resides in the ways that the maps are viewed in this film. Bergmann looks at a map as *urbs* and Manfredi sees them as *civitas*.

9. The hat belongs to an iconography of revulsion. In 1945 or 1946 (and today, too) the sight of any piece of Nazi clothing prompts a reaction of disgust. German hats were especially icons of brutality. Those who wore them could only be considered human beasts The bicycle thief in Vittorio de Sica's *Ladri di biciclette* (1948) is loathsome not only because he steals Ricci's lease on life but especially because he wears a German soldier's cap. The film infers that he might have scavenged the hat from a dead or retreating soldier. The eagle on the hat recalls the last and accented word of a German military song, "Heimatland/Sei gelobt Du roter Adler [Homeland/May your red eagle be praised]," sung by a patrol that marches through the Piazza di Spagna in the evening in front of the Spanish Steps and the church of Santa Trinità dei Monti as they are seen from the Via Condotti (1 6.19).

10. Schulz (1987, 97–122) notes the cycles were produced between the mid-1560s and the mid-1580s. Under the impetus of the Duc of Como (and with the advice of Giorgio Vasari) Egnazio Danti and Sefano Buonsignori decorated the Palazzo Vecchio in Florence with frescoes inspired by Ptolemy. Two cycles decorate the Vatican Palace in Rome, and another the Palazzo Farnese at Caprarola. In the Roman context of the film they cannot fail to be recalled.

11. Jacob (1992, 127–28; 2006, 132) deploys Michel de Certeau's principle of the "spatial story" (elaborated in 1990, 175) to show how a "periegetic" itinerary takes place in the gallery. Bergmann mimes the itinerary and then analyzes it after he reaches his desk.

12. Abraham Ortelius, in *Le théâtre de l'univers* (the French edition of 1582) of his *Orbis theatrum terrarum* encouraged his reader to fly over and about the world by going from one map to the next. In the 1606 (English) edition he writes of the way that the viewer can travel everywhere without leaving the happy confines of the room in which the atlas is consulted. At this point *Roma, città aperta* taps into a topos that links travel, cartography, and a relation of panopticism to power and control.

13. Yet by deduction the viewer cannot fail to note that the Via Tiburtina would have been seen on the first map of Rome that Bergmann and the commissioner were studying in shot 14.

14. In this sequence the gaps between the sound track and the subtitles tell much about the space and style of the film. Francesco tells Manfredi that Pina left open (*aperta*) the apartment for him after

she discovered that he was not a policeman. After Francesco reports that a leader wants Manfredi to "break all contact" with the Resistance center, Manfredi (always before the map) adds that it is an obstacle to "be blocked after so much labor [il lavoro di dovere restar re bloccato]." The subtitle translates his frustration as, "to be cut off from headquarters." The same words are taken literally in *Paisan,* in the sixth story, when one of the American soldiers tells a companion (prior to a series of figurative decapitations) that they are "cut off from headquarters" (shots 41–41, Roncoroni 1973, 322–24). A reading of the episode is taken up in Conley 1991, 114–15.

15. They are shots 505, 507, 509, 511, 513, 515, 517, 519, 523, 525, and 586 (Roncoroni 1973, 130–33). The same map is placed behind Ingrid in shots 580 and 583, in which she and Bergmann reproduce each other's itinerary to and from the threshold of the torture chamber and the desk in front of which Don Pietro is illuminated by an electric lamp.

16. For Renoir see the treatment (in chapter 2 above) of the shots of the front of Lestingois' bookstore in *Boudu sauvé des eaux.* The presence of a transcending viewpoint given on a map when treated as a work of art is taken up in Buci-Glucksmann (1996, 3–35).

17. Roncoroni (1973, 140), describing shot 557. The shape is obsessively visible in shots 557, 559, 561, 568, 570, 603, and 604 when Bergmann is in frame, and in 590, 591, 592, 594, 596, 598— the shot begging comparison when the priest makes a sign of the cross in giving absolution to his dead friend below him—in those instances where Manfredi is in frame.

18. Roncoroni, who rarely comments on the maps in the shots, notes that shot 563 begins with a "wall map seen on the background" (1973, 141).

19. "The Intelligence of the Present," foreword to Roncoroni 1973, xviii.

20. In 1953, in their *Technique of Film Editing* author-filmmakers Karel Reisz and Gavin Millar note that the technique was "at present rather out of fashion" (246). The authors of *The Film Studies Dictionary* (2001, 264) maintain that it had been popular in the 1930s and 1940s but gave way to the straight cut except where it was used for comic or archaic effects, as in Jonathan Demme's *Caged Heat* (1974).

21. It is found between shots 6 and 7 (Nannina closing the shutters of her apartment), shots 67–68 (Pina en route from the bakery to her flat), 81–82 (Marcella and Pina in the stairwell), 113–14 (Marcello and Pietro walking and being passed by a streetcar), 134–35 (Marcello going up his stairwell to the attic), 146–47 (from the resistance print shop to Marina's dressing room), 156–57 (Ingrid staring at Marina's mirror and transition to Pietro's rectory), 179–80 (from the Austrian deserter to the inside of the local church), 180–81 (Don Pietro and Pina walking on the Via Casilina), 277–78 (courtyard of Francesco's building and front of Pietro's church), 309–10 (Marcello running upstairs after a 360-degree pan in countertilt), 384–85 (Marina moving away from the window sill where she witnesses the slaughter of two lambs by pistol shot), 425–26 (from Marina in her bedroom to Manfredi sitting in a chair in the adjacent living room), and 428–29 (Manfredi crossing the street en route to the rectory).

22. Published at the time of the making of *Roma, città aperta,* Claude Lévi-Strauss's "Le Dédoublement de la représentation dans les arts de l'Asie et de l'Amérique" (1958, 269–94) offers a plausible theory of the image and of the wipe. For the indigenous mind, he argued, "décor is the face, or rather, it creates the face. That is which confers upon persons their social being, their human dignity, their spiritual meaning. The double representation of the face, considered as a graphic process, thus expresses a deeper and more essential splitting: that of the 'stupid' biological individual and that of the social personages they take to be their mission to incarnate" (285). A symbolic magic of cinema is mixed with that of the splitting of the "ego" that would be Ingrid who is Ingrid as long as she looks both at the photo (as a social being) and at her image (as vampire or malevolent force). Surely in this sequence the stylization of Ingrid could be compared to that of Gloria Grahame's face in *The Big Heat* (1954), who is the classic manifestation of a face in split representation.

23. Robert Burgoyne (1979, 36–47) analyzes the mirror-effect through the filter of Lacanian categories. The neo-real is the *reel,* while the imaginary would be the double register of Ingrid's and our desire to hold what is beheld. If the Lacanian notion of "desire" means seeing everything all over the image, then it follows that the image qualifies as a cartographic form.

4. A Desperate Journey

1. Quotations are from both the film and Gomery 1979, shot 106 (79). Where the screenplay and the film version do not coincide the latter is quoted prior to the former.

2. Study of the montage that depicts the delivery of the pardon is taken up in Conley 1991, 169–72.

3. Marie-Claire Ropars-Wuilleumier (2003, 76–77) works on this theme and draws it through the power of cinema to produce mental spaces.

4. In its reception *High Sierra* is noted to be an important film in the continuity of an "evolution" of the gangster film from its cops-and-robber character of the 1930s to the drama of the solitary and immanent figure, a person controlled by destiny, in the convention of *film noir*. To place it at a juncture of transition would simplify its spatial invention. For at this juncture (at shot 34) the Western genre inhabits the film at the same time the narrative belongs to classical myth. The DVD commentary repeats what Douglas Gomery tersely concludes from commentaries by Jack Shadoian, Robert Warshaw, and others: "Warner Brother raised Roy Earle, their new gangster figure, to a position of high tragedy (in an almost classical sense). *High Sierra* represented a nation's farewell to the gangster and the Great Depression," ultimately signaling "the end of the classical gangster film, and the beginning of film noir" (Gomery 1979, 25–26). Following Deleuze's taxonomy (1983, 282–83), the film also belongs to a modern genre, one that approaches the time-image, in which strategic conspiracies are denounced.

5. The sequence plots the economy of the film insofar as it draws into the figure of the pharmacist (Harry Hayden) an analogy with the viewing public, and in Earle the film itself (Conley 1991, 173).

6. The screenplay is geographically precise where the film is not. The officer barks, "Went north, did he? Well, we'll take no chances. If it's Earle, he's trying to get back to L. A. over the pass at Bluejay. We'll get him. I'm going to use your phone, John" (shot 248, 167). The next shot would have shown the summit of Mount Whitney in the distance.

7. Lone Pine jumps off the map in order to crystallize the film in its own history of production. From *Regeneration* (1915) to *The Big Trail* (1930) Raoul Walsh had been one of the first directors to shoot significant segments of his features on location. The cartography in the Vorkapich montage of *High Sierra* brings forward routes and places accessible to a growing population of automobile owners in southern California. For many viewers Earle's desperate journey through Lone Pine and its environs indicates that the trajectory leads the hero to a place known for being the site where thousands of Westerns had been filmed. A genre and a style of filming are folded into the topography.

8. It now belongs to a pantheon of citations. When Marie asks reporter Healy (Jerome Cowan) what it means for a man to "crash out," she rehearses the tenor of the question that Jean Seberg asks of the chief of police at the end of *A bout de souffle* (1960). The fall of the dead body anticipates the pathos of the ending of *Tirez sur le pianiste* (1960). Because it turns Mount Whitney into the site of myth the film is a "toponymic tale," a sort of secular hagiography that turns a place into a memorial space (Lestringant 1993, 109–27, and Certeau 1975, chapter 6).

9. In cartography the model is that of what David Woodward (1990, 109–22) calls a "route-enhancing map," or an itinerary drawn on or across a map.

10. The episode has a signature effect both in Walsh's cinema and in the fortunes of Hollywood

cinema. Kirk saves the men by taking a bullet from Germans rushing to the rooftop over which everyone else, the heroic woman included, have jumped. As he plummets she beholds the scene and shrieks in exactly the same way that Ida Lupino had at the sight of the fall of Humphrey Bogart at the end of *High Sierra*. In *Desperate Journey* the episode has uncanny resemblance to the leap that Scotty (James Stewart) makes in *Vertigo*, after which he is traumatized. Gilles Deleuze (1983, 276–77) argues that such sequences attest to the crisis of the image as "action" and as "movement" in classical film. The scene of the fall embodies what he calls a "mental image" in which the characters in the film, "in a way that is more or less obvious, assimilates them as spectators." They call into question the nature and status of the action in which they figure.

11. The style is associated with the maps of Richard Edes Harrison (Schulten 1998 and Thrower 1996).

12. To this point the film rehearses cartographic sequences in *Objective, Burma!* (1945) that refines the pattern given here, taken up in Conley 1991, 79–101.

13. And indeed it is a Lockheed-Hudson, a craft Flynn later identifies when he radios to headquarters after eluding ground fire and taking the plane aloft. The aircraft may have been chosen not only as a "spot" to advertise the product of the company but also an aeronautic icon. The model 14 delivered Neville Chamberlain to Munich in 1938 where he signed the treaty assuring "peace in our time." In 1939 the British Purchasing Commission ordered 250 planes, the delivery of which was interrupted by the outbreak of World War II. English flyers used the craft to patrol the coasts of the British Isles. The planes were quickly enlisted to bomb U-boats and witnessed surprising success between 1941 and 1943, according to Garner and Gustin (n.d.).

14. Language figures strongly in the camouflage. The American actors (especially Raymond Massey) imitating German soldiers speak pellucid German, the idiom with which the Australian, Flynn, is conversant where the others (especially Reagan) are not. Yet, in order to be sure that he will not be overheard or surreptitiously detected, at one point Massey, looking over the scene of the Allies' attack on the first bridge and theft of uniforms, asks his sergeant if he "understands the English language" in order to speak secretly in the prevailing tongue of Hollywood.

15. In a study whose title, "L'Opération historiographique" bears more than a superficial resemblance to Raoul Walsh's *Objective, Burma!* (often remembered as "Operation Burma") Michel de Certeau (1975, 63–120) argues that a work of history begins from a "place" it chooses to be the foundation on which it builds its effects of truth. "Here and there history remains configured by the system in which it is elaborated" (79). Much of the chronology it proposed belongs to a "masked law" (104–7) dictating that a history is written from a "founding non-place" that was "then" where the history stands "now." In *Desperate Journey* the map and city seen in the credits situate the non-place, and the camouflage—or narrative—that follows constitutes the history. The non-place is Schneidemühl, and the narrative or discourse is the journey comprised of comic and tragic scenes reflecting the very production of the film in its own milieu.

16. For Harrison's innovations and presence in cartography of spheres and of relief in general, see Thrower 1996, 210–15.

17. The last shot in the montage seems utterly out of place. The men on bicycles ride over a French terrain that is defined by the spire of a stout Romanesque or Anglo-Norman church in the background.

18. "Non-place" is a term Marc Augé (1992, 98, 117) coins to refer to areas of transit, such as waiting rooms beyond the security gates in airports or the club rooms reserved for frequent flyers of given airlines, in which are mixed feelings of privilege and anxiety: privilege, because the subject has the wherewithal to be there; anxiety, for the simple reason that the inhabitants know they are about to take a voyage whose perils and dangers are greater than what the décor might lead them to believe it to be. The non-place is to be distinguished from Gilles Deleuze's *lieu quelconque*

("any-place-whatsoever"), more typically a sordid zone, border area, *terrain vague,* or indiscriminate place, lacking identity, where humans are in the midst of detritus and trash. Deleuze's concept is close to the originary landscapes he studies in the films of Buñuel and Rossellini (1983, 181–82, 286).

19. The relation with Julien Duvivier's *Pépé le Moko* is well known. *Pépé* begins with a map of Casablanca and its casbah and effectively shuttles, as does *Casablanca,* from a present space of a tragic labyrinth in a colonial land to nostalgic reminiscence of Paris through song and words about the beauty of the underground subway. Andrew and Ungar (2005, 273) call the film a "locus classicus of desire for Paris."

20. Assayas 2001, 138–43. Olivier Assayas later directed *Irma Vep* (1996), a film that responds to the industrial aspect of American cinema in the wake of French new wave films through citation not of classic cinema but of the American underground film.

21. Assayas varies on a point that Claude Lévi-Strauss (1962, 33) makes at the outset of his *Mythologiques:* "The question is not one of sailing toward other lands, were their location unknown and their existence hypothetical: only the voyage is real, not the land, and routes are replaced by the laws of navigation."

22. In his preface to *The Branded Eye* (1993, 17) Jenaro Talens argues that from the first image the film tells the spectator that it originates from a narrative tradition "established by Paramount in the course of its history." In this line a commanding study of titles and credits, including the fortunes of the Paramount logo, is found in the essays Böhnke, Hüser, and Stanitzek assemble in their *Das Buch zum Vorspann* (2006).

23. The grammar floats as does the image of the mountain. Paramount Pictures are omnipresent in the film that they present. The name is of an enduring presence in its sustained act of presentation.

24. The film makes the most of the shot and counter shot. Jones stands in front of the blackboard; a young woman with "love you" written on her lids causes the professor to stumble and conclude that all available research gives little reason not "to date this finding as we have."

25. *Arc, ark, arc*heology, and *Marc*us are drawn across *Merca*tor: Assayas draws attention to the dialogue that lacks vivacity, "slows the action down," and even muffles any eroticism that might have been slipped into "this system of stifling morality" (143). Yet in this sequence the play of signifiers that runs from speech as it is spelled out to the referents in the image attests to a powerful allegorical machinery that makes everything follow the parabola of action. In a review of *E.T.* that he calls the *Odyssée de l'espèce* (that puts "species" in the place of *espace* or "space") Jean Narboni (1982/2001, 155) notes that for both Spielberg and Francis Coppola word-play and attention to signifiers is crafted to suggest that the cinema belongs to a cosmogony. The terrestrial globe on which *One from the Heart* began allowed the title to be read, "thanks to a simple literal permutation, as *One from the Earth,* designating a dimension of absolute creation of an artificial *world* and the cineast's cosmogonic will to power" (155). Narboni's reflections can apply also to the globe-sequence in *Raiders.*

5. Juvenile Geographies

1. The Catholic cosmographer might have obtained the woodblock from the print shop of Balthazar Arnoullet, who had published maps and city-views in Guillaume Guéroult's *Epitome de la Corographie d'Europe* eighteen years earlier in Lyons. The image made its way into at least two other works, Poldo d'Albenas's *Discours historial de l'antique et illustre cité de Nismes, en la Gaule narbonoise* (Lyons: Guillaume Rouillé, 1560) and Antoine du Pinet's mix of maps and chronicle, *Les Plantz, pourtraits et descriptions de plusieurs villes du monde* (Lyons: Jan d'Ogerolles, 1564). Mortimer, entry 445 (1964, 500–501), traces the history of the circulation of the woodblocks.

2. Truffaut had in fact shot *Une visite* (1954) with a home-movie camera. The film was not destined to inaugurate a new mode of cinema.

3. Article in *Arts* (May 15, 1957), cited by Baecque and Toubiana (2001, 219–20).

4. Truffaut 1988, 125. References to the letters will be made to this edition in the text above.

5. Robert Lachenay (born in 1930) was indeed one of Truffaut's closest childhood friends and the producer of *Les Mistons*. He was the model for the character of René Bigey in *Les 400 Coups* (Truffaut 1988, 19 and 141). In response to a letter to a Japanese student writing a dissertation on Truffaut the director admitted that "Robert Lachenay" counted among his own pseudonyms (516). The proper name was given thus to circulate between life and cinematic fiction.

6. Sigmund Freud, "A Note upon the Mystic Writing-Pad," in Freud 1955, 19:227–32. The text is glossed in Derrida 1967, 293–340, esp. 319–21.

7. The sequence shot in a manner that appears to allude to Visconti's *La Terra trëma* (1948), in which the inhabitants of Aci-Trezza are shown framed in windows in series of tilts and countertilts. No shot in the film seems to be without reference to other films.

8. Michel de Certeau explains the practice in "Utopies verbales: glossolalies," (1980, 26–37). Glossolalia is an intermediate form of speech, a private language whose incomprehensibility is part of its symbolic effect. It is also taken up in the same author's work on the possessed women of Loudun (1975, 251–53).

9. Truffaut apparently had mixed feelings of love and hate for Clouzot. In his adolescence Truffaut had seen more than half of the 200 French films shot during the Occupation. He admired "une certaine religiosité" (surely part of "a certain tendency of French cinema") associated with narratives of impossible love. He liked *Le Corbeau* because it was *noir* and "hard to see" (interview in the archives of the *Films du Carrosse,* cited in Baecque and Toubiana 2001, 50–51), and he admitted having known it by heart, shot by shot, after seeing it thirteen times (76). But for polemical reasons he had to denounce the director when he wrote "A Certain Tendency of French Cinema." Truffaut soon ranked Clouzot among the keenest adepts of "French quality," prior to "executing" him in an article titled "Clouzot au travail, ou le règne de la Terreur" (223).

10. "Entretien avec François Truffaut," originally in *Cahiers du cinéma* (December 1962), cited in Baecque and Tesson 1999, 160–61.

11. "*Chiens perdus sans collier* [Dogs Lost without their Collar] is not a piece of garbage, it's a crime perpetrated according to certain [*certaines*] rules, a theft conforming to certain [*certaines*] ambitions that are easily discerned: 'make a lot of money in hiding behind the label of quality'" (cited in Baecque and Toubiana 2001, 202). See also Baecque 2003, 162–63.

6. Michelin *Tendre*

1. Kline 1992, 24–53. Kline's reading, a point of reference for any and every study of this film, will be closely followed in these pages.

2. At times the map is referred to as "La Carte de Tendre" and at others "La Carte du Tendre," in which the longer title is compressed. I have opted for the latter because "tender" has substantive force in its usage both in the seventeenth century and in Malle's film.

3. Joan DeJean (1991) and Anne Duggan (2005) make compelling arguments for the *précieuses'* invention of a properly feminist space. The military and commercial background, evident in cartographic work of the second third of the seventeenth century, brings the hypotheses into even sharper focus. A keen reading of the allegory is found in Peters 2004.

4. Almost every pedagogical edition of the play, from the "Classiques Larousse" or "Classiques Hatier" to "Gallimard/Folio," carries an illustration of the map. When, in an interview about the film, Malle once spoke of the map as a quaint or bizarre "geographic representation of all the variations

around the theme of love," he might have been telling viewers to look again at something overlooked or that Molière had reduced to ridicule.

5. According to David Buisseret (1996, 2–3) the estate map was a transitional genre of map that grew as of the end of the sixteenth century. It came with the development of new modes of mensuration and the need for private landowners to have images of their property. The Carte du Tendre resembles an estate map insofar as the *staffage* in the lower-right corner are taken to be a group of *précieux*. They look over an allegorical domain while they entertain each other, it seems, with words that might match the toponyms above them. Their position in the ensemble resembles, too, those of the tourists who gaze upon the city-views in many of the maps in Georg Braun and Franz Hogenburg's celebrated *Civitates orbis terrarium*, a work that grew and circulated widely in the years immediately prior to Mademoiselle de Scudéry's "Carte du Tendre." See Skelton 1965.

6. Claude Filteau (1980, 206) draws two perspectival diagrams to explain how the map is at once monocular and binocular in structure. As if commenting on the play of voices in Malle's film, he notes, "it is not through precious dialogues that the value of the routes taken on the Carte will be seen, but rather *across* the precious dialogues that the strategies of sentiment will be made visible. The *Carte du Tendre* is at once dialogic and strategic." His words also pertain to the reading of the shot itself. There reigns dispute over the direction of the flow of water in the river, and hence of the spiritual itinerary. In "Le Pays de Tendre: L'enjeu d'une carte" (1979, 40–57) Filteau believes that the river (and affect) move from Tendre to Nouvelle Amitié, but clearly, as Malle's film confirms, it goes in the opposite direction, as Kline (1992, 51) astutely notes by showing that the lovers find new friendship before sharing tenderness and setting forward toward the unknown at the "dangerous hour of dawn," *dangerous* being analogue to *La Mer dangereuse* where Inclination ends and loses its name.

7. The tracking shots attest to the fact that they are *in* the mode of transport that moves on a multilayered map (of Burgundy, of Tenderness, and of recall of the cars that drive to the Château de Solognes in *La Règle du jeu*) at the same time they are outside, thus pulling the camera into the overall space of the film. The mapping impulse is even more obvious when Bernard is heard, voice-off, outside of the château, recounting to Jeanne's husband and to the guests the itinerary they took. The camera follows her bursting in laughter as she changes her clothes and moves left and right in her bedroom (just over the courtyard).

8. Panofsky 1955, 295–320, offers an inventory of its tradition of precarious beauty.

9. The art of getting lost in a landscape belongs to the tradition of the mystical fable. A person goes into a space outside of the order of cognition while remaining inside of a charted territory. Mystical stories, notes Michel de Certeau, are of spatial and often cartographic form. The reader of the tale, the person who walks in the garden, and the spectator of the landscape seek to lose themselves in their given milieus. In a telling analysis of Hieronymous Bosch's "Garden of Earthly Delights," titled "A Place in Which to Be Lost," Certeau draws on Paul Klee to discern different ways of moving about and through the painting. In a work of art, he notes of Klee in his *Theory of Modern Art*, roads are arranged for the spectator's eye to explore a landscape in the way an animal grazes a pasture. So too Bosch's garden "offers ways of getting lost. Sighting points are arranged for possibilities of wandering. Unmoored, as in a dream, from assured meanings, they come from afar" (1982, 93–94). A delightful "atopia" grounds the travel in the painting. Such, too, is the landscape in the idyllic moments of *Les Amants*, and for the good reason that the allegorical map is both a frame and a device that allows the lovers to lose themselves in an otherwise controlled space.

10. "Le pli est inséparable du vent. Ventilé par l'éventail, le pli n'est plus celui de la matière à travers lequel on voit, mais celui de l'âme dans laquelle on lit . . ., le pli de l'Evénement [The fold is inseparable from wind. Ventilated by the fan, the fold is no longer that of matter through which we see, but that of the soul in which we read . . ., the fold of the Event]," writes Gilles Deleuze

(1988, 43). Kline (1992, 31–32, 39) establishes a vital connection between the scarves worn in the film and Magritte's *Les Amants,* a painting that figures in the film much in the same way as the *Carte du Tendre.*

11. Taking leave of Jacques Lacan, Anthony Vidler (2000, 13–14, 212–13) notes that in art and architecture mirrors are always framed and thus denote the limits of their own illusory reflections. A similar sense of limit is felt here.

12. In his work on American cinema in the 1970s Raymond Bellour studies the ways that rhetorical systems are multiple and often varied within themselves. The films produce "mirages" of order (e.g., 1975, 346–47). The same "classical effect" is given here.

13. In the tradition of the emblem an image is conceived as a "silent speaker," as a voice that whispers through the mix of language and picture, notes Gisèle Mathieu-Castellani. Emblems "speak to the dream of transparency that inhabits the imagination . . . in its desire to make the world speak, to restore the mute language of signs" (1988, 29): The same effect has been studied in chapter 1 (note 20).

14. If not the *Guide vert,* then Guy Arbellot (1973, 765–91). The "tender" route that the couple takes is on the ground of a revolution in transportation and its mapping. To obtain a sense of the history of the road on which Jeanne and Bernard are driving it suffices to see the articulation of roads on the great Cassini maps (1789) of the French provinces. These maps were the basis for highway planning and for the Michelin projections of the kind that the couple studies before they enter into the light of day at the "dangerous hour of dawn."

15. In his reading of these words, Santos Zunzunegui (2001, 118–91) shows that for the novelist and the filmmaker form is totalizing. Malle makes the same point in the ending to *Les Amants.*

7. Paris Underground

1. Patrice Higonnet notes that the Exposition of 1889 set Paris "under the sign of triumphant science." Baron Haussmann's city, "the mythical capital of urban modernity, now became (in theory at least) the capital of progress, technology, science, and rationality" (2002, 358). The Exposition of 1900, he adds, was "far more phantasmagorical," and cause, with the unveiling of the east-west line of the subway and addition of electric lighting at the Place de la Concorde (360), for a greater distance from the traumatic past of the Commune and the Franco-Prussian War. In her conclusion to *Paris as Revolution* (1995) Priscilla Parkhurst Ferguson speculates that the Exposition which illuminated the Tower and inaugurated the metro strove to produce a new beginning, in a new century, bereft of a highly conflicted past that reached back to 1789.

2. Jean Starobinski (1973) studies the contradiction that philosophers of enlightenment faced when they refused to think of night and shadow that might color the experience of reason: hence the affiliation of perpetual Light with a reign of Terror (see also chapter 1, note 29). The textured light in *Les 400 coups* can be appreciated through this optic.

3. "Soleil cou coupé" [Sun neck cut off] are the final words that play on the visual, almost cinematic montage of the sun setting as if it were a sphere cut away from the heavens as might a head from its neck. Apollinaire turns Mallarmé's highly wrought description of a sunset in the form of a "handsome suicide" ["Victorieusement fuit le suicide beau"] into a compelling figure of graphic motion.

4. In "Lyrical Ideograms," on the year 1913, I argued that "Zone" "displays a cinematic aspect" through "movements established by tensions among space, line, letters, and forms in passage" (Conley 1989, 843). The effect of Apollinaire verse is close to what Giuliana Bruno describes of "filmic flow" in early cinema based on itinerary: "The geographical route is the one the motion picture took as it created a haptic language of shifting viewpoints. When one rethinks representation by way of

nautical and fluvial cartography, it comes as no surprise that early cinema, as an international phenomenon, insistently portrayed urban space by reproducing the captivating fluvial motion of cities" (2002, 183–84).

5. Denby 1969, 11. Reference to specific shots will be taken from this edition.

6. Flamand's name erupts into the film as a memory of lost time. He played the role of "Dédé" in Jean Renoir's first sound film, *La Chienne* (1931) and, by force of his own sad fate and that of the Second World War, had virtually never since been seen. His face swollen and wrinkled by the wear and tear of life and alcohol, he plays a cameo role as René Bigey's father, a man more interested in seeing friends at a "club" than spending time with his son (shots 239–44). Guy Decomble is of more recent and pertinent vintage. Having played the chief of police in Jean-Pierre Melville's *Bob le Flambeur* (1956), he embodied the force of law and order but also, as a friend of the outlaw protagonist, an admirer of truancy and a practitioner of illegalism.

7. Benton 1989, 1–5, and Bloch 1989, 6–13. In Bloch's article appears the very same map (in an English version) that in the film is to the right of Doinel who writes his inscription.

8. "En marge de 'l'érotisme au cinéma'" (April 1957), a review of Lo Duca's *L'Erotisme au cinema*, published in 1956 (Bazin 1999, 249–56).

9. In the middle of the film, in a rare moment of intimate exchange, Antoine says that he would like to join the navy. "J'aimerais voir la mer" [I'd love to see the sea] (shot 228). René responds, unconsciously referring to the maps seen in the classroom, that he has seen the English Channel, the Atlantic, and (shot 229) the Mediterranean, but not the North Sea.

10. Doinel's *mer* might be comparable to Gilles Deleuze and Félix Guattari's concept of a hypothetically "smooth space," an *espace lisse,* that needs to be thought of both geographically and psychically (1980).

11. Holland in Denby 1969.

12. The shot of Doinel's father studying his map is found in the restored version of the film and is described in the appendix of Denby (1969, 163).

13. Baecque and Toubiana 2001, 198. For Truffaut the proper name can circulate in myriad directions, offering the spectator variously inventive itineraries of interpretation.

14. Quoted by Jacob (1992, 439; 2006, 347). Jacob adds that in its first editions G. Bruno's famous *Tour de France par deux enfants,* a geographical fiction of the itinerary two orphan children lead through France lacked a map of the country. The book fits in the general context of Truffaut's juvenile geography, a point made clear by Jacques and Mona Ozouf (1997, 277–302). In *La Tour de France par deux enfants* we learn "that the grandeur of a country is not restricted to the extension of its territory but to the force of the French soul, to the generosity of their enterprises," and by "work and moral progress" (287), the very concerns of Petite-Feuille, a pedagogue overwhelmed by the chaos of his classroom.

15. In *In the Metro,* a translation of *Un ethnologue dans le métro,* Marc Augé thus writes of a person's growth and formation in the Parisian subway: "To every station are tied knots of memories that cannot be untangled, memories of these rare moments, Stendhal used to say, 'for which life is worth living,'" an observation confirmed by the fact that "[t]o speak of the metro first of all means to speak of reading and of cartography. I seem to recall that in the history atlases of my childhood, pupils were invited to measure the alternating periods of growth and decay in France. . . . There is something of an accordion effect in the image of my life presented to me by a subway map." He adds that the place-names in the subway often constitute "a more secret cartography" in which the significant moments of a person's life, like the "phases" of a painter's career, are associated with various subway stations. A "blue phase" would have as analogue the "Maubert-Mutualité" moment, and so forth (2002, 9–10).

16. One Wednesday afternoon he cut school in order to read *The Three Musketeers,* went relatively far away to avoid being seen, and happened upon a bombardment in the early evening when

everyone rallied into the metro for protection. He spent the night underground with Dumas under his arms, "without thinking about my parents," before going directly to school the next day where, in the afternoon, his mother, "dead with disquiet," awaited him. The art of prevarication that he learned in school, Truffaut's biographers observe, might have given rise to the boy's remark, fifteen years later in *Les 400 coups,* that "it's my mother . . . M'sieu [Petite-Feuille], she's dead": (Baecque and Toubiana 2001, 40). The scenes in which the parents are struck with fear when someone knocks at the door of their apartment cannot fail to recall the search tactics that Nazis and Pétainistes led in ferreting for Jews and dissidents during the Occupation (shots 123–24 in Denby 1969, 52–53).

17. Anne Gillain elegantly studies the point in *Les 400 coups* and tributary films by Truffaut through emphasis on its presentation of primal phantasies "which are inherent in the development and maturation of any human being" (2000, 149). As in a Balzacian itinerary, the film brings into the city a drama that had begun, in *Les Mistons,* in the country.

8. A Roadmap for a Road Movie

1. The same author's "Selling Maps, Selling Highways: Rand-McNally's 'Blazed Trails Programs'" (1993b, 77–89) studies the utopian strategies and "self-congratulatory rhetoric" in the design of road maps that led to the production of the national highway system.

2. At the beginning of a meticulous study of *You Only Live Once* Tom Gunning (2000, 234–35) remarks how Lang's film tends to "pare away the visual world and leave only the essentials." Lang succeeds by finding "this aspect of sight not only in his many diagrams and maps, but in his topographical shots, which view space from a point of view which facilitates its abstraction into an essential design." Gunning contrasts Lang's taste for composition, for "the graphic armature of the visual, as opposed to the delight in the textured variety of a visual field found in directors like Griffith or Renoir." Louis Menand (2003, 169–77) allies the background of French New Wave cinema with Arthur Penn's conception and realization of *Bonnie and Clyde.* Penn's film takes a road back to Lang through the landscape of the *cinema d'auteur.*

3. At first Louise seems to be a reincarnation of Cassie (Anne Sheridan), the waitress who serves coffee and terse one-liners to patrons of a truck stop along a California highway in *They Drive by Night* (d. Raoul Walsh, 1940). To her credit (so it seems) Louise works in a diner that is not a branch of Burger King, Subway, Pizza Hut, or McDonald's.

4. Elizabeth W. Spelman and Martha Minow (1996, 272) argue that the film turns on the legal issue of justifiable action. Emphasis here is that the ladies' debates about their actions lead to a didactic mission related to allegorical cartography.

5. Deleuze 1988, 27. He adds that such "is the very idea of baroque perspective."

6. Jean-Louis Leutrat and Suzanne Liandrat-Guigues (1990, 178–82) show that *Stagecoach* builds on relations of fate, seen in playing cards taken to be signs of geography given by the context of Monument Valley. The Monument Valley is a virtual "platte map" on which the action takes place.

7. The map, first printed in copperplate in 1595, is frequently reproduced on calendars that feature masterpieces of baroque cartography. See Burden 1996, 112–13, entry 88, and Karrow 1993, 376–406. The version consulted here is a facsimile in the Harvard Map Collection (M3000.1595).

8. Viewers familiar with the map would know that on the left side on the bottom (next to Thelma's chin) a map of Haiti is set on contrast to the Gulf of Mexico (stretching from the "Rio del Espiritu sanctu" or Mississippi down and around to the Yucatan peninsula).

9. In an alert but unpublished viewing of the sequence T. Jefferson Kline notes that "Zip" is a sort of "message without a code." Systems of surveillance and advertising use "zip codes" to locate where and who we are. At this moment, when they are "zipped," the two ladies are totally lost.

10. The cleanest and clearest reproduction of this monumental work (545 × 825 mm) is in

Schilder 1986, map 4. See also Schilder's comprehensive historical treatment of Visscher's carto-graphic vision (1981, 41–51). In his description of the map Rodney Shirley (1983, 317, entry 294) aptly notes that the two central hemispheres are "nearly overwhelmed by the richness and artistic invention of the border decorations," in which Europe, personified on the top, is paid homage by Indians of the other continents. It is impossible to discern much of the detail. In view is the large car-touche in the lower Pacific region of the western hemisphere. The four men who first circumnavi-gated the globe—Magellan, Cavendish, Noort, and Drake—stand about a dais on which are draped heraldic cloth printed with descriptions of their exploits. Shirley concludes that the "engraving as a whole is a masterly combination of all the emblems of the age; the two hemispheres of the world, the heavens, mythology and the classical past, the pride of recent explorers, man's duties throughout the changing seasons, and the Christian obligation of every being."

11. Thelma is attracted to the bottom of the vagrant youth (Brad Pitt) who eventually robs them. By contrast, in respect to her husband: "You could park a car in the shadow of his ass." The remark is heard when the Thunderbird approaches an intersection where the camera has panned from the sight of the two wheels of a bicycle parked by a telephone pole to catch the approaching car that dis-plays its two sets of double headlamps.

12. In *Vie des formes* (1968 [1947]), Henri Focillon characterized the baroque aesthetic as one that arches back upon and almost historicized the forms that made it possible. It refers to earlier experiment and classical solutions within its own style. In *Thelma and Louise* the baroque instance is not only found in the bent and twisted shapes that recur everywhere in the image field, as indicated by the maps, but also in the reference to many snippets of film that had defined the genre.

13. The shot attests to what Metz (1991b) called the "mobile geography of cinema." For Metz subject-positions are impossible to locate in cinema because the voice is never attached to its speaker. It ambles about the screen and thus also underscores how much the medium is one in which indirect free discourse—a point that Pasolini championed (articulated in Deleuze 1983, 106–7)—reigns. The geography of film owes much to the fact that in the field of the image speech never has specific origin or destination. In this film the point is made mystically clear on the vista of the Grand Canyon.

14. Noteworthy are the conclusions to *Colorado Territory* (1949) and *White Heat*. The sequence of *Desperate Journey* in which Alan Hale falls from a rooftop is similar in texture, and so also is a murder in *Northern Pursuit* (1943).

15. In a sequence shot in the parking lot of low-budget motel (in North Carolina) in *Bright Leaves* (2003), director Ross McElwee presents himself looking through the lens of his camera that is aimed, from what seems to be a painted parking stall on the asphalt outside of his room, at a mirror on the wall inside. The effect of a *mise-en-abyme* is given as he notes in voiceover that the pleasure of film-ing in these areas has "narcotic" attraction, an attraction in the film that fits the broader theme of nicotine addiction. A narcotic pleasure (in a room for smokers, and in Jimmy's gym in the counter-shot, where he puffs away on his cigarette) is shown, too, in this sequence of *Thelma and Louise*.

16. Although they include globes and maps, "The Astronomer" (1668) and "The Geographer" (1668) are not comparable to the paintings where women and maps are juxtaposed.

17. The viewer is reminded immediately of Gilles Deleuze's concept (1988, 6–7) of the "baroque room" in which light does not enter from a window but that is felt through harmonic folds.

18. Anthony Vidler (2000, 10–11, 230–33) writes the intersection of philosophical and psycho-analytical spaces that are "warped" in the way they are sensed subjects who live in a complex process of projection and introjection.

19. Noteworthy is that in this film the men watch television and the women do not. Their desire is not where the viewers' might be. By contrast, in Robert Siodmak's *The Killers* (1946) a long flash-back depicts the robbery of a payroll from a hat factory in Hackensack. A crane shot in a long and

complex career almost self-consciously reflects, on the windshield of a car that makes its get-away, the figure of the cameraman and his assistant poised on a crane. Siodmak uses anamorphosis to relate the memory-image to the artifice of its invention. By contrast, in this sequence Scott seems to invoke the artifice that he simultaneously represses.

20. Sharon Willis (1997, 108) remarks cogently that the film "parades" its own takeover of clichés that identify things masculine and feminine in contemporary popular culture. The two women challenge our readings of "clichéd postures" and "the effects of identification in our histories as consumers of popular culture." Willis (and also Spelman and Minow 1996) provides ample bibliographies of criticism devoted to this feature.

9. Cronos, Cosmos, and *Polis*

1. See chapter 7, and Denby 1969, 24, shot 39.

2. The reader of Luce Giard's introductions to the English editions of Michel de Certeau's two volumes of political writings (1993 and 1994) quickly intuits that they were relaunched in France in the early 1990s and in Anglophone countries later in the decade to raise political consciousness that had severely eroded since the later 1960s. "Certeau was writing," she notes, "in the context of a fully employed society, when it was all the easier to clearly denounce alienation in labor in that the latter was available to everyone" (1993, xiii). Kassovitz's *La Haine,* in the same vein, uses a mobile cartography in its backward glance to 1968 to politicize the present moment of his film.

3. All reference to the scenario will be indicated between parentheses by the number of the sequence and, respectively, that of the page on which the citation appears. This working edition of the screenplay does not always follow the final version of *Jusqu'ici tout va bien . . .*

4. Villon 1941, 215. The translation of the quatrain—no doubt the finest in the English language—is by Preston Sturges. Author of the screenplay of *If I Were King* (1938, directed by Frank Lloyd), Sturges penned translations of several of the poems of the *Testament,* including these last words and the "Ballade des pendus." Villon, played by Ronald Colman, lends a mix of elegance and wit to the scene when, en route to execution by Louis XI (Basil Rathbone), he offers the lines in response to an admiring lover (Ellen Drew) who embraces the roguish gentleman, pleading with him at this threshold of death, "Oh, please! Say something funny!"

5. The situation is reminiscent of what Michel de Certeau (1994, 68) remarked about the state of French subjects and the ruling orders of the nation in 1968: People who are the object of an ethnological investigation are "[r]éduits à n'être plus que des marginaux figés eux-mêmes dans un retour à leur histoire primitive [such would be immigrants in the suburbs] . . ., ils n'existent plus, dans la communication, qu'au titre de ce que nous disons d'eux" [reduced to being nothing more than border dwellers frozen in a return to their primitive history . . . they exist in communication only by dint of what we say about them] (1997, 33).

6. In the context of the "total social fact" of exchange, Claude Lévi-Strauss (1955, 348) staged a scenario of ritual violence that hovered between commerce and war. For opposing bands of Nambikwara Indians negotiation is not easy: "Aussi, la rencontre de deux groupes, quand elle peut se dérouler de façon pacifique, a-t-elle pour conséquence une série de cadeaux réciproques; le conflit fait place au marché" [Therefore, when it can unwind in a peaceful manner, the meeting of two groups leads to a series of reciprocal gifts; conflict gives way to commerce]. Kassovitz reverses the scenario while holding to a primal theater in which the players are exclusively male.

7. Truffaut's *Les Mistons* is exemplary, and so also *A bout de souffle* (1960) whose screenplay Truffaut had authored. But present in this context is *Pierrot le fou.* In Godard's film Pierrot sits listlessly in a theater, his copy of Elie Faure in his hands, watching newsreels of the first combat in Vietnam.

8. See Rouch 2003, 88–91, 188–95, on self and possession in this film that later inspired Jean Genet's *Les Nègres*.

9. See chapter 4 above and Lestringant 1996. Following a model given by Sartre in *Huis clos* and Genet in *Les Bonnes,* Elaine Scarry (1985) insists over and again that all representations of torture require a third party—a spectator—to maintain their symbolic effects.

10. We can again recall Marc Augé: "Parler du métro, c'est donc parler d'abord de lecture et de cartographie. . . . [L]e plan du métro, c'est aussi la carte du Tendre ou la main ouverte qu'il faut savoir plier et scruter pour se frayer un passage de la ligne de vie à la ligne de tête et à la ligne de Coeur" (2002, 18–19); [To speak of the metro first of all means to speak of reading and of cartography . . . The subway map is also the Carte du Tendre or the open hand that one has to know how to fold and study closely in order to blaze a trail from the lifeline to the headline onto the heartline (2002, 9–10)]. The reflection applies both to *Les 400 coups* and *La Haine*.

11. In "La Caméra-graffito" Jenny Lefcourt argues that in *La Haine* allusions to other films confirm an intertextual process that aligns Kassovitz's feature with cinema of the early *Nouvelle vague* and with its desire to create a "caméra-stylo" in the heritage of Alexandre Astruc's alignment of pen and camera (Lefcourt and Conley 1998). Some points of that essay are revisited in the paragraph that follows.

12. Lefcourt 2003, chapter 6. Right-wing readings, she notes, are in *Le Figaro Magazine* (10 June 1995) while the left-wing view is expressed in *Libération* (5 June 1995).

13. Lefcourt 2003 reports articles in *Le Monde* about quarter in difficulty on June 12, 13, 18–19, 20, 22, 23, 24, 27; July 6, 12, 13, 18, 27; August 9, 15, 18, 19, 20–21, 22; September 6, 9, 12, 14, 20, 21. Even Jacques Derrida contributed a leading article on the movement to save Mumia Abu-Jamal from deportation (*Le Monde,* August 9).

14. Jacob (1992, 35; 2006, 16) writes of Claudio Parmiggiani's identification of cows and maps: "Five photographs of cows are seen against a background of a pasture—white cows with black spots. Nothing appears out of the ordinary until the black spots are seen arranged in the familiar silhouettes of the Eurasian continent, Australia, the Americas, and Africa, each carefully designed and painted by the artist himself." (The work is illustrated in figure 39 of the French edition and figure 3 of the English translation.)

10. Ptolemy, *Gladiator,* and Empire

1. Deleuze (1988, 26) notes that after the eighteenth century "the fluctuation of a norm replaces the permanence of a law." Modulation becomes synonymous with new conditions of production. Basing his observations on Gilbert Simondon's studies of biological genesis and individuation, he remarks that *molding* (where a form is filled and shaped by a matrix) is tantamount to modulating in a definitive way, whereas modulating is equivalent to molding "'in a continuous and perpetually variable way.'" It is not difficult to see how political regimes of "discipline" and "control" are plotted from the analogy.

2. Marc Augé (1999, 5) steers a course between law and modulation in a short study of Georges Bataille's review of Lévi-Strauss's *Elementary Structures of Kinship*. Bataille's reading was "ego-centered." The "idea of transgression meant more for him than the rule while, clearly, for the Levi-Straussian anthropologist transgression or, more generally, the exception is of interest only in respect to the rule that serves as a measure or a point reference." By a leap of logic it can be speculated that Bataille's world is under a disciplinary regime where Lévi-Strauss's, of a modular form, is a world where "control" prevails.

3. See chapter 1, note 24. Along another line of inquiry it would be propitious to speculate that Virilio's use of *perception* is quasi-identical to Gilles Deleuze's observations (1988, 106) that "events"

take place before their actual fact for reason of the thousands of "tiny microperceptions" that precede them. "Prehensions" swarm and gather in anticipation of something that will happen.

4. It is worth recalling Deleuze's argument (1985a, 49–51, also outlined in the introduction above) that modern times are defined by the "map" or diagram that replaces an "archive." The former models and predicts behavior where the latter had accounted for and preserved its prior forms of existence.

5. It follows the theme of the enemy brothers in the Sophoclean cycle of Theban plays. In cinema conflict between the worthy inheritor who is not of the noble line and the rightful but inept heir may have its most classical expression in Anthony Mann, the director who moves, notes Jacques Rancière (2001), between classical tragedy and family romance in *The Man from Laramie* (1955). When it is seen from this perspective it shares affinities with the same director's *Fall of the Roman Empire* (1964), a principal model for *Gladiator*.

6. In *Objective, Burma!*, contrary to the dictum that "the map is not the territory," the film becomes the map—the simulacrum—of itself. The military operation is given to decipherment of the map on which the men are walking. The western is a genre that sometimes mixes with the war movie. In a collective work on Hollywood myths and the western the authors of *Le Western* (Dort et al. 1966) include a *topos* entitled "briefing," in which sheriffs, sitting on the front of their desks set in front of wall-maps of the Texas territory, Kansas, and so on, point to the images while telling their posses of the dangerous missions for which they have been chosen.

7. Jeremy Black (1997, 6) notes that in the fifteenth century Ptolemy's maps carried authority, but new findings, "accelerated by printing and European exploration," quickly turned them into historical artifacts. The 1513 edition of Ptolemy, published in Strasbourg, was the first to carry "old" and "new" maps on successive pages.

8. It is worth recalling that Erwin Panofsky (1960/1972) argued that, unlike the "revivals" of the classical world in the Carolingian and twelfth-century renascences, the Renaissance obtained the accuracy of its depiction of the Roman past through its realization that it was very much apart from it. Rome became more properly a scientific object than a living element of collective subjectivity.

9. Indeed, if it does, the proximity of *Gladiator* to *Saving Private Ryan* shows that much of the writing of the history of the latter is built upon *Jurassic Park* (1993). The panzers and half-tracks in Spielberg's film play a narrative role akin to the tyrannosaurus, stegosaurus, and other monsters that cross the paths the protagonist-tourists follow in wandering through their lost world behind enemy lines in a place in Ireland chosen to resemble Normandy.

10. The viewer of these elements of *Gladiator* finds salient analysis of their effects in Montaigne's descriptions of the games (1962, 885), built upon a reading of Calpurnius, that "S'il y a quelque chose qui soit excusable en tels excez, c'est où l'invention et la nouveauté fournit d'admiration, non pas la despence" [If there is something excusable in such excess, it is where invention and novelty furnish admiration and not expense]. "Des coches" [Of coaches], an architectural essay that militates against colonial empire, remains one of the most potent of all critiques of early modern political economies. It dovetails elegantly with the effects of simulation in *Gladiator*.

11. *Cruel lucidity* is what Michel de Certeau (1993, 21) calls a condition "that seeks respectable authorities by beginning with an examination of real situations," in which it is clear that illusion "will not lead to truth" (1997 translation, 6). He later speaks of "ocular exoticism" that is used to weave the fabric of collective reverie.

12. Once again Montaigne has critical presence in two sentences on the thumb in the Roman games in "Des pouces" [Of Thumbs], an often overlooked essay (1962, 775–76).

13. For the material that follows I am indebted to Steve Conley and the late Horace Stancil, ardent Giants football fans, who provided tickets for the NFC Championship in 2000 and obtained coveted tickets to Super Bowl XXXI in 2001.

14. The national anthem has been a ritual inauguration of sports events in America only since the end of the Second World War. For generations born after 1940 its ideology of commemoration has been less evident than that of a media-event.

Conclusion

1. In respect to what a map is I follow Harley and Woodward 1987, introduction, and Jacob 1992 and 2006, chapter 1. The former posit a working definition that allows them to distinguish a *mappa mundi* (a medieval map of the world) from a world map (that appears in print-culture of the Renaissance). The latter defines a map much as an Inuit proverbially treats of snow: he defines maps by their commanding traits and virtues without ever reducing it to a single definition or word. Père François de Dainville's enduring lexicon of geography and maps (1964) shows how maps are conceived and read differently at different times. Their icons and stenographies change over time and are in flux; so also is the textual matter that serves as their legends or is printed in their field of view. These points of reference constitute a solid foundation for the student of cartographic forms.

2. In his aptly titled *Mists of Regret* (1995) Dudley Andrew builds a monumental historical and structural study of the aesthetic and political implications of the theme in French cinema of the *entre-deux-guerres*. He and Steven Ungar build much of their cultural history of Popular Front Paris under the banner of the same theme (2005, 177–385).

.

Bibliography

Abel, Richard. 1984. *French cinema: The first wave, 1915–29.* Princeton, N.J.: Princeton University Press.

———. 1994. *The ciné goes to town.* Berkeley: University of California Press.

Akerman, James. 1991. On the shoulders of Titan: Viewing of the past in Atlas-structure. Ph.D. diss., Department of Geography, Pennsylvania State University, University Park, Pa.

———. 1993a. Blazing a well-worn path: Cartographic commercialism, highway promotion, and automobile tourism in the United States, 1880–1930. *Cartographica* 30, no. 1:10–20.

———. 1993b. Selling maps, selling highways: Rand-McNally's "Blazed Trails Programs." *Imago mundi* 45:77–89.

Alpers, Svetlana. 1987. The mapping impulse in Dutch art. In *Art and cartography: Six historical essays,* ed. David Woodward, 51–96. Chicago: University of Chicago Press.

Andrew, Dudley. 1995. *Mists of regret.* Princeton, N.J.: Princeton University Press.

Andrew, Dudley, and Steven Ungar. 2005. *Popular Front Paris and the poetics of culture.* Cambridge: The Belknap Press of Harvard University Press.

Apian, Pieter. 1551. *Cosmographie.* Paris: Gaultherot.

Apollinaire, Guillaume. 1965. *Oeuvres poétiques.* Ed. Marcel Adéma and Michel Décaudin. Paris: Gallimard/Pléiade.

Arbellot, Guy. 1973. La Grande mutation des routes de France au milieu du XVIIIe siècle. *Annales E.S.C.* 28:765–91.

Assayas, Olivier. 2001 [1981]. La Grâce perdue des aventuriers. Reprinted in *Le Goût de l'Amérique: Petite anthologie des "Cahiers du Cinéma,"* ed. Antoine de Baecque with the assistance of Gabrielle Lucantonio, 138–43. [Paris]: Cahiers du Cinéma.

Augé, Marc. 1992. *Non-lieux: Introduction à une anthropologie de la surmodernitié.* Paris: Seuil.

———. 1999. Le Triangle anthropologique: Mauss, Bataille, Lévi-Strauss. *Critique,* nos. 620–21 (Jan.–Feb.): 4–12.

———. 2002. *In the Metro.* Minneapolis: University of Minnesota Press. Translated by Tom Conley from *Un ethnologue dans le métro.* Paris: Hachette, 1986.

Aulagnier, Piera. 1975. *La Violence de l'interprétation: Du pictogramme à l'énoncé.* Paris: Presses Universitaires de France.

Baecque, Antoine de. 2003. *La Cinéphilie: Invention d'un regard, histoire d'une culture, 1944–1968.* Paris: Fayard.

Baecque, Antoine de, and Charles Tesson, eds. 1999. *La Nouvelle Vague.* Paris: Cahiers du Cinéma.

Baecque, Antoine de, and Serge Toubiana. 2001. *François Truffaut.* Paris: Gallimard/Folio.

Balzac, Honoré de. 1922–29. *Oeuvres complètes.* 35 vols. Paris: L. Conard.

Barthes, Roland. 1975. En sortant du cinema. *Communications,* no. 23:104–7.

Baudelaire, Charles. 1976. *Oeuvres completes.* 2 vols. Ed. Claude Pichois. Paris: Gallimard/Pléiade.

Bazin, André. 1989. *Jean Renoir.* Paris: Editions Gérard Lebovici.

———. 1999 (1975). *Qu'est-ce que le cinema?* Paris: Editions du Cerf.

Belleforest, François de. 1575. *Cosmographie universelle.* 2 vols. Paris: Sonnius.

Bellour, Raymond. 1975. Le Blocage symbolique. *Communications,* no. 23:235–350.

Benjamin, Walter. 1969. *Illuminations.* Trans. Harry Zohn. New York: Schocken Books.

Benton, John. 1989. Entering the date. In *A new history of French literature,* ed. Denis Hollier, 1–5. Cambridge: Harvard University Press.

Benveniste, Emile. 1966. *Problèmes de linguistique générale.* Vol. 1. Paris: Gallimard. In English as *Problems in general linguistics,* trans. Mary Elizabeth Meek. Miami Linguistics Series 8. Coral Gables, Fla.: University of Miami Press, 1971.

Billard, Pierre. 1998. *Le Mystère René Clair.* Paris: Plon.

Black, Jeremy. 1997. *Maps and history: Constructing images of the past.* New Haven: Yale University Press.

Blandford, Steve, Barry Keith Grant, and Jim Hillier. 2001. *The film studies dictionary.* New York: Oxford University Press.

Bloch, R. Howard. 1989. The first document. In *A new history of French literature,* ed. Denis Hollier, 6–13. Cambridge: Harvard University Press.

Bogue, Ronald. 2003. *Deleuze on cinema.* New York: Routledge.

Böhnke, Alexander, Rembert Hüser, and Georg Stanitzek, eds. 2006. *Das Buch zum Vorspann.* Berlin: Vorwerk 8.

Borges, Jorge Luis. 1964. *Dreamtigers.* Trans. Mildred Boyer and Harold Morland. Austin: University of Texas Press.

Brunette, Peter. 1987. *Roberto Rossellini.* New York: Oxford University Press.

Bruno, Giuliana. 2002. *Atlas of emotion.* New York: Verso Books.

Buci-Glucksmann, Christine. 1996. *L'Oeil icarien de l'art.* Paris: Galilée.

Buisseret, David. 1964. Les *ingénieurs du roy* au temps de Henri IV. *Bulletin de la Section de Géographie* 77:13–84.

———. 1992. Monarchs, ministers, and maps in France before the accession of Louis XIV. In *Monarchs, ministers, and maps: The emergence of cartography as a tool of government in early modern Europe,* ed. Buisseret, 99–123. Chicago: University of Chicago Press.

———. 1996. Defining the estate map. Introduction to *Rural images: Estate maps in the old and new worlds,* ed. Buisseret. Chicago: University of Chicago Press.

———. 2003. *The mapmaker's quest: Depicting new worlds in renaissance Europe.* New York: Oxford University Press.

———. Forthcoming. French cartography: The *ingénieurs du roi.* In *The history of cartography 3: Cartography in the European Renaissance,* ed. David Woodward. Chicago: University of Chicago Press.

Buisson, Ferdinand. 1878. *Rapport sur l'instruction primaire à l'Exposition universelle de Philadelphie en 1876.* Paris: Imprimerie nationale.

————. 1882. *Le Dictionnaire de pédagogie et d'instruction primaire*. Paris: Hachette.

Burch, Noël. 1981. *Theory of film practice*. Trans. Helen R. Lane. Princeton, N.J.: Princeton University Press.

Burden, Philip. D. 1996. *The mapping of North America*. Rickmansworth, England: Raleigh Publications.

Burgoyne, Robert. 1979. The imaginary and the neo-real. *Enclitic,* no. 3:36–47.

Casey, Edward. 1997. *The fate of place*. Berkeley: University of California Press.

————. 2000. *Representing place*. Minneapolis: University of Minnesota Press.

Cavell, Stanley. 1979. *The world viewed: Reflections on the ontology of film*. Enl. ed. Cambridge: Harvard University Press.

Céard, Jean, and Jean-Claude Margolin. 1984. *Rébus de la Renaissance: Des images qui parlent*. 2 vols. Paris: Maisonneuve et Larose.

Certeau, Michel de. 1975. *L'Ecriture de l'histoire*. Paris: Gallimard.

————. 1980. Utopies verbales: Glossolalies. *Traverses,* no. 20 (Nov.): 26–37.

————. 1982. *La Fable mystique*. Paris: Gallimard.

————. 1984. Entretien avec Alain Charbonnier et Joël Magny. *Cinéma,* no. 301 (Jan.): 19–20.

————. 1985. "Mystique." *Encyclopaedia universalis,* 873–78. 12 new ed. Paris.

————. 1987. Le revenants de la ville. *Traverses,* no. 40:74–85.

————. 1990. *L'Invention du quotidien 1: Arts de faire*. Ed. Luce Giard. Paris: Editions Gallimard.

————. 1993. *La Culture au pluriel*. Paris: Editions du Seuil. In English (1997) as *Culture in the plural*. With an introduction by Luce Giard. Trans. Tom Conley. Minneapolis: University of Minnesota Press.

————. 1994. *La Prise de parole et autres écrits politiques*. Paris: Editions du Seuil. In English (1997) as *The capture of speech*. With an introduction by Luce Giard. Trans. Tom Conley. Minneapolis: University of Minnesota Press.

Certeau, Michel de, Dominique Julia, and Jacques Revel. 1975. *Une politique de la langue: La Révolution française et les patois*. Paris: Editions Gallimard.

Chastel, André. 2001. *Le Geste dans l'art*. Paris: Presses Universitaires de France/Liana Lévi.

Château, Dominique, and Jacinto Lageira, eds. 1996. *Après Deleuze: Philosophie et esthétique du cinéma*. Paris: Editions Place Publique.

Conley, Tom. 1989. Lyrical ideograms. In *A new history of French literature,* ed. Denis Hollier, 842–49. Cambridge: Harvard University Press.

————. 1990. *L'auteur énuclée. Hors Cadre,* no. 8:77–95.

————. 1991. *Film hieroglyphs: Ruptures in classical cinema*. Minneapolis: University of Minnesota Press.

————. 1992a. Signatures de perspective. *Hors Cadre,* no. 10:217–28.

————. 1992b. *Theatres of cruelty: Wars of religion, violence, and the new world*. Chicago: The Hermon Dunlap Smith Center for the History of Cartography (The Newberry Library Slide Set 14).

————. 1996a. Laws of the game. In *Legal reelism: Movies as legal texts,* ed. John Denvir, 95–117. Urbana: University of Illinois Press.

————. 1996b. Le Cinéaste de la vie moderne: Paris as map in film. In *Parisian Fields,* ed. Michael Sheringham, 71–84. London: Reaktion Books.

————. 1996c. *The self-made map: Cartographic writing in early modern France*. Minneapolis: University of Minnesota Press.

————. 2000. *Pierrot le fou* and the madness of language. In *Focus on "Pierrot le fou,"* ed. David Wills, 81–107. Cambridge Studies on Film. Cambridge: Cambridge University Press.

————. 2001a. Cartographies de films. In *L'Art et l'hybride,* ed. Christian Doumet and Marie-Claire Ropars-Wuilleumier, 53–71. Paris: Presses de l'Université de Paris-Vincennes-à-Saint-Denis.

———. 2001b. F as in fake, A as in auteur. In *Directed by Allen Smithee*, ed. Jeremy Braddock and Stephen Hock, 127–44. Minneapolis: University of Minnesota Press.

———. 2006. Getting lost on the waterways of *L'Atalante*. In *Cinema and Modernity*, ed. Murray Pomerance, 253–72. New Brunswick, N.J.: Rutgers University Press.

Corey, Melinda, and George Ochoa, eds. 2002. *The American Film Institute desk reference*. New York: Stonesong Press.

Cosgrove, Denis. 2001. *Apollo's eye: A cartographic genealogy of the Earth in the western imagination*. Baltimore: Johns Hopkins University Press.

Courcelles, Dominique de. 2003. *Langages mystiques et avènement de la modernité*. Paris: Champion.

Curchod, Olivier, ed. 1998. *Jean Renoir "La Règle du jeu": Nouveau découpage intégral*. Paris: Livre de Poche.

Dainville, François de, S. J. 1964. *Le langage des géographes*. Paris: Picard.

———. 1968. *Le Dauphiné et ses confins vus par l'ingénieur d'Henri IV Jean de Beins*. Geneva: Droz.

Defaux, Gérard, ed. 1990. *Clément Marot, Oeuvres poétiques*. Vol. 1. Paris: Garnier.

———, ed. 1993. *Clément Marot, Oeuvres poétiques*. Vol. 2. Paris: Garnier.

DeJean, Joan. 1991. *Tender geographies: Women and the origin of the novel in France*. New York: Columbia University Press.

Deleuze, Gilles. 1983. *Cinéma 1: L'Image-mouvement*. Paris: Editions de Minuit.

———. 1985a. *Cinéma 2: L'Image-temps*. Paris: Editions de Minuit.

———. 1985b. *Foucault*. Paris: Editions de Minuit.

———. 1988. *Le Pli: Leibniz et le Baroque*. Paris: Editions de Minuit.

———. 1993. *Critique et clinique*. Paris: Editions du Minuit.

———. 2002. *L'Ile déserte et autres textes: Textes et entretiens, 1953–74*. Ed. David Lapoujade. Paris: Minuit.

———. 2003. *Deux régimes de fous: Textes et entretiens, 1975–1995*. Ed. David Lapoujade. Paris: Editions de Minuit.

Deleuze, Gilles, and Félix Guattari. 1980. *Mille plateaux: Capitalisme et schizophrénie*. Paris: Editions de Minuit.

Denby, David, ed. 1969. *The 400 blows: A film by François Truffaut*. New York: Grove Press.

Derrida, Jacques. 1967. *L'Ecriture et la différence*. Paris: Editions du Seuil.

———. 1982. Title (to be specified). *Sub-Stance*, no. 31:5–22. Published in French: 1986. "Titre à préciser." In *Parages*, 219–48. Paris: Galilée.

Dilke, O. A. W. 1987. Itineraries and geographical maps in the early and late Roman empires. In *The History of Cartography*, ed. Harley and Woodward, 234–42.

Dort, Bernard, et al. 1966. *Le Western*. Paris: Union Générale d'Editions.

Duggan, Anne. 2005. *Salonnières, furies, and fairies: The politics of gender and cultural change in absolutist France*. Newark: University of Delaware Press.

Edgerton, Samuel, Jr. 1987. From mental matrix to *Mappamundi* to Christian empire: The heritage of Ptolemaic cartography in the Renaissance. In *Art and cartography: Six historical essays*, ed. David Woodward, 10–50. Chicago: University of Chicago Press.

Edson, Evelyn. 1997. *Mapping time and space: How medieval mapmakers viewed their world*. London: The British Library.

Fahle, Oliver, and Lorenz Engel, eds. 1997. *Der Film bei Deleuze/Le Cinéma selon Deleuze*. Weimar and Paris: Verlag der Bauhaus–Universität Weimar/Presses de la Sorbonne Nouvelle.

Faulkner, Christopher. 1986. *The social cinema of Jean Renoir*. Princeton, N.J.: Princeton University Press.

Favier, Gilles, and Mathieu Kassovitz. 1995. *"Jusqu'ici tout va bien . . ."*: Scénario et photographies du film "La Haine."* Arles: Actes Sud.

Ferguson, Priscilla Parkhurst. 1995. *Paris as revolution: Writing the nineteenth-century city*. Berkeley: University of California Press.

Filteau, Claude. 1979. Le pays de Tendre: L'enjeu d'une carte. *Littérature*, no. 36 (Dec.): 40–57.

———. 1980. Tendre. In *Cartes et figures du monde*, 206–10. Paris: Musée Pompidou.

Focillon, Henri. 1968 (1947). *Vie des formes*. Paris: Presses Universitaires de France.

Foucault, Michel. 1975. *Surveiller et punir*. Paris: Gallimard.

———. 1994 (1967). Des espaces autres. In *Michel Foucault: Dits et écrits*, ed. Daniel Defert and François Ewald, 4:752–62. Paris: Gallimard.

Freud, Sigmund. 1955. *The standard edition of the complete psychological works*. 24 vols. Trans. and ed. James Strachey. London: Hogarth Press.

Garner, Forest, and Emmanuel Gustin. N.d. Aircraft and air forces: Lockheed Hudson patrol bomber. UBoat.net, http://uboat.net/allies/aircraft/hudson.htm.

Gillain, Anne. 2000. The script of delinquency: François Truffaut's *Les 400 coups* (1959). In *French Film: Texts and Contexts*, ed. Susan Hayward and Ginette Vincendeau, 142–57. London: Routledge.

Giuliani, Pierre. 1986. *Raoul Walsh*. Paris: Editions Edilig.

Godard, Jean-Luc. 1998. *Histoire(s) du cinema*. 4 vols. Paris: Gallimard/Gaumont.

Goffart, Walter. 2003. *Historical atlases: The first three hundred years, 1570–1870*. Chicago: University of Chicago Press.

Gomery, Douglas, ed. 1979. *High Sierra*. Madison: University of Wisconsin Press/Wisconsin Center for Film and Theater Research.

Goss, John, ed. 1990. *Blaeu's "The grand atlas" of the seventeenth-century world*. With a foreword by Peter Clark. New York: Rizzoli.

Guillaume, Jean. 1985. L'Escalier dans l'architecture française de la première moitié du seizième siècle. In *L'Escalier dans l'architecture de la Renaissance*, ed. Jean Guillaume, 24–47. Paris: Picard.

Guiomar, Jean-Yves. 1997. Le Tableau géographique de la France. In *Les Lieux de mémoire*, ed. Pierre Nora, 1:1073–98. Paris: Editions Gallimard.

Gunning, Tom. 2000. *The films of Fritz Lang: Allegories of vision and modernity*. London: British Film Institute.

Hale, John R. 1964. The argument of some military title pages of the Renaissance. *The Newberry Library Bulletin* 6, no. 4 (March): 91–102.

———. Forthcoming. Warfare and cartography, ca 1450 to ca 1640. In *The history of cartography 3: Cartography in the European Renaissance*, ed. David Woodward. Chicago: University of Chicago Press.

Hamilton, John. 2003. *Soliciting darkness: Pindar, obscurity, and the classical tradition*. Harvard Studies in Comparative Literature 47. Cambridge: Harvard University Studies of Comparative Literature.

Harley, J. Brian. 1988. Maps, knowledge, and power. In *The iconography of landscape*, ed. Denis Cosgrove and Stephen J. Daniels, 277–312. Cambridge: Cambridge University Press.

———. 2001. *The new nature of maps: Essays in the history of cartography*. Ed. Paul Laxton with an introduction by J. H. Andrews. Baltimore: Johns Hopkins University Press.

Harley, J. Brian, and David Woodward, eds. 1987. *The History of Cartography*, vol. 1, *Cartography in prehistoric, ancient, and medieval Europe and the Mediterranean*. Chicago: University of Chicago Press.

Harvey, David. 1990. *The condition of post-modernity: An enquiry into the origins of cultural change*. London: Basil Blackwell.

———. 2003. *The new imperialism*. New York: Oxford University Press.

Helgerson, Richard. 1992. *Forms of nationhood: The Elizabethan writing of England*. Chicago: University of Chicago Press.

Higonnet, Patrice. 2002. *Paris: Capital of the world.* Trans. Arthur Goldhammer. Cambridge: The Belknap Press of Harvard University.

Holland, Norman N. 1960. How new? How vague? *The Hudson Review* 13, no. 2 (Summer 1960).

Hollier, Denis. 1989. Birthrate and death-wish: February 6, 1934. In *A new history of French literature,* ed. Hollier, 919–24. Cambridge: Harvard University Press.

Huizenga, Johann. 1955. *Homo ludens: A Study of the play-element in culture.* Boston: Beacon Press.

Jacob, Christian. 1992. *L'Empire des cartes: Approche théorique à travers l'histoire de la cartographie.* Paris: Albin Michel.

———. 2006. *The sovereign map: Theoretical approaches in cartography throughout history.* Trans. Tom Conley and ed. Edward H. Dahl. Chicago: University of Chicago Press.

Jameson, Fredric. 1982. *The political unconscious.* Ithaca, N.Y.: Cornell University Press.

———. 1992. *The geopolitical aesthetic: Cinema and space in the world system.* Bloomington: BFI/Indiana University Press.

Jousse, Thierry. 2001. Raoul Walsh, l'effet de souffle. *Cahiers du cinema,* no. 555 (March): 63–65.

Kagan, Richard. 1998. *Urbs* and *civitas* in sixteenth- and seventeenth-century Spain. In *Envisioning the city: Six studies in urban cartography,* ed. David Buisseret, 75–108. Chicago: University of Chicago Press.

Karrow, Robert. 1993. *Sixteenth-century mapmakers and their maps.* Chicago: Speculum Press.

Kline, T. Jefferson. 1992. Remapping tenderness: Louis Malle's *Lovers* with no tomorrow. In *Screening the text: Intertextuality in new wave French cinema.* Baltimore: Johns Hopkins University Press.

Konvitz, Josef. 1987. *Cartography in France, 1660–1848.* Chicago: University of Chicago Press.

Lacotte, Suzanna Hême de. 2001. *Deleuze, philosophie et cinema: Le passage de l'image-mouvement à l'image-temps.* Paris: L'Armattan.

Lefcourt, Jenny. 2003. Keeping watch on leisure: French cinema as "Parisian populism." Ph.D. diss., Harvard University, Cambridge.

Lefcourt, Jenny, and Tom Conley. 1998. La Caméra-graffito. *Contemporary French Civilization* 22, no. 2 (Summer/Fall): 227–39.

Lestringant, Frank. 1993. *Décrire le monde à la Renaissance.* Caen: Editions Paradigme.

———. 1996. *Une sainte horreur, ou le voyage en Eucharistie, XVIe–XVIIIe siècle.* Paris: Presses Universitaires de France.

———. 2003. *Le Livre des îles. Atlas et récits insulaires de la genèse à Jules Verne.* Geneva: Droz.

Leutrat, Jean-Louis. 1997. L'horloge et la momie. In *Der Film bei Deleuze,* ed. Fahle and Engel, 407–19.

Leutrat, Jean-Louis, and Suzanne Liandrat-Guigues. 1990. *Les Cartes de l'Ouest. Un genre cinématographique: Le western.* Paris: Armand Colin.

Lévi-Strauss, Claude. 1955. *Tristes Tropiques.* Paris: Plon.

———. 1958. Le Dédoublement de la représentation dans les arts de l'Asie et de l'Amérique. Reprinted in *Anthropologie structurale 1,* 269–94. Paris: Plon.

———. 1962. *Mythologiques 1: Le Cru et le cuit.* Paris: Plon.

Lyotard, Jean-François. 1991. A l'insu (Unbeknownst). In *Community at loose ends,* ed. Miami Theory Collective, 42–48. Minneapolis: University of Minnesota Press.

Marin, Louis. 1973. *Utopiques; jeux d'espaces.* Paris: Minuit.

Mathieu-Castellani, Gisèle. 1988. La parleuse muette. *L'Esprit créateur* 28, no. 2:25–35.

McGrath, John, and Maureen Teitelbaum, eds. and trans. 1971. *The rules of the game.* Classic Film Scripts. New York: Simon and Schuster.

Menand, Louis. 2003. Paris, Texas: How Hollywood brought the cinema back from France. *New Yorker,* Feb. 17 and 24: 169–77.

Mercier, Louis-Sébastien. 1999 (1770). *L'An 2440: Rêve s'il en fut jamais*. Ed. Christophe Cave and Christine Marcandier-Colard. Paris: La Découverte.

Metz, Christian. 1974. *Language and cinema*. Trans. Donna Jean Umiker-Sebeok. The Hague: Mouton.

———. 1991a. *Film language: A semiotics of cinema*. Trans. Michael Taylor. Chicago: University of Chicago Press.

———. 1991b. *L'Enonciation impersonnelle, ou le site du film*. Paris: Meridiens/Klincksieck.

Michaelson, Annette. 1979. Dr. Crase and Mr. Clair. *October*, no. 11 (Winter): 29–53.

Monmonier, Mark. 1996. *How to lie with maps*. 2nd ed. Chicago: University of Chicago Press.

Montaigne, Michel de. 1962. *Oeuvres complètes*. Ed. Maurice Rat and Albert Thibaudet. Paris: Gallimard/Pléiade.

Mortimer, Ruth. 1964. *Harvard College Library, Department of Printing and Graphic Arts: Catalogue of books and manuscripts, part 1: French sixteenth-century books*. 2 vols. Cambridge: The Belknap Press of Harvard University.

Narboni, Jean. 1982/2001. Peut-on être et avoir E.T.? Reprinted in *Le Goût de l'Amérique: Petite anthologie des "Cahiers du Cinéma,"* ed. Antoine de Baecque with the assistance of Gabrielle Lucantonio, 149–59. [Paris]: Cahiers du Cinéma.

Negri, Toni, and Michael Hardt. *Empire*. Cambridge: Harvard University Press.

Nuti, Lucia. 1995. Le langage de la peinture dans la cartographie topographique. In *L'Oeil du cartographe et la représentation géographique du Moyen Age à nos jours,* ed. Catherine Bousquet-Bressolier, 18:53–70. Paris: C.T.H.S./Mémoires de la section de géographie physique et humaine.

Ousselin, Edward. 1999. The uses of a national icon: The Eiffel Tower in René Clair's *Paris qui dort*. *Nottingham French Studies* 36, no. 1 (Spring): 48–54.

Ozouf, Jacques, and Mona Ozouf. 1997. *Le Tour de France par deux enfants:* Le petit livre rouge de la République. In *Les Lieux de mémoire,* ed. Pierre Nora, 1:277–302. Paris: Gallimard/Quarto.

Panofsky, Erwin. 1955. Poussin and the elegiac tradition. In *Meaning in the visual arts: Papers in and on art history,* 295–320. New York: Doubleday.

———. 1960/1972. *Renaissance and renascences in western art*. New York: Harper and Row.

Pastoureau, Mireille. 1984. *Les Atlas français, XVIe–XVIIe siècles*. Paris: Bibliothèque Nationale.

Pelletier, Monique. 1998. Permanence des globes, de la Renaissance au siècle des Lumières. In *Couleurs de la terre: Des mappemondes médiévales aux images satellitales,* ed. Pelletier, 92–99. Paris: Bibliothèque Nationale de France.

———. 2001. Les globes dans les collections françaises aux XVIIe et XVIIIe siècles. In *Cartographie de la France et du monde de la Renaissance au Siècle des Lumières,* 410–12. Paris: Bibliothèque Nationale de France.

Peters, Jeffrey. 2004. *Mapping discord*. Newark: University of Delaware Press.

Pezzini, Isabella. 1996. Fra le carte. Letteratura e cartografia immaginaria. In *Cartographiques,* ed. Marie-Ange Brayer, 63–94. Paris: Réunion des Musées Nationaux.

Pichois, Claude, ed. 1975–76. *Charles Baudelaire, Oeuvres complètes*. 2 vols. Paris: Gallimard/Pléiade.

Pons, Maurice. 1955. *Virginales*. Paris: Julliard.

Ptolemy, Claudius. 1991. *The geography*. Trans. Edward Luther Stevenson. New York: Dover Reprints.

Rancière, Jacques. 2001. *La Fable cinématographique*. Paris: Galilée.

Reisz, Karel, and Gavin Millar. 1953. *Technique of film editing*. New York: Hastings House.

Renoir, Jean. 1971. *"La Grande Illusion": Découpage integral*. Paris: Seuil/l'Avant-scène du cinema.

———. 1974. *Ecrits, 1926–71*. Paris: Belfond.

Rodowick, David. 1997. *Gilles Deleuze's time-machine*. Durham, N.C.: Duke University Press.

———. 2001. *Reading after the figural, or philosophy after the new media*. Durham, N.C.: Duke University Press.

Rohdie, Sam. 2001. *Promised lands: Cinema, geography, modernism.* London: British Film Institute.

Roncoroni, Stefano, ed. 1973. *Roberto Rossellini: The war trilogy.* New York: Grossman.

Ropars-Wuilleumier, Marie-Claire. 1981. *Le Texte divisé.* Paris: Presses Universitaires de France.

———. 1997. Le tout contre la partie. In *Der Film bei Deleuze,* ed. Fahle and Engel, 243–54.

———. 2003. *Ecrire l'espace.* Paris: Presses de l'Université de Paris-VIII.

Rosolato, Guy. 1985. *Eléments de l'interprétation.* Paris: Gallimard.

———. 1996. *La Portée du désir ou la psychanalyse même.* Paris: Presses Universitaires de France.

Rouch, Jean. 2003. *Ciné-Ethnography.* Ed. and trans. Steven Feld. Minneapolis: University of Minnesota Press.

Sadoul, Georges. 1968 [1949]. *Histoire mondiale du cinéma des origines à nos jours.* Paris: Flammarion.

Scarry, Elaine. 1985. *The body in pain.* New York: Oxford University Press.

Schilder, Günter. 1981. *Three world maps by Van den Hoeye of 1661, Blaeu of 1607, Visscher of 1650.* Amsterdam: Nico Israel.

———. 1986. *Monumenta cartographica neerlandica* 6. Alphen aan den Rijn: Canaletto.

Schulten, Susan. 1998. Richard Edes Harrison and the challenge to American cartography. *Imago mundi* 50:174–88.

Schulz, Juergen. 1978. Jacobo de' Barbari's view of Venice: Map making, city views, and moralized geography before the year 1500. *The Art Bulletin* 60:425–74.

———. 1987. Maps as metaphors: Mural map cycles in the Renaissance. In *Art and cartography: Six historical essays,* ed. David Woodward, 97–122. Chicago: University of Chicago Press.

Sesonske, Alexander. 1980. *Jean Renoir: The French films, 1924–39.* Cambridge: Harvard University Press.

Shirley, Rodney. 1983. *The mapping of the world.* London: New Holland Press.

Shupe, John F., et al. 1995. *The National Geographic atlas of the world.* 6th rev. ed. Washington, D.C.: National Geographic Society.

Skelton, Raleigh A., ed. 1964. *Abraham Ortelius, "Theatrum orbis terrarum" (Antwerp 1570).* A Series of Atlases in Facsimile, 1.3. Amsterdam: World Publishing.

———, ed. 1965. Introduction to Georg Braun and Franz Hogenburg, *Civitates orbis terrarum.* Terrarum Editions. Amsterdam: Theatrum Orbis.

Spelman, Elizabeth W., and Martha Minow. 1996. Outlaw women. In *Legal reelism: Movies as legal texts,* ed. John Denvir, 261–79. Urbana: University of Illinois Press.

Starobinski, Jean. 1973. *1789, emblèmes de la raison.* Paris: Flammarion.

Talens, Jenaro. 1993. *The branded eye: Buñuel's "Un chien andalou."* Trans. Giulia Colaizzi. Minneapolis: University of Minnesota Press.

Terdiman, Richard. 1992. *Present past: Modernity and the memory crisis.* Ithaca, N.Y.: Cornell University Press.

Thrower, Norman J. W. 1996. *Maps and civilization: Cartography in culture and society.* 2nd ed. Chicago: University of Chicago Press.

Tifft, Stephen. 1992. *Drôle de Guerre:* Renoir, farce, and the fall of France. *Representations* 38 (Spring): 127–60.

Truffaut, François. 1988. *Correspondance.* Ed. Gilles Jacob and Claude de Givray. Paris: 5 Continents/Hatier.

Vidler, Anthony. 2000. *Warped space: Art, architecture, and anxiety in modern culture.* Cambridge: MIT Press.

Villon, François. 1941. *Oeuvres.* Ed. Auguste Longnon. Paris: Lemerre.

Virilio, Paul. 1982. *Logistique de la perception: Guerre et cinéma.* Paris: Gallimard/Cahiers du Cinéma.

————. 1999. *Stratégie de la déception*. Paris: Galilée.

Weber, Samuel. 1982. *The legend of Freud*. Minneapolis: University of Minnesota Press.

Williams, Linda. 1999. *Hard core: Power, pleasure, and the "frenzy of the visible."* Berkeley: University of California Press.

Willis, Sharon. 1997. *High contrast: Race and gender in contemporary Hollywood film*. Durham, N.C.: Duke University Press.

Wolff, Francis. 1997. *Dire le monde*. Paris: Presses Universitaires de France.

Wood, Denis, with John Fels. 1992. *The power of maps*. New York: Guilford Press.

Woodward, David. 1990. Roger Bacon's terrestrial coordinate system. *Annals of the Association of American Geographers* 80, no. 1:109–22.

————, ed. 2004. *The History of cartography 3: Cartography in the European Renaissance*. Chicago: University of Chicago Press.

Zunzunegui, Santos. 2001. *Robert Bresson*. Madrid: Ediciones Catédra.

Filmography

A bout de souffle [Breathless] (Jean-Luc Godard, 1960)
Les Amants (Louis Malle, 1958)
A nous la liberté (René Clair, 1931)
L'Atalante (Jean Vigo, 1934)
Ben-Hur (William Wyler, 1959)
La Bête humaine [The Human Beast] (Jean Renoir, 1938)
The Big Heat (Fritz Lang, 1953)
The Big Trail (Raoul Walsh, 1930)
Birth of a Nation (D. W. Griffith, 1915)
Black Hawk Down (Ridley Scott, 2001)
Bob le flambeur [Bob the Gambler] (Jean-Pierre Melville, 1955)
Bonnie and Clyde (Arthur Penn, 1967)
Boudu sauvé des eaux [Boudu Saved from Drowning] (Jean Renoir, 1932)
The Bowery (Raoul Walsh, 1933)
Bright Leaves (Ross McElwee, 2003)
Caged Heat (Jonathan Demme, 1974)
Le Carrosse d'or [The Golden Coach] (Jean Renoir, 1953)
Casablanca (Michael Curtiz, 1942)
La Chienne (Jean Renoir, 1931)
Chiens perdus sans collier (Jean Delannoy, 1955)
Le Ciel est à vous (Jean Grémillon, 1943)
Citizen Kane (Orson Welles, 1941)
The Cock-Eyed World (Raoul Walsh, 1929)
Colorado Territory (Raoul Walsh, 1949)
Conte d'automne [Autumn Tale] (Eric Rohmer, 1998)
Le Corbeau [The Crow] (Henri-Georges Clouzot, 1943)
Le Crime de Monsieur Lange [The Crime of M. Lange] (Jean Renoir, 1936)

Criss Cross (Robert Siodmak, 1949)
D.O.A. (Rudolph Maté, 1949)
The Deer Hunter (Michael Cimino, 1978)
Demetrius and the Gladiators (Delmer Daves, 1954)
Desperate Journey (Raoul Walsh, 1942)
Detour (Edgar G. Ulmer, 1946)
Distant Drums (Raoul Walsh, 1951)
E.T. (Steven Spielberg, 1982)
The Fall of the Roman Empire (Anthony Mann, 1964)
Les 400 coups [The 400 Blows] (François Truffaut, 1959)
Gangs of New York (Martin Scorcese, 2002)
Germany, Year Zero (Roberto Rossellini, 1947)
Gladiator (Ridley Scott, 2000)
La Grande Illusion (Jean Renoir, 1937)
Gun Crazy (Joseph H. Lewis, 1949)
La Haine (Mathieu Kassovitz, 1995)
Hallelujah! (King Vidor, 1929)
Hell's Hinges (William S. Hart, 1915)
High Sierra (Raoul Walsh, 1941)
Hiroshima, mon amour (Alain Resnais and Marguerite Duras, 1959)
The Hitchhiker (Ida Lupino, 1953)
In Old Arizona (Raoul Walsh, 1929)
In the Mood for Love (Wong Kar Wai, 2000)
India-Song (Marguerite Duras, 1975)
Indiana Jones and the Raiders of the Lost Ark (Steven Spielberg, 1981)
Irma Vep (Olivier Assayas, 1996)
Ivanhoe (Richard Thorpe, 1952)
Journal d'un curé de campagne [Diary of a Country Priest] (Robert Bresson, 1950)
Jurassic Park (Steven Spielberg, 1993)
The Killers (Robert Siodmak, 1946)
Ladri di biciclette [The Bicycle Thief] (Vittorio de Sica, 1948)
The Lady from Shanghai (Orson Welles, 1947)
M (Fritz Lang, 1931)
Les Maîtres fous (Jean Rouch, 1955)
The Man from Laramie (Anthony Mann, 1955)
La Maternelle (Marie Epstein, 1933)
Les Mistons [The Rascals] (François Truffaut, 1957)
Moonfleet (Fritz Lang, 1955)
Mystic River (Clint Eastwood, 2003)
Napoléon (Abel Gance, 1927)
North by Northwest (Alfred Hitchcock, 1959)
Northern Pursuit (Raoul Walsh, 1943)
Objective, Burma! (Raoul Walsh, 1945)
Onésime horloger (Jean Durand, 1912)
Orphée [Orpheus] (Jean Cocteau, 1950)
Païsa [Paisan] (Roberto Rossellini, 1946)
The Palm Beach Story (Preston Sturges, 1942)
Panique (Julien Duvivier, 1946)

Paris qui dort [The Crazy Ray] (René Clair, 1924)
Pépé le Moko (Julien Duvivier, 1937)
Le Plaisir (Max Ophuls, 1952)
Rancho Notorious (Fritz Lang, 1952)
Regeneration (Raoul Walsh, 1915)
La Règle du jeu [Ruler of the Game] (Jean Renoir, 1939)
Roma, città aperta (Roberto Rossellini, 1945)
Saskatchewan (Raoul Walsh, 1954)
Saving Private Ryan (Steven Spielberg, 1998)
Scarface (Howard Hawks, 1932)
Schindler's List (Steven Spielberg, 1993)
The Searchers (John Ford, 1956)
Sous les toits de Paris [Under the Roofs of Paris] (René Clair, 2002)
Spartacus (Stanley Kubrick, 1960)
Stagecoach (John Ford, 1939)
Stromboli (Roberto Rossellini, 1950)
Sullivan's Travels (Preston Sturges, 1941)
Tarzan's Secret Treasure (Richard Thorpe, 1941)
Taxi Driver (Martin Scorcese, 1976)
La Terra Trëma (Luchino Visconti, 1948)
Thelma and Louise (Ridley Scott, 1991)
Them! (Gordon Douglas, 1954)
They Drive by Night (Raoul Walsh, 1940)
The 39 Steps (Alfred Hitchcock, 1935)
Tirez sur le pianiste [Shoot the Piano Player] (François Truffaut, 1960)
To Be or Not to Be (Ernst Lubitsch, 1942)
Toni (Jean Renoir, 1934)
Trade Winds (Tay Garnett, 1938)
Triumph of the Will (Leni Riefenstahl, 1935)
Un condamné à mort s'est échappé [A Man Escaped] (Robert Bresson, 1956)
Une partie de campagne [A Day in the Country] (Jean Renoir, 1936)
Une visite (François Truffaut, 1954)
Vertigo (Alfred Hitchcock, 1958)
La Vie est à nous (Jean Renoir, 1936)
Viva l'Italia! (Roberto Rossellini, 1961)
Le Voyage imaginaire (René Clair, 1925)
Voyage to Italy (Roberto Rossellini, 1954)
What Price Glory (Raoul Walsh, 1926)
When the Clouds Roll By (Douglas Fairbanks Sr., 1919)
White Heat (Raoul Walsh, 1949)
Women of All Nations (Raoul Walsh, 1931)
You Only Live Once (Fritz Lang, 1937)
Zéro de conduite [Zero for Conduct] (Jean Vigo, 1933)

Index

255

Tom Conley is Lowell Professor of Romance Languages and Film Studies at Harvard University. His publications at the University of Minnesota Press include *Film Hieroglyphs: Ruptures in Classical Cinema* (1991; new edition, 2006) and *The Self-Made Map: Cartographic Writing in Early Modern France* (1996). His translations, also published by the University of Minnesota Press, include *The Fold: Leibniz and the Baroque,* by Gilles Deleuze; *Culture in the Plural* and *The Capture of Speech and Other Political Writings,* by Michel de Certeau; and *In the Metro,* by Marc Augé.